The Service Productivity and Quality Challenge

International Studies in the Service Economy

VOLUME 5

The titles published in this series are listed at the end of this volume.

The Service Productivity and Quality Challenge

edited by

PATRICK T. HARKER

Department of Systems Engineering,
University of Pennsylvania,
Philadelphia, Pennsylvania, U.S.A.

KLUWER ACADEMIC PUBLISHERS
DORDRECHT / BOSTON / LONDON

A C.I.P. Catalogue record for this book is available from the Library of Congress.

ISBN 0-7923-3447-7

Published by Kluwer Academic Publishers,
P.O. Box 17, 3300 AA Dordrecht, The Netherlands.

Kluwer Academic Publishers incorporates
the publishing programmes of
D. Reidel, Martinus Nijhoff, Dr W. Junk and MTP Press.

Sold and distributed in the U.S.A. and Canada
by Kluwer Academic Publishers,
101 Philip Drive, Norwell, MA 02061, U.S.A.

In all other countries, sold and distributed
by Kluwer Academic Publishers Group,
P.O. Box 322, 3300 AH Dordrecht, The Netherlands.

Printed on acid-free paper

Printed in the Netherlands

Table of Contents

Introduction   The Service Quality and Productivity Challenge

Patrick T. Harker

1. The Challenge

The popular press is awash these days over the recent world-wide recession and the impact of manufacturing on economic development. However, a few enlightened articles (e.g., *The Economist* 1992a, 1992b) have appeared that challenge the conventional wisdom that only manufacturing matters, an idea popularized in the book *Made in America* (Dertouzos, Lester, and Solow 1989). All developed economies are service-based economies and, as will be discussed below, the cause of our movement toward service-based economies is not a crisis! The true crisis lies in the low productivity that plagues many service operations. Simple answers, unfortunately, do not exist for this problem.

Our story must begin with a simple definition: what is a service? Unfortunately, even the answer to this question is not very simple as evidenced by the following attempts:

- an economic activity that produces time, place, form and/or psychological utility;
- intangible and/or perishable economic good;
- not manufacturing, mining or agriculture; and
- something that you can't drop on your foot!

1

P. T. Harker (ed.), The Service Productivity and Quality Challenge, 1–10.
© 1995 Kluwer Academic Publishers. Printed in the Netherlands.

In terms of classification, services include:
- distributive: physical (transportation, electricity, etc.) and informational (telecommunications, libraries, etc.),
- retail and wholesale trade,
- nonprofits, government, education,
- producer services,
- consumer services, and
- health care.

All in all, services constitute 70% of Gross Domestic Product (GDP) and 70-80% of employment in the United States. Other countries have a slightly lower percentage, but their rate of growth of services is faster; see Baumol (1992). The problems and opportunities facing services are a world-wide phenomenon.

Over the course of time, services have been viewed as Mom-and-Pop, "hamburger flipping'" jobs. This characterization is simply not true. Services are as capital intensive and concentrated as manufacturing; one need only consider transportation, financial services and health care for examples. Also, services are not all low-wage jobs. In the U.S. context, if one removes low-*skilled* retail and wholesale trade employment, service wages are only marginally below those of manufacturing. In addition, many different service activities occur within manufacturing organizations, where they are mistakenly classified as high-wage manufacturing jobs.The real issue for employment growth is not services versus manufacturing but rather, skilled versus unskilled jobs. Finally, services are tradeable. As the recent GATT trade talks on services illustrate, service trade constitutes an important and growing area for world commerce. In summary, services are a vital part of all developed economies and are not simply the leftovers from "real" work. The prejudice against services must first be overcome if productivity in this area is to be improved.

Why has there been this growth of services throughout the world? Several explanations have been offered in the literature (e.g., McKinsey 1992):
- as manufacturing and households have outsourced their service jobs (accounting, data processing, child care, etc.), this economic activity has been transferred from the manufacturing/ household ledger to the service ledger in our national accounts;
- increased governmental regulation has forced organizations to hire more lawyers, accountants, etc.; and
- increased customization of output due to changing consumer tastes has forced manufacturers to bundle more and more services with their goods.

While all of these explanations seem to have merit, there is one dominant reason why the percentage of GDP and employment dedicated to services has continued to increase: *low productivity*. According to *Baumol's cost disease* hypothesis (Baumol, Blackman, and Wolff 1991), the growth in services is actually an illusion. The fact is that service-sector productivity is improving slower than that of manufacturing and thus, it seems as if we are consuming more services in nominal terms. However, in real terms, we are consuming slightly less services. That is, the increase in the service sector is caused by low productivity relative to manufacturing.

The implication of Baumol's cost disease is the following. Assuming historical productivity increases for manufacturing, agriculture, education and health care, Baumol (1992) shows that the U.S. can triple its output in all sectors within 50 years. However, due to the higher productivity level for manufacturing and agriculture, it will take substantially more employment in services to achieve this increase in output. To put this argument in perspective, simply roll back the clock 100 years or so and replace the words manufacturing with agriculture, and services with manufacturing. The phenomenal growth in agricultural productivity versus manufacturing caused the employment levels in agriculture in the U.S. to decrease rapidly while producing a truly unbelievable amount of food. It is the low productivity of services that is the real culprit in its growth of GDP and employment share.

The challenge for scholars and professionals of *productivity management* (where I place almost all of the science and practice of economics, engineering and management for this purpose) is clearly to improve the productivity of services. If this effort is not made, Baumol's analysis would imply a dramatic slow-down in productivity growth as the low-productivity service-sector dominates even further the world's economies. While it has not been firmly established empirically that lagging service productivity is true and is directly to blame for our world-wide productivity slow-down (Griliches 1992), it still seems appropriate to focus our attention of service quality and productivity.

2. The Conference

In order to come to grips with the issues raised above that are faced by all modern, service-based economies in improving productivity, the Fishman-Davidson Center for the Study of the Service Sector at the Wharton School,

University of Pennsylvania, held a two day conference in October 1992. At this conference, business leaders, government officials, and leading scholars of economics, management and engineering were brought together in order to grapple with the myriad of issues surrounding service quality and productivity. This volume presents a subset of the papers that were presented at this conference.

3. This Volume

Reflecting the interdisciplinary nature of the conference, this volume presents a set of views related to the challenges of service quality and productivity. In Section I, the economy-wide problems of measuring service productivity and its impact on economic performance is addressed. In Chapter 1, Dean and Kunze describe the United States' approach for measuring service productivity as well as providing some empirical evidence to support Baumol's contention that low productivity in services is our main challenge. The Bureau of Labor Statistics (BLS) approach described by Dean and Kunze does show that, while a number of service industries have recorded strong productivity growth, many others have indeed been stagnant for the past 20 years. This viewpoint is extended in Chapter 2 by Dighe, Francois and Reinert by looking at the multiplier effects of services and interrelationships with the other sectors of the U.S. economy through use of social accounting matrices. The conclusions of this analysis show the important role that financial and business services have on the performance of all segments of the economy. Finally, Lebow and Sichel in Chapter 3 look at the input side of the service equation, namely, employment levels. In their analysis, they challenge both theoretically and empirically the conventional wisdom that increases in service employment will lead to a "recession-proof" economy; i.e., an economy with very few employment cycles. Together, these three papers present a comprehensive picture of the role of services in the economy.

The growing volume and recognition of trade and international competition in services is the subject of Section II. What exactly is service trade, and how will it be managed/policed by international organizations? This topic is first explored by Hoekman in Chapter 4 in the context of the legal, political and economic issues surrounding service trade. A major conclusion from this paper is again the vital role played by financial and business services, along with the phenomenal growth of foreign direct investment (FDI) in services, constituting over 50% of the total FDI in the world! This last point is then amplified by Li in Chapter 5 in his study of the factors that lead a country to successfully attract FDI from multinational service companies. These two studies point to the need for continued liberalization of service trade agreements in order to increase competition. As described by the papers in Section I, the relatively recent deregulation (fully or partially) of transportation, telecommunications, and financial services has led to major productivity gains therein. Chapter 6 and 7 by Apte and Mason, and Wilson, respectively, take this general knowledge of FDI and apply it in the analysis of global outsourcing of service operations, such as data processing, by many multinational firms. These papers present practical advice for managers to deal with the myriad of issues outlined by Hoekman and Li.

The first two sections have outlined the broad parameters facing the economy and individual managers as they struggle to improve service productivity in an increasingly competitive international market. However, what specific steps should they take? The first paper in Section III deals with one of the most obvious and also controversial topics in strategy formation to overcome lagging service productivity: the use of information technology (IT). Service-sector organizations have invested heavily in IT; about 85% of all installed IT in the United States exists in services. However, this investment seems not to have paid off on the bottom line of productivity (Roach 1991). This phenomena spawned Hackett (1990) to coin the term "service-sector sinkhole", that vast abyss where IT is thrown in with little or no payoff. Thus, a major paradox exists: is this massive technology investment really not paying off? While several explanations have been put forth for this phenomena (Bakos and Kemerer 1992; Brynjolfsson and Bimber 1989), it seems clear that IT investments have both an impact on measurable productivity (labor) as well as an external impact vis-a-vis enhanced customer service and value. The paper by Pennings in Chapter 8 addresses this issue in the context of IT investments by financial institutions. The second paper in this section by Borenstein, MacKie-Mason and Netz deals with another major strategic issue in services: how closely should one tie the service component of a manufactured good to the sale of the good itself. For example, as all major computer manufacturers have become service firms (Digital, Unisys, IBM, etc. now make more on their consulting services than selling computers!), this question plays an ever important role. Through an economic analysis of this issue, Chapter 9 presents both broad policy and specific managerial advice on how this bundling of goods and services should occur.

While the above strategic questions are vitally important, the real key to improving productivity in services lies in the implementation of this strategy. Thus, Section IV presents an operations management perspective on the productivity problem. First, Apte, Caveliere and Hegde show in Chapter 10 how relatively simple management science techniques can be applied to improve service production processes, in this case, claims processing in insurance. This work assumes that the objectives - the measures of productivity - are well-defined. In Chapter 11, Armstrong deals directly with the intangible nature of service production by developing and applying a model to improve service operations that ties directly to the service quality measures that have recently been developed in the marketing literature. Finally, most services cannot be inventoried. Thus, the real-time matching of supply and demand is a key factor in productivity improvement. The major technique for this matching is so-called *yield management* (see, for example, Weatherford and Bodily 1992), which has proven to be a major profit driver in the airline industry (Smith, Leimkuhler and Darrow 1992). In Chapter 12, Bitran, Gilbert and Leong show how this concept can be applied more broadly, in this case, the hotel industry.

This volume ends with a series of papers that deal with the details of productivity improvement in a variety of services. Section V presents the problems and opportunities that exist in productivity improvement in *market services* (i.e., those industries where some degree of competition and market prices exist). Chapter 13 (Fried, Lovell and Vanden Eeckaut) deal the measurement of productivity in financial services as well as showing how frontier-based productivity measures like DEA (Boussofiane, Dyson and Thanassoulis 1991) can be used to gain managerial insights into how productivity can be improved. Crandall discusses productivity performance of telecommunications in Chapter 14, and Morlok, Sammon, Spasovic and Nozick describe techniques for productivity improvement in transportation, specifically in the growing area of intermodal freight transport (Chapter 15).

Finally, the *non-market* services, a vital part of all economies, are dealt with in Section VI. Chubb and Moe (Chapter 16) confront the myriad of issues facing the educational system in the United States, and in Chapter 17, Boronico, Crew and Kleindorfer discuss the future of postal services, another large and vital government or quasi-government service. In both cases, the authors argue for some movement away from the non-market status of these services in order to generate competition-induced productivity gains.

All in all, this volume attempts to present the state-of-the-art thinking on the service productivity challenge from a variety of disciplines. Rather than a cursory view of each disciplines' perspective, the papers go into a fair amount of detail on each subject or industry. Taken as a whole, they provide a panoramic view of the problem and potential solutions. There are no simple answers for a problem this complex. However, several general trends emerge. First, measurement is important, and we need to further refine our statistical base in order to better grapple with the problems posed in Section I. Second, while measurement is important, management must be willing and able to deal directly with the "non-quantitative" aspects of investments and process improvements (Pennings and Armstrong). Third, competition is a wonderful catalyst for improvement. Perhaps Baumol's disease is not due to cost, but to the virus of over-regulation and trade barriers. As recent improvements in transportation, telecommunications and financial services attest, creative juices seem to flow when unfettered from regulatory constraints. As argued in, for example, Chubb and Moe, this is evidence that all parts of the service sector should heed.

4. The Future

The conference on service quality and productivity along with this volume is both a beginning and end of an era. It ended an era of scholarship that I can best describe as one of definition-building. The arguments as to what constitutes a service, their relationship to manufacturing, their importance to the economy, and their classification were very important in their time, but are now past. It is clear that service/ white-collar work, whether in manufacturing or traditional service sector organizations, is the dominant problem and opportunity for productivity improvement in all economies. Scholars still have a very important role in defining the extent of service work, computing its contribution to economic growth, and tracking both international and organization/sub-industry-specific trends. This is particularly the case in the need to constantly debunk the myths surrounding services. For example, all of our recent Presidential candidates in the United States reminisced of the days of high-wage manufacturing jobs versus those low-wage service jobs. Unfortunately, facts get in the way of these dreams: as stated in Section 1, excluding retailing, service wages are basically equal to those in manufacturing. The issue is not manufacturing versus services, it's skilled versus unskilled labor. Rather than debate and throw money at solving our manufacturing problem, let's invest time, talent and money in up-skilling the workforce.

While the above mentioned issues are not and should not go away, this is not where I believe the major research emphasis should and will lie in the next decade. Thus, I believe that the conference and this volume is also a beginning. For example, a panel on reengineering service processes (se, e.g., Davenport and Short 1990 for a description of the reengineering phenomena) brought together the leaders in this area, and concluded that, whether in manufacturing or the service-sector, service delivery processes are service delivery processes. Our focus must now shift to a process/ value-chain orientation in both our research and in management practice. AT&T's credit card processing techniques (recently awarded the Baldridge award), Ford's invoice handling system, etc. are all very relevant to an insurance company in benchmarking their claims processing methodology. It is not until such a process-orientation is achieved that we will fully achieve the productivity/ quality potential in services.

This need for a process-orientation is not only true at the organizational level, but for the economy as a whole (Morroni 1992). For example, if technology investments decrease profit margins in the provision of capital by banks and other financial institutions, current statistics and theory would state that technology investments led to negative productivity improvements. However, this decrease in profit margins could have been due to the fact that technology has increased competition, thus driving the "friction" out of the process of capital movement in the economy. The economy is now better off. If we insist on thinking of productivity on an organizational level, we clearly will not see improvements in the above scenario. On the other hand, by looking at capital provision as a process wherein these organization are part of the overall production system, productivity will improve. It all boils down to the unit of analysis; it must be a process if a realistic picture is to be painted of an organization or the economy.

References

Bakos, J.Y., and C.F. Kemerer (1992). "Recent applications of economic theory in information technology research," *Decision Support Systems* 8, 365-386.

Baumol, W.J. (1992). "Private affluence, public squalor," Discussion Paper, C.V. Starr Center for Applied Economics, New York University (New York, NY).

Baumol, W.J., S.A. Batey Blackman, and E.N. Wolff (1991). *Productivity and American Leadership* (MIT Press, Cambridge, MA).

Boussofiane, A., R.G. Dyson, and E. Thanassoulis (1991). "Applied data envelopment analysis," *European Journal of Operational Research* 52, 1-15.

Brynjolfsson, E., and B.A. Bimber (1989). "Information technology and the productivity paradox: an overview of issues and introduction to the literature," Technical Report, MIT Laboratory for Computer Science, MIT (Cambridge, MA).

Davenport, T.H., and J.E. Short (1990). "The new industrial engineering: information technology and business process redesign," *Sloan Management Review*, 11-27.

Dertouzos, M.L., R.K. Lester, and R.M. Solow (1989). *Made in America: Regaining the Productive Edge* (MIT Press, Cambridge, MA).

The Economist (1992a). "Cure-all or snake oil?" (October 3, 1992), 21-24.

The Economist (1992b). "More than meets the eye" (December 26, 1992), 91.

Griliches, Y. (ed.) (1992). *Output Measurement in the Services Sector* National Bureau of Economic Research Studies in Income and Wealth, vol. 56 (University of Chicago Press, Chicago, IL).

Hackett, G.P. (1990). "Investment in technology - the service sector sinkhole?" *Sloan Management Review* 31, 97-103.

McKinsey Global Institute (1992). *Service Sector Productivity* (McKinsey and Company, Inc., Washington, DC).

Morroni, M. (1992). *Production Process and Technical Change.* (Cambridge University Press, Cambridge, UK).

Roach, S.S. (1991). "Services under siege - the restructuring imperative," *Harvard Business Review* 69, 82-91.

Smith, B.C., J.F. Leimkuhler, and R.M. Darrow (1992). "Yield management at American Airlines," *Interfaces* 22, 8-31.

Weatherford, L., and S. Bodily (1992). "A taxonomy and research overview of perishable-asset revenue management: yield management, overbooking, and pricing," *Operations Research* 40, 831-844.

Chapter 1   Bureau of Labor Statistics Productivity Measures for Service Industries

Edwin R. Dean and Kent Kunze

1 . Introduction

This paper discusses the productivity measures for service industries published by the U.S. Bureau of Labor Statistics (BLS).[1]

The Bureau presently publishes productivity measures for 178 industry titles, of which 39 are for the broad service, or nongoods, sector. (For this paper the terms service industries, service sector, and the nongoods sector are synonymous.) The published measures cover about 40 percent of all workers in both the service industries and the goods-producing industries in the private business sector.

Section 2 of the paper describes the basic methodology underlying productivity measures in service industries. Section 3 gives a sector by sector description of the hours and output measures developed for specific industries.

---

[1] The authors wish to thank Charles Ardolini, retired, (past) Chief of the Division of Industry Productivity and Technology Studies of the Bureau of Labor Statistics and to John Duke, Senior Economist in the Division, for their assistance in preparing the paper and to Brian Friedman and Virginia Klarquist for their work on the tables.

P. T. Harker (ed.), The Service Productivity and Quality Challenge, 11–42.
© 1995 *Kluwer Academic Publishers. Printed in the Netherlands.*

Section 4 examines recent productivity trends in the service industries. Section 5 focuses on future directions and some of the problems which must still be addressed.

2. Methodology for Industry Productivity Measures

Service industry labor productivity measures, like labor productivity measures for goods-producing industries, are computed by dividing an index of output by an index of labor input (hours). Data for hours of labor input are readily available for service industries and generally do not present unusual problems for the construction of productivity measures. On the other hand, for a substantial number of service industries, serious problems arise in the definition and measurement of the industry's output (Sherwood, 1993).

The difficulties can be expressed simply by a basic question that seldom needs to be asked for manufacturing industries: what is the output of the industry? For manufacturing industries, output is easy to define: The output of the steel industry is tons of steel; the output of the automobile industry is the number of automobiles. But, in a service industry, there often is no simple definition of output. What, for example, is the output of an orchestra? Is it the length of time it performs? Is it the quality of the performance? Is it the size of the audience? Hill (1977) describes a service as something that changes a person or an item and involves an economic transaction. This definition would suggest that if no one attends the concert, no service is delivered, regardless of how long the orchestra plays or of the quality the performance.

However, this definition still does not solve the problem of assigning a quantifiable unit to the service. Even if output of the orchestra is defined as the size of the audience, the quality of the performance will also have an influence on the audience. In fact it may have a different impact on different people. How are these differing changes measured? These are examples of some of the difficulties that are faced when developing measures of output and productivity for service industries.

While the orchestra example might present these definitional problems in especially dramatic form, economists have identified similar problems in a number of other service industries. Additional examples could be provided for banking, insurance, education, health, and most entertainment and social services activities (Sherwood, 1993). On the other hand, some industries in transportation, communications, and utilities may present problems no greater than those found in most manufacturing industries (Mark, 1988).

2.1 Output. The Bureau of Labor Statistics has to date followed the strategy of developing service industry productivity measures for those industries that present relatively few problems in the definition and measurement of output. The Bureau's future strategy is discussed briefly at the end of this paper.

The Bureau's service industry output indexes are based on measured quantities of services provided by the industry. The unit of measurement can be either a physical quantity--such as passenger-miles, ton-miles, or kilowatt hours--or a constant dollar value of production. One of the primary objectives in developing the output measures for each industry is to start with as much detail or disaggregation of the measured outputs as possible. For example, the output index of the electric utility industry (SIC 491) is not based simply on the total number of kilowatt hours produced; instead it is derived from the number of kilowatt hours sold to each of seven types of users. The quantities sold to each type of user are aggregated with specific weights for each type of service. Similarly, the output index of hardware stores (SIC 5251) is obtained by aggregating the deflated revenues of 23 different merchandise lines from all stores. As a general rule, weights are changed every five years to correspond with the economic censuses. This is to remain consistent with manufacturing industries which are also part of the productivity measurement program.

Industry information is obtained from a wide variety of sources, public as well as private. Output indexes for trade, services, and manufacturing make extensive use of Bureau of the Census data. Other important Federal Government sources include the Department of Transportation, the Internal Revenue Service, the Department of Energy, and the Department of the Interior. For deflated value series, industry price indexes are derived from the BLS producer and consumer price indexes.

2.2 Employee hours. Indexes of hours are computed by dividing aggregate hours for each year by the base-period aggregate. Hours are treated as homogeneous and additive with no distinction made between hours of different groups of workers. Industry employment and hour indexes are developed from data compiled by BLS, the Bureau of the Census, and other sources. For most private nonagricultural industries, BLS publishes employment and average weekly hours data for production, or nonsupervisory workers, and employment data for all employees. Average annual hours of nonproduction and supervisory workers are estimated from all available data. In addition, employment and the estimated aggregate hours for the self-employed and unpaid family workers are derived from BLS and IRS data sources. In a few industries, labor input measures are simply total employee counts.

2.3   Characteristics of the measures.   The model of productivity measurement is very straight forward. However, when put to use it can become complicated. When the Bureau begins to study the possibility of developing a new industry productivity measure, the first task is to examine the available data. It is common to find that the data suffer from various deficiencies. If the deficiencies are important and not correctable, the study is ended and no measure is developed. In other instances, special efforts are made to correct the data problems.

During the study of available data, a number of issues are examined. First, it is important to find out if, for the industry in question, there have been significant changes in the Standard Industrial Classification (SIC) code over the time period considered, and, if so, whether adjustments can be made for the changes. Changes in the SIC codes indicate major changes in the type of products or services being produced, or changes in product mix. If these new products, or the changing mix of products, cannot be introduced with acceptable weights, the output index will not represent the correct changes in production over time.

Some of the industries for which the Bureau publishes measures are regulated. This is most notable in the transportation, communications, and electric, gas, and sanitary service industries. Regulated prices of outputs may not reflect competitive market conditions. This can have an adverse effect on the output measures. When value weights are being used, the regulated prices are part of the weights used to compute the output indexes. In this case the weights may not reflect relative values of production and the output indexes will not be weighted correctly.

It is difficult to determine what impact the use of weights which contain regulated prices have had on the output trends. The trend in the output index for the railroad industry was revised slightly downward when a change from revenue weights to labor cost weights was introduced in 1974. Certainly there has been some distortion in the changes of the output index for telephone communications during the regulated years when long distance rates were set artificially high to offset low local rates.

For labor input there are also a number of potential data problems. Presently, establishment surveys do not collect hours data on supervisory and nonproduction workers. The hours for supervisory and nonproduction workers are estimated for each industry. In addition, data on hours of work of self-employed and unpaid family workers are generally very thin at the industry level because they are collected by a household survey and not an establishment survey. This is a particularly acute problem for measuring labor input in the service sector where most nonfarm self-employed and unpaid family workers are working. As a result, changes in annual hours of these workers are often erratic.

The hours collected by the Bureau's establishment survey are based on hours paid, rather than on hours worked, which is the more appropriate measure for labor input. However, results from the Bureau's Hours at Work Survey show that for the private business sector the ratio of hours at work to hours paid has been reasonably stable since 1981 (Jablonski, Kunze, and Otto, 1990). Indeed, this seems to be the case even for many of the nongoods industries. Only the transportation sector has shown a significant change in the ratio of hours at work to hours paid. In this sector the ratio increased nearly 5 percentage points from 1981 to 1989[2]. Hence, actual hours of work have increased faster than hours paid. This would suggest that labor input increased 5 percentage points more than reported for this period and that labor productivity growth for industries in this sector was about 5 percentage points lower, on average, than reported for this time period.

3. Description of Service Industries

3.1 Transportation. The Bureau publishes productivity measures for five industries in the transportation sector.[3] The employment coverage of these

---

[2] Unpublished data from the Office of Productivity and Technology, Bureau of Labor Statistics.

[3] For the intercity trucking industry, SIC 4213(part), two measures are produced; one is for freight trucking alone and one is for all intercity trucking. For railroad transportation, SIC 401, two measures are produced using different output concepts, car miles and revenue ton miles. So seven measures are produced for the five industries.

measured industries is one-third of the transportation sector, based on 1991 employment (Table 1). Interestingly, the same industries represented over 50 percent of transportation employment in 1980. The decrease in coverage is attributable to declining employment in some measured industries and increasing employment in the yet unmeasured industries within the sector. For example, employment in railroads (a measured industry) has dropped from 671,000 in 1967 to 232,000 in 1991, while employment in transportation services (an unmeasured industry) has gone from 100,000 in 1967 to 345,000 in 1991.

Conceptually, the output measures for transportation industries are relatively easy to define: output is the movement of goods or passengers over distance. This is a quantifiable definition. Industry output for this sector is based on physical quantities of ton-miles, passenger-miles, or barrel-miles. In both trucking and railroads, the index of ton-miles is adjusted for changes in commodity mix being transported. The adjustment factor is the difference between the price weighted growth rate of tons of commodities and the unweighted aggregate growth rate of tons of commodities. The weighted aggregates are computed using data for more than 170 commodity lines for both railroads and trucking. For the air transportation industry four separate measures of output are aggregated using revenue weights.

Input measures are indexes of total hours for the railroad and petroleum pipeline industries. For trucking, air transportation, and bus carriers, labor input measures are indexes of annual employment only.

A potential problem specific to trucking and railroads is the lack of data on average length of haul. To the extent that unit resource requirements are different for long-distance hauls versus short hauls, a bias occurs if average length of haul changes during the period studied. The adjustment for commodity-mix changes, referred to above, may partially correct for this bias. Another possible problem, mentioned above, is the use of regulated output prices for deflating revenues or developing weights. If output prices, because of regulation, do not accurately reflect competitive market equilibrium conditions, then output measures can be biased. This problem is greater for the historical data than for recent data.

Table 1. Service industries covered by BLS productivity measures and employment coverage for major service sectors.

	1991 Employment (thousands)	Employment coverage (in percent)
SERVICE PRODUCING SECTOR	63,861	
Transportation	3,805	
Railroad Transportation, Revenue Traffic SIC 4011	232	
Railroad Transportation, Car Miles SIC 4011	232	
Bus Carriers, Class I SIC 411,13,14 (parts)	16	
Trucking, Except Local SIC 4213	444	
Trucking, Except Local, General Freight SIC 4213 (part)	275*	
Air Transportation SIC 4512,13,4522 (parts)	559	
Petroleum Pipelines SIC 4612,13	19	
, Transportation employment covered	1,270	33.4
Communications	1,287	
Telephone Communications SIC 481	905	
Communications employment covered	905	70.3
Electric, Gas, and Sanitary Services	969	
Gas and Electric Utilities SIC 491,492,493	809	
Electric Utilities SIC 491,493 (part)	605*	
Gas Utilities SIC 492,493 (part)	204*	
Utilities employment covered	809	83.5

Table 1 continued

	1991 Employment (thousands)	Employment coverage (in percent)
Trade	27,312	
Scrap and Waste Materials SIC 5093	108	
Hardware Stores SIC 5251	176	
Department Stores SIC 5311	2,047	
Variety Stores SIC 5331	168	
Retail Food Stores SIC 54	3,430	
Grocery Stores SIC 5411	3,011*	
Retail Bakeries SIC 546	181*	
Franchised New Car Dealers SIC 5511	886	
Auto and Home Supply Stores SIC 5531	365	
Gasoline Service Stations SIC 5541	690	
Apparel and Accessory Stores SIC 56	1,241	
Men's and Boy's Clothing Stores SIC 5611	99*	
Women's Clothing Stores SIC 5621	408*	
Family Clothing Stores SIC 5651	313*	
Shoe Stores SIC 5661	219*	
Home Furniture, Furnishings,and Equipment Stores SIC 57	951	
Furniture & Homefurnishings Stores SIC 571	558*	
Appliance, Radio, TV & Computer Stores SIC 572,73	393*	
Household Appliance Stores SIC 5722	92*	
Radio, Television, and Computer Stores SIC 573	301*	
Eating and Drinking Places SIC 581	6,785	
Drug and Proprietary Stores SIC 5912	635	
Liquor Stores SIC 5921	146	
Trade employment covered	17,628	64.5

Table 1 continued

	1991 Employment (thousands)	Employment coverage (in percent)
Finance, Insurance, and Real Estate	7,246	
Commercial Banks SIC 602	*1,539*	
F.I.R.E. employment covered	*1,539*	21.2
Services	23,242	
Hotels and Motels SIC 7011	*1,583*	
Laundry, Cleaning, and Garment Services SIC 721	*490*	
Beauty and Barber Shops SIC 7231,41	*762*	
Beauty Shops SIC 7231	*679**	
Automotive Repair Shops SIC 753	*816*	
Services employment covered	*3,651*	15.7
SERVICES PRODUCING SECTOR EMPLOYMENT COVERED	25,802	40.4

This employment number is included in an employment number for a more broadly-defined industry.

Note: Employment coverage of BLS measures is in italics.

Sources: Bureau of Labor Statistics

3.2   Communications.   There is only one industry measure within the communications sector. This is telephone communications (SIC 4813), which covered over 70 percent of total employment in the sector in 1991. Again, coverage has actually decreased over the past ten years due to rapid growth in the unmeasured industries (television, radio, and cable television broadcasting).

Output indexes are generated as weighted aggregates of deflated revenues collected by four different categories of telephone services: local calls, measured toll service (MTS), wide area toll service (WATS), and all other (this includes private line service). The revenue data are collected and published by the Federal Communications Commission. Deflators are derived from price indexes compiled and published by the Bureau of Labor Statistics under its producer price index program. Revenues by type of service are used as weights. Labor input is an index of total hours derived from the Bureau's establishment survey data.

Besides the possible problem of regulated prices, a measurement problem may exist because of flat-rate charges for some long distance and most local services. Flat-rate revenues may reflect changes in the service rate only and not changes in the volume of traffic or other additional services being provided. Hence changes in deflated revenues may not reflect total changes in outputs.

3.3   Electric, gas, and sanitary services.   The Bureau publishes three productivity measures for industries in this group. The industries are electric utilities (SIC 491 plus part of SIC 493), gas utilities (SIC 492 plus part of SIC 493), and the combination of the two. These measures do not include any government owned establishments. In 1991 the measures covered approximately 84 percent of total employment in this sector.

Output indexes in the electric utilities industry are weighted aggregates of seven types of electric services measured in kilowatt hours. Services are differentiated by type of customer: residential, commercial, industrial, etc. Weights are unit revenues for each service. For the gas utilities industry the output index is a weighted aggregate of four types of services; again the weights are unit revenues by type of service. The two industries' outputs are aggregated using employee weights. Output data are collected by the U.S. Department of Energy, the Rural Electrification Administration, and the American Gas Association. Input indexes are derived from employment and average hours data collected by the Bureau's establishment survey.

3.4 Trade. The trade sector is the largest of the service producing sectors. In 1991 over 27 million people worked in this area. The Bureau publishes measures for 23 different industries of which 19 are mutually exclusive. These published industries cover nearly 18 million workers, 65 percent of the trade sector. Only one of these measures--scrap and waste materials (SIC 5093)--is in wholesale trade. The remainder of the measures are for retail trade industries.

With the exception of scrap and waste materials, output indexes for the trade industries are weighted aggregates of deflated sales of merchandise lines. Sales data, available from the Census of Retail Trade and annually from Current Business Reports, are deflated by price indexes derived from CPI's. For census years the sales data are reported by merchandise lines. For non-census years more aggregated sales data are reported. For the latter, deflators are calculated by combining the prices with the base year weights. The number of merchandise lines varies by industry (Table 2).

Several types of weights are used in the BLS measures. The most commonly used weights are product-group gross margins derived from the input-output tables produced by the Bureau of Economic Analysis. Unfortunately, gross margin data are not available for all merchandise lines reported. Labor cost weights are used for some years in the retail food store measure. Employment weights are used in the franchised new car dealer measure. Detailed all employee hour weights are used for department stores. Industry all person hour weights are sometimes used to weight 4-digit measures into 2-digit measures, as in retail food stores and total apparel stores. In some industry measures, gross margin weights were not available for most of the services and products sold. For example, there are no gross-margin data for gasoline service stations. In these cases sales data are used for weighing products sold.

The labor input indexes for most of the measures in retail trade are computed from data on all person hours. The Bureau includes measures of self-employed and unpaid family workers derived from either IRS data or Current Population Survey (CPS) data. Some measures, for example department stores and franchised new car dealers, are based solely on all employee hours because of the lack of suitable self-employed and unpaid family worker information from IRS or CPS sources.

Table 2. Number of merchandise lines for retail industries

Covered retail trade industries	Merchandise lines used
Hardware stores SIC 5251	23
Department stores SIC 5311	41
Variety stores SIC 5331	33
Grocery stores SIC 5411	26
Retail bakeries SIC 546	15
Franchised new car dealers SIC 5511	7
Auto and home supply stores SIC 553	17
Gasoline service stations SIC 5541	11
Men's and boy's clothing stores SIC 5611	20
Women's ready-to-wear stores SIC 5621	19
Family clothing stores SIC 5651	22
Shoe stores SIC 5661	7
Furniture and home furnishings stores SIC 571	56
Appliance, radio, TV, & music stores SIC 572,3	36
Household appliance stores SIC 572	17
Radio, TV, & music stores SIC 573	19
Eating and drinking places SIC 58	5
Drug and proprietary stores SIC 5912	30
Liquor stores SIC 5921	6

Source: Bureau of Labor Statistics

Hardware stores (SIC 525) provide a good example of productivity measurement methods in retail sales. For a benchmark year (economic census year) annual sales are reported by merchandise line for the industry in the Census of Retail Trade. These detailed sales data are separately deflated by the appropriate CPIs and aggregated using base-year gross-margin weights. The gross-margin data are developed from the Bureau of Economic Analysis's input-output tables.

Annual measures of output for hardware stores are developed from total industry sales as reported in Current Business Reports. Annual industry sales, reported for the industry, are deflated using an aggregation of CPIs. The price indexes are weighted according to the reported merchandise line sales from the most recent census. Table 3 lists the merchandise lines and CPIs used for hardware stores. The annual output indexes are adjusted to the benchmark year indexes derived, as described above, from the more detailed sales data published in each Census of Retail Trade.

Labor input for the hardware stores measure is an index of hours of all persons working in the industry. The number of employees and the average weekly hours of nonsupervisory workers are derived directly from the Bureau's establishment survey. The number of self-employed and unpaid family workers and their respective average weekly hours are derived from Current Population Survey data. The average hours of supervisory workers are constructed from the Census of Population. These average hours are held constant between decennial census years. Average hours and employment by class of worker are simply multiplied and summed over all classes of workers in the industry.

3.5 Finance, insurance and real estate. Commercial banking (SIC 602) is the only industry in this sector that the Bureau publishes a productivity measure. In 1991 commercial banks employed 1.54 million people, or 21 percent of all workers in the finance, insurance, and real estate sector.

The output measure for this industry is based on the number of transactions for three major banking activities: time and demand deposits, loans, and trusts (fiduciaries). Each major activity is an aggregate of more refined measures. The indexes for these three activities are aggregated with fixed-year employment weights to obtain the output index for commercial banking. The employment weights were derived for 1967, 1972, 1977, 1982, and 1987, from data published in the Federal Reserve's Functional Cost Analysis (FCA).

Table 3. Merchandise lines, sales, and CPI's used for hardware stores, 1982

Merchandise Lines	1982 Sales ($1,000)	Percent	CPI's
Groceries & other foods	13,266	0.0016	Food at home
Cigars, cigarettes & tobacco	10,025	0.0012	Tobacco products
Health & beauty aids	11,478	0.0014	Toilet goods & personal care appliances
Men's & boys' clothing, except footwear	11,827	0.0015	Men's & boys' apparel
Women's & girls' wear, except footwear	6,454	0.0008	Women's & girls' apparel
Footwear, except infants'	8,256	0.0010	Footwear
Curtains, draperies & dry goods	6,977	0.0009	Textile house furnishings
Major household appliances	203,986	0.0252	Household appliances
Small electric appliances	184,128	0.0228	Office machines, small electric appliances etc.
Televisions	44,624	0.0055	Television
Audio equipment, musical instruments, supplies	32,843	0.0041	Sound equipment
Furniture & sleeping equipment	42,112	0.0052	Furniture & bedding
Floor coverings	23,680	0.0029	Floor & window coverings, infants, laundry, etc.

Table 3--continued

Merchandise Lines	1982 Sales ($1,000)	Percent	CPI's
Kitchenware & home furnishings	434,429	0.0537	Tableware, serving pieces, etc.
Jewelry	6,183	0.0008	Jewelry & luggage
Sporting goods	271,409	0.0335	Sporting goods & equipment
Hardware & tools	3,047,705	0.3766	Weighted CPI's 1
Plumbing & electrical supplies	1,640,569	0.2027	Plumbing, heating, elec. & cool. supplies
Lawn & garden equip. & supplies	784,706	0.0970	Weighted CPI's 2
Lumber & building materials	1,106,017	0.1367	Maintenance & repair commodities
Cars, trucks, power vehicles	7,401	0.0009	New vehicles
Automotive fuels & lubricants	84,774	0.0105	Motor fuel, motor oil, coolant
Auto tires, batteries & accessories	94,733	0.0117	Automobile parts & equipment
Household fuels	14,740	0.0018	Fuel oil, coal & bottled gas
Total MLS used	8,092,322	1.0000	
Total MLS reported in Census	8,335,088		
MLS used as a percent of MLS reported in Census	0.9709		

1 Weighted CPI's: lawn equipment, power tools and other hardware; miscellaneous supplies and equipment (maintenance and repair commodities).
2 Weighted CPI's: lawn equipment, power tools and other hardware; lawn and garden supplies.

The components of time deposits consist of (1) demand deposits and (2) time and savings deposits. Output indexes for both of these categories are constructed and aggregated on the basis of employment weights derived from the FCA. Time and savings deposits at commercial banks include all regular savings accounts, club accounts, certificates of deposit, and "other" time deposits.

The output measure for demand deposits consists of two components -- the number of checks written by the public and transacted through the banks, plus the number of electronic funds transfers (EFTs) to the banks' customer accounts. The two sets of numbers are added for each year, yielding the number of demand deposit transactions from 1967 forward.

The output series for the number of checks is based on three surveys conducted in 1970, 1974, and 1979, in addition to annual data published by the Federal Reserve System. The three surveys are used as benchmarks to which the Federal Reserve's annual data are adjusted by linear interpolation.

Loans are measured in terms of the number of new loans extended. The loan output measure is an aggregate of four types of loans: real estate, consumer, credit card, and, commercial and other loans. These loan outputs are aggregated by employment weights, derived from the FCA, for 1967, 1972, 1977, 1982, and 1987.

The output measure for real estate loans represents the number of residential mortgage loans, the number of construction loans, and the number of commercial mortgage loans. Data used to derive real estate loans are obtained from the Federal Housing Association (FHA) and the United States Department of Housing and Urban Development (HUD).

The index for consumer loans is a composite of the number of automobile loans, home improvement loans, personal loans, mobile home loans, and "other" installment loans. The weights used to aggregate the consumer loans output components are derived from American Bankers Association (ABA) data on the expense per average loan.

The output measure for commercial and "other" loans, for 1977 forward, is based on the number of loans as reported in the Federal Reserve's Survey of Terms of Bank Lending. Prior to 1977, no information on commercial loans is included in the banking output index.

The index of credit card services is based on the number of bank credit card transactions (both cash withdrawals and retail purchases) occurring within the

United States as reported by the VISA card network and the Mastercard Association.

The measure of trust department output is the number of accounts. The total number of accounts, by type, is combined on the basis of net income, as reported by the FCA.

Labor input in commercial banking is measured by an index of all-employee hours from 1967 forward. The number of employees and hours are derived from BLS establishment data. Average weekly hours are available only for non-supervisory workers. They are imputed to all employees. This procedure assumes that supervisory workers work the same number of average weekly hours as non-supervisory workers.

3.6 Services. The Bureau publishes only five measures in the services division of the SIC system, which includes, for example, hotels (SIC 7011) and automotive repair shops (SIC 753). The employment coverage for the services division is the lowest of all the sectors in the overall service sector at just under 16 percent. It is this sector where there are the least amount of price and quantity data and also the largest problems with defining the actual outputs of the industries.

Outputs are aggregated indexes of deflated revenues. In general, deflators are constructed from appropriate CPIs and revenue weights. Labor input indexes are derived from the Bureau's establishment survey of employment and hours, the Current Population Survey (CPS), and IRS data. The CPS and IRS data are used to estimate the number of self-employed and unpaid family workers.

An example of productivity measurement in the services division is the automotive repair shop industry (SIC 753). Annual measures of output are constructed by deflating total industry receipts, as reported in Current Business Reports, by the CPI index for the expenditure category "automotive maintenance and repair."

The annual output indexes for automotive repair shops are benchmarked every five years to the receipts data published in the Census of Service Industries. For a benchmark year, annual receipts are reported for 12 "kind of operation" groupings. The annual receipts are deflated by appropriate CPI's to the previous benchmark year, indexed, and combined to the 3-digit level using base-year paid-employee data as weights.

The receipts data available by "kind of operation" are for those "establishments with payroll". To arrive at an all establishment index, a coverage adjustment ratio is derived by dividing industry receipts of all establishments by receipts of establishments with payroll. The index of weighted receipts is multiplied by this coverage adjustment ratio to arrive at the final benchmark output index for each census period.

Labor input for automotive repair shops is an index of hours of all persons working in the industry. The number of employees and the average weekly hours of nonsupervisory workers are derived directly from the Bureau's establishment survey. The number of self-employed and unpaid family workers and the average weekly hours for both groups are derived from Current Population Survey data. The average hours of supervisory workers are constructed from the Census of Population. These hours are held constant between decennial census years. Average hours and employment by class of worker are multiplied and summed over all classes of workers in the industry.

4. Service Industry Productivity Trends

This section highlights the results of productivity, output, and hours changes in the service industries for the period 1967 to 1990. In 1967 there were 32 million people working in all the private business service industries (those which exclude nonprofit and government establishments) and 19.7 million people working in manufacturing industries. By 1991, the number of persons in the service industries had more than doubled to 63.9 million while the number working in manufacturing industries had actually dropped to 18.8 million. Within services the largest employment growth has come in the retail trade sector (which grew by 10 million) and the personal and business service sector (which grew by over 15 million during this time period). These two sectors accounted for over 75 percent of the employment growth occurring in service industries and 70 percent of the employment growth in the private business sector of the economy between 1967 and 1991.

Of the present 39 industry titles in the service sector, a total of 32 are for mutually exclusive service industries. The difference between the number of titles and industries arises from the overlap of measures for both a two-digit SIC classification and a three- or four-digit SIC classification within the two-digit group. There is at least one published measure for every major industry division in the service sector.[4] As of 1991, the BLS published industries covered over 40 percent of all workers in the service industries. For both the utilities sector and the retail trade sector the BLS has published industry productivity measures which cover over 80 percent of the workers.

Tables 4, 5, and 6 show the average growth rates of labor productivity, output, and labor input, respectively, for the published industries in the service sector. Time periods have been selected according to business cycle peaks except for 1967, which is the first year for which measures are available for most of the industries.

During the first time period, 1967-73, of the 24 industries, only one--bus carriers--experienced a productivity decline (-1.3 percent). The industry with the highest rate of productivity growth was petroleum pipelines (7.1 percent). Two industries, bus carriers and laundry and cleaning services, had negative output growth during this period. Telephone communications and electric utilities had the fastest output growth rates, 8.3 percent annual rates of increase in both cases.

During the second time period, 1973-79, 10 of the 31 industries experienced productivity declines. It is important to note that 19 of the original 24 industries had slower productivity growth during this "slowdown" period than in the earlier period. Six industries actually had output declines in this period and 19 had slower output growth rates than during the first period. The industry with the highest productivity growth rate for this period was the telephone communications industry (6.9 percent annually), which also had the largest increase in productivity growth between the two periods. Radio, television, and music stores, at 9.2 percent annually, had the fastest rate of output growth . The airline industry also showed strong growth of output and productivity, with rates of 6.8 percent and 4.8 percent respectively.

For the same time period, 1973-79, variety stores had the largest productivity decline (-2.7 percent), while family clothing stores experienced the largest decline in the annual productivity growth rate from the first to the second period (6.5 percentage points). The petroleum pipelines industry also had a large reversal in its productivity growth rate, dropping 6.5 percentage points from the previous time period. Two other industries showing poor performance during this period were gas utilities and electric utilities. The gas utilities productivity

[4] The Bureau does produce productivity measures for the Federal Government including the Postal Service. However, these measures are not included in this study. Technical notes describing detailed characteristics of all industry measures are available upon request.

rate dropped 2.9 percentage points and electric utilities dropped 3.9 percentage points from the first to the second period.

During the latest time period, 1979-90, 25 of 32 industries experienced increases in productivity. However, 17 industries had rates of productivity growth that were lower than in previous time period. Of these 17 industries, 10 also had slower productivity growth in the second period compared to the first. The service industry with the highest productivity growth rate for this period was railroad transportation with an impressive 8.3 percent rate. The industry with the slowest rate of productivity growth was gas utilities (-3.7 percent annually). This industry also had the largest decline in productivity growth from the second to the third time period.

5. Future Directions

The Bureau is proceeding simultaneously in two directions with productivity measures for service industries. One direction is enhancement of the present labor productivity measures with the development of multifactor productivity measures for industries. The other direction is to continue developing more labor productivity measures for industries not yet published.

The industry multifactor productivity measures provide information on factors underlying changes in labor productivity.[5] There are presently six multifactor measures, of which five are in manufacturing and one in services (railroads). These measures are based on gross output and a combined input index which includes labor hours, as well as capital services, energy, and other intermediate inputs, including purchased services. Multifactor productivity measures, unlike labor productivity measures, do not change as a result of substitution between measured inputs. Therefore, these measures are closer to an overall measure of industry efficiency than are the labor productivity measures. However, the development of these measures is very labor-intensive and requires significantly more data and time than labor productivity measures. Therefore we do not anticipate a rapid increase in the number of these measures in the near future.

Increasing the number of labor productivity measures for service industries has become a primary BLS goal because of the clear need for improved and more

[5] Results of these measure can be obtained from the Office of Productivity and Technology, Bureau of Labor Statistics, Washington, D.C. 20212.

detailed data for the service sector generally. However, a number of obstacles still must be overcome before significant strides can be made in this area. These obstacles can be grouped under two headings: 1) availability of data, and 2) conceptual definitions. Of course these problems often overlap. For example, problems with collecting output data can often be the result of not being able to clearly define the output in an industry. Similarly, price data cannot be collected if output cannot be defined. Aside from such complications, it is generally true that coverage of revenue and price data is scantier for service industries than for goods producing industries.

Defining the real output of some service industries continues to be a major stumbling block for both economists and statisticians alike. What do we really mean when we refer to the output of law firms, accounting firms, and recreational and entertainment concerns? How does one measure the output of educational institutions and medical delivery systems? Do the services of insurance companies increase when the deflated value of premiums rises?

Even for service industries with no definitional problems, important measurement problems may exist. For some industries, definitional problems do not exist and revenue or sales data are available. But if no appropriate price indexes exist, quantity or quality change cannot be separated from price change.

For some industries where the quality of output has been changing very rapidly, such as the computer industry, hedonic price indexes have been developed that measure price change independently of the change in the quality of the output. This avenue may provide some results in the development of price indexes for the service industries. However, hedonic price indexes are very expensive to develop and implement.

The BLS productivity measurement program relies greatly on data collected by other BLS programs and by other statistical agencies. A Federal Government initiative is presently under way to improve the service industry data prepared by these other organizations. As these improved data become more available, it will be possible for BLS to prepare additional service sector productivity measures. This initiative, however, will not necessarily lead to improved definitions of output for service sector industries; that problem deserves increased attention by the research community, including researchers within the statistical agencies.

Table 4. Output per hour for service industries, average annual rates of change (percent) [1]

Industry	Annual growth rate			Change in annual growth rate from	
	1967-73	1973-79	1979-90	1967-73 to 1973-79	1973-79 to 1979-90
Transportation					
Railroad Transportation, Revenue Traffic SIC 4011	4.9%	1.4%	8.3%	-3.5%	6.9%
Bus Carriers, Class I SIC 411,413,414 (part) [2]	-1.3	-1.3	-0.3	0.0	0.9
Trucking, Except Local SIC 4213 [2,3]	3.6	3.2	2.7	-0.4	-0.5
Trucking, Exc. Local, Gen. Freight SIC 4213 (pt) [2,3]	3.4	4.0	3.0	0.6	-1.0
Air Transportation SIC 4512,13,4522 (part) [3]	4.7	4.8	1.3	0.1	-3.5
Petroleum Pipelines SIC 4612,13	7.1	0.6	0.6	-6.5	-0.1
Communications					
Telephone Communications SIC 481	4.6	6.9	4.7	2.3	-2.2
Electric, Gas, and Sanitary Services					
Gas and Electric Utilities SIC 491,492,493	4.5	0.9	0.1	-3.7	-0.7
Electric Utilities SIC 491,493 (part)	5.2	1.3	1.4	-3.9	0.1
Gas Utilities SIC 492,493 (part)	2.8	-0.2	-3.7	-2.9	-3.6

Table 4--continued

Industry	Annual growth rate			Change in annual growth rate from	
	1967-73	1973-79	1979-90	1967-73 to 1973-79	1973-79 to 1979-90
Trade					
Scrap and Waste Materials SIC 5093			2.5		
Hardware Stores SIC 5251		2.6	1.1		-1.5
Department Stores SIC 5311	2.0	3.1	2.2	1.2	-0.9
Variety Stores SIC 5331	1.2	-2.7	1.1	-3.9	3.8
Retail Food Stores SIC 54	1.2	-0.6	-0.9	-1.8	-0.2
Grocery Stores SIC 5411		-0.3	-1.1		-0.8
Retail Bakeries SIC 546		-1.9	-0.3		1.6
Franchised New Car Dealers SIC 5511	2.9	0.3	2.0	-2.6	1.7
Auto and Home Supply Stores SIC 5531		2.3	2.5		0.2
Gasoline Service Stations SIC 5541	5.3	3.7	2.5	-1.6	-1.3
Apparel and Accessory Stores SIC 56	3.5	2.1	2.3	-1.3	0.2
Men's and Boys' Clothing Stores SIC 5611	3.7	0.8	1.6	-2.8	0.8
Women's Ready-To-Wear Stores SIC 5621	4.7	3.6	3.1	-1.1	-0.5
Family Clothing Stores SIC 5651	6.4	-0.1	2.7	-6.5	2.8
Shoe Stores SIC 5661	0.9	2.0	1.3	1.1	-0.7
Home Furniture, Furnishings, & Equip. Stores SIC 57	5.2	2.1	3.4	-3.1	1.4
Furniture & Homefurnishings Stores SIC 571	5.1	1.5	1.3	-3.6	-0.1
Appliance,Radio,TV, & Computer Stores SIC 572,73	5.5	3.0	6.4	-2.5	3.4

Table 4--continued

Industry	Annual growth rate			Change in annual growth rate from	
	1967-73	1973-79	1979-90	1967-73 to 1973-79	1973-79 to 1979-90
Household Appliance Stores SIC 5722		3.4	3.4		0.0
Radio, Television, and Computer Stores SIC 573		2.4	7.3		5.0
Eating and Drinking Places SIC 581	1.0	-0.7	-0.5	-1.6	0.2
Drug and Proprietary Stores SIC 5912	6.4	1.1	0.5	-5.3	-0.6
Liquor Stores SIC 5921		-0.7	0.2		0.9
Finance, Insurance, and Real Estate					
Commercial Banks SIC 602	2.2	0.6	2.2	-1.6	1.6
Services					
Hotels and Motels SIC 7011	1.8	1.1	-2.0	-0.7	-3.1
Laundry, Cleaning, and Garment Services SIC 721	0.5	-0.2	-1.0	-0.6	-0.8
Beauty and Barber Shops SIC 7231,41		1.1	1.0		-0.1
Beauty Shops SIC 723		0.3	1.2		1.0
Automotive Repair Shops SIC 753		-0.7	0.1		0.7

1 Compound average annual rates of change.
2 1979-89.
3 Labor input used is number of employees.

Table 5. Output for service industries, average annual rates of change (percent) [1]

Industry	Annual growth rate			Change in annual growth rate from	
	1967-73	1973-79	1979-90	1967-73 to 1973-79	1973-79 to 1979-90
Transportation					
Railroad Transportation, Revenue Traffic SIC 4011	2.2%	0.1%	1.1%	-2.1%	1.0%
Bus Carriers, Class I SIC 411,413,414 (part) [2]	-3.7	-0.9	-3.8	2.8	-2.9
Trucking, Except Local SIC 4213 [2,3]	7.0	2.0	-0.7	-5.1	-2.7
Trucking, Exc. Local, Gen. Freight SIC 4213 (pt) [2,3]	5.5	1.3	-1.2	-4.2	-2.5
Air Transportation SIC 4512,13,4522 (part) [3]	7.4	6.8	4.9	-0.6	-1.8
Petroleum Pipelines SIC 4612,13	5.1	4.0	-0.3	-1.1	-4.3
Communications					
Telephone Communications SIC 481	8.3	8.2	3.9	-0.1	-4.3
Electric, Gas, and Sanitary Services					
Gas and Electric Utilities SIC 491,492,493	6.7	2.4	1.0	-4.3	-1.4
Electric Utilities SIC 491,493 (part)	8.3	3.4	2.6	-4.9	-0.8
Gas Utilities SIC 492,493 (part)	3.2	-0.1	-3.6	-3.3	-3.5

Table 5--continued

Industry	Annual growth rate			Change in annual growth rate from	
	1967-73	1973-79	1979-90	1967-73 to 1973-79	1973-79 to 1979-90
Trade					
Scrap and Waste Materials SIC 5093			2.6		
Hardware Stores SIC 5251		4.3	1.0		-3.3
Department Stores SIC 5311	5.9	2.9	3.3	-3.0	0.4
Variety Stores SIC 5331	2.3	-5.2	-3.8	-7.5	1.4
Retail Food Stores SIC 54	2.2	1.1	1.2	-1.1	0.0
Grocery Stores SIC 5411		1.4	1.2		-0.2
Retail Bakeries SIC 546		0.3	1.7		1.4
Franchised New Car Dealers SIC 5511	4.7	0.3	2.6	-4.4	2.3
Auto and Home Supply Stores SIC 5531		5.8	4.1		-1.7
Gasoline Service Stations SIC 5541	5.1	-1.2	1.6	-6.3	2.8
Apparel and Accessory Stores SIC 56	4.7	4.3	4.1	-0.4	-0.2
Men's and Boys' Clothing Stores SIC 5611	5.4	0.5	-1.8	-5.0	-2.3
Women's Ready-To-Wear Stores SIC 5621	5.9	5.3	3.7	-0.6	-1.6
Family Clothing Stores SIC 5651	6.4	4.6	7.0	-1.8	2.4
Shoe Stores SIC 5661	2.9	4.2	2.8	1.3	-1.4
Home Furniture, Furnishings, & Equip. Stores SIC 57	7.2	4.4	5.2	-2.9	0.9
Furniture & Homefurnishings Stores SIC 571	7.7	3.0	3.0	-4.8	0.0
Appliance,Radio,TV, & Computer Stores SIC 572,73	6.4	6.6	8.5	0.1	1.9

Table 5--continued

Industry	Annual growth rate			Change in annual growth rate from	
	1967-73	1973-79	1979-90	1967-73 to 1973-79	1973-79 to 1979-90
Household Appliance Stores SIC 5722		2.1	2.9		0.8
Radio, Television, and Computer Stores SIC 573		9.2	10.5		1.3
Eating and Drinking Places SIC 581	3.8	3.2	2.3	-0.6	-0.9
Drug and Proprietary Stores SIC 5912	5.6	1.5	1.7	-4.0	0.2
Liquor Stores SIC 5921		0.8	-0.9		-1.7
Finance, Insurance, and Real Estate					
Commercial Banks SIC 602	8.1	4.6	3.4	-3.5	-1.2
Services					
Hotels and Motels SIC 7011	3.8	4.0	1.9	0.2	-2.1
Laundry, Cleaning, and Garment Services SIC 721	-4.6	-3.4	0.3	1.3	3.6
Beauty and Barber Shops SIC 7231,41		-0.2	2.5		2.7
Beauty Shops SIC 723		1.0	3.4		2.5
Automotive Repair Shops SIC 753		3.9	3.3		-0.7

1 Compound average annual rates of change.
2 1979-89.
3 Labor input used is number of employees.

Table 6. Hours for service industries, average annual rates of change (percent) [1]

Industry	Annual growth rate			Change in annual growth rate from	
	1967-73	1973-79	1979-90	1967-73 to 1973-79	1973-79 to 1979-90
Transportation					
Railroad Transportation, Revenue Traffic SIC 4011	2.6%	-1.3%	-6.6%	1.3%	-5.4%
Bus Carriers, Class I SIC 411,413,414 (part) [2]	-2.4	0.4	-3.5	2.8	-3.8
Trucking, Except Local SIC 4213 [2,3]	3.3	-1.2	-3.3	-4.5	-2.1
Trucking, Exc. Local, Gen. Freight SIC 4213 (pt) [2,3]	2.0	-2.6	-4.1	-4.7	-1.4
Air Transportation SIC 4512,13,4522 (part) [3]	2.6	1.9	3.6	-0.7	1.7
Petroleum Pipelines SIC 4612,13	-1.9	3.3	-0.8	5.2	-4.2
Communications					
Telephone Communications SIC 481	3.5	1.3	-0.8	-2.3	-2.0
Electric, Gas, and Sanitary Services					
Gas and Electric Utilities SIC 491,492,493	2.1	1.5	0.9	-0.5	-0.6
Electric Utilities SIC 491,493 (part)	2.9	2.1	1.2	-0.8	-0.9
Gas Utilities SIC 492,493 (part)	0.4	0.0	0.1	-0.4	0.1

Table--6 continued

Industry	Annual growth rate			Change in annual growth rate from	
	1967-73	1973-79	1979-90	1967-73 to 1973-79	1973-79 to 1979-90
Trade					
Scrap and Waste Materials SIC 5093			0.1		
Hardware Stores SIC 5251	3.8	1.7	-0.0	-2.1	-1.8
Department Stores SIC 5311	1.1	-0.2	1.1	-1.3	1.3
Variety Stores SIC 5331	1.0	-2.6	-4.9	-3.6	-2.3
Retail Food Stores SIC 54		1.8	2.1		0.3
Grocery Stores SIC 5411		1.7	2.3		0.6
Retail Bakeries SIC 546		2.2	2.0		-0.2
Franchised New Car Dealers SIC 5511	1.8	0.1	0.6	-1.7	0.5
Auto and Home Supply Stores SIC 5531		3.4	1.5		-1.9
Gasoline Service Stations SIC 5541	-0.2	-4.7	-0.8	-4.5	3.9
Apparel and Accessory Stores SIC 56	1.2	2.1	1.7	0.9	-0.4
Men's and Boys' Clothing Stores SIC 5611	1.7	-0.3	-3.3	-2.1	-3.0
Women's Ready-To-Wear Stores SIC 5621	1.1	1.7	0.7	0.6	-1.0
Family Clothing Stores SIC 5651	0.0	4.8	4.2	4.8	-0.5
Shoe Stores SIC 5661	1.9	2.2	1.5	0.2	-0.6
Home Furniture, Furnishings, & Equip. Stores SIC 57	2.0	2.3	1.7	0.3	-0.5
Furniture & Homefurnishings Stores SIC 571	2.5	1.5	1.6	-1.0	0.1
Appliance,Radio,TV, & Computer Stores SIC 572,73	0.9	3.4	1.9	2.5	-1.5

Table 6--continued

Industry	Annual growth rate			Change in annual growth rate from	
	1967-73	1973-79	1979-90	1967-73 to 1973-79	1973-79 to 1979-90
Household Appliance Stores SIC 5722		-1.2	-0.5		0.8
Radio, Television, and Computer Stores SIC 573		6.6	3.0		-3.7
Eating and Drinking Places SIC 581	2.8	3.9	2.8	1.1	-1.1
Drug and Proprietary Stores SIC 5912	-0.8	0.4	1.2	1.2	0.8
Liquor Stores SIC 5921		1.6	-1.1		-2.6
Finance, Insurance, and Real Estate					
Commercial Banks SIC 602	5.7	4.0	1.1	-1.8	-2.8
Services					
Hotels and Motels SIC 7011	2.0	2.8	3.9	0.8	1.0
Laundry, Cleaning, and Garment Services SIC 721	-5.1	-3.2	1.3	1.9	4.5
Beauty and Barber Shops SIC 7231,41		-1.2	1.5		2.7
Beauty Shops SIC 723		0.7	2.2		1.5
Automotive Repair Shops SIC 753		4.6	3.2		-1.4

1 Compound average annual rates of change.
2 1979-89.
3 Labor input used is number of employees.

References

Baily, Martin Neil and Robert J. Gordon (1988). "The productivity slowdown, measurement issues, and the explosion of computer power," Brookings Papers on Economic Activity 2, 347-431.

Caves, Douglas W., Laurtis R. Christensen and Michael W. Tretheway (1983). "Productivity performance of U.S. trunk and local service airlines in the era of deregulation," *Economic Inquiry* 20, 312-24.

Dean, Edwin R. and Kent Kunze (1992). "Productivity measurement in service industries," in Zvi Griliches (ed.), *Output Measurement in the Service Sector* (University of Chicago Press, Chicago, IL), 73-107.

Gollop, Frank M. and Mark J. Roberts (1981). "The sources of economic growth in the U.S. electric power industry," in Thomas G. Cowing and Rodney E. Stevenson (eds.), *Productivity Measurement in Regulated Industries* (Academic Press, New York, NY), 107-143.

Gordon, Robert J. (1992). "Productivity in the transportation sector," in Zvi Griliches (ed.), *Output Measurement in the Services Sector* (University of Chicago Press, Chicago,IL), 371-427.

Griliches, Zvi, ed. (1992). *Output Measurement in the Service Sector* (University of Chicago Press, Chicago, IL).

Hill, T.P. (1977). "On goods and services," *Review of Income and Wealth* 23, 315-38.

Jablonski, Mary, Kent Kunze, and Phyllis F. Otto (1990). "Hours at work: a new base for BLS productivity statistics," *Monthly Labor Review* 113, 17-24.

Mark, Jerome A. (1988). "Measuring productivity in services industries," in Bruce R. Gulie and James Brian Quinn (eds.), *Technology in Services: Policies for Growth, Trade, and Employment* (National Academy Press, Washington, D.C.), 139-59.

Mohr, M.F. (1992). "The measurement and deflation of services output and inputs in BEA's Gross Product Originating estimates: past practice and planned improvements," in Z. Griliches (ed.), *Output Measurement in the Services Sector* (University of Chicago Press, Chicago, IL), 25-71.

Nelson, R.A., and M.E. Wohar (1983). "Regulation, scale economics, and productivity in steam electric generation," *International Economic Review* 20, 57-79.

Sherwood, M.K. (1994). "Difficulties in the measurement of service outputs," *Monthly Labor Review* 119, 11-19.

Siegel, I.R. (1961). "On the design of consistent output and input indexes for productivity measurement," in *Output, Input, and Productivity Measurement* (Princeton University Press, Princeton, NJ), 23-46.

U.S. Department of Labor, Bureau of Labor Statistics (1992). *BLS Handbook of Methods*, Bulletin 2414 (Washington, D.C.), 89-98.

_____ (1993). *Productivity Measures for Selected Industries and Government Services*, Bulletin 2421, (Washington, D.C.).

Chapter 2   The Role of Services in U.S. Production and Trade: an Analysis of Social Accounting Data for the 1980s

Ranjit S. Dighe, Joseph F. Francois, and Kenneth A. Reinert[1]

1 . Introduction

Services represent the dominant feature of modern "industrial" economies. In such economies, the service sectors account for a substantial share of both employment and production. This pattern has been viewed in some circles of the economic policy community as cause for alarm. In the academic community, it has been viewed as cause for research. In the economic literature, explanations for the growing importance of services range from inelastic consumer demand for services to productivity growth differentials and the role of services in production.[2] Much of the attention in this literature has been devoted to changes

---

[1] We would like to thank Clinton Shiells for comments and Greg Alward and James Franklin for data.

[2] See Baumol (1967), Clague (1985), Clark (1940), Francois (1990a), and Panagariya (1988). Clark noted that the share of services in income rises with economic growth, observing that the share of labor devoted to the production of services rises with income. He emphasized the role of income levels, arguing that the reasons for this growth in the tertiary sector had to be sought on the demand side. In contrast, Baumol's cost disease model emphasizes productivity

P. T. Harker (ed.), The Service Productivity and Quality Challenge, 43–80.
© 1995 *Kluwer Academic Publishers. Printed in the Netherlands.*

in relative prices for services, and in particular for consumer services. Such changes are highly correlated with income levels, and can be explained by the pattern of productivity growth, relative factor intensities, or scale economies. In this chapter, we take a different approach. Rather than focus explicitly on productivity and price trends, we direct our attention to the structural relationship of the service sectors to production in the U.S. economy, with some examination of the apparent change in this structural relationship in the 1980s. We attempt to shed light on the role of services in production by working within a social accounting framework.

The overall pattern of structural change in the U.S. economy in the 1980s has included a decline in the importance of most services as inputs for the construction and manufacturing sectors. However, we find two notable exceptions. For the bulk of construction and manufacturing activities, the importance of finance and insurance and of business services as intermediate inputs has increased. These service sectors also have demonstrated relatively high labor productivity gains and have accounted for a rising share of employment in the 1980s. Among business services, the sectors with the strongest linkages to the construction and manufacturing sectors include computer and data processing, management and consulting, advertising, and architectural and engineering services.

We have organized the chapter as follows. We provide some background in Section 2, emphasizing U.S. employment trends related to services. In Section 3, we then examine the linkages of 76 service sectors in a 102-sector social accounting matrix (SAM) of the U.S. economy for 1989. In Section 4, we address the structural change in the role of services between 1982 and 1989 using 43-sector SAMs for those two years. In Section 5, we present our conclusions. The SAMs are described in some detail in an Appendix.

---

differences as an engine driving structural change, while Francois emphasizes the links between producer service activities and the organization and specialization of modern production activities.

2. Background

Engineering, communications, finance and management and a myriad of other services are intermediate inputs into virtually every industry. They are critical to the organization of production and to productivity gains related to specialization and returns to scale. The recent literature on growth, returns to scale, and the division of labor has placed emphasis on such reorganization and associated returns due to specialization as important mechanisms for economic growth and gains from trade.[3]

Some of the most dramatic changes in employment since World War II have occurred in these sectors. The producer services sector, which accounted for 6 percent of U.S. employment in 1949, accounted for almost 12 percent of employment and approximately 20 percent of national product in 1977. By 1985, free-standing producer service firms accounted for 14.8 percent of employment. The employment share of consumer services, in contrast, fell from 10.77 percent in 1929 to 4.99 percent in 1977, and to 4.24 percent by 1985 (see Stanback 1977 and Francois 1990a). While producer services have seen substantial growth in the post-war period relative to other service sectors, the business and professional service subsectors have also outperformed other general services subsectors in terms of postwar labor productivity growth (Baumol, Blackman and Wolff 1985).

Producer service activities also represent a growing share of the activities that are performed within manufacturing firms. Figure 1 presents the importance of non-production workers as a share of total U.S. manufacturing employment. Non-production workers accounted for a steady 18 to 19 percent of manufacturing employment in the United States between 1919 and 1949 (excepting World War II).[4] In the Post War Period, however, there has been a dramatic increase in this share. This increase parallels the growth in service employment in free-standing

---

[3] See Francois (1990a, 1990b), Gold (1981), Grossman and Helpman (1990), Lucas (1988), and Romer (1986, 1990).

[4] The Department of Labor defines production workers as working supervisors and all nonsupervisory workers engaged in actual fabricating, processing, assembling and inspection, as well as other services that are closely related to production activities, including certain distribution, recordkeeping, and power plant activities.

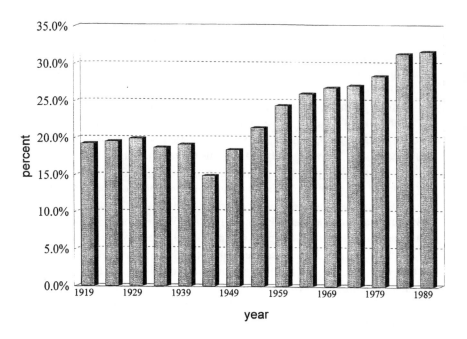

Source: *Employment and Earnings Survey*, U.S. Department of Labor, various issues

Figure 1. Indirect Labor Employed in Manufacturing as a Share of Total U.S. Manufacturing Employment.

producer service firms. Between 1949 and 1979, this share increased from 18.4 percent to 28.4 percent of manufacturing employment. Between 1979 and 1989, this share increased an additional 3.3 percent, to 31.7 percent of manufacturing employment. Comparable data for other OECD countries exhibit a similar pattern of shifting employment shares (see Francois 1990a).

3. Detailed Service Sector Linkages in 1989

In this section, we turn our attention to a 102-sector SAM for 1989 and examine the linkages of detailed producer service sectors to the construction and manufacturing sectors of the U.S. economy.[5] We first consider row and column normalizations (income and expenditure shares, respectively) of the SAM. We next examine a set of SAM multipliers and linkages to the rest of the world.

3.1 Production Linkages. To begin, denote the n x n social accounting matrix by S and a column unit n-vector by e. Then $c = e'S$ and $r = Se$ are the column-sum and row-sum vectors of S, respectively. If a caret over a vector denotes the corresponding n-dimensional diagonal matrix, then $A = S\hat{c}^{-1}$ and $B = \hat{r}^{-1}S$ represent the column-sum and row-sum normalized SAM, respectively. An element A_{ij} is the proportion of sector j's expenditure received by sector i, and element B_{ij} is the proportion of sector i's receipts paid by sector j.

We first compute the matrix B and restrict our attention to a submatrix of this row-normalized SAM. This submatrix contains those rows of B representing service sectors receiving at least one percent of their receipts from a construction or manufacturing sector. It contains those columns of B corresponding to construction or manufacturing sectors. This submatrix is presented in Table 1. The set of service sectors in the submatrix we term "detailed producer services."

---

[5] We exclude linkages to the agricultural sectors as well as those to the service sectors themselves in order to focus attention on linkages to those sectors considered most "productive" in the popular literature. Readers unfamiliar with SAMs may want to consult Pyatt and Round (1985).

Table 1. Detailed Producer Service Sector Receipt Shares from Construction and Manufacturing Sectors, 1989.

		6 construct	7 food	8 tobacco	9 textiles	10 apparel	11 lumber	12 furnit
27	railroads	0.047	0.074	0.000	0.003	0.001	0.018	0.004
29	motorfrt	0.082	0.063	0.000	0.004	0.003	0.005	0.003
30	transwater	0.020	0.037	0.000	0.002	0.001	0.003	0.000
31	transair	0.007	0.008	0.000	0.000	0.002	0.001	0.001
32	pipelines	0.013	0.002	0.000	0.000	0.000	0.002	0.000
35	communic	0.012	0.005	0.000	0.001	0.003	0.000	0.001
37	electric	0.005	0.014	0.000	0.003	0.002	0.003	0.001
38	gas	0.004	0.018	0.000	0.001	0.000	0.002	0.000
39	water	0.001	0.037	0.000	0.006	0.000	0.004	0.003
40	sanitary	0.016	0.017	0.000	0.005	0.002	0.003	0.002
41	tradewhol	0.061	0.066	0.000	0.005	0.007	0.009	0.004
42	traderet	0.151	0.001	0.000	0.000	0.000	0.001	0.000
43	banking	0.022	0.013	0.001	0.001	0.003	0.002	0.002
45	brokers	0.001	0.008	0.002	0.000	0.001	0.001	0.003
46	insurecarr	0.012	0.004	0.000	0.000	0.000	0.001	0.001
50	hotels	0.005	0.003	0.000	0.000	0.001	0.000	0.000
51	laundrclsh	0.001	0.012	0.000	0.001	0.002	0.001	0.001
57	rprmisc	0.067	0.025	0.000	0.007	0.003	0.006	0.003
58	bldgsvcs	0.001	0.009	0.000	0.001	0.001	0.001	0.001
59	personnel	0.005	0.013	0.000	0.010	0.008	0.002	0.003
60	compdata	0.016	0.010	0.000	0.001	0.002	0.000	0.002
61	mgtconsult	0.019	0.013	0.001	0.001	0.002	0.002	0.001
62	detprotect	0.000	0.024	0.001	0.006	0.007	0.013	0.005
63	equiprentl	0.147	0.030	0.000	0.002	0.004	0.008	0.003
64	photo	0.005	0.000	0.000	0.001	0.004	0.000	0.001
65	othbussvcs	0.000	0.012	0.000	0.006	0.001	0.000	0.010
66	advertise	0.000	0.085	0.012	0.002	0.003	0.000	0.003
68	enginarch	0.707	0.009	0.000	0.001	0.000	0.001	0.000
69	acctaudbk	0.012	0.020	0.000	0.002	0.004	0.001	0.006
95	uspostal	0.006	0.015	0.001	0.002	0.007	0.001	0.002
100	govtothsl	0.005	0.017	0.000	0.001	0.000	0.000	0.000

Table 1 (Cont.)

		13 paper	14 printpb	15 chemicl	16 petrlref	17 rubberpl	18 leather	19 stone
27	railroads	0.050	0.009	0.062	0.012	0.023	0.000	0.028
29	motorfrt	0.019	0.008	0.037	0.009	0.014	0.000	0.027
30	transwater	0.007	0.001	0.027	0.022	0.006	0.000	0.007
31	transair	0.005	0.008	0.013	0.002	0.002	0.000	0.002
32	pipelines	0.001	0.001	0.045	0.436	0.001	0.000	0.002
35	communic	0.001	0.005	0.004	0.001	0.001	0.000	0.001
37	electric	0.014	0.003	0.027	0.005	0.010	0.000	0.009
38	gas	0.015	0.001	0.039	0.020	0.003	0.000	0.019
39	water	0.028	0.000	0.089	0.021	0.014	0.000	0.006
40	sanitary	0.027	0.002	0.026	0.005	0.006	0.000	0.008
41	tradewhol	0.018	0.010	0.029	0.007	0.010	0.000	0.006
42	traderet	0.000	0.000	0.002	0.001	0.000	0.000	0.001
43	banking	0.002	0.004	0.011	0.006	0.003	0.000	0.003
45	brokers	0.002	0.000	0.010	0.005	0.005	0.000	0.002
46	insurecarr	0.000	0.002	0.002	0.000	0.001	0.000	0.000
50	hotels	0.001	0.005	0.004	0.000	0.000	0.000	0.000
51	laundrclsh	0.002	0.002	0.005	0.000	0.002	0.000	0.001
57	rprmisc	0.013	0.007	0.026	0.011	0.009	0.000	0.011
58	bldgsvcs	0.003	0.002	0.007	0.000	0.003	0.000	0.002
59	personnel	0.005	0.005	0.010	0.002	0.005	0.000	0.005
60	compdata	0.004	0.015	0.012	0.004	0.003	0.000	0.003
61	mgtconsult	0.006	0.008	0.047	0.007	0.006	0.000	0.005
62	detprotect	0.010	0.006	0.022	0.002	0.007	0.000	0.009
63	equiprentl	0.011	0.015	0.020	0.004	0.010	0.000	0.008
64	photo	0.002	0.030	0.006	0.000	0.001	0.000	0.002
65	othbussvcs	0.000	0.012	0.034	0.002	0.002	0.000	0.002
66	advertise	0.007	0.011	0.096	0.010	0.009	0.000	0.002
68	enginarch	0.004	0.001	0.006	0.004	0.005	0.000	0.005
69	acctaudbk	0.007	0.009	0.050	0.004	0.004	0.000	0.004
95	uspostal	0.004	0.034	0.011	0.002	0.003	0.000	0.003
100	govtothsl	0.005	0.001	0.005	0.002	0.001	0.000	0.001

Table 1 (Cont.)

		20 metalpr	21 metalfb	22 indmch	23 eleceq	24 transeq	25 instrum	26 mfgmsc
27	railroads	0.081	0.019	0.011	0.010	0.016	0.007	0.002
29	motorfrt	0.030	0.017	0.015	0.011	0.020	0.009	0.004
30	transwater	0.022	0.003	0.002	0.001	0.003	0.001	0.000
31	transair	0.003	0.007	0.018	0.018	0.015	0.006	0.001
32	pipelines	0.002	0.001	0.002	0.001	0.001	0.001	0.000
35	communic	0.001	0.005	0.007	0.006	0.004	0.005	0.001
37	electric	0.031	0.010	0.011	0.011	0.011	0.005	0.001
38	gas	0.029	0.008	0.005	0.004	0.006	0.002	0.000
39	water	0.024	0.011	0.011	0.016	0.015	0.005	0.000
40	sanitary	0.011	0.007	0.006	0.004	0.007	0.006	0.003
41	tradewhol	0.029	0.021	0.035	0.031	0.032	0.015	0.005
42	traderet	0.000	0.000	0.001	0.000	0.006	0.000	0.000
43	banking	0.005	0.007	0.014	0.014	0.014	0.005	0.001
45	brokers	0.003	0.004	0.006	0.008	0.005	0.001	0.003
46	insurecarr	0.002	0.002	0.002	0.001	0.002	0.001	0.000
50	hotels	0.001	0.004	0.011	0.011	0.012	0.002	0.000
51	laundrclsh	0.002	0.003	0.004	0.004	0.003	0.003	0.000
57	rprmisc	0.025	0.019	0.018	0.011	0.015	0.008	0.001
58	bldgsvcs	0.004	0.005	0.012	0.005	0.006	0.005	0.001
59	personnel	0.008	0.012	0.024	0.016	0.013	0.011	0.002
60	compdata	0.006	0.008	0.028	0.027	0.022	0.012	0.001
61	mgtconsult	0.006	0.014	0.027	0.027	0.034	0.015	0.002
62	detprotect	0.022	0.024	0.033	0.030	0.042	0.017	0.003
63	equiprentl	0.012	0.018	0.028	0.022	0.021	0.015	0.002
64	photo	0.000	0.011	0.020	0.010	0.005	0.013	0.002
65	othbussvcs	0.004	0.006	0.010	0.007	0.004	0.008	0.000
66	advertise	0.003	0.006	0.006	0.009	0.014	0.011	0.005
68	enginarch	0.010	0.018	0.038	0.025	0.025	0.011	0.001
69	acctaudbk	0.005	0.013	0.011	0.013	0.006	0.010	0.002
95	uspostal	0.005	0.007	0.011	0.016	0.016	0.007	0.002
100	govtothsl	0.002	0.003	0.003	0.003	0.003	0.002	0.000

Note: For sector descriptions, see Table A-1 of the Appendix.

To highlight the potential importance of construction and manufacturing sectors for producer service receipts, we consider management and consulting services (sector 61) and engineering and architectural services (sector 68). Nearly 5 percent of management and consulting services receipts in 1989 were from the chemicals and allied products sector (15). Approximately 3 percent of this sector's receipts came from each of the industrial machinery and equipment (22), electronic and other electric equipment (23), and transportation equipment (24) sectors. Over 70 percent of engineering and architectural services receipts in 1989 were from the construction sector, but this sector also received approximately 3 percent of its receipts from sectors 22, 23, and 24.

We next compute the matrix **A**. We again focus on a submatrix defined by the detailed producer service rows and construction and manufacturing columns. These expenditure shares are presented in Table 2. A number of construction and manufacturing sectors are intensive in either railroad or motor freight services.[6] These include construction (6), food and kindred products (7), paper and allied products (13), chemicals and allied products (15), rubber and miscellaneous plastics products (17), stone, clay and glass products (19), primary metal industries (20), and fabricated metal products (21). Not surprisingly, petroleum refining (16) is intensive in pipeline services.[7] Many of these sectors are also intensive in either electric or gas services. These are paper and allied products (13), chemicals and allied products (15), petroleum refining (16), rubber and miscellaneous plastics products (17), stone, clay and glass products (19), and primary metal industries (20). Most every column sector in Table 2 is intensive in wholesale trade, while construction (6) and lumber (11) are intensive in retail trade.[8]

---

[6] We (arbitrarily) define a construction or manufacturing sector to be "intensive" in the use of a detailed producer service input if at least one percent of its expenditures are on that service input.

[7] The input-output accounts used in the construction of the SAM (see Appendix) are "margined". Therefore, production of any good requires intermediate inputs of trade and transportation for final delivery. This should be kept in mind when considering these service linkages.

[8] Within the construction sector, the largest consumers of retail services are: maintenance and repair, other facilities; new residential structures; and new industrial and commercial buildings.

Table 2. Construction and Manufacturing Sector Expenditure Shares on Detailed Producer Service Sectors, 1989.

		6 construct	7 food	8 tobacco	9 textiles	10 apparel	11 lumber	12 furnit
27	railroads	0.002	0.006	0.000	0.001	0.000	0.007	0.003
29	motorfrt	0.015	0.019	0.002	0.006	0.003	0.007	0.008
30	transwater	0.001	0.005	0.000	0.002	0.000	0.002	0.000
31	transair	0.001	0.002	0.001	0.001	0.002	0.001	0.003
32	pipelines	0.000	0.000	0.000	0.000	0.000	0.000	0.000
35	communic	0.002	0.002	0.000	0.002	0.003	0.000	0.003
37	electric	0.001	0.006	0.001	0.009	0.003	0.007	0.005
38	gas	0.000	0.003	0.000	0.001	0.000	0.002	0.001
39	water	0.000	0.002	0.000	0.002	0.000	0.001	0.002
40	sanitary	0.000	0.000	0.000	0.001	0.000	0.000	0.000
41	tradewhol	0.043	0.081	0.012	0.037	0.034	0.052	0.048
42	traderet	0.132	0.001	0.000	0.000	0.000	0.012	0.001
43	banking	0.006	0.006	0.007	0.003	0.004	0.005	0.007
45	brokers	0.000	0.001	0.006	0.000	0.001	0.001	0.005
46	insurecarr	0.002	0.001	0.000	0.000	0.000	0.001	0.002
50	hotels	0.000	0.000	0.000	0.000	0.001	0.000	0.001
51	laundrclsh	0.000	0.000	0.000	0.000	0.000	0.000	0.000
57	rprmisc	0.002	0.001	0.000	0.002	0.000	0.001	0.002
58	bldgsvcs	0.000	0.000	0.000	0.000	0.000	0.000	0.000
59	personnel	0.000	0.000	0.000	0.004	0.002	0.000	0.001
60	compdata	0.001	0.002	0.001	0.002	0.001	0.000	0.004
61	mgtconsult	0.002	0.003	0.003	0.002	0.002	0.003	0.003
62	detprotect	0.000	0.000	0.000	0.001	0.000	0.001	0.001
63	equiprentl	0.007	0.002	0.000	0.001	0.001	0.003	0.002
64	photo	0.000	0.000	0.000	0.000	0.000	0.000	0.000
65	othbussvcs	0.000	0.001	0.001	0.004	0.000	0.000	0.010
66	advertise	0.000	0.028	0.048	0.003	0.004	0.001	0.008
68	enginarch	0.080	0.001	0.000	0.001	0.000	0.001	0.001
69	acctaudbk	0.000	0.002	0.000	0.001	0.001	0.001	0.006
95	uspostal	0.000	0.001	0.002	0.001	0.002	0.000	0.002
100	govtothsl	0.000	0.000	0.000	0.000	0.000	0.000	0.000
	value added	0.369	0.209	0.392	0.307	0.210	0.355	0.339

Table 2 (Cont.)

		13 paper	14 printpb	15 chemicl	16 petrlref	17 rubberpl	18 leather	19 stone
27	railroads	0.012	0.003	0.006	0.002	0.007	0.000	0.013
29	motorfrt	0.017	0.009	0.014	0.006	0.015	0.003	0.045
30	transwater	0.002	0.000	0.005	0.007	0.003	0.000	0.006
31	transair	0.004	0.008	0.004	0.001	0.002	0.000	0.003
32	pipelines	0.000	0.000	0.001	0.021	0.000	0.000	0.000
35	communic	0.001	0.006	0.002	0.001	0.002	0.001	0.002
37	electric	0.016	0.006	0.014	0.005	0.016	0.001	0.022
38	gas	0.008	0.001	0.010	0.010	0.003	0.000	0.022
39	water	0.005	0.000	0.007	0.003	0.003	0.000	0.002
40	sanitary	0.003	0.000	0.001	0.000	0.001	0.000	0.002
41	tradewhol	0.060	0.047	0.045	0.019	0.044	0.015	0.041
42	traderet	0.002	0.002	0.003	0.004	0.004	0.000	0.009
43	banking	0.003	0.008	0.006	0.006	0.005	0.002	0.008
45	brokers	0.001	0.000	0.002	0.002	0.003	0.000	0.002
46	insurecarr	0.000	0.002	0.001	0.000	0.001	0.000	0.001
50	hotels	0.000	0.004	0.001	0.000	0.000	0.001	0.000
51	laundrclsh	0.000	0.000	0.000	0.000	0.000	0.000	0.000
57	rprmisc	0.002	0.001	0.002	0.001	0.002	0.000	0.004
58	bldgsvcs	0.000	0.000	0.000	0.000	0.000	0.000	0.000
59	personnel	0.001	0.001	0.001	0.000	0.001	0.001	0.002
60	compdata	0.002	0.011	0.003	0.002	0.002	0.001	0.003
61	mgtconsult	0.004	0.007	0.013	0.003	0.005	0.002	0.006
62	detprotect	0.000	0.000	0.000	0.000	0.000	0.000	0.001
63	equiprentl	0.002	0.005	0.002	0.001	0.003	0.000	0.004
64	photo	0.000	0.004	0.000	0.000	0.000	0.000	0.000
65	othbussvcs	0.000	0.005	0.005	0.000	0.001	0.001	0.001
66	advertise	0.006	0.013	0.040	0.007	0.011	0.002	0.004
68	enginarch	0.002	0.001	0.001	0.001	0.003	0.000	0.005
69	acctaudbk	0.002	0.004	0.007	0.001	0.002	0.000	0.002
95	uspostal	0.001	0.013	0.001	0.000	0.001	0.001	0.001
100	govtothsl	0.000	0.000	0.000	0.000	0.000	0.000	0.000
	value added	0.315	0.419	0.318	0.158	0.281	0.157	0.348

Table 2 (Cont.)

		20 metalpr	21 metalfb	22 indmch	23 eleceq	24 transeq	25 instrum	26 mfgmsc
27	railroads	0.015	0.003	0.001	0.001	0.001	0.001	0.001
29	motorfrt	0.020	0.011	0.006	0.004	0.005	0.008	0.009
30	transwater	0.007	0.000	0.000	0.000	0.000	0.000	0.000
31	transair	0.001	0.004	0.006	0.006	0.003	0.005	0.002
32	pipelines	0.000	0.000	0.000	0.000	0.000	0.000	0.000
35	communic	0.001	0.003	0.003	0.002	0.001	0.005	0.003
37	electric	0.029	0.009	0.006	0.006	0.004	0.006	0.003
38	gas	0.013	0.003	0.001	0.001	0.001	0.001	0.000
39	water	0.003	0.001	0.000	0.001	0.000	0.001	0.000
40	sanitary	0.001	0.000	0.000	0.000	0.000	0.000	0.001
41	tradewhol	0.077	0.054	0.051	0.050	0.032	0.054	0.040
42	traderet	0.001	0.002	0.003	0.000	0.007	0.004	0.000
43	banking	0.005	0.007	0.007	0.008	0.005	0.007	0.004
45	brokers	0.001	0.001	0.001	0.002	0.000	0.001	0.003
46	insurecarr	0.001	0.001	0.000	0.000	0.000	0.001	0.000
50	hotels	0.000	0.001	0.002	0.002	0.002	0.001	0.000
51	laundrclsh	0.000	0.000	0.000	0.000	0.000	0.000	0.000
57	rprmisc	0.003	0.002	0.001	0.001	0.000	0.001	0.000
58	bldgsvcs	0.000	0.000	0.000	0.000	0.000	0.001	0.000
59	personnel	0.001	0.001	0.002	0.001	0.000	0.002	0.001
60	compdata	0.002	0.003	0.006	0.007	0.003	0.007	0.001
61	mgtconsult	0.003	0.007	0.007	0.008	0.006	0.010	0.003
62	detprotect	0.001	0.001	0.001	0.001	0.001	0.001	0.000
63	equiprentl	0.002	0.003	0.003	0.002	0.001	0.004	0.001
64	photo	0.000	0.000	0.000	0.000	0.000	0.001	0.000
65	othbussvcs	0.001	0.001	0.001	0.001	0.000	0.003	0.000
66	advertise	0.002	0.004	0.002	0.004	0.004	0.011	0.012
68	enginarch	0.004	0.007	0.009	0.006	0.004	0.006	0.001
69	acctaudbk	0.001	0.003	0.001	0.002	0.000	0.003	0.002
95	uspostal	0.001	0.001	0.001	0.002	0.001	0.002	0.001
100	govtothsl	0.000	0.000	0.000	0.000	0.000	0.000	0.000
	value added	0.229	0.372	0.311	0.315	0.232	0.253	0.282

Note: For sector descriptions, see Table A-1 of the Appendix.

The printing and publishing sector (14) is intensive in computer and data processing services. Chemicals and allied products (15) and instruments and related products (25) are intensive in management and consulting services (61). The furniture sector (12) is intensive in other business services (65). Food and kindred products (7), tobacco (8), printing and publishing (14), chemicals and allied products (15), rubber and miscellaneous plastics products (17), instruments and related products (25), and miscellaneous manufacturing industries (26) are those sectors intensive in advertising services (66). The construction sector (6) is intensive in engineering and architectural services (68), and printing and publishing (14) is intensive in U.S. postal services.

We next divide the n accounts of the SAM into two groups: m endogenous accounts and k exogenous accounts. Following convention, we define the k exogenous accounts as the government, capital, and rest-of-the-world accounts.[9] All remaining accounts, including the household account, are endogenous. Define the submatrix of $\mathbf{A}$ consisting of the m endogenous sectors as $\mathbf{A}_{mm}$. The multiplier matrix is given by $\mathbf{M} = (\mathbf{I}_m - \mathbf{A}_{mm})^{-1}$, a representative element (M_{ij}) of which gives the direct and indirect effects on sector i income caused by an exogenous unit increase in sector j income.[10] We examine the submatrix of $\mathbf{M}$ with rows corresponding to the detailed producer service sectors and columns corresponding to the construction and manufacturing sectors. The elements of this submatrix are presented in Table 3.

---

[9] "In models based on the SAM, an important question is which accounts are to be assumed exogenous. Standard practice is to pick one or more of the government, capital, and rest of the world accounts, justifying the choice on the basis of macroeconomic theory" (Robinson, 1989, p. 902).

[10] It is important to recognize that the matrix M is not the standard Leontief multiplier matrix, since a number of institutional accounts (value added, enterprises, and households) are endogenous. For more on this distinction, see Roland-Holst (1990).

Table 3. Linear Multipliers of Detailed Producer Service Sectors for Changes in Construction and Manufacturing Final Demand.

		6 construct	7 food	8 tobacco	9 textiles	10 apparel	11 lumber	12 furnit
27	railroads	0.012	0.017	0.008	0.011	0.006	0.018	0.013
29	motorfrt	0.052	0.061	0.029	0.042	0.027	0.039	0.041
30	transwater	0.011	0.018	0.007	0.013	0.007	0.013	0.010
31	transair	0.023	0.023	0.020	0.021	0.016	0.020	0.022
32	pipelines	0.002	0.002	0.001	0.002	0.001	0.002	0.002
35	communic	0.038	0.036	0.030	0.034	0.027	0.032	0.034
37	electric	0.051	0.052	0.041	0.056	0.035	0.050	0.048
38	gas	0.025	0.027	0.019	0.026	0.016	0.024	0.023
39	water	0.007	0.009	0.006	0.011	0.005	0.007	0.008
40	sanitary	0.005	0.007	0.004	0.007	0.004	0.005	0.005
41	tradewhol	0.158	0.210	0.109	0.154	0.119	0.167	0.159
42	traderet	0.282	0.147	0.131	0.135	0.095	0.152	0.133
43	banking	0.057	0.056	0.052	0.049	0.037	0.051	0.052
45	brokers	0.019	0.020	0.025	0.018	0.013	0.019	0.023
46	insurecarr	0.039	0.036	0.032	0.033	0.023	0.035	0.034
50	hotels	0.015	0.014	0.012	0.013	0.010	0.013	0.013
51	laundrclsh	0.005	0.005	0.004	0.004	0.003	0.004	0.004
57	rprmisc	0.009	0.010	0.005	0.010	0.006	0.008	0.008
58	bldgsvcs	0.007	0.006	0.005	0.006	0.004	0.006	0.006
59	personnel	0.008	0.008	0.006	0.012	0.008	0.007	0.008
60	compdata	0.023	0.021	0.018	0.020	0.014	0.018	0.022
61	mgtconsult	0.027	0.025	0.022	0.026	0.018	0.024	0.024
62	detprotect	0.004	0.004	0.003	0.004	0.003	0.005	0.005
63	equiprentl	0.016	0.011	0.007	0.010	0.007	0.012	0.011
64	photo	0.004	0.003	0.003	0.003	0.003	0.003	0.003
65	othbussvcs	0.015	0.015	0.013	0.019	0.011	0.013	0.024
66	advertise	0.045	0.070	0.093	0.048	0.032	0.035	0.042
68	enginarch	0.093	0.011	0.007	0.010	0.006	0.010	0.010
69	acctaudbk	0.016	0.017	0.011	0.016	0.011	0.013	0.019
95	uspostal	0.012	0.013	0.013	0.012	0.010	0.011	0.013
100	govtothsl	0.005	0.005	0.004	0.004	0.003	0.004	0.004

Table 3 (Cont.)

		13 paper	14 printpb	15 chemicl	16 petrlref	17 rubberpl	18 leather	19 stone
27	railroads	0.024	0.014	0.017	0.008	0.018	0.004	0.023
29	motorfrt	0.054	0.046	0.050	0.028	0.053	0.018	0.087
30	transwater	0.014	0.010	0.017	0.017	0.015	0.004	0.018
31	transair	0.024	0.032	0.025	0.016	0.023	0.009	0.022
32	pipelines	0.002	0.002	0.003	0.024	0.002	0.000	0.002
35	communic	0.033	0.042	0.034	0.024	0.034	0.014	0.034
37	electric	0.062	0.054	0.060	0.041	0.062	0.019	0.066
38	gas	0.033	0.026	0.035	0.028	0.028	0.009	0.048
39	water	0.012	0.007	0.015	0.008	0.011	0.003	0.008
40	sanitary	0.009	0.006	0.007	0.004	0.006	0.002	0.007
41	tradewhol	0.176	0.169	0.153	0.091	0.157	0.063	0.144
42	traderet	0.138	0.152	0.140	0.109	0.137	0.056	0.148
43	banking	0.048	0.058	0.053	0.042	0.051	0.021	0.053
45	brokers	0.018	0.019	0.021	0.016	0.022	0.008	0.020
46	insurecarr	0.033	0.038	0.033	0.025	0.033	0.014	0.034
50	hotels	0.013	0.018	0.014	0.009	0.013	0.006	0.013
51	laundrclsh	0.004	0.005	0.004	0.003	0.004	0.002	0.004
57	rprmisc	0.009	0.009	0.008	0.006	0.009	0.003	0.010
58	bldgsvcs	0.006	0.007	0.006	0.004	0.006	0.002	0.006
59	personnel	0.008	0.009	0.008	0.005	0.008	0.004	0.009
60	compdata	0.020	0.033	0.022	0.016	0.021	0.008	0.021
61	mgtconsult	0.025	0.030	0.038	0.019	0.030	0.011	0.027
62	detprotect	0.004	0.004	0.004	0.002	0.004	0.001	0.005
63	equiprentl	0.011	0.015	0.011	0.007	0.012	0.004	0.012
64	photo	0.003	0.008	0.004	0.002	0.003	0.001	0.003
65	othbussvcs	0.013	0.021	0.019	0.010	0.015	0.006	0.014
66	advertise	0.042	0.053	0.083	0.033	0.056	0.019	0.039
68	enginarch	0.011	0.009	0.010	0.010	0.013	0.003	0.015
69	acctaudbk	0.015	0.018	0.022	0.010	0.016	0.005	0.015
95	uspostal	0.011	0.026	0.012	0.008	0.012	0.006	0.012
100	govtothsl	0.005	0.005	0.004	0.003	0.004	0.002	0.004

Table 3 (Cont.)

		20 metalpr	21 metalfb	22 indmch	23 eleceq	24 transeq	25 instrum	26 mfgmsc
27	railroads	0.028	0.015	0.009	0.009	0.009	0.011	0.007
29	motorfrt	0.058	0.048	0.034	0.032	0.033	0.042	0.031
30	transwater	0.021	0.012	0.008	0.007	0.008	0.009	0.007
31	transair	0.020	0.024	0.024	0.024	0.021	0.026	0.015
32	pipelines	0.002	0.002	0.001	0.001	0.001	0.002	0.001
35	communic	0.030	0.035	0.031	0.030	0.027	0.037	0.024
37	electric	0.075	0.058	0.045	0.044	0.041	0.049	0.032
38	gas	0.039	0.029	0.021	0.020	0.019	0.023	0.015
39	water	0.010	0.008	0.006	0.007	0.006	0.007	0.004
40	sanitary	0.006	0.005	0.004	0.004	0.004	0.006	0.004
41	tradewhol	0.191	0.174	0.151	0.145	0.132	0.169	0.112
42	traderet	0.127	0.139	0.118	0.113	0.116	0.130	0.090
43	banking	0.048	0.053	0.048	0.047	0.043	0.052	0.034
45	brokers	0.018	0.020	0.017	0.018	0.015	0.018	0.016
46	insurecarr	0.031	0.034	0.029	0.028	0.026	0.031	0.022
50	hotels	0.012	0.015	0.014	0.014	0.013	0.014	0.009
51	laundrclsh	0.004	0.004	0.004	0.004	0.003	0.004	0.003
57	rprmisc	0.010	0.009	0.007	0.006	0.006	0.008	0.004
58	bldgsvcs	0.006	0.006	0.006	0.005	0.005	0.006	0.004
59	personnel	0.007	0.009	0.008	0.007	0.006	0.009	0.005
60	compdata	0.020	0.022	0.024	0.024	0.020	0.027	0.013
61	mgtconsult	0.023	0.028	0.027	0.027	0.026	0.034	0.017
62	detprotect	0.005	0.005	0.004	0.004	0.004	0.005	0.002
63	equiprentl	0.011	0.012	0.011	0.010	0.009	0.013	0.007
64	photo	0.003	0.004	0.004	0.003	0.003	0.005	0.003
65	othbussvcs	0.013	0.015	0.013	0.012	0.011	0.016	0.009
66	advertise	0.034	0.038	0.031	0.033	0.032	0.047	0.036
68	enginarch	0.015	0.018	0.018	0.015	0.013	0.017	0.007
69	acctaudbk	0.014	0.016	0.013	0.013	0.011	0.017	0.010
95	uspostal	0.010	0.012	0.010	0.011	0.010	0.013	0.009
100	govtothsl	0.004	0.004	0.003	0.003	0.003	0.004	0.003

Note: For sector descriptions, see Table A-1 of the Appendix.

The Table 2 results provided estimates of the direct effects of changes in construction and manufacturing final demand on the producer service sectors. In contrast, Table 3 gives estimates of direct and indirect effects of changes in these final demands on the producer service sectors. The indirect effects include those from other intermediate linkages as well as linkages via increased household demand. For example, whereas the direct effect of changes in final demand for food and kindred products (7) on motor freight (29) is estimated to be approximately 2 percent, the direct and indirect effects are estimated to be approximately 6 percent. Examination of Table 3 reveals the set of producer service sectors with the strongest linkages to the construction and manufacturing sectors of the U.S. economy. These are the transportation services sectors, the utility sectors, the trade and financial sectors, computer and data processing, management consulting, advertising, and engineering and architectural services. While none of these structural features should be surprising, it is worthwhile to illustrate them with some detail and precision since they are so often overlooked in debates on the role of "burger-flipping" service sectors.

3.2 Trade Linkages. To complete this section of the chapter, we address the direct and indirect linkages of the detailed producer service sectors to the rest of the world.[11] Define f_i as the export final demand for commodity i and $\mathbf{f}$ as the column vector of these elements. The coefficient $\emptyset_i = f_i/\mathbf{f}\mathbf{e}$ gives the share of commodity i in total export demand, and the column vector $\emptyset$ contains the full set of these coefficients. A subvector of $\emptyset$ corresponding to the detailed producer service sectors is presented in the first column of Table 4. Only five of these

---

[11] As explained in the Appendix, effort was made to include the best data available on U.S. trade in services into the 1989 SAM. The following results make use of this data.

Table 4. External Linkages of Detailed Producer Services, 1989.

Sector	ϕ^a	Ωb	γ^c	μ^d
27 railroads	0.00	0.01	0.03	0.15
29 motorfrt	0.00	0.04	0.00	0.11
30 transwater	0.03	0.06	0.26	0.48
31 transair	0.05	0.08	0.17	0.29
32 pipelines	0.00	0.00	0.00	0.14
35 communicat	0.01	0.04	0.05	0.14
37 electric	0.00	0.05	0.00	0.13
38 gas	0.00	0.02	0.03	0.20
39 water	0.00	0.01	0.00	0.12
40 sanitary	0.00	0.01	0.00	0.11
41 tradewhol	0.00	0.14	0.00	0.10
42 traderet	0.00	0.13	0.00	0.10
43 banking	0.00	0.05	0.00	0.11
45 brokers	0.01	0.04	0.03	0.14
46 insurecarr	0.00	0.04	0.01	0.10
50 hotels	0.04	0.05	0.20	0.28
51 laundrclsh	0.00	0.00	0.00	0.13
57 rprmisc	0.00	0.01	0.03	0.20
58 bldgsvcs	0.00	0.01	0.00	0.12
59 personnel	0.00	0.01	0.00	0.11
60 compdatapr	0.00	0.03	0.00	0.12
61 mgtconsult	0.00	0.03	0.00	0.12
62 detprotect	0.00	0.00	0.00	0.13
63 equiprentl	0.00	0.01	0.00	0.11
64 photo	0.00	0.00	0.00	0.12
65 othbussvcs	0.00	0.01	0.00	0.12
66 advertise	0.00	0.04	0.00	0.13
68 enginarch	0.00	0.02	0.01	0.11
69 acctaudbk	0.00	0.01	0.00	0.10
95 uspostal	0.00	0.01	0.00	0.12
100 govtothsl	0.00	0.00	0.00	0.13

[a] Share in total export demand. [b] Weighted average, direct and indirect effect of increasing export demand by one dollar. [c] The share of expenditures to the rest of the world (direct import leakages). [d] Total import leakages resulting from the direct and indirect effects of a dollar increase in exogenous final demand for the sector in question.

sectors has a positive $\emptyset_i$ coefficient. These are water transportation (30), air transportation (31), communication, except radio and TV (35), security and commodity brokers (45), hotels and lodging places (50). These coefficients represent the direct effect of an increase in export final demand.

The column vector $\Omega = \mathbf{M}\emptyset$ gives the weighted average, direct and indirect effect on sector i of increasing export demand by one dollar, holding its sectoral composition constant. A subvector of Ω corresponding to the detailed producer service sectors is presented in the second column of Table 4. Indirect effects via intermediate and household demands cause positive coefficients in almost every cell of this vector. The two most export-sensitive sectors turn out to be wholesale and retail trade (41 and 42), despite the fact that they have no direct export linkages. These are followed by water transportation (30) and air transportation (31).

On the import side, define γ_j as the share of expenditures by endogenous sector j to the rest of the world (import leakages) and γ as the row vector of such expenditure shares. A subvector of γ corresponding to the detailed producer service sectors is presented in the third column of Table 4. The sectors with the largest direct import leakages are water transportation (30),[12] air transportation (31), and hotels and lodging places (50).

The leakage multiplier vector is given by $\mu = \gamma \mathbf{M}$. This row vector gives the total import leakages resulting from the direct and indirect effects or a dollar increase in the exogenous final demand for good i. The detailed producer service

---

[12] For additional analysis of water transportation imports in a general equilibrium context, see Francois, Arce, Reinert, and Flynn (1992).

subvector of μ is presented in the last column of Table 4. The sectors with the largest total import leakages are again water transportation, air transportation, and hotels and lodging places. Changes in final demand for gas production and distribution (38) and miscellaneous repair shops (37) also generate a large total import leakage.

While producer services are not traded directly, they are tied to the economy's merchandise imports and exports via indirect linkages.[13] These indirect linkages are implicit in Table 3, but have been brought to the fore in Table 4.

4. Structural Change in the Service Sectors, 1982-1989

We next turn to the changes in producer service linkages in the 1980s. For this purpose, we compare two 43-sector SAMs for the years 1982 and 1989, focusing on the finance and insurance (32) and the business services (35) sectors.[14] We begin by calculating the percent change in receipt shares for services, presented in Table 5.

In general, the results of Table 5 demonstrate a decline in the receipt shares of the service sectors from the construction and manufacturing sectors during the 1982-1989 period. Notable exceptions to this pattern exist. First each service

---

[13] See Francois (1993) for more on the pattern of U.S. international trade in producer services. Overall, services represent a substantial share of total world trade. However, the measurement of international service flows is generally imprecise at best.

[14] The business services sector includes: miscellaneous repair shops; services to dwellings and other buildings; personnel supply services; computer and data processing services; management and consulting services; detective and protective services; equipment rental and leasing services; photofinishing labs, photocopy, and commercial photography; advertising; legal services; engineering, architectural, and surveying services; and accounting auditing and bookkeeping services.

Table 5. Percent Change in Receipt Shares for Services, 1982-1989.

	6 construct	7 food	8 tobacco	9 textiles	10 apparel	11 lumber	12 furnit
27 transport	-20.55	2.19	-64.00	-55.85	182.43	0.22	-16.98
28 communic	-34.78	-19.21	-65.51	-84.53	568.08	-15.06	-26.57
29 radioandtv	-	-	-	-	-	-100.00	-100.00
30 utilities	-24.83	-9.31	-54.09	-46.65	170.49	2.87	-1.28
31 trade	74.09	-4.08	-52.32	-64.77	237.03	27.29	-8.94
32 finaninsur	-46.88	-0.12	-36.00	-71.79	333.33	4.66	-4.49
33 realestate	-60.08	-52.11	-75.00	-89.47	82.60	-45.71	-50.00
34 hotelsrepr	-66.59	-60.24	-78.12	-86.94	20.43	-55.91	-58.20
35 businservc	-7.42	-12.64	-64.15	-62.76	242.35	8.91	-14.76
36 eatingdrin	-31.68	-8.55	-60.00	-72.85	253.84	1.03	-18.34
37 autorepair	-42.13	-46.20	-71.07	-82.43	158.33	-11.88	-49.56
38 amusement	-44.44	33.33	-71.42	-66.66	-	-	-28.30
39 healedusoc	-75.00	-52.27	-80.00	-76.19	-	-28.57	-50.00
40 fedgovtent	-29.66	-9.63	-58.53	-81.32	470.90	-	-15.17
41 statlocgov	-54.26	-42.63	-73.01	-66.91	210.00	-25.00	-48.00

	13 paper	14 printpb	15 chemicl	16 petrlref	17 rubberpl	18 leather	19 stone
27 transport	-5.81	-18.56	-1.73	-56.20	17.77	-35.84	0.74
28 communic	-22.12	-31.43	-6.45	-58.56	-	-51.42	-19.25
29 radioandtv	-100.00	-	-	-	-100.00	-	-100.00
30 utilities	13.70	10.35	2.48	-59.90	26.97	-33.33	-12.93
31 trade	7.31	21.02	18.26	-27.49	32.89	-34.61	16.93
32 finaninsur	4.73	3.51	26.63	-40.03	38.94	-46.15	13.33
33 realestate	-48.83	-36.26	-35.75	-79.67	-35.51	-80.00	-46.31
34 hotelsrepr	-63.32	-53.47	-53.37	-79.85	-55.93	-65.15	-60.89
35 businservc	-8.94	-14.90	3.65	-53.74	11.54	-48.75	-2.96
36 eatingdrin	-14.50	-19.48	10.73	-54.23	12.69	-50.00	-9.66
37 autorepair	-26.82	-20.72	-31.40	-71.42	-25.88	-73.07	-42.43
38 amusement	307.14	313.15	16.98	100.00	61.53	-	50.00
39 healedusoc	-35.71	-40.00	-34.88	-70.58	-35.71	-100.00	-41.66
40 fedgovtent	-13.89	-20.66	2.78	-55.19	8.33	-63.91	-5.50
41 statlocgov	-30.27	-33.51	-29.43	-70.26	-28.74	-41.53	-41.95

Table 5 (Cont.)

	20 metalpr	21 metalfb	22 indmch	23 eleceq	24 transeq	25 instrum	26 mfgmsc
27 transport	16.83	-13.41	-13.05	-13.87	-8.91	86.66	-21.25
28 communic	-9.67	-24.92	-29.81	-12.55	-24.01	95.23	-40.61
29 radioandtv	-60.00	-71.47	-33.33	-66.66	-16.66	-	-
30 utilities	7.49	-3.63	-11.83	9.87	6.17	108.29	-25.54
31 trade	20.00	-2.51	-6.43	2.50	16.63	127.16	-20.20
32 finaninsur	11.21	-6.65	14.23	23.30	5.57	133.57	-2.41
33 realestate	-37.20	-52.19	-46.64	-42.21	-55.45	22.66	-64.28
34 hotelsrepr	-57.55	-60.44	-44.94	-53.84	-56.39	-10.34	-68.96
35 businservc	12.50	-6.13	-0.52	5.34	2.54	91.25	-42.02
36 eatingdrin	9.47	-20.00	-12.52	-0.23	-15.44	96.14	-34.53
37 autorepair	-23.30	-45.28	-37.53	-20.72	-41.65	-2.53	-51.30
38 amusement	40.00	71.73	-6.89	40.54	3.35	99.02	326.47
39 healedusoc	-27.27	-44.18	-40.00	-40.90	-49.18	-6.52	-62.96
40 fedgovtent	8.70	-8.26	-12.63	-2.20	-7.56	97.47	-34.36
41 statlocgo	-27.84	-33.78	-40.20	-31.03	-33.08	34.64	-55.66

Note: For sector descriptions, see Table A-2 of the Appendix.

sector experienced an increased receipt share from the apparel sector (10).[15] Many of the service sectors also experienced an increased receipt share from the instruments and related products sector (25). The business service sector (35) shows increased receipt shares from apparel (10), lumber and wood products (11), chemicals and allied products (15), rubber and miscellaneous plastic products (17), primary metal industries (20), electronic and other electrical equipment (23), transportation equipment (24), and instruments and related products (25). The finance and insurance sector (32) shows increased receipt shares from lumber and wood products (11), paper and allied products (13), printing and publishing (14), chemicals and allied products (15), rubber and miscellaneous plastic products (17), stone, clay and glass products (19), primary metal industries (20), electronic and other electrical equipment (23), transportation equipment (24), and instruments and related products (25).

We next calculate the percent change in expenditure shares for the 1982-1989 period. These are presented in Table 6. The overall pattern discernible from this table is a decline in the service intensity of construction and manufacturing sectors. However, we again find two notable exceptions. For approximately 70 percent of the construction and manufacturing sectors, the finance and insurance intensity of production increased. Also, for approximately 70 percent of the construction and manufacturing sectors, the business service intensity of production increased. For approximately 60 percent of the construction and manufacturing sectors, both the finance and insurance intensity *and* the business service intensity of production increased. Therefore, those service sectors which demonstrated relatively high post-war productivity growth also were those which became more important in construction and manufacturing production in the 1980s.

---

[15] Note, however, that apparel expenditure shares on services did not in general increase (see Table 6).

Table 6. Percent Change in Expenditure Shares on Services, 1982-1989.

	6 construct	7 food	8 tobacco	9 textiles	10 apparel	11 lumber	12 furnit
27 transport	-21.45	26.85	-56.80	11.13	-48.42	-9.32	-27.57
28 communic	-32.61	5.23	-54.63	-59.18	29.80	-19.51	-32.74
29 radioandtv	-	-	-	-	-	-	-
30 utilities	-44.12	-15.62	-58.50	0.61	-62.89	-30.19	-35.48
31 trade	91.55	32.56	-36.51	-1.25	-30.72	28.20	-11.69
32 finaninsur	-39.25	43.29	-11.88	-17.57	-8.30	9.62	-3.71
33 realestate	-57.38	-36.24	-70.34	-70.27	-63.71	-47.47	-54.12
34 hotelsrepr	-63.40	-44.94	-72.65	-63.81	-75.23	-55.03	-59.69
35 businservc	19.60	41.71	-44.27	22.39	-17.11	28.84	-3.01
36 eatingdrin	-32.63	12.79	-53.20	-31.69	-35.27	-9.23	-28.59
37 autorepair	-54.49	-47.19	-72.23	-65.07	-62.50	-36.60	-65.24
38 amusement	-	133.33	-46.15	33.33	600.00	100.00	-12.79
39 healedusoc	-75.00	-22.00	-57.53	-20.31	-76.58	-12.08	-40.56
40 fedgovtent	-16.27	35.00	-40.54	-43.38	25.96	8.69	-11.19
41 statlocgov	-38.46	-	-55.81	13.79	-16.66	-5.88	-37.50

	13 paper	14 printpb	15 chemicl	16 petrlref	17 rubberpl	18 leather	19 stone
27 transport	-9.12	-28.64	-0.06	-3.64	6.90	-18.79	7.69
28 communic	-21.26	-37.12	-0.47	-4.80	-5.13	-35.84	-10.06
29 radioandtv	-	-	-	-	-	-	-
30 utilities	-17.73	-27.23	-21.84	-33.87	-13.65	-37.39	-30.28
31 trade	15.21	18.16	33.92	77.28	34.21	-9.55	38.97
32 finaninsur	16.76	5.14	48.83	52.73	46.38	-21.29	39.60
33 realestate	-47.20	-39.75	-29.76	-51.78	-36.96	-65.51	-38.38
34 hotelsrepr	-60.57	-54.55	-47.18	-50.00	-55.60	-50.92	-53.98
35 businservc	15.01	-2.45	37.78	33.06	32.53	-15.67	35.76
36 eatingdrin	-18.05	-29.66	12.17	0.41	2.00	-37.97	-3.88
37 autorepair	-44.10	-44.92	-44.44	-49.42	-46.55	-74.33	-51.22
38 amusement	428.57	414.81	63.63	600.00	100.00	-	120.00
39 healedusoc	-18.51	-28.70	-12.66	-16.00	-22.03	-35.29	-13.95
40 fedgovtent	-	-16.17	25.86	18.18	18.09	-45.52	21.76
41 statlocgov	-6.57	-19.23	-	-8.00	-9.09	3.33	-14.70

Table 6 (Cont.)

	20 metalpr	21 metalfb	22 indmch	23 eleceq	24 transeq	25 instrum	26 mfgmsc
27 transport	37.97	0.75	-9.51	-15.30	-25.17	18.92	-21.04
28 communic	11.60	-8.39	-23.57	-9.77	-34.57	30.17	-37.84
29 radioandtv	-	-50.00	-	-	-	-	-
30 utilities	-4.84	-15.87	-31.19	-18.94	-34.68	-0.39	-43.85
31 trade	57.68	26.33	8.39	12.20	6.69	61.13	-10.78
32 finaninsur	51.91	25.59	37.56	40.27	0.27	72.22	13.17
33 realestate	-20.38	-40.28	-40.48	-38.69	-60.70	-16.45	-61.49
34 hotelsrepr	-44.33	-48.77	-36.27	-49.48	-60.17	-36.52	-65.13
35 businservc	73.56	42.79	35.39	35.43	10.12	59.24	-24.10
36 eatingdrin	29.48	-7.18	-9.33	-2.14	-30.80	24.55	-34.37
37 autorepair	-27.94	-49.53	-48.28	-38.20	-61.96	-50.77	-61.47
38 amusement	133.33	178.57	33.33	96.00	19.35	77.77	492.30
39 healedusoc	7.14	-13.88	-17.33	-22.89	-44.82	-22.54	-51.36
40 fedgovtent	53.33	28.09	9.77	15.38	-8.55	51.25	-20.80
41 statlocgov	19.04	6.45	-16.66	-4.76	-22.22	16.66	-37.50

Note: For sector descriptions, see Table A-2 of the Appendix.

Finally, we calculate the percent change in linear multipliers for the 1982-1989 period. Again, we define the exogenous accounts as the government, capital, and rest-of-the-world accounts. Table 7 presents a submatrix of **M** as defined above for the service sector rows and construction and manufacturing columns of the 43-sector SAM. We again focus on the finance and insurance (32) and the business services (35) sectors. The largest percent change in multiplier (direct and indirect) linkages for finance and insurance occurred for changes in primary metal industries (20) final demand. This was followed by changes in final demand for textiles (9) and instruments and related products (25). The largest percent change in multiplier linkages for business services occurred for changes in instruments and related products (25) final demand. This was followed by changes in final demand for primary metal industries (20) and textiles (9). The textiles, primary metal, and instrument industries therefore figured prominently in the increased demand for these two producer service sectors. Other industries with relatively large increases in linkages to *both* the finance and insurance and the business service sectors are food and kindred products (7), lumber and wood products (11), paper and allied products (13), chemicals and allied products (15), petroleum refining and related industries (16), rubber and miscellaneous plastic products (17), stone clay and glass products (19), fabricated metal products (21), and transportation equipment (24).

5. Concluding Comments

The economic literature on the growth of the service sector has been focused on final expenditure patterns. In this chapter, we have instead examined the structural relationship of services to production. Working with social accounting data on the U.S. economy, we have examined the basic structural relationship of services to manufacturing production and construction as well as the apparent change in this relationship in the 1980s. While the service intensity of the construction and manufacturing sectors has declined in the 1980s for most service sectors, we find that substantial linkages exist between producer services and the construction and manufacturing sectors of the United States. The importance of business services, finance, and insurance as inputs to the construction and manufacturing sectors has grown over the period.

Table 7. Percent Change in Expenditure Multipliers, 1982-1989.

	6 construct	7 food	8 tobacco	9 textiles	10 apparel	11 lumber	12 furnit
27 transport	-15.16	-4.00	-29.74	1.37	-38.84	-15.32	-20.59
28 communic	-2.77	-0.40	-9.79	-5.71	-26.98	-1.79	-12.85
29 radioandtv	-34.32	-32.07	-46.66	-27.08	-53.84	-34.00	-41.37
30 utilities	-31.91	-31.68	-38.00	-19.39	-51.85	-33.79	-36.73
31 trade	27.13	10.78	-4.29	11.20	-26.78	8.40	-4.14
32 finaninsur	2.01	7.20	-0.19	14.58	-23.13	5.19	-1.78
33 realestate	1.69	-4.20	-3.83	8.83	-29.34	-0.96	-8.41
34 hotelsrepr	-15.34	-15.24	-17.85	-10.00	-44.18	-13.38	-24.54
35 businservc	29.60	30.90	-14.76	42.23	-8.88	27.32	14.27
36 eatingdrin	-8.00	-6.08	-12.64	-1.04	-35.15	-7.28	-16.87
37 autorepair	-29.06	-28.56	-34.46	-21.75	-48.47	-27.44	-37.12
38 amusement	14.82	11.34	2.25	22.14	-20.58	10.54	1.49
39 healedusoc	27.64	29.41	30.55	40.22	-10.63	30.37	16.78
40 fedgovtent	18.37	19.26	-11.93	6.11	-13.10	15.18	2.56
41 statlocgov	19.15	17.85	11.60	32.50	-13.17	22.97	9.50

	13 paper	14 printpb	15 chemicl	16 petrlref	17 rubberpl	18 leather	19 stone
27 transport	-15.15	-18.74	-9.40	-10.97	-7.19	-30.95	-5.14
28 communic	-4.96	-11.69	0.66	0.77	-3.22	-29.07	-4.39
29 radioandtv	-36.53	-38.09	-32.14	-32.35	-33.96	-51.72	-35.84
30 utilities	-32.54	-31.84	-32.77	-36.90	-30.31	-47.93	-37.61
31 trade	5.56	5.29	10.80	15.78	8.23	-21.26	7.83
32 finaninsur	5.21	4.66	11.38	11.71	8.54	-22.28	6.34
33 realestate	-1.32	-2.23	-0.53	-11.38	-3.18	-27.55	-3.16
34 hotelsrepr	-19.48	-23.32	-15.35	-10.57	-18.48	-38.84	-18.24
35 businservc	22.81	17.24	32.81	27.75	30.96	-4.67	27.08
36 eatingdrin	-10.51	-14.61	-4.66	-6.22	-8.90	-34.18	-10.28
37 autorepair	-29.07	-28.77	-25.98	-25.80	-28.35	-47.36	-30.89
38 amusement	12.09	15.30	17.09	16.47	10.59	-20.69	9.37
39 healedusoc	27.22	25.41	30.25	34.69	22.75	-9.42	24.54
40 fedgovtent	11.00	-3.66	19.58	17.42	15.89	-24.82	13.73
41 statlocgov	14.03	17.12	21.16	22.65	17.01	-8.47	15.17

Table 7 (Cont.)

	20 metalpr	21 metalfb	22 indmch	23 eleceq	24 transeq	25 instrum	26 mfgmsc
27 transport	12.24	-6.75	-19.48	-18.22	-16.41	-	-28.08
28 communic	7.03	-2.78	-14.40	-9.76	-5.20	5.78	-23.09
29 radioandtv	-29.54	-37.09	-41.50	-40.00	-36.17	-31.37	-47.72
30 utilities	-22.37	-29.21	-38.69	-35.09	-33.55	-25.27	-45.05
31 trade	24.57	8.92	-5.04	-1.69	4.08	16.10	-14.17
32 finaninsur	17.37	7.58	-2.42	1.46	5.40	13.02	-10.06
33 realestate	6.75	-0.62	-11.68	-9.49	-0.13	-1.18	-19.22
34 hotelsrepr	-9.85	-18.63	-25.82	-26.44	-22.49	-16.60	-33.01
35 businservc	48.06	33.71	20.78	23.79	24.17	48.29	-3.61
36 eatingdrin	-0.74	-9.44	-18.90	-15.33	-11.77	-3.40	-26.18
37 autorepair	-21.19	-28.10	-35.50	-32.16	-33.27	-28.74	-41.00
38 amusement	20.06	11.73	-1.43	3.57	10.54	16.76	6.20
39 healedusoc	34.20	24.67	10.35	14.70	26.94	20.24	3.98
40 fedgovtent	30.14	18.02	5.11	9.19	10.33	29.64	-10.12
41 statlocgov	28.91	19.34	5.54	9.77	18.15	20.05	-2.91

Note: For sector descriptions, see Table A-2 of the Appendix.

Appendix.   Social Accounting Matrix Construction

The analysis of this paper utilizes three different social accounting matrices: a 102-sector SAM for 1989, a 43-sector SAM for 1982, and a 43-sector SAM for 1989.‎ The 102-sector 1989 SAM is constructed according to the sectoring scheme presented in Table A-1. This sectoring scheme is designed to provide maximum possible detail in the service sectors. This SAM includes 76 service sectors at the 6-digit Bureau of Economic Analysis (BEA) level, and the remainder of the economy is aggregated to the 2-digit SIC level. The 43-sector SAMs include 17 service sectors at the 2-digit BEA level, with the remainder of the economy again aggregated to the 2-digit BEA level. The sectoring scheme for these two SAMs is presented in Table A-2.

Construction of the 1982 SAM was described in Reinert and Roland-Holst (1993), and we will not provide any further details here. The two 1989 SAMs are aggregations of a detailed, 487-sector SAM, similar in broad structure to that constructed for 1988 by Reinert and Roland-Holst (1992). The remainder of this section will briefly describe the construction of the detailed 1989 SAM, giving particular emphasis to differences from the Reinert and Roland-Holst (1992) effort.

Construction of the detailed 1989 SAM began with the transformation of the 1989 U.S. National Income and Product Accounts (NIPA) into a macroeconomic SAM.[16] The macroeconomic SAM provided control totals for each submatrix of the detailed SAM, as well as scalar inter-institutional transfers. The transformation of the NIPA accounts into the SAM framework was accomplished with a modification of the mapping presented in Hanson and Robinson (1991).

To construct the detailed accounts, we relied on IMPLAN input-output tables from the U.S. Forest Service of the U.S. Department of Agriculture for 1982 and a host of other data sources for 1989.[17] 1989 activity output data were taken from the U.S. Department of Labor at the level of 226 sectors and were disaggregated to the 487 sectors based on IMPLAN gross output shares for 1982. To obtain commodity outputs, the 1982 IMPLAN make matrix was row normalized and premultiplied by a row vector of the activity outputs. The 1982

---

[16] Stone (1981 and 1986) describes macroeconomic SAMs.

[17] At the time of this work, the U.S. Bureau of Economic Analysis benchmark input-output table for 1982 was not yet available.

IMPLAN make matrix was then updated to 1989 using the RAS procedure with the 1989 activity and commodity output vectors as control totals.[18]

For the value-added submatrix, control totals were taken from the 1989 macro SAM. The 1989 value-added data for approximately 60 sectors are taken from the U.S. National Income and Product Accounts. Values for those sectors were further allocated to the 487 sectors by 1989 activity output shares. The sectoral totals were allocated among labor income, property income, and indirect business taxes based on shares from the 1982 IMPLAN data. Finally, the value-added submatrix was balanced to the macro-SAM control totals using the RAS procedure.

To estimate the 1989 import and export submatrices, control totals for both were taken from the 1989 macro SAM. Data on merchandise imports and exports for 1989 by 7-digit TSUSA lines and Schedule B, respectively, were extracted from U.S. Bureau of the Census data tapes and concorded to BEA merchandise sectors 1.0100 to 64.1200. The difference between the resulting totals and the NIPA merchandise control totals were allocated among the merchandise sectors in proportion to their shares in the resulting totals.

The data on trade in non-factor services came from various government sources, notably DiLullo and Whichard (1990), Murad (1990), and Nicholson (1990).[19] From Murad we obtained general data on imports and exports of selected services, including communications, finance, insurance, and education. From DiLullo and Whichard we obtained more specific figures on trade in transportation, travel, and some business services. From Nicholson we obtained detailed information on trade in business services. After concording this data with the service sectors, the differences between the resulting totals and the services control totals for imports and exports were allocated among the service sectors in proportion to their shares in the resulting totals.

The final demand submatrix was updated using control totals from the 1989 macro SAM. For those commodities without intermediate deliveries, total final demand was set equal to estimated commodity supply. Total final demand less exports for each of these sectors was then distributed over household, government, and capital-goods demand based on 1982 shares. For the remaining sectors, 1989 non-export final demand by type less the corresponding final

---

[18] The RAS procedure is described in Stone and Brown (1965).

[19] Trade in factor services is included in the interinstitutional submatrix of the SAM.

demand for sectors without intermediate deliveries was first allocated among approximately 80 sectors based on shares from the 1986 input-output tables. It was then further allocated to the 487 sectors based on 1982 shares.

The last step was to update the 1982 IMPLAN use matrix to 1989. For the row control vector, the estimated vector of commodity output, plus the import vectors, and less the final demand vectors was used. For the column control vector, the activity output vector, less the value-added and error vectors was used. With these control vectors, we updated the use matrix using the RAS procedure.

Both the 1982 and 1989 SAMs were consolidated by elimination of activity accounts. Using the apportionment procedure described in Pyatt (1985), the resulting transactions matrix of interindustry accounts represents an activity technology (see UNSO 1968).

Table A-1. Sectoring Scheme for 102-Sector 1989 SAM.

Sector Number	Description	Reference Classification
1	Agriculture, forestry and fishing	SIC 01,02,07,08,09
2	Metal mining	SIC 10
3	Coal mining	SIC 12
4	Oil and gas extraction	SIC 13
5	Nonmetallic minerals, except fuels	SIC 14
6	Construction	SIC 15,16,17
7	Food and kindred products	SIC 20
8	Tobacco	SIC 21
9	Textiles	SIC 22
10	Apparel	SIC 23
11	Lumber and wood products, except furniture	SIC 24
12	Furniture and fixtures	SIC 25
13	Paper and allied products	SIC 26
14	Printing and publishing	SIC 27
15	Chemicals and allied products	SIC 28
16	Petroleum refining and related industries	SIC 29
17	Rubber and miscellaneous plastics products	SIC 30
18	Leather and leather products	SIC 31
19	Stone, clay, and glass products	SIC 32
20	Primary metal industries	SIC 33
21	Fabricated metal products	SIC 34
22	Industrial machinery and equipment	SIC 35
23	Electronic and other electric equipment	SIC 36
24	Transportation equipment	SIC 37
25	Instruments and related products	SIC 38
26	Miscellaneous manufacturing industries	SIC 39
27	Railroads and related services	BEA 650100
28	Local, interurban passenger transit	BEA 650200
29	Motor freight transportation and warehousing	BEA 650300
30	Water transportation	BEA 650400
31	Air transportation	BEA 650500
32	Pipe lines, except natural gas	BEA 650600
33	Other transportation services	BEA 650701
34	Arrangement of passenger transportation	BEA 650702
35	Communications, except radio and TV	BEA 660000

Table A-1 (Cont.)

Sector Number	Description	Reference Classification
36	Radio and TV broadcasting	BEA 670000
37	Electric services (utilities)	BEA 680100
38	Gas production and distribution (utilities)	BEA 680200
39	Water supply and sewerage systems	BEA 680301
40	Sanitary services, steam, irrigations systems	BEA 680302
41	Wholesale trade	BEA 690100
42	Retail trade	BEA 690200
43	Banking	BEA 700100
44	Credit agencies other than banks	BEA 700200
45	Security and commodity brokers	BEA 700300
46	Insurance carriers	BEA 700400
47	Insurance agents, brokers and services	BEA 700500
48	Owner-occupied dwellings	BEA 710100
49	Real estate	BEA 710200
50	Hotels and lodging places	BEA 720100
51	Laundry, cleaning, and shoe repair	BEA 720201
52	Funeral service and crematories	BEA 720202
53	Photo studios and misc. personal services	BEA 720203
54	Electrical repair shops	BEA 720204
55	Watch, clock, jewelry, furniture repair	BEA 720205
56	Beauty and barber shops	BEA 720300
57	Miscellaneous repair shops	BEA 730101
58	Services to buildings	BEA 730102
59	Personnel supply services	BEA 730103
60	Computer and data processing services	BEA 730104
61	Management and consulting services	BEA 730105
62	Detective and protective services	BEA 730106
63	Equipment and rental leasing	BEA 730107
64	Photofinishing, commercial photography	BEA 730108
65	Other business services	BEA 730109
66	Advertising	BEA 730200
67	Legal services	BEA 730301
68	Engineering, architectural services	BEA 730302
69	Accounting, auditing and bookkeeping, n.e.c.	BEA 730303
70	Eating and drinking places	BEA 740000
71	Automotive rental and leasing	BEA 750001
72	Automotive repair shops and services	BEA 750002

Table A-1 (Cont.)

Sector Number	Description	Reference Classification
73	Automobile parking and car washes	BEA 750003
74	Motion pictures	BEA 760100
75	Dance halls, studios and schools	BEA 760200
76	Theatrical producers, bands etc.	BEA 760201
77	Bowling alleys and pool halls	BEA 760202
78	Commercial sports except racing	BEA 760203
79	Racing and track operations	BEA 760204
80	Membership sports and recreation clubs	BEA 760205
81	Other amusement and recreation services	BEA 760206
82	Doctors and dentists	BEA 770100
83	Hospitals	BEA 770200
84	Nursing and personal care facilities	BEA 770301
85	Other medical and health services	BEA 770302
86	Elementary and secondary schools	BEA 770401
87	Colleges, universities, professional schools	BEA 770402
88	Other educational services	BEA 770403
89	Business associations	BEA 770501
90	Labor and civic organizations	BEA 770502
91	Religious organizations	BEA 770503
92	Other membership organizations	BEA 770504
93	Residential care	BEA 770800
94	Social services, n.e.c.	BEA 770900
95	U.S. Postal Service	BEA 780100
96	Federal electric utilities	BEA 780200
97	Other federal government services	BEA 780400
98	Local government passenger transit	BEA 790100
99	State and local electric utilities	BEA 790200
100	Other state and local government enterprises	BEA 790300
101	Government industry	BEA 820000
102	Household industry	BEA 840000

Table A-2. Sectoring Scheme for 43-Sector SAMs.

Sector Number	Description	Reference Classification
1	Agriculture, forestry and fishing	SIC 01,02,07,08,09
2	Metal mining	SIC 10
3	Coal mining	SIC 12
4	Oil and gas extraction	SIC 13
5	Nonmetallic minerals, except fuels	SIC 14
6	Construction	SIC 15,16,17
7	Food and kindred products	SIC 20
8	Tobacco	SIC 21
9	Textiles	SIC 22
10	Apparel	SIC 23
11	Lumber and wood products, except furniture	SIC 24
12	Furniture and fixtures	SIC 25
13	Paper and allied products	SIC 26
14	Printing and publishing	SIC 27
15	Chemicals and allied products	SIC 28
16	Petroleum refining and related industries	SIC 29
17	Rubber and miscellaneous plastics products	SIC 30
18	Leather and leather products	SIC 31
19	Stone, clay, and glass products	SIC 32
20	Primary metal industries	SIC 33
21	Fabricated metal products	SIC 34
22	Industrial machinery and equipment	SIC 35
23	Electronic and other electric equipment	SIC 36
24	Transportation equipment	SIC 37
25	Instruments and related products	SIC 38
26	Miscellaneous manufacturing industries	SIC 39
27	Transportation and warehousing	BEA 65
28	Communications, except radio and TV	BEA 66
29	Radio and TV broadcasting	BEA 67
30	Electric, gas, water, and sanitary services	BEA 68
31	Wholesale and retail trade	BEA 69
32	Finance and insurance	BEA 70
33	Real estate and rental	BEA 71
34	Hotels; personal and repair services, except auto	BEA 72
35	Business services	BEA 73
36	Eating and drinking places	BEA 74

References

Baumol, W.J. (1967). "Macroeconomics of unbalanced growth: The anatomy of urban crisis," *American Economic Review* 57, 415-426.

_____ (1986). "Productivity growth, convergence, and welfare: What the long-run data show," *American Economic Review* 76, 1072-1085.

Baumol, W.J., S.A.B. Blackman, and E.N. Wolff (1985). "Unbalanced growth revisited: Asymptotic stagnancy and new evidence," *American Economic Review* 75, 806-817.

Clague, C.K. (1985). "A model of real national price levels," *Southern Economic Journal* 51, 998-1017.

Clark, C. (1940). *The Conditions of Economic Progress* (Macmillan, London).

DiLullo, A.J. and O.J. Whichard (1990). "U.S. international sales and purchases of services," *Survey of Current Business* 70, 37-72.

Francois, J.F. (1990a). "Producer services, scale, and the division of labor," *Oxford Economic Papers* 42, 715-729.

_____ (1990b). "Trade in producer services and returns due to specialization under monopolistic competition," *Canadian Journal of Economics* 23, 184-195.

_____ (1992). "Explaining the pattern of trade in producer services," *International Economic Journal,* forthcoming.

Francois, J.F., H.M. Arce, K.A. Reinert, and J.F. Flynn (1992). "Commercial policy and the domestic carrying trade: A general equilibrium assessment," Research Division Working Paper 92-03-A, U.S. International Trade Commission (Washington, D.C.).

____ (1990b). "Trade in producer services and returns due to specialization under monopolistic competition," *Canadian Journal of Economics* 23, 184-195.

____ (1993). "Explaining the pattern of trade in producer services," *International Economic Journal* 7, 23-31 forthcoming.

Francois, J.F., H.M. Arce, K.A. Reinert, and J.F. Flynn (1992). "Commercial policy and the domestic carrying trade: a general equilibrium assessment," Research Division Working Paper 92-03-A, U.S. International Trade Commission (Washington, D.C.).

Gold, B. (1981). "On size, scale, and returns: a survey," *Journal of Economic Literature* 19, 5-33.

Grossman, G.M., and E. Helpman (1990). "Comparative advantage and long-run growth," *American Economic Review* 80, 796-815.

Hanson, K., and S. Robinson (1991). "Data, linkages, and models: U.S. National Income and Product Accounts in the framework of a social accounting matrix," *Economic Systems Research* 3, 215-232.

Lucas, R.E., Jr. (1988). "On the mechanisms of economic development," *Journal of Monetary Economics* 22, 3-42.

Murad, H. (1990). "U.S. international transactions, second quarter 1990," *Survey of Current Business* 70, 73-85.

Nicholson, R.E. (1990). "U.S. international transactions, first quarter 1989," *Survey of Current Business* 70, 66-74.

Panagariya, A. (1988). "A theoretical explanation of some stylized facts of economic growth," *Quarterly Journal of Economics* 103, 509-526.

Pyatt, G. (1985). "Commodity balances and national accounts: a SAM perspective," *Review of Income and Wealth* 31, 155-169.

Pyatt, G., and J.I. Round (eds.) (1985). *Social Accounting Matrices: A Basis for Planning* (The World Bank, Washington, D.C.).

Reinert, K.A., and D.W. Roland-Holst (1992). "A detailed social accounting matrix for the United States: 1988," *Economic Systems Research* 4, 173-187.

_____ (1993). "Structural change in the United States: social accounting estimates for 1982-88," *Empirical Economics* 18, forthcoming.

Robinson, S. (1989). "Multisectoral models," in H. Chenery and T.N. Srinivasan (eds.), *Handbook of Development Economics* (Elsevier, Amsterdam), 885-947.

Roland-Holst, D.W. (1990). "Interindustry analysis with social accounting methods," *Economic Systems Research* 2, 125-145.

Romer, P.M. (1986). "Increasing returns and long-run growth," *Journal of Political Economy* 94, 1002-1037.

_____ (1990). "Endogenous technological change," *Journal of Political Economy* 98, S71-S102.

Stanback, T.M., Jr., P.J. Bearse, T.J. Noyelle, and R.A. Karasek (1981). *Services: The New Economy* (Allanheld, Osmun and Company, Totawa, New Jersey).

Stone, R. (1981). *Aspects of Economic and Social Modelling* (Librarie Droz, Geneva).

_____ (1986). "The accounts of society," *Journal of Applied Econometrics* 1, 5-28.

Stone, R., and A. Brown (1965). "Behavioural and technical change in economic models," in E.A.G. Robinson (ed.), *Problems in Economic Development* (Macmillan, London), 428-439.

Summers, R. (1985). "Services in the international economy," in R.P. Inman (ed.), *Managing the Service Economy* (Cambridge University Press, Cambridge), 27-52.

United Nations Statistical Office (1968). *A System of National Accounts* (United Nations, New York).

Williamson, J.G. (1991). "Productivity and American leadership: a review article," *Journal of Economic Literature* 29, 51-68.

Chapter 3   Is The Shift Toward Employment In Services Stabilizing?

David E. Lebow and Daniel E. Sichel[1]

1. Introduction

In the United States, as in other countries, the share of employment in service-producing industries has increased over time. While the implications of this sectoral shift for issues such as productivity and wages has received attention, there has been little work considering the implications of this shift for economic stability. This paper takes a step toward filling the gap.

To the extent that economists have considered the question posed by the title of this paper, there appears to be an emerging conventional wisdom that the economy will become more stable as the service share increases (see Moore, 1987, Zarnowitz and Moore, 1986). As is clear from figure 1, employment in the service-producing sector has more than tripled over the postwar period, and has grown relatively smoothly. In contrast, employment in the goods-producing sector has increased only about 40 percent, and has fluctuated widely. It is easy to see why these basic facts have suggested to many a prima facie case that as employment shifts to the comparatively stable service-producing sector,

---

[1]We would like to thank Barry Bosworth, David Romer, Bill Wascher and seminar participants at the Federal Reserve Board and the Wharton Conference on Services for useful discussions and suggestions. The views in this paper represent those of the authors and not of the Board of Governors or its staff.

P. T. Harker (ed.), The Service Productivity and Quality Challenge, 81–112.
© 1995 *Kluwer Academic Publishers. Printed in the Netherlands.*

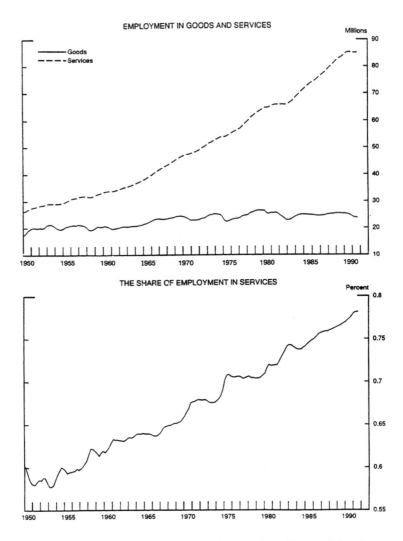

Figure 1. Employment in Goods and Services and the Share of Employment in Services.

aggregate employment will become more stable over time--that is, the business cycle will be attenuated.

This paper has two goals. First, it demonstrates that the conventional wisdom does not logically have to be correct; it is possible for the sectoral shift to be destabilizing. In section 2 we present a simple accounting framework to demonstrate this point. If the sectoral shift affects the structure of the economy in a way that boosts the variance of employment in the goods sector or the services sector (or the covariance between the sectors), then the shift may not be stabilizing. In section 3, we present a two-sector model that provides an analytic framework for analyzing sectoral shifts in employment shares. While our focus is on the cyclical implications of the sectoral shift, the model also provides insights into the causes of the shift.

The model in section 3 highlights three reasons why the sectoral shift could be less stabilizing than the conventional wisdom suggests. To the extent that the sectoral shift owes to manufacturers becoming more likely to outsource their business services, or to rapidly increasing purchases of more cyclically-
sensitive luxury services, then the service sector itself may have become less stable over time. Further, regardless of the source of the shift, if monetary policy has a smaller effect on services than on goods, then to achieve a certain amount of disinflation monetary shocks may have had to increase over time. These larger monetary shocks could offset the stabilizing influence of the mix shift.

The paper's second goal is to determine whether the shift toward employment in services stabilized employment to a significant degree; that is, whether--as an empirical matter--the conventional wisdom is correct. We do this in section 4. If not for our three offsets, we estimate that the sectoral shift toward services would have reduced the variance of payroll employment growth noticeably over the sample period from the early 1960s to the late 1980s. But we also find that these other factors have offset most of this stabilization. Hence, we conclude that, overall, the shift toward employment in services has not been an important factor in stabilizing employment.

2. A Simple Accounting Framework

In this section, we show in very general terms the source of the conventional wisdom that an increase in the share of employment in services has stabilized aggregate employment, and why this conventional wisdom is not necessarily correct. Aggregate employment is defined as the sum of employment in the goods- and service-producing sectors (E ≡ E^s + E^g). We can rewrite that equation in terms of growth rates as follows:

(1) $\Delta e = \lambda \Delta e^s + (1 - \lambda) \Delta e^g$,

where lower-case letters denote logarithms (so Δe is approximately equal to the growth rate of total employment) and λ is the share of employment in services. Assuming for the moment that the services share λ is constant, the variance of total employment is given by:

(2) $\text{Var } \Delta e = \lambda^2 \sigma_s^2 + (1 - \lambda)^2 \sigma_g^2 + 2\lambda(1 - \lambda)\sigma_{sg}$,

where σ_s^2 and σ_g^2 , and σ_{sg} represent the variance of employment growth in the two sectors and the covariance between the sectors, respectively. Holding the sectoral variances and covariance constant, the change in the variance of total employment growth is then given by:

(3) $d\text{Var}(\Delta e) = [2\lambda\sigma_s^2 - 2(1 - \lambda)\sigma_g^2 + 2(1 - 2\lambda)\sigma_{sg}]d\lambda$.

Equation (3) shows what we refer to as the simple mix-shift effect. For realistic values of the covariance σ_{sg}, as long as the services sector is more stable than the goods sector $(\sigma_s^2 < \sigma_g^2)$, then the expression on the right hand side is negative.[2]   That is, as the relatively stable component of employment becomes a larger share of the total, total employment becomes more stable. No doubt, it is this mix-shift effect that underlies the conventional wisdom that the aggregate economy will become more stable as the share of services increases.

But the decomposition in equation (3) is incomplete, because it takes the sectoral variances and covariance to be constant; indeed, the next section

---

[2] A sufficient condition for this statement to hold is that σ_{sg} be positive with magnitude in between the two sectoral variances, as is in fact the case in the sample we consider. (See table 1).

highlights several reasons why changes in λ may lead to changes in the cyclicality of the two sectors. If that is true, then we can write:

$$\sigma_s^2 = \sigma_s^2 (\lambda, z) \text{ , and}$$

$$d\sigma_s^2 = \left(d\sigma_s^2 / d\lambda \right) d\lambda + \left(d\sigma_s^2 / dz \right) dz \text{ ,}$$

where z represents exogenous variables and shocks that are unrelated to λ; similar equations can be written for σ_g^2 and $d\sigma_{sg}$. Then the full decomposition of the change in Var(Δe) can be written as:

(4)
$$\begin{aligned} dVar \; \Delta e = & \left[2\lambda \sigma_s^2 - 2(1-\lambda)\sigma_g^2 + 2(1-2\lambda)\sigma_{sg} \right] d\lambda \\ & + \left[\lambda^2 d\sigma_s^2 / d\lambda + (1-\lambda)^2 d\sigma_g^2 / d\lambda + 2\lambda(1-\lambda) d\sigma_{sg} / d\lambda \right] d\lambda \\ & + \left[\lambda^2 d\sigma_s^2 / dz + (1-\lambda)^2 d\sigma_g^2 / dz + 2\lambda(1-\lambda) d\sigma_{sg} / dz \right] dz \end{aligned}$$

The terms on the first line of equation (4) correspond to the simple mix-shift effect shown in equation (3). But the terms on the second line show how the variance of employment growth would be affected if changes in λ were to affect the variance of services, the variance of goods, or the covariance--that is, if changes in λ were to induce changes in the structure of each sector of the economy. Since these terms on the second line of (4) could be positive and large, the shift toward services is not necessarily stabilizing. Hence, as a matter of logic, the conventional wisdom need not be true. In addition, the third line of (4) makes clear that changes in other variables, unrelated to λ, also could affect the variance of employment in each sector.

3. The Two-Sector Model

In this section, we present a simple two-sector model that provides an analytic framework for studying the effects of sectoral shifts in employment shares. We assume that trend output growth is the same in both the goods and service sectors, increasing over time with the growth in population (Δn) and in aggregate productivity ($\Delta \rho$). This assumption holds the long-run output share of each sector constant. In fact, in postwar data, the share of total services in output has increased a little, but not nearly as much as the <u>employment</u> share. The assumption of constant output share--while not literally true--makes the model much more transparent. In any case, we do not maintain this assumption in our empirical work.

Using the trend growth rate $(\Delta n + \Delta \rho)$,[3] the demand side of the model is:

(5a) $y_t^s = \alpha_o^s + (\Delta n + \Delta \rho)T + \alpha^s d_t$

(5b) $y_t^g = \alpha_o^g + (\Delta n + \Delta \rho)T + \alpha^g d_t$,

where the superscripts g and s represent goods and services, respectively, and T is a time trend. Equations (5a) and (5b)indicate that output in each sector (lower case letters represent logs) has both a trend and a cyclical component.The trend component was discussed above. The cyclical component of output is given by the response to a demand shock(d). In section 3.2 below we will consider movements in the federal funds rate to be the only source of cyclical variability; for now, d_t may be viewed as representing any demand shock.

We define aggregate productivity growth as a weighted average of productivity growth in each sector, using the employment shares as weights. That is,

$$\Delta \rho = \lambda \Delta \rho^s + (1 - \lambda)\Delta \rho^g   ,$$

where λ is the employment share in services. The log level of productivity in the two sectors is given by:

(6a) $\rho_t^s = \rho_o^s + \Delta \rho^s T$

(6b) $\rho_t^g = \rho_o^g + \Delta \rho^g T$.

Productivity is assumed to grow more rapidly in the goods sector; that is, $\Delta \rho^g > \Delta \rho^s$. This productivity assumption will be seen to drive the fact that the

---

[3] This is the same growth rate as in Solow's model (1957). We could specify the trend to be stochastic without affecting any of our results.

share of employment in services increases over time. The model would not change qualitatively if, in line with actual experience, we were to add a cyclical component to productivity; for simplicity, we have chosen not to do so.

The log of employment in each sector is equal to the log of output minus the log of productivity:

(7a) $\quad e_t^s = \left(\alpha_0^s - \rho_0^s\right) + \left(\Delta n + \Delta\rho - \Delta\rho^s\right)T + \alpha^s d_t$

(7b) $\quad e_t^g = \left(\alpha_0^g - \rho_0^g\right) + \left(\Delta n + \Delta\rho - \Delta\rho^g\right)T + \alpha^g d_t$

Writing these equations in terms of growth rates, and defining aggregate employment growth as a weighted average of the sectoral growth rates, we obtain:

(8a) $\quad \Delta e_t^s = \left(\Delta n + \Delta\rho - \Delta\rho^s\right) + \alpha^s \Delta d_t$

(8b) $\quad \Delta e_t^g = \left(\Delta n + \Delta\rho - \Delta\rho^g\right) + \alpha^g \Delta d_t$

(8c) $\quad \begin{aligned} \Delta e_t &= \lambda \Delta e_t^s + \left(1 - \lambda\right)\Delta e_t^g \\ &= \Delta n + \left[\lambda\alpha^s + \left(1 - \lambda\right)\alpha^g\right]\Delta d_t \end{aligned}$

Although this paper focuses on cyclical properties of the model, we first look at the trend movements in output, employment, and productivity. These trend movements are very similar to those derived by Baumol (1967). [4] The trend rate of growth of aggregate output is $\Delta n + \Delta\rho$, while trend employment grows at the slower rate Δn. The difference, of course, reflects aggregate productivity gains. Trend output growth is assumed to be the same in both sectors, but productivity in the goods sector is assumed to rise more rapidly than

---

[4] In other early work, Fourastie (1957) looked at the relationsip between productivity and relative prices for goods and services.

in services. Thus, employment in services rises faster than employment in goods--that is, λ increases over time.[5]

As written, the model assumes that differential productivity growth in the two sectors is the only reason for the secular increase in λ. While this surely is the most important reason for the shift, two other reasons also have been identified by previous researchers (see, for example, Fuchs, 1969). First, if the income elasticity of demand for services is larger than for goods, then as per capita income increases, demand for services rises more than for goods. As mentioned above, the output share of services in the U.S. has risen a bit in the postwar period, although this may not be a robust feature of economic growth.[6] Second, there may be an increasing tendency to measure employment as occurring in the service-producing sector that was previously measured as occurring in the goods-producing sector or as non-market activities. Examples include outsourcing of business services, and increased purchases of household services associated with rising labor force participation rates of married women. While we could explicitly include these additional factors in the trend component, nothing important is lost by leaving them out. We will, however, return to these other factors in our discussion of the cyclical component of the model.

Turning to that cyclical component, the key assumption is that α^g is larger than α^s ; that is, output and employment in the goods sector are more sensitive to demand shocks than are output and employment in the service sector. An obvious reason for the difference between α^g and α^s is the much greater durability--or storability--of goods than of services. Even so-called nondurable goods, such as clothing, are nearly always more durable than services. Households can enjoy the flow of services from the stocks of durable goods currently held, even if they slash their purchases of new durable goods in response to a negative shock. In contrast, consumption of services can only be maintained by continuing to purchase services. To say this another way,

---

[5] If we were to assume that the output share of services increased over time, then the employment share λ would increase even more rapidly than in the model above.

[6] Summers and Heston (1988) provide cross-country evidence that the share of services in consumption does not increase with per-capita income. Baumol, Blackman, and Wolff (1991) examine a group of services with especially slow productivity growth, and demonstrate that the share of these "stagnant" services in output has not increased in post-war U.S. data.

purchases of most goods can be more easily postponed than many types of services; therefore, goods are likely to be more sensitive than services to demand shocks.[7]

We analyze the cyclicality of employment in this model by examining the variance of aggregate employment growth:

$$(9) \qquad \text{Var } \Delta e_t = \alpha^{*2} \text{ Var} \left(\Delta d_t \right)$$

$$\text{where } \alpha^* = \lambda \alpha^s + \left(1 - \lambda \right) \alpha^g \quad .$$

To see how this variance depends on λ, we first examine the derivative holding constant the parameters α^s and α^g and the variance of the shocks:

$$(10) \qquad d\text{Var} \left(\Delta e_t \right) = \left[2\alpha^* \text{ Var} \left(\Delta d_t \right) \left(\alpha^s - \alpha^g \right) \right] d\lambda < 0 \quad .$$

Equation (10) gives the mix-shift effect analogous to the first line of equation (4) in the accounting framework. Since the demand shock has a smaller effect on services employment than on goods employment--that is, $\alpha_s < \alpha_g$ --aggregate employment growth becomes more stable as the service share grows.

However, as the accounting framework shows, it is possible for λ to affect the sectoral variances as well. In the context of this model, it is possible for λ to affect either the parameters (α^s and α^g) or the size of the shocks (Var(Δd)). The remainder of this section will discuss three possible reasons why this may occur.

3.1   Outsourcing and luxury services.

In addition to differential productivity growth in the two sectors, a reason posited for the shift in employment toward services is increasing outsourcing of business services. That is, goods-producing firms are now purchasing externally some business

---

[7] The ability of firms to hold inventories of goods--but not of services-- is another reason that goods could be more cyclically sensitive than services. While a great deal of research has posted that firms hold inventories to smooth production, Blinder and Holtz-Bakin (1986) have shown that inventory investment contributes importantly to swings in output at business cycle frequencies.

services that used to be produced in-house.[8] As goods-producing firms outsource more, employees will be classified as working in the service sector rather than the goods sector, boosting reported employment growth in the service sector. Further--as we show below--the volatility of employment in these jobs is higher than in the rest of the service sector. This may reflect a closer tie between business services and the more volatile goods sector of the economy, or may indicate that employment in these jobs is inherently more volatile than employment in other parts of the service sector. Thus, as more and more business services are outsourced, the cyclical sensitivity of employment in the service sector will increase, as the service sector comes to look more like the goods sector. Outsourcing might also affect the cyclicality of the goods sector, although that will not be our focus.

Another reason posited for the shift in employment toward services is that consumption (and output) of luxury services--items with an income elasticity greater than unity--has increased as income has grown. That is, as household income and wealth have risen, luxury items have become a larger share of purchases, raising employment in industries producing luxury services. In addition to rapid growth, it also seems likely that luxury services (like vacations) are more easily postponed than many other types of services; that is, luxury services have a higher intertemporal elasticity of substitution.[9] Hence, luxury services are likely to be more volatile and cyclically sensitive than other types of services. Again, if employment in luxury services increases, the overall cyclical sensitivity of the service sector could increase.[10]

Both of these arguments suggest that the structure of the service sector may be changing in such a way as to make employment more sensitive to demand shocks than was previously the case. Focussing on the cyclical component of

[8] See Kutscher (1988) for a discussion.

[9] Interestingly, analysts of aggregate consumption behavior often make the simplifying assumption of a constant intertemporal elasticity of substitution, thereby assuming away the effect we are considering.

[10] Our story about luxury services may be particularly applicable to the 1980s. Anecdotal evidence suggests that consumption of luxury services by "yuppies" increased dramatically during the mid 1980s, as incomes of those individuals grew rapidly. However, the anecdotes also suggest that these purchases were slashed equally dramatically during the late 1980s and early 1990s, as the recession hit.

our model, α^s may be an increasing function of λ. If this is true, then the change in the variance of total employment is no longer given by equation (10), but by:

$$
\begin{aligned}
(11) \quad \text{dVar } \Delta e_t = & \left[2\alpha^* \text{ Var} \left(\Delta d_t \right) \left(\alpha^s - \alpha^g \right) \right] d\lambda \\
& + \left[2\alpha^* \text{ Var} \left(\Delta d_t \right) \lambda \, da^s / d\lambda \right] d\lambda \quad .
\end{aligned}
$$

In addition to the stabilizing mix-shift effect (represented by the term on the first line of (11)), there is an offsetting effect owing to the increase in α_s (captured on the second line). If the term on the second line is large and positive, this expression need not be negative.

3.2 Changing influence of monetary policy. In addition to possible offsets from outsourcing and luxury services, the increasing share of employment in the service sector may change the influence of monetary policy. In this section, we show that this changing influence could offset part of the stabilization owing to the mix-shift effect.

To demonstrate this channel, it is necessary to add a bit more detail to the model. We write down a simple supply function in which the rate of inflation rises when aggregate employment is above its trend level. In first difference form, we have:

$$
(12) \qquad \Delta \pi_t = \beta \left(\Delta e_t - \Delta n \right)
$$

where π is the rate of inflation. Writing down a single aggregate supply function assumes an identical supply response in the two sectors; this restriction is relaxed in our empirical work, yielding qualitatively similar conclusions.

We also specify a monetary policy reaction function:

$$
f_1 = \gamma \left(\pi - \pi_t^* \right) \text{ , or in difference form,}
$$

$$
\begin{aligned}
(13) \quad \Delta f_t = & \, \gamma \Delta \pi_t - \gamma \Delta \pi_t^* \\
= & \, \gamma \Delta \pi_t - \Delta \delta_t \quad .
\end{aligned}
$$

The reaction function states that the monetary authority adjusts the federal funds rate (f) whenever the level of inflation rises above its target π^*. The "error term" $\Delta\delta$, defined equal to $\gamma\Delta\pi^*$, captures changes in the inflation target over time, and is our measure of monetary shocks. We have previously ignored the distinction between changes in demand stemming from the federal funds rate or other sources and focused on the composite shock d. Here, to demonstrate this channel most clearly, we set $\Delta d = -\Delta f$ and assume that changes in the federal funds rate--that is, changes in the inflation target as captured by $\Delta\delta$--are the only shocks hitting the model. In addition, we temporarily shift our focus to the response of employment growth to a single monetary shock ($\Delta\delta$), in contrast to the earlier focus on the variance of employment growth resulting from a series of shocks. Combining equations (12) and (13) with equation (8c) above, comparative-statics results for the model are:

(14a) $\Delta e_t = \Delta n + [\alpha^*/(1+\alpha^*\beta\gamma)]\Delta\delta_t$

(14b) $\Delta\pi_t = [\alpha^*\beta/(1+\alpha^*\beta\gamma)]\Delta\delta_t$

(14c) $\Delta f_t = [-1/(1+\alpha^*\beta\gamma)]\Delta\delta_t$.

   To see the effect of the growing share of service-sector employment (increasing λ) on the cyclical sensitivity of employment growth, take the derivative of $\Delta e / \Delta\delta$ with respect to λ:

(15) $\dfrac{d(\Delta e/\Delta\delta)}{d\lambda} = [1/(1+\alpha^*\beta\gamma)]^2(\alpha^s - \alpha^g) < 0$.

where we are again holding α^s constant. Equation (15) illustrates the basic mix-shift effect: Since α^g exceeds α^s, the expression is negative. That is, the response of total employment growth to a given shock $\Delta\delta$ decreases as a larger share of the workforce is employed in the more stable service sector.

   Now, consider the following thought experiment. Suppose the monetary authority wants to reduce the inflation rate by 1 percentage point, and sets $\Delta\delta$ such that $\Delta\pi = -1$. Then it is easy to show that the comparative-statics results in equations (14a-14c) reduce to:

(16a) $\Delta e_t = \Delta n - 1/\beta$

(16b) $\Delta \pi_t = -1$

(16c) $\Delta f_t = 1/(\alpha^*\beta)$.

The derivatives with respect to λ are given by:

(17a) $\dfrac{d \Delta e}{d\lambda} = 0$

(17b) $\dfrac{d \Delta \pi}{d\lambda} = 0$

(17c) $\dfrac{d \Delta f}{d\lambda} = -1/(\beta \alpha^*)^2 (\alpha^s - \alpha^g) > 0$.

As equation (17a) shows, Δe does not depend on λ. That is, with this policy function, the stabilizing effect of the shift toward services would be completely offset by changes in monetary policy as λ increases. This offset occurs for the following reason. As employment shifts towards services, total employment becomes less cyclically sensitive; however, because the supply schedule is the same for both sectors, total employment must decline by a given amount to achieve a given disinflation. Therefore, in this model, as employment shifts toward services and the economy becomes less cyclically sensitive, the monetary authority would have to induce larger and larger increases in the federal funds rate to achieve the reduction in total employment that generates the desired amount of disinflation.[11]   That is, the derivative in equation (17c) is positive. In this example, the larger increases in the federal funds rate exactly offsets the stabilizing mix-shift effect.

---

[11] Interestingly, the magnitude of the rise in the federal funds rate prior to recessions has tended to increase in the postwar period. Prior to the recession of 1948-49, the federal funds rate moved up 60 basis points: prior to the 1979-80 recession, the federal funds rate moved up 700 basis points (Romer, 1989). One notable exception is the recession beginning July 1990, in which the federal funds rate began moving down well before the onset of the recession.

The above analysis is done in differentials; we now shift our focus back to variances, which retains consistency with our earlier analysis of outsourcing and luxury services. The story in variances depends on the monetary authority engaging in the following type of monetary rule. The inflation target is allowed to drift up until inflation reaches some critical, unacceptable level, at which point monetary policy is tightened until inflation is reduced substantially. Such a monetary rule has much in common with the comparative statics exercise above, because variability is being generated by a period of monetary looseness followed by disinflation of a set magnitude.[12]

Writing down and solving a model with this reaction function is difficult, however. For our purposes, it is sufficient to note that this story can roughly be captured in equation (13), if we allow the variance of the inflation-target shock $\Delta\delta$ to be an increasing function of λ. We saw above that as the share of employment in services increases, it takes larger and larger federal funds movements to achieve a given disinflation. It follows that, in the type of reaction function just described, there will be larger swings--both positive and negative--in the federal funds rate as λ increases. That is, the variance of $\Delta\delta$ is increasing in λ. Returning to the comparative-statics solution for Δe in equation (14a), it is evident that the variance of aggregate employment growth can be expressed as:

$$(18) \qquad \text{Var } \Delta e_t = \left(\frac{\alpha^*}{1+\alpha^*\beta\gamma} \right)^2 \text{Var}\left(\Delta\delta_t\right) \quad .$$

To see how this variance is affected by λ, differentiate to obtain:

$$(19) \qquad \begin{aligned} \text{dVar } \Delta e_t = & \left[\frac{2\alpha^*}{\left(1+\alpha^*\beta\gamma\right)^3} \left(\alpha^s - \alpha^g\right) \text{Var}\left(\Delta\delta_t\right) \right] d\lambda \\ & + \left[\left(\frac{\alpha^*}{1+\alpha^*\beta\gamma} \right)^2 \text{dVar}\left(\Delta\delta_t\right)/d\lambda \right] d\lambda \quad . \end{aligned}$$

Since α^g is assumed to be greater than α^s, the first term on the right-hand side is negative. However, since the variance of $\Delta\delta$ is increasing in λ, the second term

---

12 Such a characterization of monetary policy--that the monetary authority tightens on those occasions when inflation reaches an unacceptable level--is in the spirit of Romer and Romer (1989).

is positive, and there is no guarantee that the overall change in the variance of aggregate employment growth will decrease as the share of services increases.

4. Estimates of the Size of the Mix Shift and the Potential Offsets

The second goal of this paper is to quantify the effects of the shift in employment shares. Before explicitly measuring those effects, consider how the variability of employment growth has changed over the sample. Figure 2 presents rolling five-year variances and standard deviations of total and sectoral employment growth.[13] Two things are of note in this chart. First, there does appear to have been some small degree of stabilization in total employment growth over the sample. And second, at all times during the sample employment growth in the goods sector is substantially more variable than in the service sector, suggesting that the mix-shift effect could be of quantitative importance.

Quantifying this mix-shift effect is relatively straightforward. However, getting a quantitative handle on our suggested offsets requires measuring the influence of a structural change in the economy, which is difficult, and consequently, controversial.[14] This is so for two reasons. First, the shift in the employment share is likely to affect the economy in very subtle ways, and it may be difficult to capture these effects in a dynamic model estimated with aggregate data. Second--as highlighted in the third line of equation (4) of the accounting framework--many features of the economy have changed since World

---

[13] In these calculations, as elsewhere in the paper, we measure employment as quarterly averages of monthly nonfarm payrolls from the Bureau of Labor Statistics survey of establishments. We define the goods sector to include manufacturing, construction, and mining, and the rest of the non-farm economy (i.e., transportation and public utilities, wholesale and retail trade, finance, insurance, and real estate, services, and government). We focus on variances and covariances of four-quarter growth rates of employment, because some of the disaggregated employment data we use later are only available without seasonal adjustment. By using four-quarter growth rates, we exclude seasonal volatility.

[14] The debate about whether the economy is more stable after World War II than before provides a good example of the difficulty and controversy associated with measuring the effect of structural change. See, Romer (1989) and Balke and Gordon (1989).

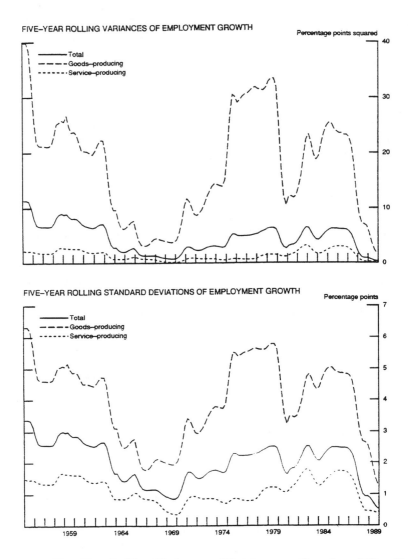

Figure 2. Five-Year Rolling Variances of Employment Growth and Five-Year Rolling Standard Deviations of Employment Growth

War II in addition to the shift in employment shares. Therefore, it may be difficult to determine whether a change in the volatility of employment growth reflects the shift toward services or one of these other factors.

Having said this, we still want to gauge the magnitude of both the mix-shift and the offsets described in this paper, and we use two empirical techniques to do this. The first technique follows in the spirit of the simple accounting framework described in section 2. For this approach, we calculate sectoral variances and covariances over the sample, and plug these pieces into the first line of equation (4) in the accounting framework to obtain an estimate of the mix-shift effect. A more complicated version of this technique is used to measure the size of the offsets. The second technique relies on the model presented in section 3. After estimating a dynamic version of the model, simulation experiments can be used to measure the size of the mix-shift and the offsets.

Both of these techniques, however, face the difficulties just described. The accounting-framework technique requires few assumptions, but controls for none of the factors other than employment shares that might have changed the variance of employment growth in the post-war period. The model simulation technique imposes a lot of structure on the problem and requires taking a stand on exactly how the shift in employment share affects a dynamic macro model. On the other hand, this technique is able to control for some--but by no means all--of the other factors that might affect the variance of employment growth.

4.1 How large is the mix-shift? Table 1 presents an estimate of the size of the simple mix-shift effect, using a quantification of the first line of equation (4). Panel A of the table presents the sectoral variances and covariance of employment growth over the period 1961:Q2 to 1989:Q4.[15] As the column labeled "variances"shows, the service sector is much more stable than the goods sector. Namely, the standard deviation of four-quarter growth rates of services employment is 1.2 percentage points over the sample, compared with 3.9 percentage points for goods. We measure the change in the services share of employment (λ) as the change from the average value between the first five years of data (1961:2 to 1966:1) and the last five years (1985:1 to 1989:4). As shown in the column labeled "shares," the service share has increased from .64 to .76

---

[15] We began our quantitative analysis in 1961 because data on the federal funds rate, used later in the paper, are not available for the earlier period.

Table 1. Basic Mix Shift

Reduction in the Variance of Employment Growth from a Mix-Shift
(1961:2-1989:4)

Panel A
The Necessary Pieces

	Variances		Shares	
Sector	Over full sample		Average over full sample	Change in share over sample[2]
Goods	$\sigma_g^2 = 15.1$	$(\sigma_g = 3.9)$	$1-\lambda = .306$	$-\Delta\lambda = -.121$
Services	$\sigma_s^2 = 1.4$	$(\sigma_s = 1.2)$	$\lambda = .694$	$\Delta\lambda = .121$
Covariance (goods.svcs)	$\sigma_{gs} = 3.6$			
Memo: total	$\sigma^2 = 3.5$	$(\sigma = 1.9)$		

Panel B
The formula[3]

$$\Delta Var(\Delta e) = [\ 2\lambda\ \sigma_s^2\ -\ 2(1-\lambda)\sigma_g^2\ +\ 2(1-2\lambda)\sigma_{gs}\ ]\ \Delta\lambda$$

$$= -1.2$$

---

[1] Variances and covariances are calculated for four-quarter growth rates.

[2] Difference between the average value of λ over the first five years of the sample and the last five years of the sample.

[3] In the text, the formula is computed using differentials. To operationalize the formula it is necessary to use first differences. As indicated, the formula in panel B uses the average value of λ over the full sample, which is analogous to an arc elasticity.

over this period, an increase of 12 percentage points. Plugging these values into the formula--shown in panel B--we find that the simple mix-shift effect has reduced the variance of total employment growth by 1.2 units of variance (percentage points squared).

4.2   Offsets: outsourcing and luxury services.   As shown below, outsourcing of business services and increased consumption of luxury services have contributed to increases in the services share of total employment. Further, employment in these areas will be seen to be more volatile than in the rest of the service sector.   Therefore, other things equal, the rapid growth in service-sector employment has been accompanied by shifts in employment shares within the sector that have increased the volatility of total service-sector employment growth.   The influence of these offsets can be measured using the accounting framework of section 2.[16]

4.2.1.   How large is the offset from outsourcing of business services?   As illustrated in table 2, the share of employment in business services (λ_b) is quite small, but has increased rapidly over the sample period.[17] Further, the volatility of employment in these jobs is higher than in the rest of the service sector, for the reasons described in section 3.1.   In fact, as shown in the variance column of table 2, the standard deviation of growth in business services over the sample was 3.1 percentage points, compared with 1.1 percentage points for the rest of the service sector and 3.9 percentage points for the goods sector.

To measure how much the rise of employment in business services offsets the stabilizing effect of the simple mix shift, we again return to equation (4) of the simple accounting framework.   In terms of the second line of that equation,

---

[16] We also tried to measure these offsets with dynamic model simulations; however, this required estimating models with time-varying parameters, and the effort bore little edible fruit.

[17] Business services--which includes such industries as advertising, personnel supply services, and computer and data processing services--is where many outsourced employees would be classified.   But this may be an understatement of the true amount of outsourcing because there are other industries, such as legal services and accounting, which are not included in business services but may also contain outsourced employees.   Unfortunately, data are less complete for these other industries so they could not be included.

we have provided a reason why the variance of service sector employment growth will increase as λ rises. Denoting business services and other services with the subscripts b and o, the service share (λ) is now split into two: $\lambda = \lambda_b + \lambda_o$.

Noting that σ_s^2 and σ_{sg} can be decomposed as

$$\sigma_s^2 = \lambda_b^2 \sigma_b^2 + \lambda_o^2 \sigma_o^2 + 2\lambda_b \lambda_o \sigma_{ob} \text{ and}$$

$$\sigma_{sg} = \lambda_b \sigma_{gb} + \lambda_o \sigma_{go} \quad .$$

we can quantify the magnitude of the increase in these two variables owing to the especially rapid growth of business services. The first two lines of equation (4) can be shown to equal:

$$dVar(\Delta e) = \left[2\lambda_s^2 - 2(1-\lambda)\sigma_g^2 + 2(1-2\lambda)\sigma_{sg} \right] d\lambda$$
$$+ \left[2\lambda^2 (\lambda_b \sigma_b^2 + \lambda_o \sigma_{ob}) + 2\lambda(1-\lambda)\sigma_{gb} \right] d\lambda_b$$
$$+ \left[2\lambda^2 (\lambda_o \sigma_o^2 + \lambda_b \sigma_{ob}) + 2\lambda(1-\lambda)\sigma_{go} \right] d\lambda_o \quad .$$

Again, the first line of this equation denotes the mix-shift effect, and the rest captures the offset due to outsourcing. Plugging in the parts to this equation in table 2, we estimate that, with this channel operative, the variance of total employment growth has been reduced by about 1.1 units of variance. The mix shift alone was seen to cause a reduction of 1.2 units. Thus, the offset due to outsourcing is estimated to be about 0.1 unit of variance, roughly 10 percent of the stabilization of the two-sector mix shift.

4.2.2   How large is the offset from luxury services? Turning to luxury services, the story is similar. We have defined luxury services to include personal services (such as cleaning services and beauty shops), eating and drinking places, airline transportation, and motion picture theaters. This is surely an incomplete list, but, again, data availability limits our choice.[18]

---

[18] Employment data for these industries--based on the Bureau of Labor Statistics' establishment survey--only go back to 1972.

Table 2. Outsourcing

Estimating the Offset from the Increasing Share of Business Services
(1961:2-1989:4)

Panel A
The Necessary Pieces[1]

Sector	Variances[1] Over full sample		Shares Average over full sample	Change in share over sample[2]
Goods	$\sigma_g^2 = 15.1$	$(\sigma_g = 3.9)$	$1-\lambda = .306$	$-\Delta\lambda = -.121$
Business services	$\sigma_b^2 = 9.8$	$(\sigma_b = 3.1)$	$\lambda_b = .025$	$\Delta\lambda_b = .028$
Other services	$\sigma_o^2 = 1.3$	$(\sigma_o = 1.1)$	$\lambda_o = .669$	$\Delta\lambda_o = .094$
Covariance (goods.bus)	$\sigma_{gb} = 9.6$			
Covariance (goods.oth)	$\sigma_{go} = 3.4$			
Covariance (oth.bus)	$\sigma_{ob} = 2.5$			

Panel B
The Formula

$$\Delta Var(\Delta e) = [2\lambda\sigma_s^2 - 2(1-\lambda)\sigma_g^2 + 2(1-2\lambda)\sigma_{sg}] \Delta\lambda$$
$$+ [2\lambda^2(\lambda_b\sigma_b^2 + \lambda_o\sigma_{ob}) + 2\lambda(1-\lambda)\sigma_{gb}] \Delta\lambda_b$$
$$+ [2\lambda^2(\lambda_o\sigma_o^2 + \lambda_b\sigma_{ob}) + 2\lambda(1-\lambda)\sigma_{go}] \Delta\lambda_o$$
$$= -1.1$$

Mix shift alone (from table 1)	-1.2
Offset	0.1

[1] "b" and "o" denote business and other services. respectively. The share of goods is $1-\lambda$. Variances and covariances are calculated for four-quarter growth rates.

[2] Differences between the average values of λ's over the first five years of the sample and the last five years of the sample.

As shown in table 3, employment in these industries has grown more rapidly than in the rest of the service sector. Further, the volatility of employment growth in luxury services is higher than in the rest of services. Between 1973 and 1989 luxury services had a standard deviation of 1.8 percentage points, compared with 1.2 percentage points for the rest of the service sector.

Analogously to the case of outsourcing, we have divided service-sector employment into two subsectors (luxuries and other), and we estimate the extent to which the variance of service-sector employment growth (and the covariance with the goods sector) increases with the sectoral shift. As shown in table 3, we estimate almost exactly the same amount of stabilization since 1972 as in the simple mix shift from section 4.1.[19]   Evidently, employment in luxury services is too small a share of total employment--and the difference in cyclical variability was not large enough to generate much of an offset to the simple mix shift.

4.3   How large is the offset from the changing influence of monetary policy? As discussed in section 3.2 above, the increasing share of employment in the service sector may change the influence of monetary policy. To gauge the magnitude of this offset, we estimate and simulate a dynamic version of the simple analytic model of that section.

For this model, the demand equations are essentially the same as in the simple analytic model, except that the equations are now dynamic, include terms for relative prices of goods and services, and include terms for real exports.

---

[19] This offset is calculated for the 1972-1989 period, about two-thirds of the full 1961-1989 sample used to calculate the mix-shift effect. The offset is small enough that making assumptions about its magnitude over the earlier period would not affect any of the results.

Table 3. Luxury Services

Estimating the Offset from the Increasing Share of Luxury Services
(1973:1-1989:4)

Panel A
The Necessary Pieces[1]

Sector	Variances Over full sample		Shares Average over full sample	Change in share over sample[2]
Goods	$\sigma_g^2 =$ 19.4	$(\sigma_g = 4.4)$	$1-\lambda =$ .275	$-\Delta\lambda =$ -.091
Luxury services	$\sigma_1^2 =$ 3.1	$(\sigma_1 = 1.8)$	$\lambda_1 =$ .068	$\Delta\lambda_1 =$ .020
Other services	$\sigma_o^2 =$ 1.6	$(\sigma_o = 1.2)$	$\lambda_o =$ .656	$\Delta\lambda_o =$ .071
Covariance (goods.lux)	$\sigma_{g1} =$ 6.0			
Covariance (goods.oth)	$\sigma_{go} =$ 4.3			
Covariance (oth.lux)	$\sigma_{o1} =$ 1.6			

Panel B
The Formula

$$\Delta Var(\Delta e) = [2\lambda\sigma_s^2 - 2(1-\lambda)\sigma_g^2 + 2(1-2\lambda)\sigma_{sg}] \, \Delta\lambda$$
$$+ [2\lambda^2(\lambda_1\sigma_1^2 + \lambda_o\sigma_{o1}) + 2\lambda(1-\lambda) \, \sigma_{g1}] \, \Delta\lambda_1$$
$$+ [2\lambda^2(\lambda_o\sigma_o^2 + \lambda_1\sigma_{o1}) + 2\lambda(1-\lambda) \, \sigma_{g1}] \, \Delta\lambda_o$$
$$= -1.1$$

Mix shift alone (over this sample) = -1.1

Offset = .0

[1] "1" and "o" denote luxury and other. respectively. The share of goods is $1-\lambda$. Variances and covariances are calculated for four-quarter growth rates.

[2] Differences between the average values of λ's over the first year of the sample and the last year of the sample.

These equations are:

(20a) $e_t^s = \beta_0^s + \beta_1^s(L)e_{t-1}^s + \beta_3^s(L)pr_{t-1}^s + \beta_4^s(L)x_t + \epsilon_t^s$

(20b) $e_t^g = \beta_0^g + \beta_1^g(L)e_{t-1}^g + \beta_2^g(L)f_{t-1} + \beta_3^g(L)pr_{t-1}^g$

$\qquad + \beta_4^g(L)x_t + \epsilon_t^g$

where, as before, e and f represent (log) employment and the federal funds rate. In addition, pr_t is the relative price of goods or services and x_t represents (the log of) total real exports. The lag-operator polynomials are constructed to include four lags of each variable on the right hand side. Note that for real exports in this equation (x_t), and for the price of oil below, the equations also include the contemporaneous value on the right-hand side, since these variables are taken to be exogenous.[20]

Unlike the simple analytic model, each sector has its own supply equation. In addition, the supply equations include cross quantity terms and oil price terms. The supply equations are:

(21a) $\pi_t^s = \phi_0^s + \phi_1^s(L)\pi_{t-1}^s + \phi_2^s(L)\Delta e_{t-1}^s + \phi_3^s(L)\Delta y_{t-1}^g$

$\qquad + \phi_4^s(L)\Delta poil_t + \eta_t^s$

(21b) $\pi_t^g = \phi_0^g + \phi_1^g(L)\pi_{t-1}^g + \phi_2^g(L)\Delta e_{t-1}^g + \phi_3^g(L)\Delta y_{t-1}^s$

$\qquad + \phi_4^g(L)\Delta poil_t + \eta_t^g$

where the same notational conventions have been used as for the demand equations. In addition, π_t^g and π_t^s are the inflation rates in the goods and services

---

[20] The federal funds rate is the average rate throughout the quarter. Prices are measured using the quarterly fixed-weight price index for personal consumption expenditures for goods and for services, as published by the Bureau of Economic Analysis (BEA). The relative price of goods is defined as (pg-p), and analogously for services, where lowercase letters denote logarithms. Exports of goods and services are measured in 1982 dollars, published by the BEA.

sectors, respectively, and $poil_t$ is the (log) relative price of oil.[21] In the analytic model of section 3.2, we specified the change in inflation to depend on the growth rate of employment. Such a relationship can be captured in equations (21a-b), since no restrictions are imposed on the coefficients on the lagged dependent variables

Finally, a stylized policy rule for the monetary authority is given by:

$$(22) \qquad f_t = \theta_0 + \theta_1 (L) f_{t-1} + \theta_2 (L) \pi_t + \upsilon_t \quad ,$$

where π_t is the overall inflation rate in the economy.

These equations were estimated over the period 1961:Q2 to 1989:Q4 by ordinary least squares using quarterly data.[22] Note that for the employment variables, we used one-quarter growth rates to estimate the model. The results of the model are summarized in figure 3, which shows the estimated impulse responses of employment and inflation in the two sectors to a federal funds shock.[23] As can be seen in the top panel, a 100 basis point increase in the federal funds rate has its maximal effect on the goods sector about 10 quarters after the shock, and leads to a 1.5 percent decline in employment in that sector. In the service sector, however, the maximal effect comes after about 15 quarters, and leads only to a 0.6 percent decline in employment. That is, federal funds shocks are estimated to have an effect on employment in the goods sector that is about two and a half times larger than in the services sector. And, as is clear from the bottom panel, the shock also reduces inflation in the goods sector by more than in the services sector; here the difference is a factor of two (0.5 percentage point versus 0.2 percentage point).

---

[21] The relative price of oil is computed as the ratio of the producer price index (PPI) for crude petroleum to the PPI for all commodities, after first converting both of the monthly PPI series to a quarterly average.

[22] Regression output is available from the authors upon request.

[23] Impulse responses from a VAR containing the five endogenous variables of the system (employment and inflation in the two sectors and the federal funds rate) give similar results.

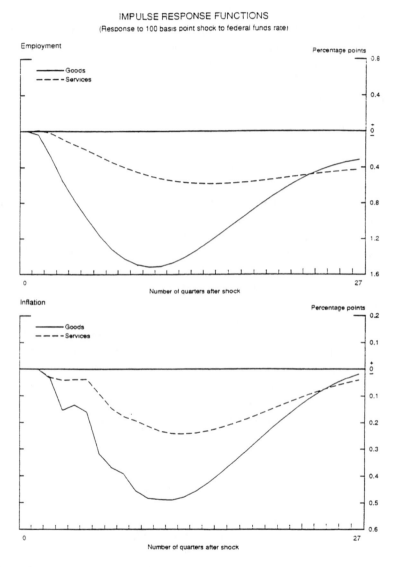

Figure 3. Impulse Response Functions

These impulse responses confirm the basic premise of the simple model described above; namely, that monetary shocks have a larger effect on employment and inflation in the goods sector than in the services sector. We now confirm a corollary of that simple model: federal funds shocks have increased over time as the services share has grown. We see this by regressing the squared residuals from the federal funds equation (22) against the services share of employment (λ), obtaining:

$$(23) \qquad \hat{v}_t^2 = \underset{(-1.1)}{-5.2} + \underset{(1.3)}{9.0} \quad \lambda_t \qquad \qquad RSQ = .015$$

While the estimated coefficient on λ is only marginally significant, it is quantitatively large: as λ increases from .64 at the beginning of the sample to .76 at the end, the predicted variance of the federal funds shock more than triples, rising from 0.57 to 1.66 units (the average variance over the sample period is 1.09 units).

How much of an offset to the simple mix shift can come from this increasing variance of federal funds shocks? To answer this question, we perform some simulations of the estimated model given by equations (20a-b), (21a-b), (22), and (23). The simulations are done over the sample period, and use shocks drawn from the estimated variance-covariance matrix of residuals (shown in the appendix).

We first simulate the basic model in which the variance of federal funds shocks is constant over the sample (referred to as case 1 in table 4). We calculate the variance of the simulated four-quarter growth rates of sectoral and total employment during a five-year window at the beginning (from 61:Q2 to 66:Q1) and the end (85:1 to 89:4) of the sample. We perform 1000 repetitions of this exercise, and calculate the mean of these variances over these repetitions. As shown in table 4, the variance of total employment growth is simulated to fall by 1.6 units (from 4.8 to 3.2 units of variance) between these two periods; this decline reflects a combination of the simple mix-shift effect and differences

Table 4. Monetary Policy Shocks

Model Simulations:
Estimating the Offset from Increasing Federal Funds Shocks

Case 1. Simple model

Variance of shocks in the federal funds equation: 1.09

Simulation results (percentage points. mean over 1000 repetitions):

	61:Q2-66:Q1	85:Q1-89:Q4	Change
$\text{Var}(\Delta e)$[1]	4.8	3.2	-1.6
$\text{Var}(\Delta e^g)$	17.2	15.3	-1.9
$\text{Var}(\Delta e^s)$	1.5	1.1	-.4
$\text{Cov}(\Delta e^s, \Delta e^g)$	4.0	2.4	-1.5

Case 2. Putting λ in the federal funds shock

Variance of shocks in the federal funds equation: $-5.2 + 9.0 \lambda$

Simulation results (percentage points. mean over 1000 repetitions):

	61:Q2-66:Q1	85:Q1-89:Q4	Change
$\text{Var}(\Delta e)$[1]	4.5	3.6	-.8
$\text{Var}(\Delta e^g)$	16.0	17.3	1.3
$\text{Var}(\Delta e^s)$	1.4	1.2	-.2
$\text{Cov}(\Delta e^s, \Delta e^g)$	3.7	2.9	-.8

The size of the offset

Change in $\text{Var}(\Delta e)_{\text{case 2}}$ - Change in $\text{Var}(\Delta e)_{\text{case 1}}$

$$= -.8 - (-1.6) = .8$$

[1] Variances and covariances of employment are calculated for four-quarter growth rates.

in the exogenous variables or in the shocks drawn during these two five-year periods.[24]

We then repeat this exercise allowing the variance of the federal funds shock to depend on λ as in equation (23) above (referred to as case 2 in table 4). The variance of the simulated total employment growth in this case declines by only 0.8 unit between the two periods. We started the random-number generator with the same seed as in case 1, and of course the exogenous variables also are the same as in case 1; therefore, any differences between the two cases comes from the fact that the federal funds shock is allowed to depend on λ. Comparing the figures for case 1 and case 2, we compute that the increasing variance of federal funds shocks has raised the variance of total employment growth by about 0.8 unit.

An important caution must be noted here. We demonstrated that the sectoral shift toward services could have reduced the influence of monetary policy, thereby necessitating larger monetary shocks to achieve a given amount of disinflation. However, as discussed in Bosworth (1989), several of the factors also may have contributed to a reduced effect of monetary policy, such as the increasing prevalence of adjustable rate mortgages and the removal of deposit rate ceilings at mortgage-lending institutions in the 1980s. Since we have not included these factors explicitly, we may be attributing some of their influence on the impact of monetary policy to the sectoral shift story. In any case, the sectoral-shift story should certainly be added to the list of structural changes reducing the influence of monetary policy.

---

[24] It is possible to separate the mix-shift effect from the effect of the exogenous variables and shocks by simulating another version of the model in which λ is constrained not to trend up over time. This yielded a measure of the mix-shift effect similar to that derived in table 1.

4.4 Summing up: the mix shift and its offsets. The table below summarizes our empirical results, reporting the mix-shift and offsets in units of variance (percentage points squared).

Mix shift:	-1.2
Outsourcing:	.1
Luxury services:	.0
Monetary policy shocks:	.8
Total	-.3

As the table shows, the sectoral shift from goods to services implies a reduction in the variance of total employment growth of 1.2 units from the beginning to the end of the sample. We estimate that three-fourths of this stabilization, however, is offset by the factors identified in the table.

We can gain a sense of how large these numbers are by looking back at chart 2, which shows the actual variances of aggregate and sectoral employment growth over five-year rolling samples. A decline of 1.2 units of variance over the sample period owing to the mix-shift effect would be noticeable, if not extremely large. But when our estimated offsets are included, the final stabilization of 0.3 unit of variance is negligible. The increasing share of employment in services has not contributed much to whatever stabilization of the economy has occurred over the postwar period.

5. Conclusion

This paper investigated whether the shift toward employment in the service sector has stabilized overall employment. According to the conventional wisdom, total employment indeed should have become more stable as employment shifted toward the more stable service sector. In the first part of this paper we demonstrated that--as a matter of logic--the shift toward services does not have to be stabilizing. We suggested three factors that could offset the stabilizing effect implicit in the conventional wisdom. For example, two areas within the service sector that have experienced rapid growth--thereby contributing to the shift toward services--are business services and luxury services. Employment growth in both of these areas is more volatile than in the rest of the service sector, so that as employment in these areas grows, the volatility of employment growth in the full service sector increases. Further, if monetary policy has a smaller effect on services than on goods, then to achieve a certain amount of disinflation, monetary shocks may have had to increase overtime.

In the second part of the paper, we quantified the magnitude of the stabilizing effect of the sectoral shift toward services. While the mix-shift appears to have reduced the volatility of overall employment, other factors--also related to the shift in employment toward services--appear to have offset much of this stabilization. Of these factors, the monetary policy channel seems far and away the most important.

On balance, it appears that the shift toward services has not done much to stabilize total employment. Whatever stabilization has occurred likely reflects factors other than the shift in employment shares. Hence, the conventional wisdom about the stabilizing effect of the shift toward services appears to be incorrect.

References

Balke, N., and R. Gordon (1989). "The estimation of prewar Gross National Product: Methodology and new evidence," *Journal of Political Economy* 97, 38-92.

Baumol, W. (1967). "Macroeconomics of unbalanced growth: The anatomy of urban crisis," *American Economic Review* 57, 415-426.

Baumol, W., S.A.B. Blackman, and E.Wolff (1991). *Productivity and American Leadership: The Long View* (The MIT Press, Cambridge, MA).

Blinder, A., and D. Holtz-Eakin (1986). "Inventory fluctuations in the United States since 1929," in R. Gordon, (ed.), *The American Business Cycle: Continuity and Change*, (National Bureau of Economic Research and University of Chicago Press, Chicago, IL), 183-236.

Bosworth, B. (1989). "Institutional change and the efficacy of monetary policy," *Brookings Papers on Economic Activity* 1, 77-124.

Fourastie, J. (1957). *Productivity, Prices, and Wages* (The European Productivity Agency of the Organization for European Economic Cooperation, Paris, France).

Fuchs, V. (1968). *The Service Economy* (National Bureau of Economic Research).

Kutscher, R. (1988). "Growth of services employment in the United States," in *Technology in Services* (National Academy of Engineering), 47-75.

Moore, G. (1987). "The service industries and the business cycle," *Business Economics* (April), 12-17.

Romer, C. (1989). "The prewar business cycle reconsidered: New estimates of Gross National Product, 1869-1908," *Journal of Political Economy* 97, 1-37.

Romer, C., and D. Romer (1989). "Does monetary policy matter: A new test in the spirit of Friedman and Schwartz," in *NBER Macroeconomics Annual*, 121-170.

Romer, D. (1989). "Comment," *Brookings Papers on Economic Activity* 1, 114-119.

Solow, R. (1957). "Technical change and the aggregate production function," *Review of Economic Studies* 39, 312-330.

Summers, R., and A. Heston (1988). "The international demand for services," Discussion Paper No. 32, Fishman-Davidson Center for the Study of the Service Sector, University of Pennsylvania (Philadelphia, PA).

Zarnowitz, V., and G. Moore (1986). "Major changes in cyclical behavior," in R. Gordon, (ed.), *The American Business Cycle: Continuity and Change* (National Bureau of Economic Research and University of Chicago Press, Chicago, IL), 519-582.

Chapter 4   Regional Liberalization of Trade in Services

Bernard Hoekman[1]

1 . Introduction

Competition is usually regarded as an important force underlying investment in-
- or pursuit of -- productivity and quality enhancement by producers. For
countries that maintain significant trade barriers, liberalization of international
trade is frequently an obvious and important means of increasing the
contestability of markets. As entry is facilitated for foreign firms, incumbents
are forced to rationalize -- and may find it easier to do so insofar as the cost of
sourcing inputs, technology and know-how from abroad has declined. If foreign
direct investment (FDI) is liberalized as well, the contestability of markets will
increase further. Again, the likely effects on the productive efficiency of firms
are positive, as the extent of technology transfer is often greater when foreign
firms supply markets via a local establishment rather than from abroad.

The foregoing "conventional wisdom" is usually applied to the manufacturing sector, but applies as much to services. There are differences between
goods and services, however, that may influence the design and scope of
liberalization efforts. One difference is that the nonstorable nature of many
services implies that establishment is often necessary to supply services, and

---

[1] This paper was written when the author was with the GATT secretariat. The
views expressed are personal and do not necessarily reflect those of the GATT or
its contracting parties. I am grateful to Susan Kollins, Pierre Sauvé and Robert
Stern for helpful comments on the draft of the paper presented at the October
1992 Fishman-Davidson conference.

P. T. Harker (ed.), The Service Productivity and Quality Challenge, 113–137.
© 1995 *Kluwer Academic Publishers. Printed in the Netherlands.*

that liberalization must therefore encompass foreign direct investment policies as well as trade barriers *per se*. Another important difference is that the intangible nature of services has led to the creation of regulatory regimes that are intended to establish minimal quality standards for service providers. Some of the regulations that are imposed may have a protectionist rationale, but in most instances this will not be the intention. Indeed, insofar as foreign providers of services are permitted to contest a market (i.e., access is allowed), often such regulations will be applied in identical fashion to domestic and foreign service providers (i.e., national treatment applies). Market access barriers then arise as the result of the differences in standards across countries.

Notwithstanding these differences, the general political economy of liberalization of trade in services is similar to merchandise trade liberalization. Export-oriented industries and consumers of importables will tend to support it, import-competing firms can be expected to oppose it, and the influence of consumers of services will generally be quite limited. In practice, therefore, the reciprocal liberalization path will be easier to pursue for governments than unilateral efforts, as interest groups that benefit from greater access to foreign markets are given an incentive to counter lobbying by those opposed to liberalization. There are two types of reciprocal liberalization, regional (or preferential) and multilateral. The first involves only a limited number of countries, the second a much larger set.

This paper starts in Section 2 with a conceptual discussion of why those countries that have sought to enhance the productivity and efficiency of their service sectors through liberalization have pursued the regional route towards reciprocal liberalization of market access more intensively (and so far more successfully) than the multilateral one.[2] A potential problem with a regional approach towards liberalization of access to service markets is that interest groups that are opposed to greater competition may attempt to increase the barriers facing firms originating in non-member countries and/or exclude their

---

[2] Regional agreements to liberalize international transactions in services include the United States-Canada free trade agreement, the Australia-New Zealand Closer Economic Relations trade agreement, the EC-1992 program, and the North American Free Trade Agreement. All of these agreements are recent, the oldest (the EC-1992 project) entering into force in 1987, the most recent (NAFTA) yet to be implemented. No multilateral agreement yet exists, although a draft General Agreement on Trade in Services has been negotiated as part of the Uruguay Round.

industry from the reach of market opening measures altogether. A number of criteria can be identified to help determine the scope that exists for such "capture" of regional agreements. These include: (1) the sectoral coverage of the regional agreements and the modalities of liberalization that are pursued; (2) the degree to which regional preferences are extended to third parties through multilateral negotiations, or, alternatively put, the regional policy stance vis-a-vis outsiders; and (3) the existence of a liberal accession clause, foreseeing the expansion of the regional agreement to new members. Section 3 summarizes the main elements of existing regional agreements between OECD countries to liberalize access to service markets. Section 4 investigates the extent to which they satisfy the three criteria mentioned earlier. The greater the internal liberalization, the more this is "multilateralized" and the more liberal accession procedures, the higher the rates of growth in productivity, quality and variety of services offered to consumers are likely to be. Section 5 concludes.

2. Conceptual Issues

The choice between pursuing a regional as opposed to a multilateral trade liberalization agreement depends on numerous factors. A regional trade agreement (RTA) by definition involves substantially fewer countries than a multi-lateral one; indeed, some RTAs have only two members. Insofar as the countries involved are relatively like-minded on specific issues, achieving agreement may be much more straightforward in the regional context. And, because the number of players is small, tradeoffs across issues may be easier to achieve as well. Indeed, one characteristic of RTAs is that their agendas tend to be much wider than multilateral agreements. Moreover, the more similar are countries in their endowments and income levels, the likelier it is that intra-industry trade will be significant. Consequently the adjustment costs for such countries associated with preferential liberalization are likely to be much lower than under multilateral liberalization.[3] This facilitates regional approaches, as opposition by industry is likely to be lower, while globally-oriented exporting firms are left indifferent as long as external trade barriers are not raised. RTAs

---

[3] This hypothesis is often postulated in the literature and has been supported by empirical studies. See Greenaway and Hine (1991) for a recent survey of the theory and evidence in the EC context.

may also allow more credible commitments to be made, insofar as it is easier to monitor the implementation of the agreement. Fewer countries and geographical proximity is likely to imply that industries are better informed regarding actions taken by rivals or foreign governments that are deemed to violate the negotiated agreement.

These "standard" explanations of why regional or preferential trade liberalizing agreements are observed are quite general, and should be independent of whether the agreement pertains to merchandise or to service trade flows. For example, available data on trade in services suggest that intra-industry trade is quite high. Table 1 reports data revealing that intra-industry trade in services between OECD countries is comparable to that of merchandise. The measure of intra-industry trade in services used in Table 1 is the Grubel-Lloyd index, defined as

$$GL = \frac{\Sigma_i (X_i + M_i) - \Sigma_i |X_i - M_i|}{\Sigma_i (X_i + M_i)}$$

where X_i and M_i are a country's exports and imports of industry i, respectively. The index ranges between 0 and 100, intra-industry trade being greater the closer the index is to 100.[4] It can be seen from Table 1 that intra-industry trade is quite high for all countries except Spain. Intra-industry trade indices for merchandise, drawn from Greenaway and Hine (1991), which are based on data for 28 goods-producing sectors are also reported in Table 1 for comparison purposes.[5] On average, it appears that the magnitude of intra-industry trade in services is very similar to that in merchandise for the countries reported. Intra-industry trade is significantly greater than for merchandise in Canada, Denmark, and Germany, while the opposite holds only for Spain. It is well known that intra-industry trade in merchandise has grown substantially over the last two decades. The

[4] The number of disaggregated service categories reported by countries varies. The EC countries report 14 such categories, Canada 15, and the United States 21. However, for the United States this coverage is only available for recent years. Up to 1985 the United States reports only 10 categories.

[5] It should be kept in mind that the smaller number of service categories as compared to merchandise items may bias the service indices upward. However, the difference between the number of service and merchandise sectors for the most recent years is relatively small.

mean Grubel-Lloyd index for merchandise trade of the OECD countries for which we have services data was 67.4 in 1970, 70.4 in 1980 and 75.4 in 1985. The average index for services also demonstrates an upward trend, but increases are smaller. The average of the services indices increased from 72 in 1979 (the first year for which EC data are available) to 74.2 in 1985 to 76.7 in 1989.[6]

Table 1. Grubel-Lloyd Intra-Industry Services Trade Indices

	Services					Merchandise	
	1980	1983	1985	1987	1989	1980	1985
Belguim-Lux	84.2	86.3	87.1	84.4	83.8	84.1	86.7
Denmark	77.5	73.9	80.2	82.3	79.3	67.4	72.6
France	85.0	82.3	81.1	85.6	85.7	86.1	85.5
Germany	71.0	76.4	76.6	73.6	74.6	55.4	68.2
Italy	62.0	59.3	64.0	71.2	79.5	69.6	69.5
Netherlands	69.2	72.0	68.3	68.9	68.8	77.9	76.3
Spain	52.0	49.6	47.6	45.2	51.8	50.4	68.2
U.K.	80.8	85.3	82.9	83.5	80.9	80.8	84.3
Canada	88.2	81.4	85.6	83.8	85.3	64.5	76.4
U.S.	78.3	70.6	69.0	73.9	77.7	68.2	66.5

Source: Services trade data are drawn from EUROSTAT (1990) and OECD (1992); merchandise intra-industry indices are from Greeaway and Hine (1991).

An extensive literature exists on the pro's and con's of regional (preferential) liberalization from the perspective of both the welfare of member and non-member countries.[7] What is of interest here is the services dimension of such

---

[6] For more discussion of data on intra-industry and intra-regional trade in services, see Hoekman (1992a).

[7] See, e.g., the contributions in Anderson and Blackhurst (1993) for a recent discussion and references to the literature.

agreements, an aspect that has been relatively neglected. The key issues in this connection are the importance of FDI as a mode of contesting service markets and the regulatory regimes that are applied by countries to their service sectors. FDI is often required to contest a market, if not for technical reasons (i.e., the service is not tradable), than for practical ones. Thus, in many instances even if cross-border trade is technically feasible, FDI may be the most efficient mode of supply.

The importance of foreign direct investment as a mode of supply for service providers and the existence of regulatory barriers to entry may alter the specifics of the political economy of liberalization efforts. In the short-run, it is generally assumed that sector-specific factors of production employed in inefficient protected industries will oppose liberalization of market access. In the services-context this may not be the case. To the extent that establishment (FDI) is the most efficient mode of contesting a market, sector-specific labor may be less opposed to liberalization, insofar as it is expected that net employment in the sector will not change much upon liberalization due to the establishment of foreign-owned firms. This is likely to be the case in particular when establishment is the only feasible mode of contesting a market. Moreover, because it is more difficult to control industries that are located in foreign jurisdictions, regulators may prefer that establishment is *required* as a mode, even if FDI is neither technically required nor the preferred mode of supply for a given service firm.

Given the importance of FDI in effectively contesting service markets it should not come as a surprise that FDI in services already accounts for a substantial share of global direct investment flows. FDI in services varies between 25 and 80 percent of the total stock of inward FDI in most host countries. As of the late-1980s over 40 percent of the world stock of FDI was in services. Services-related FDI has also been growing faster than FDI in manufacturing. A large share of this investment is in the financial services sector (banking, insurance, financial intermediation). Financial services account for some 50 percent or more of total inward FDI in services in many OECD countries (UNCTAD and World Bank, 1994). In conjunction with the relatively low volume of trade in financial services, this suggests that many of these services are not readily tradable.[8] Of particular relevance in the context of this paper is that by far the largest share of FDI flows originate in the major OECD countries and go to other industrialized nations (Table 2).

Table 2.   Stocks of FDI by Source Country and Host Region, various years
(percentage of total and US $ billion)

Country	Period	Developed Countries			Developing Countries			Total (US $bn)
		Primary	Manufac.	Services	Primary	Manufac.	Services	
Canada	1975	16.1	46.2	14.3	4.9	4.2	14.1	10.7
	1989	11.0	42.4	32.8	2.6	2.5	9.4	66.9
Germany	1975	1.5	35.3	37.1	2.6	13.0	4.7	20.0
Fed. Rep	1990	1.2	33.6	49.7	1.1	9.6	4.8	143.4
Japan	1975	10.9	8.8	26.5	17.2	23.6	13.0	16.0
	1990	2.5	17.7	48.5	3.5	8.5	19.3	310.8
Nether-	1973	40.4	33.7	9.5	7.1	5.5	3.7	15.8
lands	1990	28.9	19.7	39.9	3.5	4.3	3.7	100.0
United	1974	7.0	49.3	22.4	4.3	11.5	8.0	23.6
Kingdom	1984	27.5	27.3	26.9	5.9	4.5	8.0	101.1
United	1975	19.9	36.6	14.4	3.8	8.4	7.0	124.2
States	1990	7.5	24.5	24.7	4.3	6.4	10.9	550.5

Source: UNCTAD and World Bank (1994).

---

[8] There are, of course, very large capital and foreign exchange flows between countries on a daily basis. But this does not constitute trade in services.

The magnitude of intra-OECD cross-hauling of FDI and the growth in such flows over the last decade reflects relatively low and falling barriers to inward FDI. These barriers have been reduced in the context of cooperation in the OECD context, under whose auspices a number of "codes" have been established requiring, inter alia, national treatment. More importantly, barriers to FDI and trade in services in Western Europe were reduced through the EC-92 Single European Market initiative and its expansion to the EFTA countries (excepting Switzerland) via the negotiation of the European Economic Area Agreement. Not only have these agreements spurred investment flows by reducing discrimination against foreigners, but the European integration efforts made it much more attractive to locate production facilities within that region. From the perspective of this paper what matters is that negotiated liberalization of FDI has largely been an intra-OECD affair. Geographical and cultural proximity and similarity in regulatory regimes and objectives as well as levels of per capita income greatly facilitated the reciprocal liberalization of FDI and international transactions of services.

In some instances FDI may not be the preferred mode of contesting a market, but may be necessary to satisfy regulatory requirements. And in other cases FDI may be impossible even after the abolition of general measures discriminating against establishment by foreign firms because entry into an industry - by domestic or foreign firms - is prohibited by a government. Regulatory regimes *per se* are then an additional, if not the primary, barrier to accessing a particular market. Regulatory bodies may support or oppose liberalization in general. If they support it, they may prefer regional efforts, especially if liberalization involves a need for regulatory convergence and/or deregulation. To the extent that a precondition for liberalizing market access is harmonization of regulatory regimes (or agreement to recognize the standards and regulations of partner countries) a clear preference can be expected for RTAs on the part of regulators.

A distinction between regulated and non-regulated service sectors is therefore useful to make. Liberalization of the latter can be achieved in either a regional or a multilateral context.[9] For the former the scope of multilateral liberalization efforts will inherently be limited, as the most that can realistically be sought is the application of the principles of national treatment and most-favored-nation

---

[9] Thus, regional progress in liberalizing access to such service markets can in principle be extended to third countries in a multilateral setting.

(MFN) treatment. National treatment implies the foreign firms seeking to contest a domestic market will be subjected to the same regulations as local firms. MFN implies that all foreign firms will be treated in the same manner. Going beyond national treatment - e.g., pursuing a policy of mutual recognition of regulatory standards - will generally only be possible in the small numbers context of a regional arrangement. The EC experience illustrates the limitations of national treatment in liberalizing access to service markets; as recognized in the EC-92 program (see below) in practice mutual recognition is a necessary condition for the effective liberalization of regulated service sectors.

It is well known that from an efficiency (and thus productivity-enhancing) perspective, regional liberalization will generally be inferior to multilateral liberalization.[10] This standard presumption must be qualified to some extent when services enter into the picture, insofar as mutual recognition may the most effective way of liberalizing access to regulated service markets and this will be difficult to achieve in the multilateral context. But, notwithstanding this qualification, it is certainly the case that the first best option is to seek to expand (regional) mutual recognition regimes to as many countries as possible. From the perspective of maximizing the contestability of markets, and thus enhancing the pressure to increase productivity in service sectors, it is therefore important that mechanisms exist to expand regional arrangements to additional countries over time.

Three criteria can be identified to help determine whether regional liberalization efforts focusing on the service sector will be pro-competitive in the long run. The first is that the sectoral coverage of the agreement be comprehensive, i.e., all services are affected, and that the rules and principles that are embodied in the agreement (the modalities of liberalization) imply that covered service markets actually become contestable for foreign service providers. The greater the coverage of the agreement, the greater the presumption that it will enhance productive efficiency and not be a vehicle for industries to create rents. The second criterion is that there be a willingness to extend regional preferences and procedures to the multilateral setting. The degree to which regional preferences are extended to third parties in the multilateral context, or, alternatively put, the region's policy stance vis-a-vis outsiders, will be important in determining the economic impact of regional integration. The third criterion is the openness of the region to additional membership. This implies the

---

[10] See, e.g., Bhagwati (1992).

existence of a formal accession mechanism. The more liberal such accession clauses are, the less worrisome regional agreements will be.

3. Existing RTAs Involving OECD Countries

The extent to which existing RTAs satisfy these criteria can only be determined by a close reading of their provisions. This section summarizes the main provisions of the regional agreements between OECD countries liberalizing access to service markets. The extent to which these agreements satisfy the three criteria noted above is discussed in Section 4.

3.1   The Treaty of Rome and the Single Market Program.   The main objective of the Treaty of Rome establishing the European Economic Community is the realization of the four freedoms: free internal movement of goods, services, labor and capital, including the right of establishment. In principle, the freedom to provide services applies to all services, with the exception of transportation services for which the primacy of national policies was recognized until a common EC-wide regime was established. As a result, there has been only limited intra-EC competition in transportation services, governments frequently setting tariffs (e.g. in rail), imposing and enforcing quotas (road transport), or agreeing to bilateral market sharing arrangements (air transport). Nor was much progress made to effectively liberalize intra-EC trade and investment in other services. For example, Article 61 of the Treaty of Rome stated that liberalization of financial services was to be affected in step with the progressive liberalization of capital movements - on which little progress was made (Roth, 1988). More generally, the main liberalizing principle of the Treaty of Rome - nondiscrimination/national treatment - proved to be insufficient to lead to an increase in competition in services, as most of the regulations that restricted market access did not discriminate between domestic and foreign (other EC) firms. Writing in the mid-1980s, Hindley (1987, p. 471) noted that "it is widely accepted that progress to [attain the] liberalization of services transactions is so slow as to raise serious doubts as to whether it will ever arrive at its destination." Lack of progress was due to a lack of enthusiasm on the part of many EC members, who argued in the EC Council that a necessary condition for liberalization was the adoption of common regulatory policies for specific services. Efforts to agree to harmonized policies proved relatively unfruitful.

The adoption of the Single Market or '1992' program can be characterized as an attempt to achieve the original objectives of the Treaty of Rome (Winters, 1992). However, it goes beyond the original treaty by defining the concept of the 'internal market,' adopting qualified majority voting in the EC Council on most issues relating to the establishment and functioning of the internal market, and introducing the concepts of minimum standards, mutual recognition and 'home country control' for regulatory regimes.[11]   The adoption of the Single European Act reflected a marked change in the stance of European business. As noted by Sandholtz and Zysman (1989), as of the mid-1980s both services and goods-producing industries in many EC countries had come to the conclusion that to be able to withstand Japanese and American competition it was necessary to reap the potential economies of scale implicit in the creation of a European-wide single market. Managerial innovations such as 'just-in-time' inventory control and advances in information and communication technologies increased the marginal costs of maintaining artificially segmented markets in Europe. The increasing costs of R&D in sectors such as informatics required structures in which European firms could cooperate. Through the Roundtable of European Industrialists, business interests actively pushed for the creation of EC-supported cooperative arrangements and the liberalization of intra-EC transactions in domestic political markets.

A significant dimension of the '1992' liberalization of service markets concerns financial services. The second Coordinating Banking Directive made home countries responsible for prudential supervision (setting and enforcing liquidity and solvency standards) subject to the requirements of other EC Directives that established minimum standards in this regard. It therefore allows any credit institution authorized in one EC Member State to establish branches and provide banking services anywhere in the EC (the so-called single passport). However, foreign financial institutions remain subject to the host country's business rules - such as reporting requirements and restrictions on permissible products and activities. As noted by Chrystal and Coughlin (1992) this potentially limits the extent to which there will be a genuine single market for financial services. In addition to banking, there are also directives on investment

---

[11] See Pelkmans (1990) for a summary description and discussion of the Single Market program.

services (securities markets), mutual funds, and insurance. The first of these has proven more difficult to formulate than the banking directive, in large part because the activities it covers are more diverse as are existing regulatory structures in individual EC Member States.

The 1992 program is clearly potentially far-reaching in terms of liberalizing intra-EC service markets. Majority voting should reduce the influence of national interest groups that oppose specific EC directives, and in contrast to the past there now appears to be a greater confluence of interest between business and the Commission. It should result in significant liberalization of European service markets. Moreover, it does not appear that the 1992 program will result in greater market access barriers for non-EC service providers.[12]

3.2   The Canada-United States Free Trade Agreement (CUSFTA).
The CUSFTA was negotiated in 1987 and entered into force in early 1989.[13] It contains four chapters related to trade in services, one on services *per se*, one on financial services, one on temporary entry for business travel and one on investment. The investment chapter is general, covering both services and goods-related establishment. As is the case for the Treaty of Rome, the main principle that is applied is that of national treatment, i.e., service providers from either country were to be treated no less favorably than domestic providers of a given service. However, the immediate effect of this obligation was severely restricted because it only applied to new measures adopted by either country after the entry into force of the agreement is 1989. That is, existing nonconforming measures were 'grandfathered'. The agreement takes a 'positive list' approach to sectoral coverage, its obligations only applying to those services that are explicitly listed in an annex. Important service activities such as transportation, basic telecommunications, legal and medical services (doctors, dentists) were excluded.

The one service sector where some immediate progress was made is financial services. The agreement has a separate chapter on financial services: banking, investment banking, and loan and trust companies.[14] Its provisions formally

---

12 See Pelkmans (1990) for a sector-by-sector discussion.
13 See Schott and Smith (1988) for a review of the agreement's provisions on services.
14 Insurance is not covered, instead being covered by the general chapter on services.

grandfather the existing market access situation - which was already relatively liberal, with banks from both countries being active in each other markets - but commit both parties to further liberalization. Canadian banks operating in the United States were provided with the right to underwrite and deal in securities of the Canadian government, and guaranteed national treatment consequent to any changes in the Glass-Steagal Act. American firms are exempted from various investment restrictions (e.g. a 12 percent ceiling on the size of the foreign bank sector). Disputes were not covered by the general dispute settlement provisions of the agreement but were to be handled by the respective finance ministries.

Even if existing measures pertaining to service sectors had not been grandfathered, the EC experience illustrates that national treatment is not likely to be sufficient to ensure effective liberalization of service markets. As no general provisions or procedures were established for harmonization or mutual recognition of regulations, the CUSFTA could only achieve limited progress at best in increasing the contestability of service markets.[15] In any event, the agreement has been superseded by NAFTA.e

3.3   The North American Free Trade Agreement (NAFTA). The NAFTA negotiations were concluded in September 1992. NAFTA diverges from the CUSFTA in three significant ways as far as services are concerned. First, a negative list approach is used to determine the coverage of liberalization obligations: all service sectors are covered by the NAFTA except for those that are explicitly listed in annexes to the agreement. One consequence of this is that there is no general grandfathering of existing 'nonconforming measures'. Instead all such measures must be listed by parties to the agreement. This ensures a much higher degree of transparency than was the case under CUSFTA. Second, although no general obligations are imposed on public procurement of services, the procurement of some services is covered for a significant number of government agencies. Under the CUSFTA services were largely excluded.[16] This is important, as public procurement often accounts for a substantial share of total service sector turnover in a country. Third, the rules and obligations are

---

[15] See Whalley (1991) for a similar conclusion.

[16] Only services incidental to the sale of a product were covered in CUSFTA. A positive list approach to entity coverage and a negative list approach for services coverage in procurement contracts is taken under the NAFTA. Services that are excluded include most transportation, storage, communication, financial, R&D, legal, education and health services.

based on a clearer conceptual foundation. A distinction is made between national treatment, MFN, and nondiscriminatory measures that restrict access to a service market. The latter are called 'quantitative restrictions' in the agreement. National treatment and MFN are general obligations. In contrast, parties are unconstrained with respect to quantitative restrictions subject to the condition that these are listed in an annex. Such nondiscriminatory measures are to be the subject of periodic negotiation. Finally, the NAFTA incorporates 'ratcheting' in that a party's obligations are automatically adjusted to the liberalization of any domestic measure.

The negative list approach required the inclusion of a rather daunting set of annexes pertaining to exceptions and reservations. Annex I has reservations and specific commitments for existing nonconforming measures. Annex II lists reservations for future measures (i.e., 'nonnegotiable' exceptions). Annex III embodies activities reserved for the State. Annex IV is for exceptions from MFN, while Annex V relates to existing nondiscriminatory quantitative restrictions. There is also one sector-specific annex relating to reservations and specific commitments for financial services. What is relevant of course is not the number of such annexes, but their content. Perusal of the various annexes reveals that the number of services that are excluded from the coverage of the agreement is relatively limited. For example, the only sectors of economic significance Canada has reserved in Annex I are air and water transport; social services, telecommunications transport networks, basic telecommunications services, policies implying preferences for aboriginal and minority populations, nonscheduled air transport, and maritime cabotage of goods and persons. Only maritime transport and telecommunication services are excluded from the MFN requirement (Annex IV). Finally, in Annex V (nondiscriminatory quantitative restrictions) Canada has listed its postal services monopoly, licensing requirements for radio communications and oil/gas pipelines, provincial monopoly for retail distribution of alcoholic beverages, and extra-provincial public passenger land transit.

Clearly the foregoing includes a number of important service sectors on which future negotiations will undoubtedly focus. But it is noteworthy that the majority of services are in principle covered by the NAFTA. Mexican and U.S. reservations are somewhat different from those of Canada, reflecting national preferences and economic structure. However, the same conclusion applies. The number of excluded sectors is relatively limited. The primary sectors that are reserved are again air and water transport, and basic telecommunications.

There is a separate chapter dealing with financial services that covers both investment and cross-border trade. It largely duplicates the general provisions of the agreement, but takes into account some of the specificities of financial services (e.g., need for prudential supervision). National treatment and MFN obligations apply to both establishment and cross-border trade. A negative list approach is again taken with respect to nonconforming measures. Allowance is made for recognition of prudential measures, subject to the condition that another Party be permitted to negotiate accession to recognition agreements.

3.4   Australia-New Zealand Closer Economic Relations Trade Agreement (ANZCERTA).

ANZCERTA's goal is to progressively liberalize trade between Australia and New Zealand.[17] It came into force in January 1983 and was extended to cover trade in services in 1988. In contrast to the CUSFTA, a negative list approach was followed to determine the coverage of the agreement (i.e., all service sectors are covered unless specifically exempted). Excluded sectors include basic telecoms, air transport, maritime cabotage and postal services. In contrast to other regional agreements, these sectoral exclusions are not indefinite, as there are provisions to bring these sectors within the scope of the protocol in the future. Also excluded from the national treatment obligation are taxation measures, subsidies and government procurement.

Parties are required to provide national treatment, MFN treatment for excluded (reserved) sectors, and market access for covered services. Market access is defined as granting persons and services of the partner country access rights no less favorable than those allowed to domestic providers. National treatment is defined conventionally, except that allowance is made (as in the other agreements) for differences in treatment that nonetheless result in effectively equal treatment between foreign and domestic service providers, and for differences that are motivated by prudential, health or safety considerations. While there is no mention of non-discriminatory regulations (quantitative restrictions) as impediments to market access, the market access article implicitly allows such restrictions to be maintained.

Service providers originating in a member state are free to choose their preferred mode of supply, including establishment. Although the agreement

---

[17] See Lloyd (1991) for a detailed treatment. What follows draws on Hoekman and Sauvé (1994).

includes a right of establishment -- this being recognized as a critical element of the provision of many services -- such establishment is subject to the foreign investment policies maintained by each country. As do the CUSFTA and the NAFTA, ANZCERTA incorporates the principle of non-establishment. Measures requiring establishment are forbidden if the measure constitutes a means of arbitrary or unjustifiable discrimination or a disguised restriction on trade between the member states in services. Similar to the EC, Australia and New Zealand form a common labor market, nationals from one country being free to seek employment in the other. The common labor market obviates the need for CUSFTA/NAFTA-type provisions on temporary entry and the removal of citizenship and/or permanent residency requirements associated with the licensing of service providers.

A standstill was imposed on export subsidies and other direct assistance affecting trade in covered services, and member states were required to work towards the elimination of all such measures. The agreement also contains "best efforts" language regarding licensing and certification requirements, which was all that was feasible given the sovereignty of Australian states with respect to numerous licensing and certification matters. Parties agreed to endeavor to ensure that such measures do not act to discriminate against persons of another Party when these seek access to licensing or certification. Parties are also encouraged -- but not required -- to recognize qualifications obtained in the other member state, though the Agreement contained no specific procedures aimed at facilitating such recognition.

Monopolies that are excluded from the coverage of the Protocol -- i.e., are featured in the annexes listing excluded sectors and activities -- are still required to provide services to consumers of another Party on a non-discriminatory and transparent basis. The two countries have agreed to endeavor to prevent such monopoly providers from cross-subsidizing services that are sold in competition with private companies originating in either country.

4. Evaluating the Regional Agreements

Three criteria were identified earlier to help determine the extent to which regional liberalization efforts can be expected to enhance the contestability of service markets in the medium and long run, as well as in the short run. The criteria were: (1) the sectoral coverage and modalities of liberalization; (2) the region's external policy stance; and (3) the existence and wording of an accession clause.

4.1 Sectoral coverage and modalities of liberalization. The ANZCERTA and NAFTA take a negative list approach to coverage; the CUSFTA a positive list. While either approach can lead to the same outcome, a negative list is more transparent. It forces parties to list all nonconforming measures and excluded sectors, whereas a positive list approach does not. Aside from this major difference, the non-EC agreements appear to be rather similar with respect to coverage. The same sectors tend to be excluded: basic telecommunications, air and water transport, social services, government procurement.[18] These have also been the sectors where the EC has encountered difficulties in liberalizing market access. NAFTA makes some progress on road transport, but does not open up air or maritime transport (cabotage). Although transport is formally covered by the EC-92 liberalization program, even in that context it is proving difficult to make significant changes (Messerlin, 1990). Before '1992' transport was effectively excluded from the scope of liberalization in the EC context, and it was excluded in the CUSFTA.

Although some industries therefore succeeded in being exempted from the reach of liberalization efforts, many services are affected by the RTAs. In part this reflects active support of liberalization initiatives by influential service industries such as the financial services industry. In part this support was driven by a desire to obtain greater access to foreign markets, which in turn was driven by recent advances in information and telecommunication technologies that augmented the tradability of many financial services - both at the retail and the wholesale level. American financial services firms - both banks and insurance companies - have been especially active in *both* regional and multilateral services negotiations. They were prime movers behind the formation of the Coalition of Service Industries, and created a Financial Services Group in mid-1989 to lobby American negotiators. The industry was influential in opposing attempts by the United States Treasury to have financial services excluded from a multilateral agreement on trade in services (Westlake, 1990) and was able to induce the American government to oppose the reciprocity provisions of the EC Commissions first draft of the Second Banking Directive. As mentioned earlier, the CUSFTA and the NAFTA contain similar language on financial services that

---

[18] With the partial, but noteworthy, exception of the NAFTA.

goes a bit beyond the general provisions of the agreements in terms of liberalizing access to markets.

As with sectoral coverage, the agreements reviewed in this paper also are all broadly similar insofar as the basic instruments or modalities of liberalization are concerned. Key principles that are found in most or all agreements include national treatment, MFN, and freedom in principle for providers of services to use any mode of supply. However, there are significant differences in the extent to which the reach of such principles is restricted for individual sectors or measures. NAFTA allows for MFN derogations, the EC and ANZCERTA do not. In the case of NAFTA the need for a derogation arose mainly because of concerns of the telecommunications and maritime transport industry regarding potentially unbalanced market access opportunities in other countries involved in negotiations.

In contrast to the EC, the other agreements do not mandate the harmonization or mutual recognition of regulatory regimes pertaining to licensing and certification of professional services providers. NAFTA goes further than the ANZCERTA in that it contains a generic blueprint aimed at assisting all professions to achieve mutual recognition of licenses and certifications and incorporates separate work programs aimed at liberalizing the provision of foreign legal consulting and engineering services. However, there is no obligation under the NAFTA to recognize credentials of professional service providers from another member country.

Summing up, there has clearly been substantial opening of service markets in Western Europe, North America and the Tasman area through the various regional agreements. But the scope of the regional efforts remains limited, especially outside Western Europe. Indeed, it is by comparing the other agreements with the EC/European Economic Area that the "holes" they contain become obvious. Major "holes" are the exclusion of sectors such as air and maritime transport and basic telecommunications from the reach of liberalization, as well as the limited degree to which mutual recognition of regulatory regimes is pursued. While a right of establishment and implementation of the national treatment principle are certainly steps forward, for regulated services in particular this may be inadequate to make markets contestable. Given the incompleteness of regional efforts, the external policy stance of each region becomes of particular importance in determining whether the initial effect of preferential liberalization in increasing the contestability of service markets will endure.

4.2   The external dimension. At the same time that most OECD countries were involved in establishing regional agreements to liberalize access to service markets, these countries also actively pursued the creation of multilateral disciplines in this area. Services were included as an agenda item of the Uruguay Round of multilateral trade negotiation that were launched in late 1986. A draft General Agreement on Trade in Services (GATS) emerged from the negotiations at the end of 1991. Attention here will focus largely on the position taken by "regional" industrialized countries in the GATS negotiations, as in the short to medium run this will be the main indicator of the extent to which non-member countries will be discriminated against. Although negotiations continue at the time of writing (spring 1993) regarding the sectoral coverage of the GATS, most of its content has broad-based support and is not likely to be changed significantly in the final stages of the Uruguay Round. Nonetheless, it should be emphasized that the discussion that follows is based on the 1991 draft.[19]

A core obligation imposed on members of the GATS is unconditional most-favored-nation treatment (MFN). The agreement applies to four "modes of supply:" the cross-border supply of a service (that is, not requiring the physical movement of supplier or consumer); provision implying movement of the consumer to the location of the supplier; services sold in the territory of a member by (legal) entities that have established a commercial presence there but originate in the territory of another member; and provision of services requiring the *temporary* movement of *natural* persons. These modes are covered in principle only. Tne extent to which specific modes can be used by foreign suppliers to provide individual services is determined by a member's schedule of commitments.

There are two main articles in Part III of the GATS on Specific Commitments, entitled Market Access and National Treatment. These obligations apply *only* to services that are included in the schedules of contracting parties, subject to whatever qualifications or conditions are listed. The first requires that a member does not maintain any of six types of prohibited measures. These include limits on the number of firms allowed, the magnitude

---

[19] For a detailed discussion of the draft GATS, see Hoekman (1992b). The agreement that eventually emerged is discussed in Hoekman and Sauvé (1994). It does not differ substantially from the 1991 draft.

of sales or employment, and restrictions on equity participation by foreigners. However, if desired, such measures may continue to be applied, but must be listed individually. Market access commitments are therefore country- and sector-specific, "free" market access (implicitly) being equated with the absence of prohibited restrictions on any of the possible modes of supply.

National treatment is defined as treatment no less favorable than that accorded to like domestic services and service providers. Such treatment may or may not be identical to that applying to domestic firms, in recognition of the fact that identical treatment may actually worsen the conditions of competition for foreign-based firms (e.g., a requirement for insurance firms that reserves be held locally). In part, the use of separate market access and national treatment obligations reflects one of the distinguishing characteristics of service markets: the fact that the contestability of such markets is frequently restricted by nondiscriminatory regulations. The market access article explicitly covers one type of such regulation - quantitative restrictions - that were felt to be of particular importance by negotiators.

A major difference between the CUSFTA, NAFTA and the ANZCERTA on the one hand and the GATS on the other is that national treatment is a general obligation in the regional agreements but may be applied selectively under the GATS. As a result, the schedules of commitments of the member countries of the GATS are very important in terms of determining the extent of the resulting market access opportunities. Unfortunately, the contents of the schedules remain under negotiation at the time of writing. Nonetheless, the initial offers that were on the table as of the end of 1992 provide an indication of the agreement's likely coverage and the extent to which unilateral/regional liberalization will be multilateralized in the GATS.

As of early 1993, some 40 developing countries and all OECD countries had presented an initial offer. A number of summary indicators can be constructed to compare country offers. The most straightforward is to simply count the number of subsectors mentioned in an initial offer and express this as a share of the total number of subsectors in the GATS indicative list of service activities. This list distinguishes 11 major service categories and 154 sub-sectors.[20] The

[20] The major categories are business services (including professional and computer-related services), communication services (including postal, telecom and audiovisual services), construction, distribution services, education, environmental services, financial services, health and related services, tourism, recreation, and transportation. UNCTAD and World Bank (1994) reproduces the

initial offers of developing countries as of the end of 1992 had "coverage ratios" ranging from 1 to 50 percent, the average being about 20 percent. The average unweighted coverage ratio of initial offers of industrialized countries exceeds 75 percent (UNCTAD and World Bank, 1994).

Coverage ratios of this kind are of course extremely crude indicators of the relative magnitude of country offers. They do not take into account the restrictions on national treatment and market access that continue to be maintained, or the relative size of countries. Moreover, they give each subsector equal weight, something that is clearly inappropriate. But from the perspective of this paper the ratios suggest that OECD countries are ready to make significant offers in the multilateral context, substantially more than developing countries. An implication is that the regional experiments are not intended to close off markets from third parties. Indeed, the fact that the main sectors that are likely to excluded from the reach of GATS disciplines by OECD countries (and the United States and the EC in particular) are the same as those on which no agreement could be attained in the regional context - e.g., transport and basic telecoms - supports this.

4.3   Accession clauses and procedures. All of the regional agreements discussed earlier have an accession clause. That of the EC is limited to European countries. It has been used quite extensively, the EC expanding as a result from the six original members, to twelve currently, with over a half-dozen additional countries in the queue for accession. A necessary condition for countries aspiring to membership is that they accept all of the EC's existing rules, disciplines and procedures (the acquis communautaire). Negotiations center largely on the length of transitional periods for implementation of provisions affecting "sensitive" sectors and the magnitude of financial contributions, not on the substantive rules of the game.

The NAFTA also has an accession clause allowing other countries or groups of countries, within or outside the Western Hemisphere, to join the NAFTA by accepting the same obligations as other member countries. As with that of the EC, it locks in the previously agreed rules and liberalization commitments, ensuring that negotiations will not start from zero. The ANZCERTA also has an accession clause providing for the future association of other countries. The terms of such accession are to be negotiated jointly between the potential entrant and existing members. As under NAFTA there are no geographic requirements.

GATS classification list.

Although both the NAFTA and the ANZCERTA accession clauses are relatively liberal, it is noteworthy that the GATS does not contain a requirement that integration agreements be 'open' in principle (i.e., contain an accession clause). This is arguably an important 'hole' in the GATS. Given the difficulty of determining simple, quantifiable criteria to ensure that integration agreements that liberalize both trade and factor flows not be detrimental to non-members, requiring that such an accession clause be included would be one of the most straightforward ways of ensuring that the systemic effects of economic integration attempts are positive. Its absence, as well as the rather weak disciplines imposed by the GATS on preferential agreements liberalizing access to service markets, suggests that member countries of regional arrangements did not desire to significantly constrain their degree of discretion in this domain.

5 . Concluding Remarks

Are the RTAs beneficial from an efficiency-cum-productivity perspective by greatly enhancing the contestability of service markets? In the short run the answer is positive, even though the sectoral coverage of most of the agreements remains incomplete. While preferential liberalization of service markets is inferior in economic terms to multilateral (non-discriminatory) market opening, it is easier to attain in the regional context. It is noteworthy, however, that with the exception of the EC, the extent to which mutual recognition is foreseen -- let alone pursued -- is quite limited, suggesting that liberalization of regulated sectors is a difficult issue no matter what forum is chosen.

The current uncertainty regarding the sectoral coverage of the GATS makes it difficult to come to clearcut conclusions regarding the longer-term impact of the RTAs. It is unclear to what degree regional preferences will be extended to non-member countries. The fact that national treatment and market access obligations under GATS are specific rather than general obligations, and that the excluded sectors tend to be the same in both the RTAs and in the GATS suggests that there is some cause for concern regarding the ability of governments to overcome the power of those vested interests that are opposed to the liberalization of such key services as transport and basic telecommunications.

The negotiating history of the various agreements illustrates that a necessary (but not sufficient) condition for liberalization is pressure by export-oriented service industries - the lead role having been taken by the financial service sector.

Progress towards liberalization in both the regional and multilateral contexts was driven by firms desiring greater access to foreign markets, complemented by users of service inputs (producer services) seeking to lower their production costs. For some industries - e.g., financial services - pushing for reciprocal liberalization was part of a strategy of seeking changes in the domestic regulatory structure. Such changes were considered to be more likely to occur in the quid pro quo context of regional or multilateral negotiations. While export-oriented service industries such as financial services were somewhat successful in achieving their objectives, they did not dominate opposition on the part of industries seeking to keep 'their' home market to themselves. Users played an major role as well in convincing regulators and policy makers that changes were required. Indeed, a perception that greater competitiveness required that average service input costs (quality) be reduced (increased) was an important factor explaining regulatory changes in general, and the willingness to allow greater access to service markets in particular.

The main policy issue then is to ensure that export-oriented firms and users of services continue to make their voice heard at the policy-making level. It is these two groups that have the greatest stake in maintaining the momentum of liberalization, and in particular in seeking to augment the contestability of those markets where industry lobbies managed to prevent substantial market opening from occurring. Ensuring that regional preferences are "multilateralized" is the obvious way to maintain and increase the external pressures on locally established services firms, thus inducing them to pursue the investments in quality upgrading and productivity enhancement that will benefit both producers and consumers generally.

References

Anderson, K., and R. Blackhurst, (eds.) (1993). *Regional Integration and the Global Trading System* (Harvester-Wheatsheaf, London, UK).

Bhagwati, J. (1992). "Regionalism and multilateralism: An overview," presented at a World Bank/CEPR conference on New Dimensions in Regional Integration, Washington D.C., April 2-3.

Crystal, K.A., and C. Coughlin (1992). "How the 1992 legislation will affect European financial services," *Economic Review* (Federal Reserve Bank of St. Louis), (March/April), 62-77.

EUROSTAT (Statistical Office of the European Communities) (1990). *International Trade in Services: EUR12 from 1979 to 1988* (EUROSTAT, Luxembourg).

Greenaway, D., and R. Hine (1991). "Intra-industry specialization, trade expansion and adjustment in the European economic space," *Journal of Common Market Studies*, 29, 603-22.

Hindley, B. (1987). "Trade in services within the European Community," in H. Giersch (ed.), *Free Trade in the World Economy* (J.C.B. Mohr, Tubingen).

Hoekman, B. (1992a). "Regional versus multilateral liberalization of trade in services," CEPR Discussion Paper No. 749, Center for Economic Policy Research (London,UK).

Hoekman, B. (1992b). "Market access through multilateral agreement: From goods to services," *The World Economy* 15, 727-47.

Hoekman, B., and P. Sauvé (1994) "Regional and multilateral liberalization of service markets: Complements or substitutes," *Journal of Common Market Studies*, September.

Lloyd, P. (1991). *The Future of CER: A Single Market for Australia and New Zealand*. Committee for Economic Development of Australia Monograph No. 96, (Victoria University Press, Wellington).

Messerlin, P. (1990). "The European Community," in Patrick Messerlin and Karl Sauvant (eds.), *The Uruguay Round: Services in the World Economy* (The World Bank and United Nations Center for Transnational Corporations, Washington D.C.).

Organization for Economic Cooperation and Development (1992). *OECD Countries International Trade in Services 1970-1989* (OECD, Paris).

Pelkmans, J. (1990). "Europe 1992: Internal and external," in F. Laursen (ed.), *EFTA and the EC: Implications of 1992* (European Institute of Public Administration, Maastricht).

Roth, W. (1988). "The European Economic Community's law on services: harmonization," *Common Market Law Review* 25, 35-94.

Sandholtz, W., and J. Zysman (1989). "1992: Recasting the bargain," *World Politics* 42, 95-127.

Schott, J., and M. Smith (1988). "Services and investment," in J. Schott and M. Smith (eds.), *The Canada-United States Free Trade Agreement: The Global Impact* (Institute for International Economics, Washington D.C.).

UNCTAD and World Bank (1994). *Liberalizing International Transactions in Services: A Handbook* (United Nations, Geneva).

Whalley, J. (1991). "Services and the U.S.-Canada relationship beyond the FTA," University of Western Ontario (February), mimeo.

Winters, L.A. (1992). "The European Community: a case of successful integration?" CEPR Discussion Paper No. 755, Center for Economic Policy Research (London).

Westlake, M. (1990). "Towards a new financial order," *Euromoney* (November), 74-78.

Chapter 5 **An Empirical Analysis of Foreign Direct Investment in Service Industries**

Jiatao Li[1]

1. Introduction

Services play an increasingly important role in modern economies (Bhagwati, 1984; Francois, 1990), leading not only to intensified international competition, but also to growing concern over the nature and extent of government intervention in service trade and investment. Recognition of the impact of government restrictions on market access, as well as other trade barriers, have led to proposals for services liberalization (Sampson and Snape, 1985; Hoekman, 1992a,b; Rivera-Batiz and Rivera-Batiz, 1992). However, these proposals have been countered by some protectionist sources in the United States, who are concerned that the influx of foreign capital will lead to a decline in U.S. competitiveness. This paper represents a contribution to the debate on the liberalization of international service trade and investment.

[1] I thank Joseph Francois, Bernard Hoekman, Susan Kollins, Patrick Harker, and participants at the 1992 Wharton Conference on Service Productivity and Quality Challenge for helpful comments and Karen Kelsky for research assistance. This chapter is based in part on a large research project prepared for the United Nations and I thank Stephen Guisinger, Karl Sauvant, Padma Mallampally, and Jorg Weber for their contributions to the research project. All errors remain my own.

P. T. Harker (ed.), The Service Productivity and Quality Challenge, 139–168.
© 1995 *Kluwer Academic Publishers. Printed in the Netherlands.*

Service industries have certain characteristics in common which distinguish them from manufacturing industries, and which make it possible to analyze them as a whole. Most importantly, services are intangible and non-storable. Although the electronic transfer of information has recently made it possible for some service providers and receivers to be separated (Bhagwati, 1984), the qualities of intangibility and non-storability still almost always require that the production and consumption of services occur at the same time and in the same place (Bhagwati, 1984; Feketekuty, 1988). One result of this is that direct interaction and close physical proximity are almost always necessary between the service provider and user (Bhagwati, 1989). Those service sectors exhibiting such location-boundedness (simultaneous production and consumption) will require local facilities (Rivera-Batiz and Rivera-Batiz, 1992; Boddewyn et al., 1986).

Two other factors are important when considering services. First, national governments may strictly control the extent and form of foreign involvement in service industries (Feketekuty, 1988). Second, services supplied by multinational corporations (MNCs) to local customers may need to be adapted to a greater extent than manufacturing products, in order to accommodate different languages and cultural backgrounds.

Because they often already possess a comparative advantage through their MNCs, developed countries have actively pursued liberalization of foreign direct investment (FDI) in services. As a result, FDI in services grew to account for 50 percent of total FDI flows during the 1980's, and by the 1990 it accounted for 40 percent of the world's stock of foreign direct investment. FDI is now more important than trade in delivering services to foreign markets, at least for the most important developed countries (Sauvant, 1989). FDI, which encompasses all sales of services produced by the foreign affiliates of MNCs (Dunning, 1989), constitutes the best way for firms to control acquisition or utilization of intangible assets across national boundaries (Dunning, 1988).

Technological developments are behind much of the rapid internationalization of service activities. International communication through telematics enables companies in sectors such as banking and insurance to establish close links between the various branches and subsidiaries of MNCs operating in different markets. It also enables financial and insurance companies worldwide to communicate more easily with their client MNCs in the manufacturing sector. Once established abroad, they can act as a relay in a global network of information flows and business connections internal to individual companies or shared by the majority of companies in the industry.

The recent theoretical literature on trade in services includes Bhagwati (1984, 1989), Deardorff (1985), Francois (1990, 1993), Hoekman (1992a,b), Rivera-Batiz and Rivera-Batiz (1992), and Sampson and Snape (1985). Bhagwati (1984) has suggested that producer services appear to be a growing sector in part because firms are externalizing service activities once performed within the firm itself. Francois (1990) argues that the post-war expansion of the producer service sector in modern industrial economies may be a result of both the integration of internal markets and the expanded opportunities for trade that have accompanied post-war trade liberalization. Francois (1993) examines the role of market size, cultural differences, geography, and country similarity in determining the pattern of trade in services. Rivera-Batiz and Rivera-Batiz (1992) show that FDI in the service sector has a positive effect on national welfare that investment in manufacturing may lack. Dunning suggests an "eclectic paradigm" which examines relations and interactions between the service MNC's competitive advantage, the location advantages of potential host countries, and economies of the common governance of cross-border activities (Dunning, 1989).

In the literature on multinational enterprises much has been written on foreign direct investment in manufacturing industries. However, FDI in services has yet to receive the same attention. The objective of this study is to fill this gap by examining the determinants of foreign direct investment in service industries. In this study we will analyze foreign investment decisions by testing hypotheses on nine major factors affecting service FDI using a logistic regression model. The study will encompass 210 of the largest service MNCs in several developed countries and eleven service industries over the period of 1980-1986. While the present study, due to limitations in the data, focuses exclusively on service direct investment in developed countries, many of the factors examined here also have important implications for service FDI in developing countries[2].

The paper is organized as follows: In Part Two we will examine the impact of nine key factors on foreign investment decisions of service MNCs. These factors are: market size, home country business presence, cultural distance,

---

[2] Service FDI in developing countries has grown rapidly and has important implications for government policies (UNCTC, 1988). See also Bhagwati (1984), Hoekman (1992b), and Li and Guisinger (1993).

government regulations, competitive advantage of service industries, oligopolistic reaction, industry concentration, tradability of services, and growth of firm size. These nine factors have been identified in previous studies as determinants of FDI in both manufacturing and service industries such as banking, advertising, and insurance. They in turn lead us to suggest nine related testable hypotheses. In Part Three we discuss the empirical research design and the logistic regression model used to analyze the data and test the hypotheses. In Part Four, we discuss the results of the empirical tests, examining the determinants of service FDI by both home and host countries and by major industry groups. We also make certain policy recommendations based on our findings. Finally, in Part Five, differences in the international behavior of service MNCs are analyzed and policy implications are further discussed.

2. Theories and Hypotheses

Extending an earlier study (Li and Guisinger, 1992), we identify nine factors that may influence the foreign investment decisions of service MNCs. These factors lead logically to nine hypotheses that we test in a subsequent section. The factors and hypotheses are drawn from a variety of theories on FDI, including the eclectic paradigm (Dunning, 1988), internalization theory (Buckley and Casson, 1976) and oligopolistic reaction theory (Knickerbocker, 1973). Other hypotheses are based on more recent research concerning cultural distance (Hofstede, 1980; Kogut and Singh, 1988) and firm strategy (Kogut, 1988; Porter, 1990).

We also examine factors specific to service FDI, such as the client-following hypothesis and the location boundedness or non-tradability of service industries. Other factors include the tighter host government controls on trade and investment in services (the degree of openness of the host markets), and the need for local responsiveness or adaptation of services to the needs of local customers (cultural distance). The influence of these factors on service foreign investment has been discussed in the literature, but has been subjected to only limited empirical testing.

2.1 Market size. Previous studies have revealed that the market size of the host country has a positive impact on the inflow of manufacturing FDI (Scaperlanda and Mauer, 1969; Agarwal, 1980; Davidson, 1980; Culem, 1988). Market size also affects the international activities of services, as has been shown in the case of multinational banks (Gray and Gray, 1981), international advertising agencies (Weinstein, 1977; Terpstra and Yu, 1988), and transnational insurance firms (Schroath and Korth, 1989). The size of potential markets has also been shown to affect the location choice for offices of international companies (Dunning and Norman, 1987). **First Hypothesis**: The market size of the host country is expected to have a positive impact on the location decision of new FDI of service MNCs.

2.2 Home country business presence. One of the earliest motives for overseas ventures among service firms is the need to follow home country clients abroad. Insurance, banking, and advertising firms, for example, frequently venture abroad to supply the same services to foreign affiliates that they had previously supplied to the parent companies. Previous empirical studies in international banking and advertising have consistently observed this client-following motive (Weinstein, 1977; Goldberg and Sanders, 1980; Ball and Tschoegl, 1982; Nigh et al., 1986; Terpstra and Yu, 1988), demonstrating that it is usually the first stage in the international expansion process of service MNCs. Because they reduce uncertainty in the foreign market, such pre-established relationships are very beneficial to service MNCs.

It is important to note, however, that this client-following behavior is only an initial stage in international expansion, which is generally followed by a secondary "market-seeking" stage. In this second stage, service MNCs which have followed home country client firms abroad begin to extend their services to local firms and/or other foreign firms in the host market. This two-stage process suggests that following the client is most important as a motive only in the early stages of service internationalization. Because service MNCs based in the triad nations may be at different stages of internationalization, differences in the impact of this client-driven hypothesis are also expected. **Second Hypothesis**: Foreign investment of service MNCs is positively related to the home country business presence in the host country.

2.3 Cultural differences. Service MNCs need to adapt their services to local customers' different cultures, tastes, living habits, and industrial needs (Hofstede, 1980; Prahalad and Doz, 1987). Cultural differences have been shown to affect both the entry strategies of MNCs (Kogut and Singh, 1988) and the performance of foreign subsidiaries (Li and Guisinger, 1991). A pattern is clear among both manufacturing and service MNCs to initially expand into culturally similar countries, and then later to move international investments into less developed, culturally distant countries. This suggests that the impact of cultural differences on service FDI may diminish over time. **Third Hypothesis**: Cultural distance between home and host countries has a negative impact on foreign investment of service MNCs.

2.4   Government regulations. Changes in national regulatory patterns on controls and impediments of inward FDI have to be considered as factors affecting the location of service activities by MNCs (OECD, 1982, 1987a; UNCTC, 1988; Hoekman, 1992a,b). Widespread government control of the form and extent of foreign involvement in service industries is the case in many countries, particularly when the industry is considered politically or culturally sensitive.   Such sensitive service industries often include banking, transportation, and telecommunications (UNCTC, 1988; Hoekman, 1992a). One previous study shows that U.S. involvement in banking abroad is significantly dependent on the openness of the host country to new foreign branches (Nigh et al., 1986).   Other barriers to foreign investment by service MNCs include fiscal policies which favor indigenous companies (Feketekuty, 1988), performance requirements, or self-imposed barriers to entry.   These barriers may include requiring membership to local professional associations, controlling licensing, restricting access to legal, accounting and other business services, and carefully supervising the structure and practices of banks, insurance firms and other financial companies (UNCTC, 1988; Dunning, 1989). **Fourth hypothesis**: Foreign investment of service MNCs is positively related to openness of the host country to the establishment of new foreign service subsidiaries.

2.5   Competitive advantage of service industries. Every country has it own unique competitive advantages. FDI can help service MNCs to utilize and add value to the competitive advantages brought from the home country, either to supply services to local customers or to serve a regional or global market. As global competition in services grows, national competitive advantage in services will assume increased importance to firms and nations alike (Porter, 1990). Dunning (1989) has already provided a thorough listing of ownership, location and internalization advantages for several service industries.

As Kogut (1988) has noted, firms are likely to exploit the same skills and methods in international competition which have already proven successful in their home market. If the international competitive advantage is embedded in specific organizational routines unique to a specific firm, or is culturally and institutionally embedded, it is not likely to be "exportable" to different firms or countries. **Fifth Hypothesis**: Foreign investment of service MNCs is positively related to the international competitiveness of the service industry in the home country.

2.6   Global oligopolistic reaction.   Many scholars, beginning with Hymer (1960), have suggested that international competition is frequently characterized by oligopolistic interdependence. Oligopolistic interdependence means that the number of firms within a given industry is small enough to allow each firm to recognize the impact of its actions on its rivals and on the entire market (Caves, 1982). Such circumstances tend to result in a pattern of "tit-for-tat" investment matching in major markets (Knickerbocker, 1973), as well as a "follow the leader" or "exchange of threats" strategy of mutual intrusion into rival firms' territories (Knickerbocker, 1973; Flowers, 1976; Graham, 1978).

Thus oligopolists are likely to undertake foreign direct investment in order to "counter, check, or forestall a move by some rival oligopolist" (Graham, 1978, 1985). This pattern is substantiated for FDI in the U.S. advertising industry (Terpstra and Yu, 1988). Any empirical analysis of international competition must account for this oligopolistic effect--both within a single region and on an international scale--in order to discover possible national patterns of competitive behavior. **Sixth hypothesis**: Foreign investment of service MNCs is positively related to the global oligopolistic reaction in the host country.

2.7   Industry concentration.   The same factors that create barriers to entry may also encourage foreign investment by creating high industry concentration (Caves, 1982). Conditions surrounding high industry concentration--such as advertising intensity, capital costs, scale economies and R&D intensity (Dunning, 1988)--are likely to encourage firms to expand abroad. Multinational firms often have some advantages over newly organized firms or single-nation firms in getting past barriers to entry (Shapiro, 1983). Therefore, the height of entry barriers and the extent of foreign investment activity should be highly correlated (Caves, 1982), and foreign investment and industry concentration are expected to be closely associated.

The empirical evidence clearly supports this hypothesis. Fishwick (1981) reports high correlations between industry concentration and foreign investment in Great Britain, France, and West Germany. Additionally, previous studies have shown that the degrees of industry concentration are also correlated among developed countries (Pryor, 1977). **Seventh Hypothesis**: Service foreign investment is positively related to the degree of industry concentration.

2.8   Tradability of service industries.   International involvement in both manufacturing and service is of course not limited to FDI, but can also take the forms of export (trade) and licensing (Dunning, 1989). The export, or trade, of final services may require that the foreign customer travel to the exporting country, although service firms can also expand abroad through equity or non-equity foreign involvements. Trade is particularly important in investment banking, insurance, and advertising. There are other services which can be traded to a limited extent, or which, although tradable in theory, are inhibited by cross-border transaction costs (Buckley and Casson, 1976). "Non-tradable" services include hotels, wholesales, and retailing. In cases such as these, MNCs can provided services to customers by either licensing an indigenous firm, or by engaging in foreign direct investment. The absence of tradability in some service industries may spur some service MNCs to invest abroad to exploit their technological advantages and other forms of intangible assets. **Eighth hypothesis**: Foreign investment of service MNCs is negatively related to the tradability of service industries.

2.9   Firm size and growth.   Previous studies have suggested that, in manufacturing, large firms are more likely than smaller ones to invest abroad (Horst, 1972; Bergsten, Horst and Moran, 1978; Grubaugh, 1987; Culem, 1988). In an early study, firm size was found to be the only significant characteristic related to a firm's decision to invest abroad (Horst, 1972). Researchers have also identified firm size as an important variable in the international behavior of several service industries such as banking and advertising (Ball and Tschoegl, 1982; Terpstra and Yu, 1988). Because the definition of firm size is not consistent across different service industries, we use a dynamic measure--the growth of firm size over the 1980-1986 period--in the model. **Ninth hypothesis**: Foreign investment among service MNCs is positively related to growth in firm size.

3.   Empirical Analysis

This study examines the major factors influencing international expansion of service MNCs. In particular, the study focuses on the increasing presence of a service MNC in a foreign region over time. The decision to establish a new foreign subsidiary is expressed as a binary dependent variable, with one (1) indicating a service MNC's decision to increase its presence in a foreign region over a specific period of time and zero (0) representing the lack of such decision.

3.1   Research design. We compiled data for 210 of the largest service MNCs in eleven service industries for the 1980-1986 period. While there are increasing flows of service foreign investment between developed and developing countries, data limitations have forced us to focus exclusively on developed countries. Future research is recommended to extend the present study to developing countries.

The number of foreign subsidiaries possessed by each service MNC in developed host countries was recorded for two separate years: 1980 and 1986. This study considers five host regions: the United States, Canada, Japan, Western Europe and "Other Developed Countries," and focuses on service MNCs whose home base is in the triad regions: Japan, Western Europe and the United States. Firms from the triad regions account for 95 percent of the largest service MNCs in these eleven industries.

The industries covered in this study include finance-related industries (insurance, reinsurance, and securities); trade-related industries (trading and retailing); business services (accounting and advertising); and other service industries (construction, publishing, airlines, and hotels). Multinational banks are not examined due to data limitations.

For the 1980-1986 period, the value of our dependent variable, foreign investment (P[FI=1]), is one (1) if a service MNC increased its number of subsidiaries in a given host region between 1980 to 1986, and zero (0) otherwise. Because we specify our dependent variable as the change in foreign presence in a certain host region over the 1980-1986 period, most of our independent variables were measured at the beginning of the period (1980). The market size of a host country is measured by Gross Domestic Product (GDP) in 1980 (World Bank, 1982). Since disaggregate data are not available for each host country in Western Europe, U.S. and Japanese service firms are assumed to invest in Europe as a region (the European market), rather than in individual countries.

Table 1. Global Competition in the Service Industries: A Summary of Sample Data, 1980-1986, Number of Parent Service MNCs

| | Home Country of Service MNCs | | | |
	U.S.	Japan	Europe	Total
Finance-Related				
Insurance	14	7	9	**3 0**
Reinsurance	5	1	9	**1 5**
Securities	1 0	8	1	**19**
Trade-Related				
Wholesale	-	13	3	**16**
Retail	1 8	5	6	**29**
Business Services				
Accounting	6	-	1	**7**
Advertising	1 1	2	6	**19**
Other Services				
Construction	6	8	6	**2 0**
Publishing	8	-	5	**1 3**
Airlines	9	2	8	**1 9**
Hotels	17	-	6	**2 3**
Total	**104**	**46**	**60**	**210**

The home country business presence in a host region (FDI) is measured by the book value of the FDI position from the home country in 1980. Data are collected from U.S. Department of Commerce (1984), OECD (1987b), and UNCTC (1988).

The measures of cultural distance (CD) between the home and host countries are drawn from the work of Hofstede (1980). Hofstede found that differences in national cultures vary substantially along four dimensions: tolerance of power distance, uncertainty avoidance, individualism, and masculinity. Using Hofstede's four dimensions and following the methodology of Kogut and Singh (1988), a composite index was formed, based on the deviation along each of four cultural dimensions, to measure the cultural distance between home and host countries[3].

An openness index (OPEN) was developed to measure the openness of service industry (i), in country (j), to the establishment of new foreign service subsidiaries. The degrees of government controls and impediments affecting inward FDI in each service industry were estimated on an integer scale of one to four, one representing industries with the most restrictive control and four representing industries with little or no controls and impediments on inward FDI in 1980. The openness index rests on subjective evaluations of the importance of two categories of policies: (1) controls over entry, establishment, and ownership of foreign investment in service industries; and (2) policies bearing on the operations and competitive opportunities of foreign affiliates. The major sources of data are OECD (1982, 1987a), with supplementary data from USTR (1984, 1986) and UNCTC (1983-1988). Obviously, this index is a crude proxy for measuring the degree of government restrictions on inward service foreign investment.

Domestic profitability and export performance should not be considered reliable indicators of international competitive advantage because of differences in accounting conventions and government interventions between countries. Rather, we can judge the international success of a given national industry by examining that industry's competition worldwide, seeking evidence of either substantial and sustained exports to a wide array of other nations, or significant outbound foreign investment based on skills and assets in the home country (Porter, 1990). Since, as we mentioned earlier, many service industries are not tradable, the first criterion--exports--is unfeasible. Therefore, this study measures service competitiveness by the second criterion: significant outward foreign investment.

This study developed a new measure for international competitiveness of service MNCs. The international competitive index (ICI) combines Balassa's revealed comparative advantage (RCA) (Balassa, 1965, 1977; Balassa and Bauwens, 1987) and the intra-industry foreign direct investment (IIFDI) index as developed by Dunning (1988). The international competitiveness index (ICI_{ij}) is

---

[3] Language difference has emerged as a significant influence on international activity in several other empirical studies. This would be an interesting area to extend the current paper.

defined as:

$$ICI_{ij} = (Q_{ij} - I_{ij})/(Q_{ij} + I_{ij})$$

where Q_{ij} is the number of subsidiaries in industry i formed overseas by firms based in country j; and I_{ij} is the number of subsidiaries in industry i formed in country j by firms not based in country j.

Table 2 presents the ICI index for the eleven service industries for both 1980 and 1986, using data from UNCTC (1988). Only data for 1980 were used in the regression. The ICI index permits industry-level comparisons of the international competitiveness of different countries' service industries. This index should be regarded as only generally indicative of competitiveness. Since service industries are regulated by governments, the ICI index contains protectionist biases.

The global oligopolistic reaction (OLIGOP) can be measured as follows:

$$OLIGOP_{ij} = C_{ij} / P_{ij}$$

where C_{ij} is the number of other foreign parents with affiliates in service industry i, host country j, excluding the service MNC in question; P_{ij} is the total number of all foreign parent service firms with a potential for establishing affiliates in industry i, host country j, in 1980. In other words, P_{ij} includes all other firms in the sample not based in a particular country.

The degree of industry concentration is measured by the ratio of sales accounted for by the top four firms over sales of the world's top 100 service firms in a service industry. Data were derived from the UNCTC (1990). Tradability of service industries is measured by the ratio of export sales over total foreign sales (export plus foreign affiliates) in a service industry. Formally, $TRADE_{ij} = T_{ij} / (T_{ij} + S_{ij})$, where T_{ij} -- export sales in service industry i; S_{ij} -- sales by foreign affiliates in industry i; $TRADE_{ij}$ -- tradability of service industry i. TRADE takes continuous values between 0 and 1, with "0" representing services which are location-bounded and which cannot be traded. Data were obtained from the U.S. Office of Technology Assessment (1986) and George and Schorth (1991)[4].

---

[4]It should be noted that data regarding the tradability of service industries is very limited. The trade-based data provided by the Office of Technology Assessment (1986) is somewhat ad hoc. The Department of Commerce trade in services data

Table 2.   Global Competition in the Service Industries International Competitiveness Index

$$ICI_{ij} = (Q_{ij} - I_{ij}) / (Q_{ij} + I_{ij})$$

Q_{ij} -- the number of subsidiaries in industry i formed overseas by
   firms based in country j;

I_{ij} -- the number of subsidiaries in industry i formed in country j by
   firms not based in country j.

Industry	U.S.		Home Country of Service MNCs Japan		E.C.	
	1980	1986	1980	1986	1980	1986
Finance-Related						
Insurance	0.35	0.19	0.54	0.25	0.07	-0.03
Reinsurance	0.11	0.31	0.00	1.00	0.25	-0.05
Securities	0.83	0.71	1.00	0.99	-0.91	-0.94
Trade-Related						
Trading	-1.00	-1.00	0.99	0.99	0.04	-0.28
Retail	0.83	0.53	1.00	0.60	-0.39	-0.20
Business Services						
Accounting	n/a	0.82	n/a	-1.00	n/a	-0.39
Advertising	0.99	0.85	-0.17	0.78	-0.80	-0.64
Other Services						
Construction	0.34	-0.30	0.91	0.95	-0.41	-0.02
Publishing	-0.07	-0.24	-1.00	-1.00	0.03	0.27
Airline	-0.40	-0.48	-1.00	0.00	0.12	0.09
Hotels	n/a	-0.01	n/a	-1.00	n/a	0.04

Note: $-1 < ICI_{ij} < 1$, when $ICI_{ij}=-1$, industry i in home country j is the least competitive among world competitors; when $ICI_{ij}=1$, industry i in home country j is the most competitive among world competitors.

---

for 1986 is based on a benchmark survey and is more comprehensive (Wichard, 1988; Krueger, 1989). Unfortunately for our purpose here, the FDI/export breakdown was not provided in the data.

The growth of firm size (GSIZE) was measured by the annual growth rate in revenues (sales) of service MNCs over the 1980-1986 period. Data were derived from UNCTC (1988). In most cases, sales were used to measure the size of each service firm. In some other cases, however, measures other than sales were used. For accounting firms, for example, the total fee income was used because it was considered a more appropriate measure of size for accounting firms (UNCTC, 1988).

3.2 Statistical analysis. We apply a logistic regression model to foreign investment decisions of service multinationals over the 1980-1986 period. Results of the overall analysis and the individual analyses for U.S., Japanese and European service MNCs are reported in Tables 3-4. The study then groups the eleven service industries into four industry groups: finance-related, trade-related, business services and other service industries. Separate analyses were performed for each industry group (Tables 5-6).

The descriptive statistics and correlation matrices of the study variables for overall and regional models are presented in Appendix I. As expected, some of the exploratory variables are highly correlated. Because the home country business presence variable is measured by the book value of foreign direct investment from home country, it is correlated with many of other exploratory variables such as market size and cultural distance. For this reason caution is advised in interpreting our results. Because of the presence of multicollinearity in the data, we provide two models for each analysis. We feel that doing so will present a better picture of important variables than can be observed in a single model[5].

Another issue is related to our specification of the dependent and exploratory variables. Because the dependent variable is specified as the change in foreign presence over the 1980-1986 period, most of exploratory variables were measured at the beginning of the period (1980). The 1980 data were used to measure market size, home country business presence, global oligopolistic reaction, the openness index, and the international competitiveness index[6]. Measures for other

---

[5]Although only two alternative model specifications are reported in the tables, we have run many other models as well. The results are consistent.

[6]An alternative theoretical specification is to define some of the exploratory variables as changes over the 1980-1986 period, such as changes in market size. For simplicity of the presentation here, we leave different specifications of the

variables are limited by the extent of data availability and are used as a proxy. These include cultural distance, the tradability index, and industry concentration. Because the definition of firm size is not consistent across different service industries, we use the growth of firm size over the 1980-1986 period in the model.

4. Results and Discussion

Logistic regressions were performed for service foreign direct investment in the host regions. The total number of observations for the 1980-86 period in the overall models comes to 892. Separate regional analyses were also performed for foreign investment activities by the U.S., Japanese and European service MNCs.

4.1 General analysis and recommendations. The results of estimation for the overall sample are shown in Table 3. The chi-square scores of models indicate that the models are generally accurate: over 79 percent of foreign investment decisions can be correctly predicted by factors we examine. These results suggest that the factors identified in this study are significant in explaining variation in service FDI decisions. These results should therefore be of use to government policy makers and international managers in decisions concerning service MNC investments.

Foreign investment of service MNCs is found to be positively related to the market size of the host country (GDP). The results are consistent with findings of previous empirical studies in single service industries (e.g., Terpstra and Yu, 1988, for advertising). They reveal that service industries follow the example of manufacturing in demonstrating market-seeking behavior.

Cultural distance is found to have a significant negative impact on FDI of service MNCs. These results reiterate the findings of Kogut and Singh (1988) on foreign entry modes and Li and Guisinger (1991) on the performance of foreign subsidiaries. It is clear that managers of service MNCs who are formulating international strategy must be alert to differences in culture. We would also recommend that the governments of culturally dissimilar host countries should take steps to reduce barriers which are based on cultural differences.

---

model to a further study.

Table 3. Logistic Regression Estimation of International Service Expansion, 1980-1986.

	Overall Sample		U.S. Service MNCs	
Variable	Model 1	Model 2	Model 1	Model 2
Intercept	-3.1573***	-4.7444***	-3.7415***	-4.9042***
	(0.5244)	(0.4796)	(1.0933)	(0.9321)
GDP	0.0002**		0.0002	
	(0.0001)		(0.0003)	
FDI	-0.0064**	0.0028	-0.0111	0.0017
	(0.0032)	(0.0025)	(0.0109)	(0.0041)
CD	-0.2031*	0.0476	-0.0884	0.2842*
	(0.1074)	(0.0803)	(0.3135)	(0.1646)
OPEN	0.4466***	1.1899***	0.6528*	1.4369***
	(0.1554)	(0.1194)	(0.3560)	(0.2901)
ICI	0.2740	0.1724	0.9213**	1.6355***
	(0.1993)	(0.1836)	(0.4692)	(0.4195)
OLIGOP	2.8067***		3.3806***	
	(0.4639)		(0.8673)	
CONC	0.8690	4.0148***	2.0964	5.1358***
	(0.9160)	(0.7580)	(1.6304)	(1.3750)
TRADE	-0.5036	-0.8366***	-1.2555	-2.5030***
	(0.3322)	(0.3134)	(0.7942)	(0.7045)
GSIZE	0.0014**	0.0015**	0.0012	0.0011
	(0.0006)	(0.0006)	(0.0015)	(0.0014)
Chi-Square	230.64	176.81	116.06	100.19
D.F.	9	7	9	7
Model p<	0.0001	0.0001	0.0001	0.0001
Hit Ratio	79.0	75.5	80.8	78.5
Observations	892	892	408	408

***: $p < 0.01$; **: $p < 0.05$; *: $p < 0.10$.
Standard errors are in parentheses.
Independent Variables: GDP-market size; FDI-home country business presence; CD-cultural distance; OPEN-openness index; ICI-international competitiveness index; OLIGOP-global oligopolistic reaction; CONC-industry concentration; TRADE-tradability of service industries; GSIZE-firm size growth.

Table 4. Logistic Regression Estimation of International Service Expansion, 1980-1986.

Variable	Japanese MNCs		European MNCs	
	Model 1	Model 2	Model 1	Model 2
Intercept	14.1155	-12.942***	-2.0975***	-2.7122***
	(22.225)	(4.1642)	(0.8047)	(0.7825)
GDP	0.0039		0.0004***	
	(0.0036)		(0.0001)	
FDI	-2.3723	-0.0307		0.0839***
	(2.0877)	(0.1526)		(0.0224)
CD	-8.0858	1.8672	-0.4023**	-0.2362
	(8.5526)	(1.2374)	(0.2007)	(0.1743)
OPEN	1.9246***	2.3538***	0.1145	0.5496***
	(0.6628)	(0.5780)	(0.2443)	(0.1914)
ICI	-1.1391	-1.0972	0.5256	0.2686
	(0.8943)	(0.8105)	(0.5899)	(0.5764)
OLIGOP	4.0947***		1.8179**	
	(1.3861)		(0.7676)	
CONC	1.2991	8.4851***	0.0590	1.6346
	(3.4113)	(2.3490)	(1.4007)	(1.2877)
TRADE	-1.8619*	-1.8260	0.1442	-0.2499
	(1.0473)	(0.9403)	(0.5598)	(0.5452)
GSIZE	0.0012	0.0004	0.0058***	0.0065***
	(0.0023)	(0.0022)	(0.0020)	(0.0020)
Chi-Square	74.80	64.73	73.40	67.57
D.F.	9	7	8	7
Model p<	0.0001	0.0001	0.0001	0.0001
Hit Ratio	83.8	81.1	77.2	76.2
Observations	184	184	300	300

***: $p < 0.01$; **: $p < 0.05$; *: $p < 0.10$.
Standard errors are in parentheses.

Openness (OPEN) is a significant determinant of foreign investment of service MNCs, with host government policies constituting one of the major factors considered by managers of service MNCs when they pursue international expansion. The results suggest that the liberalizing of national restrictions can substantially encourage inward FDI. This positive impact should encourage host governments to further liberalize their controls on inward service foreign investment. The result is also consistent with findings of Rivera-Batiz and Rivera-Batiz (1992).

Global oligopolistic reactions are shown to have a positive impact on foreign investment, suggesting that many service MNCs, like manufacturing MNCs, follow both their domestic and international competitors abroad as a defensive strategy (Knickerbocker, 1973; Flowers, 1976; Graham, 1978). It is clear that service MNCs must consider the international strategies and possible responses of major competitors in both domestic and foreign markets. The effect of global oligopolistic reactions is likely to increase with the continuing integration of the world economy, the globalization of markets, and improving communications technology (Hout, Porter and Rudden, 1982).

The degree of industry concentration in home countries is shown to be positively related to foreign investment of service industries. Because industry concentration results in uncertainties in the competitive environment, firms in concentrated industries are more likely to seek expansion on an international scale. These results are consistent with previous findings in manufacturing industries (Caves, 1982).

As expected, there is a negative relationship between the tradability of the service and establishment of foreign subsidiaries by the MNCs which provide it. This result shows a significant departure from the findings for manufacturing firms; the location-boundedness of certain services requires firms in those industries to expand abroad by establishing foreign subsidiaries.

The growth in firm size (GSIZE) is statistically significant, showing a positive sign in the regression models. This means that international expansion is one of the major growth strategies for service MNCs. The results are consistent with findings of foreign investment by manufacturing firms (Horst, 1972; Grubaugh, 1987).

Unexpectedly, our results show that client-following behavior--although it has been observed in the early stages of most U.S., Japanese and European service firm investments abroad--has a negative impact on service FDI in the models. This unexpected finding may be partially explained by discrepancies and inconsistencies in the measurement and comparability of foreign investment positions across countries, due to different reporting standards (Dunning and Cantwell, 1987). A second factor is the problem of multicollinearity, which, as we mentioned earlier, causes the effect of home country business presence to disappear when dropping the market size variable in the second model.

Most importantly, the unexpected result may be due to the declining importance of the factor during the period under examination. The initial objective of FDI by service multinationals to follow their home country clients abroad may be fulfilled at an early stage, and lose relevance as time passes.

4.2 Regional differences. This section analyzes FDI of service MNCs based in different home countries. The results are similar to those of the previous general analysis, but do show some interesting differences. We caution the reader, however, that the regional analysis can only be conducted by forming smaller subsets of the overall sample. Despite this limitation, however, we feel the results are still informative and potentially useful.

In the case of the United States, service FDI (Table 3) is positively related to four factors: openness of the host markets, the index for international competitiveness, global oligopolistic reaction, and industry concentration. It is negatively related to the tradability of service industries. This suggests that strategies of U.S. service MNCs in developed countries have shifted from the market-seeking and client-following behaviors of the earli r period. They are now increasingly linked to host country government policies, industry competitive structures, and reactions of major competitors.

Cultural distance proves to have a positive effect on U.S. service FDI, suggesting that U.S. MNCs, having already established a presence in culturally similar developed market economies, are now investing in culturally dissimilar countries. Of course, increasing experience in international operations may also offset the negative effect of cultural differences. As expected, home country business presence (FDI) and foreign market size (GDP) are highly correlated and are not included in the same model.

In the case of Japan, service FDI (Table 4) appears driven by the competitive factors of oligopolistic market structure and industry concentration, and the openness of the host country's policies. Location decisions of Japanese service MNCs have been significantly influenced in recent years by the increasing liberalization of host government policies in other parts of the triad. As expected, tradability was negatively related to Japanese service FDI. The cultural distance variable was not found to have a significant impact. It may be that cultural distances between Japan and Western countries are all uniformly large; the variation in this variable between individual Western country is perhaps small relative to total cultural distance measure.

It is interesting to note that the home country business presence variable is not significant for Japanese service MNCs over the 1980-1986 period. It is possible that the early stage of client-following behavior predates this study's time frame, or that service MNCs in Japan lead rather than follow manufacturing. Further research is needed to shed light on this important issue.

For European service MNCs, FDI (Table 4) appears to be positively influenced by five factors--market size, home country business presence, openness of foreign markets, oligopolistic market structure, and the growth of their own firms--and negatively influenced by cultural distance. Because the accumulated value of foreign direct investment (FDI) is highly correlated with the size of foreign markets, the two variables were not included in the same model. When we rerun the model without including the size of foreign market (GDP) variable (model 2), the parameter for the FDI variable becomes positive and significant.

Global oligopolistic reaction and host government regulations are the only two variables significant in each of the three regional models as well as in the overall analysis. These results reiterate the importance of host government policies and competitive strategic interactions among major competitors in service industries, but also show that there remain major differences in investor motivation between the three regions.

4.3 Industry groups. This study clustered the sample firms in eleven service industries into four industry groups: finance-related, trade-related, business services, and "other services" (UNCTC, 1988). The finance-related group includes service MNCs in insurance, reinsurance, and securities. The trade-related group includes service MNCs in trading and retailing industries. Business services include advertising and accounting firms. Construction, publishing, airlines and hotels are grouped into the "other" category. Although the statistical analysis at the industry level is hampered by reduced variations and a smaller number of observations, the results are still informative. We present by industry group (Table 5-6).

Our results show that finance-related FDI is positively related to global oligopolistic reaction and openness of the host markets (Table 5), and market size and tradability of services. However, the effect of the international competitiveness index is negative. It is likely that the heavily regulation of finance-related services across countries due to government restrictions biases the measurement of the international competitiveness index. FDI in trade-related services is also positively related to global oligopolistic reaction and openness of the host markets. As expected, the tradability of services has a negative effect in this industry group as well.

As in the previous two industry groups, business service FDI is positively related to global oligopolistic reaction (Table 6). Because industry concentration also shows a positive impact on FDI of business service MNCs, we can predict that the significance of competitive industry structures will increase.

The final category comprises service MNCs in construction, publishing, airlines and hotels. The similarities between these four industries are not as clear as in the industry groups analyzed above; nevertheless, the results are informative. We find that service FDI of MNCs in these four industries is positively related to market size, openness of the host markets, the index for international competitiveness, and growth of the firm size. It is negatively related to cultural distance and tradability of services (Table 6).

Table 5. Logistic Regression Estimation of International Service Expansion, 1980-1986 By Industry Groups

Variable	Finance-Related		Trade-Related	
	Model 1	Model 2	Model 1	Model 2
Intercept	-1.4813**	9.3239*	-4.5626***	9.3033*
	(0.6906)	(5.4452)	(1.0008)	(5.4431)
GDP	0.0003**		-0.0001	
	(0.00015)		(0.0001)	
FDI		0.0043		0.0039
		(0.0048)		(0.0046)
CD	-0.2025	0.0522	0.0041	
	(0.1676)	(0.1391)	(0.2372)	
OPEN		1.1160***	0.8724**	1.1171***
		(0.2098)	(0.3439)	(0.2110)
ICI	-0.9131**	-0.8149	0.3095	-0.7718
	(0.4318)	(0.5073)	(0.4856)	(0.4952)
OLIGOP	2.9361***		2.7963***	
	(0.8521)		(0.8798)	
CONC	-1.5699			
	(1.3008)			
TRADE		-16.014**		-15.904**
		(7.0517)		(7.0421)
GSIZE	0.0011	0.0011	-0.0014	0.0011
	(0.0012)	(0.0012)	(0.0024)	(0.0011)
Chi-Square	60.06	46.51	61.80	46.37
D.F.	6	6	6	5
Model p <	0.0001	0.0001	0.0001	0.0001
Hit Ratio	77.1	75.1	81.7	74.6
Observations	271	271	189	189

***: $p < 0.01$; **: $p < 0.05$; *: $p < 0.10$.
Standard errors are in parentheses.

Table 6. Logistic Regression Estimation of International Service Expansion, 1980-1986 By Industry Groups.

	Business Services		Other Services	
Variable	Model 1	Model 2	Model 1	Model 2
Intercept	-3.4888***	-4.4175***	-0.1372	-4.2557***
	(1.0678)	(1.3870)	(0.9373)	(0.7969)
GDP	0.0004		0.0005***	
	(0.0003)		(0.0001)	
FDI		0.0114		0.0017
		(0.0084)		(0.0051)
CD	-0.2539		-0.6160***	0.1089
	(0.2435)		(0.2419)	(0.1947)
OPEN		0.5530		1.2840***
		(0.4422)		(0.2636)
ICI	0.5323	0.2799	1.1373**	-0.1091
	(0.4319)	(0.4372)	(0.4718)	(0.5600)
OLIGOP	4.1635***		0.9243	
	(1.2958)		(0.8463)	
CONC		7.1580*	-5.9870**	
		(3.7443)	(2.9656)	
TRADE				-1.0295**
				(0.5005)
GSIZE	0.0074	0.0066	0.0044*	0.0026
	(0.0070)	(0.0063)	(0.0024)	(0.0025)
Chi-Square	38.28	28.12	49.41	50.04
D.F.	5	5	6	6
Model p<	0.0001	0.0001	0.0001	0.0001
Hit Ratio	83.2	78.2	74.7	72.6
Observations	111	111	321	321

***: $p < 0.01$; **: $p < 0.05$; *: $p < 0.10$.
Standard errors are in parentheses.

5. Conclusions

This study has shown that firms in service industries, like firms in manufacturing industries, prefer to pursue overseas expansion in large, culturally similar markets, to supply preestablished client firms from their own country, and to be subject to a minimal amount of government restrictions. Oligopolistic market structure can be considered one of the principal variables explaining the geographic location of service investments. We suggest that our findings of the significance of oligopolistic forces in the two-way movement of investment may be of relevance to the debate over the alleged decline of U.S. competitiveness that is said to result from the inflow of services FDI. Many individuals, such as Stephen Roach, argue that the recent surge in foreign investment can only mean that "the balance of globalization is tipping in favor of foreign service companies, putting U.S. companies at a distinct disadvantage" (1991: 88). Our findings suggest otherwise. We argue that decades of rapid and accelerated movement of U.S. service firms abroad (reflecting U.S. competitive advantage in key industries such as financial services, data processing and transportation), are finally being countered, in classic oligopolistic fashion, by firms in other countries beginning to enter the U.S. home market. The policy implications arising from this oligopolistic response explanation of investment flows are clear. Inward investment by service firms should not be resisted through restrictions but actively encouraged through liberalization.

References

Agarwal, J.P. (1980). "Determinants of foreign direct investment: a survey," *Weltwirtschaftliches Archiv* 4, 733-739.

Balassa, B. (1965). "Trade liberalization and 'revealed' comparative advantages," *The Manchester School* 33, 99-123.

Balassa, B. (1977). " 'Revealed' comparative advantage revisited: an analysis of relative export shares of the industrial countries," *The Manchester School* 45, 327-44.

Balassa, B., and L. Bauwens (1987). "Intra-industry specialization in a multi-country and multi-industry framework," *Economic Journal* 97, 923-39.

Ball, C.A., and A.E. Tschoegl (1982). "The decision to establish a foreign bank branch or subsidiary," *Journal of Financial and Quantitative Analysis* (September), 411-424.

Bergsten, C.F., T. Horst, and T. Moran (1978). *American Multinationals and American Interests* (Brookings Institution, Washington, DC).

Bhagwati, J.N. (1989). "The role of services in development," in *Services and Development: The Role of Foreign Direct Investment and Trade* (United Nations, New York), 5-9.

Bhagwati, J.N. (1984). "Splintering and disembodiment of services and developing nations," *The World Economy* 7, 133-144.

Boddewyn, J.J., M.B. Halbrich, and A.C. Perry (1986). "Service multinationals: conceptualization, measurement and theory," *Journal of International Business Studies* (Fall), 41-58.

Buckley, P.J., and M. Casson (1976). *The Future of the Multinational Enterprise* (Holmes and Meier, London).

Caves, R.E. (1982). *Multinational Enterprise and Economic Analysis* (Cambridge University Press, Cambridge).

Culem, C.G. (1988). "The locational determinants of direct investments among industrialized countries," *European Economic Review* 32, 885-904.

Davidson, W.H. (1980). "The location of foreign direct investment activity," *Journal of International Business Studies* (Fall), 9-22.

Deardorff, A.V. (1985). "Comparative advantage and international trade and investment in services," in R.M. Stern (ed.), *Trade and Investment in Services: Canada/U.S. Perspectives* (Ontario Economic Council, Toronto), 39-71.

Dunning, J.H. (1988). *Explaining International Production* (Unwin Hyman, London).

Dunning, J.H. (1989). *Transnational Corporations and Growth of Services: Some Conceptual and Theoretical Issues* (United Nations, New York).

Dunning, J.H., and J. Cantwell (1987). *The IRM Directory of Statistics of International Investment and Production* (MacMillan, London).

Dunning, J.H., and G. Norman (1987). "The location choice of office of international companies, " *Environment and Planning* 19, 613-631.

Feketekuty, G. (1988). *International Trade in Services* (Ballinger Publication, Cambridge, MA).

Fishwick, F. (1981). *Multinational Companies and Economic Concentration in Europe* (Institute for Research and Information on Multinationals, Paris).

Flowers, E.B. (1976). "Oligopolistic reactions in European and Canadian direct investment in the U.S.," *Journal of International Business Studies* (Fall/Winter), 43-55.

Francois, J.F. (1990). "Trade in nontradeables: proximity requirements and pattern of trade in services," *Journal of International Economic Integration* 5, 31-46.

Francois, J.F. (1992). "Explaining the pattern of trade in producer services," *International Economic Journal* forthcoming.

George, A.M., and C.W. Schroth (1991). "Managing foreign exchange for competitive advantage," *Sloan Management Review* 2, 105-116.

Goldberg, L.G., and A. Saunders (1980). "The causes of U.S. bank expansion overseas," *Journal of Money, Credit and Banking* 12, 630-643.

Graham, E.M. (1978). "Transatlantic investment by multinational firms: a rivalistic phenomenon," *Journal of Post-Keynesian Economics* 1, 82-99.

Graham, E.M. (1985)."Intra-industry direct foreign investment, market structure, firm rivalry and technological performance," in A. Erdilek, (ed.), *Multinationals as Mutual Invaders* (Groom Helm, Kent).

Gray, J.M., and P. Gray (1981). "The multinational bank," *Journal of Banking and Finance* (March), 33-63.

Grubaugh, S.G. (1987). "Determinants of direct foreign investment," *The Review of Economics and Statistics* 69, 149-152.

Hoekman, B.M. (1992a). "Policies affecting trade in services: a review and assessment of principal instruments," Institute of Public Policy Studies, Research Forum on International Economics Discussion Paper No. 303, University of Michigan (Ann Arbor, MI).

Hoekman, B.M. (1992b). "Conceptual and political economy issues in liberalizing international transactions in services," Institute of Public Policy Studies, Research Forum on International Economics Discussion Paper No. 303, University of Michigan (Ann Arbor, MI).

Hofstede, G. (1980). *Culture's Consequences* (Sage Publications, Beverly Hills. CA).

Horst, T.E. (1972). "Firm and industry determinants of the decision to invest abroad," *The Review of Economics and Statistics* (August), 258-266.

Hout, T., M.E. Porter, and E. Rudden (1982). "How global companies win out," *Harvard Business Review* (September-October), 98-108.

Hymer, S.H. (1960). *The International Operations of National Firms: A Study of Direct Foreign Investment* (The M.I.T. Press, Cambridge, MA).

Knickerbocker, F.T. (1973). *Oligopolistic Reaction and the Multinational Enterprise* (Harvard University Press, Boston, MA).

Kogut, B. (1988). "Country patterns in international competition: appropriability and oligopolistic agreement," in N. Hood & J. Vahlne, (ed.), *Strategies in Global Competition* (Croom Helm, London).

Kogut, B., and H. Singh (1988). "The effect of national culture on the choice of entry mode," *Journal of International Business Studies* (Fall), 411-432.

Krueger, R.C. (1989). "U.S. international transactions, first quarter, 1989," *Survey of Current Business* (June), 50-92.

Li, J.T., and S. Guisinger (1992). "The globalization of service multinationals in the 'triad' regions: Japan, Western Europe and North America," *Journal of International Business Studies* 23, 675-96.

Li, J.T., and S. Guisinger (1993). "The transnationalization of service industries," (United Nations, New York).

Li, J.T. and S. Guisinger (1991). "Comparative business failures of foreign-controlled firms in the United States," *Journal of International Business Studies* 22, 209-224.

Nigh, D., K.R. Cho, and S. Krishnan (1986). "The role of location-related factors in U.S. banking involvement abroad," *Journal of International Business Studies* (Fall), 59-72.

OECD (1982). *Controls and Impediments Affecting Inward Direct Investment in OECD Member Countries* (OECD, Paris).

OECD (1987a). *Controls and Impediments Affecting Inward Direct Investment in OECD Member Countries* (OECD, Paris).

OECD (1987b). *Recent Trends in International Direct Investment* (OECD, Paris).

Porter, M.E. (1990). *Competitive Advantages of Nations* (The Free Press, New York, NY).

Prahalad, C.K., and Y. Doz (1987). *The Multinational Mission* (The Free Press, New York, NY).

Pryor, F. (1971). "An international comparison of concentration ratios," *Review of Economic and Statistics*, 130-140.

Riddle, D.I., and K.J. Brown (1988). "From complacency to strategy: retaining world class competitiveness in services," in M.K. Starr, (ed.), *Global Competitiveness* (W.W. Norton and Co., New York, NY).

Rivera-Batiz, F.L., and L.A. Rivera-Batiz (1992). "Europe 1992 and the liberalization of direct investment flows: Services versus manufacturing," *International Economic Journal* 6, 45-58.

Roach, S.S. (1991)."Services under siege--the restructuring imperative," *Harvard Business Review* (September/October), 82-91.

Sampson, G.P., and R. H. Snape (1985). "Identifying the issues in trade in services," *The World Economy* 8, 171-181.

Sauvant, K.P. (1989). "Foreign direct investment and transnational corporations in services," in *Services and Development: The Role of Foreign Direct Investment and Trade* (United Nations, New York), 12-15.

Scaperlanda, A.E. and L.J. Mauer (1969). "The determinants of U.S. direct investment in the E.E.C.," *The American Economic Review* (September), 558-568.

Schroath, F.W., and C.M. Korth (1989). "Managerial barriers to the internationalization of U.S. property and liability insurers," *Journal of Risks and Insurance* 56, 630-648.

Shapiro, D.M. (1983). "Entry, exit, and the theory of the multinational corporation," in C.P. Kindleberger and D. Andretsch (eds.), *The Multinational Corporations in the 1980's* (The M.I.T. Press, Cambridge, MA).

Terpstra, V., and C.M. Yu (1988). "Determinants of foreign direct investment of U.S. advertising agencies," *Journal of International Business Studies* (Spring), 33-47.

UNCTC (1983-1988). *National Legislation and Regulations Relating to Transnational Corporations*, vols. 1-6 (United Nations, New York, NY).

UNCTC (1988). *Transnational Corporations in World Development: Trends and Prospects* (United Nations, New York, NY).

UNCTC (1990). *Directory of the World's Largest Service Companies* (Moody's Investors Service, New York, NY).

U.S. Department of Commerce (1984). *International Direct Investment: Global Trends and the U.S. Role* (U.S. Government Printing Office, Washington, DC).

U.S. Office of Trade Representative (1984). *United States National Study on Trade in Services* (USTR, Washington, DC).

U.S. Office of Trade Representative (1986). *Report on Foreign Trade Barriers* (USTR, Washington, DC).

U.S. Office of Technology Assessment (1986). *Trade in Services: Exports and Foreign Reserves* (Government Printing Office, Washington, DC).

Weinstein, A.K. (1977). "Foreign investments by service firms: the case of the multinational advertising agency," *Journal of International Business Studies* (Spring/Summer), 83-92.

Wichard, O.G. (1988). "International services: new information on U.S. transactions with unaffiliated foreigners," *Survey of Current Business* (October), 27-34.

World Bank (1978-1982). *World Development Report* (World Bank, Washington, DC).

Chapter 6   Global Outsourcing of Information Processing Services

Uday M. Apte and Richard O. Mason

1. Introduction

The low productivity growth and competitive weaknesses of U.S. manufacturing industry and the associated loss of blue-collar jobs to the Pacific rim and European countries during the last two decades are well documented and debated (Hayes and Wheelwright, 1984; Thurow, 1991). In contrast, the service sector of the U.S. economy has proved to be the engine of growth for decades, and hence, Americans have taken the growth of service sector jobs for granted. Given this, the recent reports on the unimpressive performance of the service sector (Nasar, 1991) and the growing migration of certain white-collar jobs overseas are disquieting indeed (Shereff, 1989; Wysocki, 1991).

These white-collar jobs are characterized by their use of information technology. They can be categorized into two types: information systems-related and information processing-related services. The first category of information systems services encompasses managing of information technology - hardware, software and telecommunications technology. This includes activities such as development and maintenance of software, and operating a computer and communications facility.

The second category of information processing services involves using information systems to transform, store or generate information. Thus, the clerical, back-office jobs, such as data entry, transaction processing, database

169

P. T. Harker (ed.), The Service Productivity and Quality Challenge, 169–202.
© *1995 Kluwer Academic Publishers. Printed in the Netherlands.*

creation or updating, and using information systems to make simple, routine decisions, belong to this category. These information processing service jobs are gradually moving to countries such as Barbados, the Philippines, India, and Ireland, where wages are low, talented and English-speaking labor is plentiful, and where a telecommunications infrastructure is generally available for linking to a host company's computer in the United States.

Information, unlike products such as automobiles or bags of grain, can be transported quickly and cheaply. Modern communications and computation technologies make this possible. Thus, many information intensive tasks can be conceivably moved halfway across the world if it makes economic sense. Today more economic factors are weighing in its favor. The trend towards global electronic outsourcing (i.e., selectively turning over certain functions to a subcontractor) of information services can be traced primarily to three factors: cost reduction pressure, advances in information technology, and improvements in information technology's cost/performance ratio. Faced with increasing pressure to reduce costs, a growing number of U.S. companies are finding the option of global outsourcing of information services quite attractive since the wage rates in many underdeveloped and newly industrialized countries are significantly lower than those in the United States. For example, wages of data-entry clerks in the Philippines can be as low as one-fifth of their wages in the United States (Hamilton, 1988). The progress of information technology has also been an important factor enabling this trend. Telecommunications advances, especially the laying of global fiberoptic and other networks, have allowed some companies, for example, to move information processing abroad without causing disruption to end users' work (McMullen, 1990).

Which jobs are likely to be outsourced? A job classification scheme proposed by Reich (1991) sheds some light. He argues that the standard classification scheme being used by U.S. Bureau of the Census is no longer suitable for analyzing trends in the emerging global economy. He proposes three categories: routine production services, in-person services, and symbolic-analytic services. Routine production services entail low skill, repetitive tasks performed for material transformation or information processing. These jobs roughly account for about a quarter of the total U.S. jobs. The information processing jobs, including data entry and clerical jobs referred to earlier, fall in this category. As we argue later, these jobs are excellent candidates for outsourcing. The second category, in-person services, accounts for 30% of total U.S. jobs. Since these jobs necessarily involve person-to-person interaction, they hold small potential for global outsourcing. The third category includes all problem identifying, problem-solving, strategic decision making and brokering activities. These jobs account for about twenty percent of jobs and cover professions including software engineer, research scientist, investment bankers, lawyers, and so forth. The jobs referred to earlier as information systems services mostly fall in this category. Since symbolic analysts rarely need to come in direct contact with the ultimate beneficiaries of the work, many of these jobs are suitable for global outsourcing.

This discussion simply points to the emerging trend of Americans becoming part of an international labor market. The competitiveness of Americans in this global market is essentially going to depend on the functions they can perform, and the value they can add, within the global economy. The corporate executives of today and tomorrow, therefore, should not only be cognizant of this global outsourcing trend but also be able to face the challenges posed by, and to take advantage of the opportunities made available by, the global outsourcing of information systems and processing services.

The phenomenon of global outsourcing is discussed here from the viewpoint of a U.S. business, and guidelines are developed to help managers deal with this issue. These guidelines, however, are equally useful for managers from other developed countries. Similarly, for brevity, the discussion focuses on the information systems services, although the conclusions drawn are equally applicable to a wide range of information processing services. Following this discussion, various types of information services being currently outsourced are reviewed, and advantages and disadvantages of outsourcing option are analyzed. Next, various examples of global outsourcing phenomenon are presented and guidelines for managing global outsourcing are developed. We end the paper by presenting our conclusions, a summary, and some comments on the national policy implications of the trend towards global electronic outsourcing of information services.

2. Outsourcing of Information Services

Tracing its roots to the traditional timesharing and professional services of the 1960s, outsourcing has become a valid option today in all areas of information services (Apte, 1991). Outsourcing is an umbrella term which covers many information processing and information systems services.

- *Information Processing* services include data entry, transaction processing, and back-office clerical tasks. These tasks are typically well defined, routine and require little interaction between outsourcer and vendor.
- *Contract Programming* addresses software development and maintenance activities including systems analysis, design, programming, testing, implementation and subsequent maintenance including porting and conversion of systems.
- *Facilities Management* agreement places the responsibility of operation and support of a system, or data center functions including hardware, software, networking and personnel, with a subcontractor.
- *System Integration* involves development of a fully-integrated system (hardware, software, and/or networking) from design through implementation. Once the system is implemented, the vendor typically turns the system over to the customer.
- *Support Operations* for maintenance/service and disaster recovery are sometimes covered under a facilities management agreement, but more frequently these are treated as specialties. Other special services include: training and education, telephone "hot-line" support, PC support, and so forth.

As seen from the above list, the term outsourcing covers the entire spectrum of information services. It ranges from leasing a whole IS department, down to just having a programmer or two develop a simple application, or having a clerk enter non-time-critical data.

The growth of outsourcing as an important strategy can be attributed to a number of factors. Cost reduction pressures often trigger companies to consider outsourcing of information services. Other important reasons include the difficulty of finding suitable information systems professionals, the need for access to a leading-edge information technology, and the increased availability of outsourcing services in the marketplace. Outsourcing also has a number of drawbacks; most particularly the loss of control and the natural resistance of information systems executives to outsourcing option.

The factors underlying the attractiveness and growth of outsourcing are:

- *Cost reduction, containment and predictability.* Double-digit growth in the information system (IS) budget was the norm in 1980s; but given the current recession, the present trend is towards flat or low growth IS budgets

(Rifkin, 1991). The challenge for IS management today is to accomplish more with less resources. This mounting cost pressure is seen as the most significant factor driving today's corporate interest in outsourcing (Wilder, 1990). Even if the cost of outsourcing is not significantly less than an in-house effort, it tends to become more predictable because the responsibility of cost overruns often gets placed on the vendor (Clermont, 1991). The vendor may also be contractually obliged to meet deadlines, preventing costly delays. The lessened need for in-house IS staff is a significant benefit of outsourcing given the growing shortage of skilled IS professionals in the United States.

• *Improved focus on the strategic use of IT.* Even the IS departments fortunate enough to have a group of experienced and productive IS professionals find outsourcing to be an important and useful alternative. Outsourcing allows management to focus the available IS talent on IT activities promoting competitiveness, rather than spend time on routine activities of systems maintenance or operations.

• *Access to leading-edge technology and know-how.* Outsourcing IS functions to an appropriate vendor provides immediate access to the latest in technology and increases the competitiveness of one's product offerings through the use of state-of-the-art technology that may not be easily available in-house.

• *Availability of outsourcing services.* Recent years have seen a dramatic increase in the number of outsourcing vendors. Aside from the traditional vendors such as Anderson Consulting, EDS, and the big six accounting firms, outsourcing market has attracted the traditional hardware vendors including IBM, Digital and Unisys. As estimated by The Yankee Group, a consulting firm, the size of the outsourcing market in U.S. alone was about $26 billion in 1989. The market is expected to grow annually at about 15% rate to reach $50 billion by 1994. In the same time frame, the global outsourcing market is expected to grow from $101 billion in 1989 to $240 billion in 1994 (McMullen, 1990).

In short, outsourcing offers a variety of ways for a corporation to better leverage its resources, manage its costs, and focus on core applications to increase IT's value to corporate objectives. While many outsourcing vendors exist in the U.S., the global outsourcing of selected information system functions, discussed subsequently at length, can potentially offer even greater benefits.

Despite the benefits listed above, IS executives frequently resist outsourcing. They see outsourcing as a clear threat to their own and to their subordinates' long-term career prospects (McCusker, 1991; Mead, 1990). After all, by adopting the outsourcing approach they are disbanding their own organization with the likelihood that many IS professionals will not find suitable jobs, or promising career paths, in other functional areas of the corporation. The personnel displacement caused by outsourcing discourages IS executives from taking an objective approach in evaluating outsourcing decisions. More often than not, therefore, evaluation of outsourcing options are initiated by business executives (Clermont, 1991). Often, the impetus comes from the chief executive office or the chief financial officer.

The costs of negotiating and monitoring the outsourcing contract with the vendor, and the cost of reverting to the insourcing option, should outsourcing fail, can also be substantial. In practice, a company considering outsourcing option and deciding to do so often finds its best IS staff being absorbed by the outsourcing vendor or jumping the ship to a competitor. The residual staff that is required to monitor the outsourcing contract or to focus on strategic applications is often woefully inadequate to make insourcing a viable option if the company later finds itself to be unhappy with the outsourcing vendor. Thus, the only option available may be to select another outsourcing vendor. This irreversibility of outsourcing decisions is also considered as a serious risk of outsourcing.

IS executives also complain that outsourcing reduces their control over the quality of the software and the project's timetable since the work is now being carried out by another organization. The company that chooses to outsource a major portion of its IS function can also lose touch with the advances in information technology. A significant shortcoming; if IT is strategically important.

The merits and drawbacks of outsourcing option can be more systematically analyzed using the Transaction Cost theory (Williamson, 1985; Kleeper and Hartog, 1991; Apte, 1991). Transaction cost theory explains the relative benefits of carrying an economic activity within the firm (using the governance structure of organizational hierarchy) or through the market exchange mechanism (using the market-based governance structure). In comparing the "make" versus "buy" options, a total of production plus transaction costs[1] of these alternatives

---

[1] Transaction costs are the costs of negotiating, monitoring and enforcing an agreement or contract.

are compared and the alternative having a smaller total cost is hypothesized to be the predominant governance structure.

As discussed in Apte (1991), the outsourcing option generally has smaller production costs and higher transaction costs as compared to the insourcing option. Some important conclusions of the transaction cost analysis of outsourcing are:

• The activities that are well defined and that have significant economies of scale in production are good candidates for outsourcing since the lower production costs of a service provider tend to dominate the slightly higher transaction costs of dealing with the service provider. Some examples of information systems services: data center or network operations.

• Lowering transaction cost is the key to success in outsourcing. Some options are: (1) to choose an activity that is likely to have well-defined requirements, (2) to create a process whereby the requirements become clearly known to the service provider, and consequently the uncertainty is reduced, and (3) to develop a long-term, partnership arrangement to reduce the frequency-related transaction costs.

The discussion in this section dealt with the option of outsourcing in general. In the next section we take a closer look at the global outsourcing options and the additional advantages and disadvantages that it offers.

3. Global Outsourcing

The significant disparity of salary levels of personnel between developed and underdeveloped countries is one of the primary reasons behind interest in foreign outsourcing. As we note in Table 1, the salary levels of underdeveloped and newly industrialized countries are considerably lower than the salary levels in the developed countries.[2] Vendors from underdeveloped and newly industrialized countries see outsourcing as a very lucrative target market for their IS services and their pricing advantage has made global outsourcing a small but rapidly growing segment of the overall outsourcing market.

---

[2] It should be noted, however, that in comparing the total labor-related costs, one should add the fringe benefits (which range from 20% to 40% of salary) and the additional cost of telecommunications and travel to the basic salary.

Table 1.   Comparison of Wages in Selected Countries (1988-89)[a]

| Country[c] | Annual Wages in U.S. $000 | |
	Clerical	Professional[b]
Canada	25.5	35.3
China	0.4	0.4
Dominican Republic	2.5	8.8
France	15.5	37.2
Germany, Fed. Rep. of	22.5	44.6
India[d]	N/A	5.5
Ireland	12.9	20.3
Japan	15.9	38.3
Korea	12.2	39.1
Mexico[e]	1.5	N/A
Netherlands[f]	N/A	19.5
Philippines	1.6	3.1
Singapore	5.3	14.0
Trinidad and Tobago	5.8	N/A
United Kingdom	11.9	27.0
United States[g]	25.0	35.0

Notes

[a]   The original wage data, in the currency of the country, is converted to U. S. dollars using the then prevalent exchange rate.

[b]   Wages in this column are for occupations indicated as "professional" for certain countries and "commercial specialist" for other countries. It is assumed that IT professionals' wages are comparable to these wages.

[c]   The wage data pertaining to China, Germany, Japan, Philippines and Singapore is for the year 1988. The wage data for other countries is for the year 1989.

[d]   Estimated wages of an IT professional are based on Senn [1991].

[e]   Wage level in 1987.

[f]   Average wage for all services in 1989.

[g]   Estimated wages based on interviews with industry executives.

Sources: 1. Foreign Labor Trends, Published by U. S. Department of Labor, Bureau of International Labor Affairs. 2. 1987 Statistical Yearbook, Publishing Division, United Nations, New York, 1990

Not all information systems activities are suitable for global outsourcing. For example, facilities management would suffer from the geographic limitations inherent in a global setting. The telecommunication costs would be simply too high for global outsourcing of facilities management to be cost competitive. On the other hand, the data entry and contract programming, and to some extent the systems integration and support activities, are arenas where vendors from underdeveloped countries can certainly compete. And compete they do with vigor, especially in data entry and contract programming services.

Data entry was one of the earliest task to be globally outsourced. Data entry requires the lowest level of computer literacy. It also requires very little interaction between the customer and the vendor. The customer can mail data forms to the vendor, and the vendor in turn can send the computerized data back via telecommunication lines or by mailing magnetic tapes. Use of systems for data entry or processing of simple forms can be accomplished without the strict need for a common language requirement. For example, Pacific Data Services has been contracting data entry services from China since 1961 (Noble, 1986). Even with the trouble that Chinese have with the English language, the Pacific Data Services guarantees 99% accuracy rate for data entry tasks. Today, vendors from many countries participate in data entry partnerships. For example, Mead Data Central has citizens of South Korea, Jamaica, Haiti, and Barbados entering information for its large databases, such as Nexis (Noble, 1986).

Outsourcing has not been limited to simple data entry. Semi-skilled jobs are also being globally outsourced. For example, New York Life Insurance and Cigna Corporation have claims processing operations in Ireland (Lohr, 1988; Wysocki, 1991). An interesting illustration of a high-skill end of the back office work being performed overseas is the Quarterdeck Office Systems' technical-support staff in Ireland, that handles technical queries from users of Quarterdeck System from all around the world including U.S. (Wysocki, 1991).

A small, yet growing trend is also observed in outsourcing of software development activities. India's distinct advantages in this regard are again the existence of very low salaries and abundant availability of English-speaking, technically trained graduates, numbering about a quarter of a million new technical graduates per year (Senn, 1991; Hazarika, 1991). Some of the major problems faced by operations in India, however, include inadequate and unreliable telecommunications infrastructure and the shortage of mainframe computers.

Several well-known American companies, including Hewlett-Packard, Texas Instruments, Digital Equipment Corporation and more recently IBM, have set up operations in cities of Bangalore and Bombay in India. Digital Equipment Corporation writes diagnostic software used in the entire company. To overcome the telecommunications problems, both DEC and TI have each acquired a dedicated satellite link. The recent announcements of incentives and liberalization of ownership requirements has led to a joint venture between IBM and Tata Industries, an Indian industrial house, for production of PS/2 computer hardware and other software.

Design work is also being outsourced. Texas Instruments employs Indian engineers to write computer aided design software which is used for designing integrated circuits in the company's semi-conductor group. Boeing Company, in a joint project with a vendor in the Philippines, is developing an air-base inventory-management system. In this project, Filipinos will train Americans in system's use after its development and implementation (Hamilton, 1988).

Many of the outsourcing vendors already have significant command of the English language. Vendors from the Philippines, Singapore, India and Ireland, for example, pose no communication problems for companies from English-speaking countries such as the United States, United Kingdom, or Canada. The language barrier for companies from non-English-speaking countries such as Germany, France or Japan, however, may be a stumbling block for the same vendors. As shown by the Quarterdeck's example earlier, some of these countries can also provide hot-line telephone support for software products of American companies, assuming of course that suitable arrangements for the high-quality, reliable telephone lines are made.

3.1   Global outsourcing: further advantages and disadvantages.
The advantages listed earlier for IS outsourcing in general are also valid for global outsourcing. But there are additional considerations:

*   *Substantial cost reduction.* The pricing structures of global outsourcing vendors tend to be extremely attractive. This can lead to significant additional cost saving for an outsourcer. Another way to think about this is that with the same budget, an outsourcer can clear backlog and broaden the portfolio of projects it can complete by using the services of a global outsourcing vendor.
*   *Global outsourcing provides a good option for developing and operating a global information systems essential for global operations.* Managing global IS, an essential element of global operations, can be very difficult and expensive. Having a global outsourcing vendor can be beneficial in this case. For example, a U.S.-based software package vendor may sell its products around the world and then contract an outsourcing vendor for providing the after-sales support.
*   *Access to the a large pool of skilled professionals well versed with latest technology.* Given the economic conditions of some of the third world countries, this benefit may seem counter-intuitive. However, a typical American IS professional is now burdened with old software development

technology and habits -- an ironic disadvantage of being a first user of information technology. For example, it is relatively easy to find a COBOL programmer but it is hard to find, at a reasonable cost, a programmer knowledgeable in networking, object-oriented programming, or UNIX environment. In comparison, India, a late-entrant to information technology field, has a sizable pool of software developers trained in the latest high-tech knowledge and techniques. From the perspective of a U.S. based company, an added advantage of labor market in the third world countries is the low turnover rate caused by higher unemployment rates.

- *Faster cycle time for development.* Given the size of human resource pool that the foreign vendors of contract programming can tap into and deploy, and the advanced software engineering methodologies that at least some of them do utilize, product development can proceed rapidly.
- *Access to foreign markets.* Protectionism is still an obstacle that the companies interested in global operations must overcome. Many countries do not allow foreign companies to enter the country and market products without substantial tariffs. Others have strict limits on the ownership of companies. Outsourcing partnerships can provide an appropriate foothold in the growing, sizable and lucrative marketplace of the third world countries.

Thus, there are substantial gains to be made through the selective use of global information outsourcing: significant cost savings and capital market gains, faster cycle time, help in developing or operating global information systems, and the access to foreign markets and a skilled labor pool. These benefits have encouraged many companies to begin use of, or investigation into, the global outsourcing option. However, with advantages come certain disadvantages:

- *Difficulties in communication and coordination.* Even if we assume that the system requirements are well specified, the specifications often change while the system is being designed or programmed. Hence, constant communication -- both inter-personal and data communication -- between the user, the designers and the programmer becomes a key for developing quality software. The poor telecommunications infrastructure, a common problem in the underdeveloped countries, can be a serious drawback in this case. High quality, reliable telephone lines necessary for data communication are still rare although available at a premium on a leased-line basis from telephone companies. In developing a large and complex system, the problem of coordinating activities of multiple teams is always a difficult one. These difficulties are only magnified in a global setting.

- *Potential for violation of intellectual property rights.* Many third world countries have lax regulations and laws regarding the honoring of intellectual property rights. For example, for all practical purposes, Taiwan has no copyright protection law. Under these circumstances, an unscrupulous outsourcing vendor may be tempted to violate the intellectual property rights by possibly sharing the software specification with the outsourcer's competitor. Thus, global outsourcing arrangement may leave an outsourcer open to the risk of theft of its strategic information systems technology. This risk is considered to be a significant drawback of global outsourcing.

- *Lack of control on software quality and project timetable.* With inadequate or ever-changing system specifications, the outsourcing vendor may not be able to deliver the quality software that the outsourcer desires on time. The physical remoteness also makes it difficult to monitor a project's progress and to take corrective actions. Hence, the worry of possible project delays and a sense of having no control over the quality of software is always at the back of mind of an outsourcer.

- *Unclear governmental attitudes toward transborder data flows and IS services.* Underdeveloped countries are becoming aware of the potential for increasing their national income by taxing information systems products and services created within their borders. The United States and Europe are lobbying for reducing these duties, but no clear resolution of the conflict has been accepted.[3]

- *Difficulty in Managing Cultural Diversity*: Global outsourcing, almost always, involves dealing with people from different parts of the world having different culture and customs. Managing this cultural diversity can be a difficult task for a manager whose entire experience may be limited to dealing with people and companies only from their own country; unless the manager is fully committed to understanding the other culture.

The outsourcer should, therefore, approach global outsourcing option with sufficient care. As indicated above, there are many problems in managing the global outsourcing relationship which are not found in the in-house software development or in dealing with the U.S.-based outsourcing vendor. In the next section we will examine the managerial considerations pertaining to the global outsourcing option.

---

[3] At the current writing it appears that with the resolution of disagreement between the U.S. and the European Community concerning agricultural subsidies, the issue of Trade in Services is likely to come to table as the GATT round of negotiations continues.

4. Global Outsourcing: Managerial Considerations

Managers, in dealing with global outsourcing, are faced with three main implementation issues: identifying the activities that can and should be globally outsourced; choosing the right service providers and countries; and creating appropriate organizational arrangements and coordination mechanisms between the domestic and foreign entities. These issues, in a broader context of disaggregation of services, are also discussed in Apte and Mason (1992a).

4.1   Identify candidate activities. As Daniel Bell noted in "The Coming of Post-Industrial Society" (1979), and for which authors like Machlup (1980), Porat (1977), and Kling (1990) have provided evidence, the number and importance of information intensive jobs is increasing throughout the global economy. A preliminary analysis of the global outsourcing examples cited earlier indicates that the white-collar service jobs being globally outsourced are characterized by high information-intensity (Porter and Millar, 1985; Linder and Ives, 1987) and low customer contact needs (Chase, 1981). As discussed earlier, information can be transported easily and inexpensively using the modern telecommunications technology. The concomitant advances in information technology, such as data storage, imaging, or artificial intelligence, have also made it easier to deal with information. Thus, information intensive activities that require little customer contact can be easily outsourced globally, if that makes economic sense and is technologically feasible. Executives like Thomas Spencer, Director of Operations Research, at AT&T have a homey way of assessing the possibilities. In deciding which of his employees can effectively work at home or other remote locations, he estimates the "computnik" to consulting ratio and allows heavy "computnik" jobs to be geographically dispersed.

Thus, a simple two dimensional model that explains the characteristics of the jobs that indicate the potential for global electronic outsourcing is shown in Figure 1. Indicated in this figure are selected job categories as mentioned by Kling (1990). In general, we hypothesize that the jobs that are characterized by medium to high information intensity and low customer contact need have a higher potential for global electronic outsourcing. Based on the data provided by Kling, concerning the number of people employed in the information sector (about half of total jobs in the United States), and our preliminary analysis as suggested by the "information intensity - customer contact" framework, we

conclude tentatively that as high as 12% of information service sector jobs in the United States are vulnerable to global outsourcing (see Table 2 for analysis).
Not all information systems and processing services should be outsourced. The decision should be guided by two considerations: strategic importance of a service to the company, and the relative efficiency with which the company can perform that service. Consider a service such as the payroll processing.

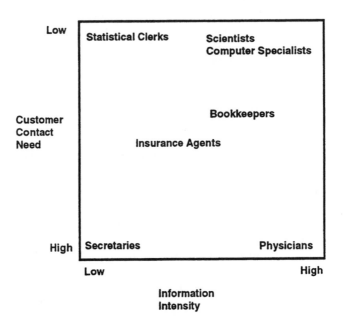

Figure 1.   Characterization of Services for Global Disaggregation

Table 2:   Potential Number of Jobs That May Be Globally Outsourced

Job Category	Number of Jobs (000)	Job Category	Number of Jobs (000)
High Potential		**Low Potential**	
Accountants	1,076	Physicians,Dentists	803
Scientists	594	Health Technologists	588
Operations & Sys Res	173	Nurses, Dietitians	1,607
Architects	92	Teachers	4,012
Writers, Artists	1,313	Lawyers and Judges	558
Computer Specialists	598	Various Administrators	7,702
Bookkeepers	1,942	Blue Collar Supervisors	1,754
Statistical Clerks	396	Various Semi-prof	1,022
Telephone Operators	323	Real Estate Agents	598
Stenographers	65	Personnel	461
		Inspectors, Collectors	288
		Secretaries	3,944
Medium Potential		Sales Agents	1,143
Engineers	1,472	Sales Workers	3,149
Financial Managers	659	Cashiers	1,592
Research Workers	180	Blue Collar Information	
Engineering Tech.	1,127	Workers	2,082
Sales Reps and Managers	1,656	Various Clerical	6,611
Insur. Agents/Underwriters	543		
Insurance Claims Adjusters	179		
Typists	1,043		
Other Clerical Workers	1,899		
Clerical Supervisors	245		
Billing Clerks	165		

Notes: To compute the potential number of jobs vulnerable to global outsourcing, we assume the following percentages: High (40%), Medium (20%), Low (5%).

Source: Kling (1990) data for employment in U.S. information sector is based on U.S. Bureau of Census, 1980.

This service is normally considered to be strategically unimportant, since performing it at a level better than certain minimum required level does not add to the competitiveness of the company. Neither can a small to medium company hope to perform payroll processing at a cost lower than an outsourcing vendor, such as ADP, who has specifically set up operations that are fine-tuned to carry out payroll service at a large volume and a great efficiency. Thus, it may be appropriate to outsource the payroll processing function.

In general, the higher the strategic importance of a function, and higher the relative efficiency of performing that function, the less desirable it is as an outsourcing candidate. The actions preferable under different combinations of two underlying factors are given in Figure 2 (adapted from Walker, 1988). Thus,

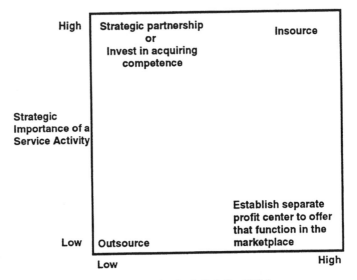

Figure 2.   Insourcing versus Outsourcing

a function that scores low (high) on both the dimensions should, in general, be outsourced (insourced). If a function is strategically important and if it cannot be performed with a relative efficiency, the company should make the necessary investment so that it can be performed internally with efficiency. Other option is to establish strategic partnership with another company that can perform it with a relative efficiency. In the final case when a function is not strategically important but can be performed with a great relative efficiency, the company may want to become an outsourcing vendor for that service. Thus, it may want to establish a separate profit center for offering it in the marketplace.

Global outsourcing provides information systems managers with new options for meeting their needs. The type of work being outsourced can vary with a company's familiarity with the global environment; with the experience, knowledge, and size of its IS department; and with the profile of information system development needs. We have seen in the examples described earlier that a variety of IS activities can be globally outsourced. We believe that the most important requisites of a successful outsourcing relationship are the cost savings potential, and the ability to manage the communications process. The simplest way to ensure good communications is to outsource only those activities that are well structured and specified. Thus, global outsourcing of data entry or claims processing activities have a good chance of being successful. The facilities management services such as data center operation are well structured but the cost savings potential, due to geographic remoteness, is either very small or nonexistent. Hence, these facilities management services are normally not globally outsourced. Similarly, the outsourcing of abstract design tasks may also meet with greater difficulties because the foreign designer may not have immediate access to the users of the system, and therefore, may not clearly understand the system requirements.

We can view the systems life cycle as a continuum of activities, from the most abstract to the most structured (See Figure 3). We propose that in general the structured activities are more amenable for global outsourcing than the abstract activities.

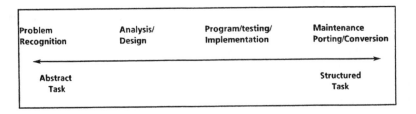

Figure 3. System Development Activities

Problem recognition requires an in-depth knowledge of the company to spot the inherent causes of problems, as opposed to the mere symptoms, and to understand which solutions are feasible. While one could imagine asking a consultant to come and study a company, it is doubtful if such consultant could be a foreign one. Cultural and language barriers would make the task that much more difficult for a foreign consultant.

The design phase is also a very abstract process. One must work closely with the users to guarantee the development of a system that meets their needs. Too many systems have failed because of a lack of communication between the designers and the users. This problem would be exacerbated by having the two teams on opposite sides of the world, speaking different languages.

Once the specifications have been fully developed, the programming can become a fairly straight-forward process and therefore this activity is considered a good candidate for global outsourcing. While the specifications are bound to change over time, these changes can be managed with well-defined change control procedures. This would improve the communication between individuals and mitigate the possibility of confusion.

Testing and implementation are well-structured activities. These tasks may not require as highly trained individuals, nor is there need for much interaction between the outsourcer and the vendor. Subsequent to system implementation the training of outsourcer's employees can be done by those people in the vendor firm most fluent in the language and customs of the outsourcer. The activities such as porting and conversion of systems arehighly structured since the task is essentially to move system from one hardware/operating/database environment to another. Also given that the current system is usually in operation, the time pressure on system completion is somewhat less. Hence, porting and conversion of systems are considered some of the most ideal activities for global outsourcing of information systems services.

4.2 Choose the service provider. The next important issue that faces a global outsourcer is the choice of the service provider. In addition to the obvious factor such as pricing, there are several important characteristics of a service provider that must be analyzed:

- *Track record.* The companies most likely to successfully complete a software project are those with previous experience in outsourcing. Hence, the previous track record of the service provider is a very important fac tor. In this task one can check the references to determine the quality of outsourcing service previously provided by the service provider.
- *Human and technology resources.* In essence, the basic resource that an outsourcer is purchasing from the vendor is human skills and capacity. Hence, in outsourcing decisions, both the project management skills and experience, and the specific software engineering skills, such as languages, databases, networking skills, etc., should be verified. The technology resources should also be checked. For example, if the task involves use of a particular type of a mainframe, it is imperative that the service provider must either own or have guaranteed access to the required type of that mainframe.
- *Staying power of the service provider.* Outsourcing an information system function to a service provider who then becomes bankrupt while the work is half complete is one of the worst scenarios for the outsourcer. Hence, the

financial strength and the overall sustaining power of the service provider should be verified. This factor assumes added importance due to the global setting with its inherent uncertainties regarding the bonafides of the entities.

In addition to the above-mentioned characteristics, the outsourcer must be aware of the political and social environment of the service provider's home-base country. Working with developing countries can create difficulties not typically encountered in dealing with the developed countries. Some important factors related to the home-base country are:

- *Stability of the political and social environment.* This is a very important consideration since a stable environment is the requisite foundation for achieving a beneficial and continued relationship. For example, a change in the style of political governance means a tremendous shock to the economy of the country. Even changes seemingly for the better (such as those found in today's Eastern Europe) do not guarantee increased stability. Countries with sharply divided populations along religious or racial lines are also generally unstable.
- *The attitude of the host country's government towards foreign investment and collaborations in IT.* The attitude of the country government can make the alliance easy or difficult to manage. Many of the third world countries have been creating incentives to encourage foreign investment. India has created special incentives and has relaxed ownership rules for foreign companies (Hazarika, 1991). Ireland has financed the upgrading of its telecommunications infrastructure and is offering loan guarantees, interest subsidies, and a maximum corporate tax rate of 10% (Wysocki, 1991). The Singaporean government's role in implementing a series of national computer plans designed to make Singapore an economic power in the post-industrial information age is particularly noteworthy (Gurbaxani et. al., 1990). In specific, the government has emphasized development of necessary IT infrastructure (including advanced telecommunications and human resource development) and maintenance of a favorable investment climate to attract IT producers and sophisticated IT users to the island.
- *Foreign currency restrictions and volatility.* An important aspect of the business environment, especially in a case where the outsourcer chooses to establish a wholly owned subsidiary, is the guarantee that the host country's central bank provides access to and allows repatriation of the money earned

in the venture. Some governments have dismal histories of nationalization of foreign-owned businesses, while others have stringent restrictions on the foreign exchange. The currency must also be convertible. The volatility of a currency's value in U.S. dollars is an important consideration, since, as the foreign exchange rate changes, the outsourcing decisions made earlier based on an older rate may no longer be as beneficial.

- *Size of the pool of skilled software professionals.* Low average salaries of professionals is one of the strongest incentive for global outsourcing. However, in addition to cost advantage, the host country must have a large population of well-educated, underemployed citizens with a sizable pool of skilled professionals. Many countries also have large groups of well-educated women of all ages who are traditionally unemployed.

- *Communications.* The necessity of appropriate telecommunication infrastructure is discussed earlier. Other consideration is the question of command over the common language, as the software projects typically require a substantial amount of verbal communication between the outsourcer and the vendor. Many countries support English as their primary or secondary language, so this is not a great limitation for English-speaking customers. In projects which are quite self-contained, such as data entry, the workers' ability to speak the language is not as important. However, the vendor management must share the language with the outsourcer to ensure that the work is up to standard.

- *Time zone difference.* Another consideration is the time difference between the customer and vendor if it can be used as an advantage in designing the working arrangements with the service provider. An appropriate time difference and an on-line environment with shared databases can allow for around-the-clock work, resulting in fast turn-around times. Additionally, if the vendor is using the outsourcer's computers for development, the time difference can allow vendor's employees an access to the computer during the outsourcer's off-peak hours, and thereby reduce the ultimate cost to the outsourcer.

Having suggested a number of factors important in analyzing the suitability of the home-base country, we can identify several countries which seem prime candidates for outsourcing relationships. For simple data entry tasks the countries such as Philippines, Jamaica, Haiti, Barbados, and Ireland have proven records. For more sophisticated design, programming testing and conversion activities, the countries such as Ireland, India, Singapore, the Philippines, the Netherlands, and Australia are good choices.

4.3   Organizational arrangements and cultural diversity.   Having identified appropriate activities to outsource and selected appropriate service providers, the next task is to weave these pieces together within a coherent organizational form.   Three organizational arrangements have generally proven more suitable for global outsourcing: networked organizations, strategic alliances, and customer-vendor contracts. Operating in a global economy also means that ultimately, the effectiveness of these organizational arrangements is highly influenced by the way cultural diversity is managed. Consequently, brief comments on management of multi-cultural teams are also included.

Bartlett and Ghoshal (1989) have found that the particular organizational form employed by firms operating in multiple countries depends on their individual strategies and capabilities:

*   Firms building on economies of scale and scope tend to seek cost advantages through centralized global-scale operations. They employ a multi-divisional form (M-form) organization in which overseas nodes are used to carry out parent company strategies. (Matsushita is an example.)
*   Firms building on a strong local presence in various countries by means of sensitivity and responsiveness to national differences tend to be decentralized with each node being self-sufficient. (Unilever is an example.)
*   Firms exploiting the parent company's knowledge and intellectual capital through worldwide diffusion and adaptation tend to rely on core competencies that are centralized, augmented by unique decentralized competencies. (General Electric is an example)

Many managers today, however, question the long term effectiveness of the these organizational forms. Indeed, critical questions can be raised as to whether the hierarchical, M-form will continue to be the most effective in the global, post-industrial, information economy. Generally speaking, the M-form organization does not have the speed and agility necessary to compete in a time-based manner. Stalk and Hout (1990) and Keen (1986), for instance, present convincing arguments as to why speed and agility are essential to compete effectively in today's global markets and as to why traditional organizational models may be inappropriate. The M-form, for example, emphasizes high volume economies. It does not stress adding value by applying knowledge dynamically throughout a firm's value-added chain. Thus, it lacks the flexibility and swiftness to be responsive to a rapidly changing global environment.

Meeting these requirements of flexibility and swiftness as well as efficiency and effectiveness requires an approach that modularizes business activities, establishes communication links among these activities, and insures that the appropriate information is routed to each work task in a timely manner. At least three organizational structures that purport to satisfy these needs have been proposed. Collectively they are called networked organizations. Bartlett and Ghoshal (1989) developed the concept of a "transnational firm," Miles and Snow (1986) developed the idea of "dynamic network organizations," and Reich (1991) developed the notion of an "enterprise web." A successful transnational, network, or web organization is more flexible and more capable of learning from its diverse environment than any of the organizational structures described above. These firms' assets and capabilities are clustered in nodes which have three general characteristics. They are (1) dispersed, (2) interdependent, and (3) specialized. Differential contributions are made by each of the overseas and domestic nodes, and these contributions are coordinated and integrated into worldwide operations. Generally speaking, learning is conducted and knowledge is developed jointly by the nodes and is shared worldwide. This calls for a flatter organization consisting of many semi-autonomous nodes.

One firm that is experimenting with a form of integrated network configuration based on electronic communication is Texas Instruments (TI) (see Apte and Mason, 1992b). TI is one of the largest manufacturers of electronics components and equipment in the world and has operations in the United States, Central and South America, Europe and Asia. Design Automation Division (DAD) is a division of TI that has the responsibility of designing Computer Aided Design (CAD) software for the design of integrated circuits. Five years ago, DAD was organized along the traditional, geographic lines. Since then DAD has reorganized itself into a networked organization along the lines of its "worldwide strategies" or projects, where each "strategy" organization potentially consists of professionals drawn from five geographically dispersed organizations. In forming a project team, the skills and experiences required for a project are matched with the unique strengths and availability of individual DAD members. This dynamic network organization approach not only ensures that DAD members learn continuously by gaining exposure to a wide range of projects, but also that the project teams can be frequently reassembled to meet the complex and changing strategic requirements of the semiconductor marketplace.

The experience of companies such as TI has created a need to understand globally networked organization better. Reich (1991) provides imagery for such a networked organization. Instead of a pyramid, his "new web of enterprise" looks more like a spider's web. Strategic brokers (executives who manage ideas rather than things and who dynamically link problem identifiers together with problem solvers) are at the center, but there are all sorts of connections that do not involve them directly, and new connections are being spun all the time. At each point of connection are a relatively small number of people -- depending on the task, from a dozen to several hundred. The concept, however, is still evolving. As Miles and Snow explain, new organizational forms are arising to cope with the global environmental conditions.

A more complete description of how this new type of organization works is provided by Miles and Snow. Their "dynamic network organization" has four major features: (1) vertical disaggregation of business functions, (2) brokers organizing business functions, (3) market mechanisms used to hold groups together, and (4) full disclosure computer information systems. The dynamic network organization requires a new managerial approach. To be effective it must be balanced. For the individual firm (or component, or node), the primary benefit of participation in the network is the opportunity to pursue its particular distinctive competence. A properly constructed network can display the technical specialization of the functional structure, and the balanced orientation characteristic of the matrix. Therefore, each component can be seen as complementing rather than competing with the other components.

Balance and dynamism are achieved through continual and active organizational learning. Knowledge and information are accumulated at each node and either communicated to other nodes or used as a resource in negotiating contracts and alliances. Each node, consequently, represents a unique combination of skills that can be drawn upon when required. Direct ownership and control of each node in the web are not essential, perhaps not even preferred. Contractual and other agreements can serve just as well.

Miles and Snow conclude that in order to keep the organization balanced its major nodes must be "assembled and reassembled (frequently) to meet complex and changing competitive conditions." This requires forming strategic alliances with organizations well beyond the organization's boundaries and engaging in global brokering.

Strategic Alliances are associations and agreements that form relationships between two independent entities. Frequently this is done by enforceable contract; occasionally it is accomplished by simple verbal agreement. Strategic alliances are coalitions an organization forms with other organizations in order to achieve one or more of its strategic goals. An assumption of most large scale, M-form corporations is that they must own and carefully control the assets and capabilities at very node in their network. Globalization is challenging this assumption. A corporation need not own every node in its value-added network (or even most of them) as long as each node delivers its output on time and within cost objectives, and it meets quality standards. In fact, there are several reasons why in the global environment, alliances are preferred to ownership. Alliances offer special capabilities that the firm can not acquire otherwise. They can be formed and disbanded quickly in order to respond to changing market conditions. They force a clear pinpointing of responsibility between nodes. And, by forming (or holding open the option to form) multiple alliances a firms can use competitive pressure to hold down costs and manage risk.

Reich identifies five basic forms of relationships between the organization and the nodes in its global network:

1. Independent Profit Center in which authority and for product development and sales is pushed down to each node. In this case the node is owned but is rather autonomous.
2. Spin-off Partnerships in which independent businesses are spawned from the main organization using former employees and assets. The node then contributes to the organization on a contractual basis.
3. Spin-in Partnerships in which ideas and unique assets from external groups are acquired and become nodes in the organization itself.
4. Licensing in which headquarters contracts with independent businesses to use its brand name, sell its special formulas, or otherwise market (that is, find applicable problems for) its technologies.
5. Pure Brokering in which headquarters contracts with independent businesses for problem solving and identifying as well as for production.

   The various organizational arrangements identified above provide an outsourcer with different degrees of control (see Figure 4 below). Information processing jobs of data entry or claims processing tend to be well-defined, simple and repetitive. Therefore, the need for control over vendor for these jobs is relatively small. Hence, a simple customer/vendor contract is adequate in this situation. The arrangements required for information systems services, however, are different and more complicated. A software development project requires a significant amount of project management and control to ensure success. Conceptually, there are two ways of managing a software project: by controlling outcome or by controlling process.

   Outcome standards create clear specifications for what is acceptable work, and what is an acceptable schedule. For the customer/vendor relationship this is an obvious choice of control. Development specifications, deliverables and dates

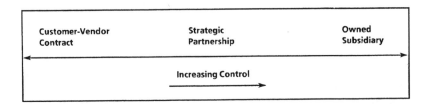

Figure 4. Contractual Arrangements

of delivery must be clearly stated. These should include functionality, documentation, and so forth. Appropriate penalties should be outlined for any deviation from the contract.

If the customer has more control over the outsourcing vendor, then the development process itself can be more closely managed and thereby the quality of outcome is assured. This will take more effort on the part of the outsourcer than the effort required to control through outcome specification. However, it can help prevent the waste of time and money incurred when a project is belatedly found to be out of specifications and behind schedule. Project management techniques which help control budget and structure tasks can be implemented. Project milestones can be checked regularly to ensure that the project is progressing smoothly.

An added advantage of subsidiary or partnership arrangement is that the risk of intellectual property rights violation is minimized. It can be seen that the owned subsidiary arrangement gives the maximum amount of control over process. As opposed to this, the standard customer-vendor contract may only allow for control of outcome. Hence, depending on the strategic importance of systems being outsourced, and the rules and regulations of the vendor's home-base country, an appropriate contractual arrangement for dealing with the vendor may be chosen.

As the TI experience indicates, the need to manage multi-cultural teams is a reality facing managers of global outsourcing. The concept of culture has been extensively studied in the field of Anthropology (see Spradley and McCurdy, 1975). Following Hofstede (1986), we consider "organizational culture" as a holistic construct that describes the shared knowledge and knowledge structures which organizational members use to perform tasks and generate social behavior. Since the values, attitudes and behavior are different for people belonging to different cultures, the styles of leadership, decision making, organizing and controlling must be suitably tuned for managing multi-cultural teams.

Cultural diversity in a work group has both positive and negative implications for the productivity of a group. Multi-cultural groups have more potential for higher productivity than homogeneous groups, but they also bear the risk of greater losses due to faulty processes (Adler, 1986). As shown in Table 3, the task of a manager in dealing with global outsourcing is to encourage the factors that have positive impact, and mitigate those that have negative impact, on the productivity of a multi-cultural group.

TABLE 3. Advantages and Disadvantages of Cultural Diversity

Advantages	Disadvantages

Diversity Permits
Increased Creativity
- Wider range of perspectives
- More and better ideas
- Less "groupthink"
	Diversity Causes
	a Lack of Cohesion
	- Mistrust
	  - Lower interpersonal
	    attractiveness
	  - Stereotyping
	  - More within culture
	    conversations

Diversity Forces Enhanced
Concentration
- To understand others'
  - Ideas
  - Meanings
  - Arguments
	- Miscommunication
	  - Slower Speech
	    - Non-native speakers
	    - Translation problems
	  - Less accurate
	- Stress
	  - More counterproductive
	    behavior
	  - Less disagreement on content
	  - Tension

Increased Creativity Can *Lead To:* - Better problem definitions - More alternatives - Better solutions	*Lack of Cohesion Causes* *Inability To:* - Validate ideas and people - Agree when agreement is needed - Gain consensus on decisions - Take concerted action
Groups Can Become: - More effective - More productive	*Groups Can Become*: - Less efficient - Less effective - Less productive

Source: Adapted from Adler (1986).

5. Summary and Conclusions

Outsourcing of information systems functions has recently captured the imagination of information systems and corporate executives. Outsourcing has always been a solution to the problem of increasing capacity or lowering costs without undertaking additional fixed cost burden. The information systems executives, faced with significant cost containment pressures, see outsourcing as an important option as it allows them to better leverage their resources, manage their costs, and focus on core applications to increase IT's value to corporate objectives. This has given rise to a large and growing IS outsourcing industry in the U.S.

Several countries have large pools of IS professionals who are well-trained and whose salary expectations are significantly less than those of their U.S. counterparts. Vendors from these countries see outsourcing as a very lucrative target market for their IS services, and their pricing advantage has made global outsourcing a small but rapidly growing sector of the overall market.

Global outsourcing can lead to substantial benefits: significant cost savings and capital market gains, faster cycle time, help in developing and operating global information systems, and the access to foreign markets and skilled labor pool. These benefits have encouraged many companies to begin use of, or investigation into, the global outsourcing option. However, with advantages come certain pitfalls which await the unwary. Some of the main drawbacks are problems of communication and coordination, lack of control over quality and timetable, possible violation of intellectual property rights, and rules, regulations and infrastructure within the vendor's home country.

In managing the global outsourcing option the outsourcer is faced with three main issues: identifying the candidate activity for global outsourcing, choosing the right service provider, and finally creating the appropriate organizational arrangements. In determining if a given activity is suitable for global outsourcing, a manager should consider the following characteristics of an activity: information intensity, need for customer contact, its strategic importance, the relative efficiency with which the company can perform that activity, and if the activity is well-structured or specified. In choosing the service provider, a manager should consider the provider's track record, its resource level, and its staying power. The economic and political environment of the home-base country of the service provider is also very important. In arriving at the suitable organizational arrangement, a manager should consider the degree of control that is desired for the activity. To ensure better conformance to quality and timetable, and to ensure that intellectual property rights are not violated, the approach of creating a owned subsidiary is preferable. Finally, to ensure successful global outsourcing, attention needs to be paid to multi-cultural dimension of the organizational arrangement.

At a more general level, the national policy implications raised by the global outsourcing phenomenon are enormous (Metzger and von Glinow, 1988). The migration of back office jobs may mean that a typical entry level position is no longer available. Similarly, what happens to young people unqualified to secure a managerial position, if there exists only a few entry level jobs? The phenomenon also has implications for the education policy: what training in information technology related skills is necessary? These issues reflect a sense of adverse implications for the population of a developed economy such as the United States. But the same phenomenon of global outsourcing also represents an enormous opportunity for economic development through increased trade in information services for less developed countries such as Barbados, Ireland, India or Philippines. These and a range of strategic, social and ethical questions must be researched and addressed before the true potential of global outsourcing of information services can be properly harnessed.

References

Adler, N. J. (1986). *International Dimensions of Organizational Behavior* (Kent Publishing Company, Boston, MA).

Apte, U. M. (1991), "Global outsourcing of information systems and processing services," *The Information Society* 7, 287-303.

Apte, U. M., and R. O. Mason (1992a). "Global disaggregation of information intensive services," Working Paper, Cox School of Business, Southern Methodist University (Dallas, TX).

Apte, U. M., and R. O. Mason (1992b). "Texas Instruments (India) private limited," Working Paper, Cox School of Business, Southern Methodist University (Dallas, TX).

Bartlett, C. A., and S. Ghoshal (1989). *Managing Across Borders: The Transnational Solution* (Harvard Business School Press, Boston, MA).

Bell, D. (1973). *The Coming of Post-Industrial Society: A Venture in Social Forecasting* (Basic Books, New York, NY).

Chase, R. (1981). "The customer contact approach to services: Theoretical bases and practical extensions," *Operations Research* 21 (4), 698-705.

Clermont, P. (1991). "Outsourcing without guilt," *Computerworld* (September 9, 1991).

Gurbaxani, V., et. al., (1990). "Government as the driving force toward the information society: National computer policy in Singapore," *The Information Society* 7 (2), 59-73.

Hamilton, J. M. (1988). "Jobs at computer terminals link Philippines and US," *Christian Science Monitor* (August 8, 1988).

Hayes, R., and S. C. Wheelwright (1984). *Restoring Our Competitive Edge: Competing Through Manufacturing* (J. Wiley & Sons, New York, NY).

Hazarika, S. (1991). "In Southern India, a glimpse of Asia's high-tech future," *The New York Times* (October 6, 1991).

Hofstede, G. (1986). *Cultural Consequences: International Differences in Work Related Values* (Sage Publishing, Beverly Hills, CA).

Johnson, W. B. (1991). "Global work force 2000: The new world labor market," *Harvard Business Review* (March/April), 113-127.

Keen, P. G. W. (1986). *Competing in Time: Using Telecommunications for Competitive Advantage* (Ballinger, New York, NY).

Kleeper, R., and C. Hartog (1991). "Some determinants of MIS outsourcing behavior," Working Paper, MIS Department, Southern Illinois University (Edwardsville, IL).

Kling, R. (1990). "More information, better jobs?: Occupational stratification and labor-market segmentation in the United States' information labor force," *The Information Society* 7(2).

Linder, J., and B. Ives (1987). "Information intensity: A framework for competitive advantage," Unpublished Working Paper.

Lohr, S. (1988). "The growth of the global office," *The New York Times* (October 18, 1988).

McCusker, T. (1991). "There is life after outsourcing," *Datamation* (April 1, 1991).

McMullen, J. (1990). "New allies: IS and service suppliers," *Datamation* (March 1, 1990).

Machlup, F. (1980). *Knowledge: Its Creation, Distribution and Economic Significance,* vol. 1, *Knowledge and Knowledge Production* (Princeton University Press, Princeton, NJ).

Mead, T. (1990). "Will your job be outsourced?" *Datamation* (December 15, 1990).

Metzger, R.O., and M.A. von Glinow (1988). "Off-site workers: At home and abroad," *California Management Review* (Spring), 101-111.

Miles, R. E., and C. C. Snow (1986). "Organizations: New concepts for new forms," *California Management Review* XXVII(B) (Spring).

Nasar, S. (1991). "American revival is seen in U.S. report," *The New York Times* (February 5, 1991).

Noble, K. (1986). "America's service economy begins to blossom -- overseas," *The New York Times* (December 14, 1986).

Pollack, A. (1992). "Technology transcends borders, raising tough questions in U.S.," *The New York Times* (January 1, 1992).

Porat, M. V., and M. R. Rubin (1977). *The Information Economy,* 9 vols., U.S. Department of Commerce, Office of Telecommunications Special Publication 77-121(1-9), U.S. Government Printing Office (Washington, DC).

Porter, M., and V. Millar (1985). "How information gives you competitive advantage," *Harvard Business Review* (July-August).

Reich, R. B. (1991). *The Work of Nations* (Alfred A. Knopf Publishing, New York, NY).

Rifkin, G. (1991). "Heads that roll if computers fail", *The New York Times* (May 14, 1991).

Senn, J. (1991). "The emerging software passage to India," *SIM Network* VI(1) (January/February).

Shereff, R. (1989). "Creative clerical solutions: Service firms open up satellite global offices," *Management Review* (August).

Spradley, J. P., and D. M. McCurdy (1975). *Anthropology: The Cultural Perspective* (Wiley & Sons, New York, NY).

Stalk, G., Jr., and T. M. Hout (1990). *Competing Against Time: How Time-Based Competition is Reshaping Global Markets* (Free Press, New York, NY).

Thurow, L. (1991). Keynote address at ORSA/TIMS annual conference, Anaheim, CA.

Walker, G. (1985). "Strategic sourcing, vertical integration and transaction costs," *Interfaces* 18(3), 62-73.

Werner, M. (1986). "Transborder data flows: A cost benefit analysis," *Canadian Banker* 93(5).

Wilder, C. (1990). "Outsourcing: Fad or fantastic," *Computerworld* (January 1, 1990).

Williamson, O. E. (1985). *The Economic Institutions of Capitalism* (The Free Press, New York, NY).

Wysocki, B. (1991). "Overseas calling," *The Wall Street Journal* (August 14, 1991).

Chapter 7   The Office Farther Back: Business Services,
               Productivity, and the Offshore Back Office

Mark I. Wilson [1]

1. Introduction

Insurance in Ireland. Back offices in Barbados. Software in Seoul. The
routinization and mass production of services, combined with the spatial
flexibility afforded by communications, is changing the structure and location
pattern of the service economy. Basic paperwork and information processing is
increasingly performed away from corporate headquarters in North America and
Europe, and placed in low cost locations offshore. Back offices exemplify
several current characteristics of the service economy, such as growing
international trade, application of advanced technology to services production,
and the spatial separation of operations that comprise production networks.

Advanced communications serves as a vehicle for firms to access low cost
labor in the Caribbean, Asia, and Ireland for the production of back office
services. Back office services produced offshore are unique in that their location

[1] This research is funded, in part, by grants from the MSU Foundation and the
Institute for Public Policy and Social Research (MSU). The research assistance
of K.C. Chan and Daniel Koblin contributed to this paper, as did the excellent
field work in the Caribbean by Oumatie Marajh. The comments of two
anonymous referees were also useful in the revision of this chapter.

P. T. Harker (ed.), The Service Productivity and Quality Challenge, 203–224.
© 1995 Kluwer Academic Publishers. Printed in the Netherlands.

is determined not by a desire to serve markets overseas but for their ability to serve domestic demand at lower cost. Offshore offices offer considerable cost savings of one third to one half over domestic costs, with greater production flexibility due to less restrictive regulations and labor practices. The attractiveness to many firms of offshore production is further enhanced through public policy incentives offered by governments eager to generate employment and economic development.

Globalization of services is not a new phenomenon. American service firms have a long history serving foreign markets from both domestic and international locations. What is new, however, is the use of offshore locations to produce services that are inputs to domestic production. While offshore manufacturing is well documented, as is the international sale of services, there is little written about the economic and political determinants of the offshore location of producer services. Offshore production of back office services represents the use of advanced telecommunications to access low cost, primarily low wage,locations overseas with additional financial inducements offered by host governments to increase employment and development.

Back offices collect, manage, and process information as an intermediate input to the production of goods and services. Activities commonly undertaken by back offices include data entry and processing, database management, accounting and financial services, processing of magazine subscriptions and insurance claims, and computer software development. While back offices are frequently established to serve internal firm requirements for information, they are also designed to assemble and manage information that is sold to other firms. For example, McGraw-Hill uses a back office in Ireland to maintain its subscription database, while National Demographics uses its database services in Barbados to prepare market research information sold to clients. The growing importance of accurate and immediate information on firm operations and clients, and the sale of information as a commodity, has greatly increased demand for back office services. Simultaneously, firms report that the cost of producing back office services in the United States has increased due to labor shortages and the cost of wages and benefits. In addition, competitive pressures to innovate and control services costs in a range of industries, such as transportation and publishing, has led in some cases to the development of offshore back offices.

The benefits of offshore production for United States firms lie in two areas, cost and flexibility. Firms moving tasks offshore can save as much as 50% over domestic production, with average costs being at least one third less. Woodward (1990) analyzes international data entry costs by equating input costs to output of verified keystrokes. This approach takes into account differences in efficiency across locations, with some areas using low cost labor in labor intensive double entry systems (Asia),while more advanced locations use better educated workers to maintain efficiency (Ireland). Cost comparisons are presented in Table 1, showing lowest costs in China, the Philippines, and the Caribbean, contrasting costs of 50% to 100% more in Europe, United States, Canada, and Japan. It is not just the cost savings that attracts firms, however, as offshore locations also offer advantages in the organization of production.

Table 1. International Data Entry Costs

Country/Region	Price per 1000 Verified Keystrokes
Caribbean	$1.00 - 1.75
China	$0.90 - 1.25
Europe	$1.60 - 2.00
Philippines	$0.90 - 1.25
USA/Canada	$1.50 - 3.50
Japan	$1.50 - 3.50

Source: Woodward (1990)

Also important is the flexibility that offshore production affords, with offshore operations designed to take into account peaks and troughs in demand through employment practices, contracting out in slack periods, and use of domestic facilities in off peak hours. Flexible production has already been widely recognized in manufacturing, but only recently applied to services. Coffey and Bailly (1991) note characteristics of flexible production of producer services as externalization, spatial relocation, and the social division of labor; factors significant in the operations of offshore back offices. Moving services production offshore gains cost savings, the shifting of some risk to foreign governments that share set up costs, and less rigid labor and employment practices. The disadvantages include reduced actual or perceived control due to distance from domestic operations, potential for political and social disruption of production, and exchange rate fluctuations that create uncertainty about costs or erode cost savings. The costs and benefits of offshore production will be further evaluated in a later discussions of the implications this trend.

Offshore back offices are a dramatic example of the globalization of services production, and the ability of firms to control costs and gain flexibility through the reorganization of production. The shift offshore is a recent phenomenon, however, and while it is currently not substantial in terms of employment, it is an instructive example of how services production can become footloose. Domestic production remains the predominant source of data and information processing output in the United States. Data processing employs approximately 212,000 workers in 1992 at the industry level (SIC 7374), although many firms use in-house sources so this figure underestimates the employment for this task [Bureau of Labor Statistics (1992b)]. Occupation data for 1991 reveal greater employment levels for data processing, with over 750,000 computer equipment operators, 2.4 million financial records processors, and 4.4 million secretaries in the United States [BLS (1992a)]. In comparison, offshore back office employment for the United States market does not exceed 35,000 workers. The importance of studying the development of offshore offices lies not in its present scale but in its suggestion of the future organization and globalization of services production.

This chapter concentrates on United States based firms and their offshore subsidiaries and suppliers to illustrate the factors influencing the production of offshore back office services. The chapter continues by describing the character of offshore back offices, followed by discussion of production and location factors. Offshore operations are determined primarily by the economic, political, and social environment surrounding three factors: 1) communications and transportation; 2) labor markets; and 3) public policy, with secondary influences being corporate culture, political stability, and foreign exchange fluctuations. The role of each location factor in the offshore production of services is illustrated using evidence collected through surveys and a series of interviews with US firms having offshore data and information processing operations in Asia, the Caribbean, and Ireland. The discussion is supported by information gathered from interviews with public officials attracting offshore back offices to Ireland, Barbados, and Jamaica. Following analysis of production determinants is a discussion of the implications of this spatial reorganization of services production.[2]

---

[2] Additional information on offshore office development can be found in Wilson (1992a), with case studies of Ireland and the Caribbean in working papers by Wilson and Bagchi-Sen (1990) and Wilson (1992b) respectively.

2. Offshore Operations

Firms in many countries utilize offshore back offices for service inputs, for example, British firms utilize the Caribbean back office for basic clerical tasks, while Australian organizations use Asian sources for publishing and printing services. While widespread, much back office work tends to be occasional and for major projects, such as data entry for a library card catalogue. The leading consumers of back office services, and developers of the most sophisticated form of back offices, tend to be American multinational firms. The United States leads in this industry for several reasons, including the scale of its economy, access to low cost communications, and its lack of restrictions on trade and information flows. Many European countries place significant restrictions on transborder data flows and have expensive communications charges from state owned telecommunications suppliers.

Offshore back offices are organized in two ways, as local firms overseas operating under contract to US based businesses, or subsidiaries of multinational firms. Historically, offshore offices started during the 1970s when US firms sent occasional batch work to the Caribbean for processing. This was a time consuming method as documents were transported by sea, with a two week journey in each direction. The industry remained quite small until the early 1980s when advances in communications and transportation overcame the cost and time limitations to offshore clerical work and information processing. The industry initially relied on local office services in the Caribbean and Asia to develop working relationships with US firms, but this was expensive due to the information costs associated with finding offshore suppliers, and management problems of long distance production systems. Offshore management difficulties later provided a niche for US based agencies to link domestic consumers to offshore producers.

Agencies are a response to the information and organizational costs of establishing a contract offshore back office. Lack of knowledge about offshore operators, the potential for delays and errors, and misunderstandings about terms and conditions slowed the growth of contract offices. Agencies are able to avoid most of these problems by establishing working relationships with a number of offshore facilities to handle a range of data and information processing needs. Agencies contract directly with firms for office tasks and then subcontract work to a range of offshore producers throughout the Caribbean and Asia. The unconnected back offices of the 1970s are now frequently associated through agencies to provide consistent services to the North American and European markets. Contract back offices are found primarily in Asia (India, Philippines, Korea, and China) and the Caribbean (Jamaica).

More recently, back offices emerged as direct subsidiaries of multinational firms, primarily American, but also some European and Canadian firms. Corporations establish offshore offices that tend to be totally dedicated to serving internal requirements for office services, although excess capacity is often sold to other firms. These facilities are usually fully integrated into firm operations in terms of both organization, and constant communication and computer connection. In many cases, offshore back offices are indistinguishable from domestic operations in terms of process and real time access. American firms most likely to establish offshore back offices tend to be in profit squeezed industries such as insurance, aviation, publishing, market research, and financial services. Offshore offices of US firms tend to be concentrated in Barbados, Jamaica, Dominican Republic, the Philippines, and Ireland. The preceding chapter by Apte and Mason offers a detailed analysis of the decision making process to outsource production.

Employment in offshore back offices mirrors domestic operations with most workers being young and female. These workers are expected to average 7,000-11,000 keystrokes per hour with high levels of accuracy. Female workers predominate for several reasons, including the need for keyboard skills that males are less likely to obtain; the location of back offices in relatively isolated areas with limited employment opportunities for women, such as small towns and suburbs; and the preference for less costly part-time and temporary workers, with firms able to benefit from the work limitations that family responsibilities often create.[3] Both domestically and offshore, firms seek locations with an over supply of female workers to guarantee a workforce without cost pressures on wages.

The size of back offices varies, with offshore subsidiaries larger than local operations, having 50 to 500 workers compared to less than 50 workers in many locally owned and operated facilities. The subsidiaries tend to be more formal in operation with full-time permanent positions, although excess capacity is met using temporary and part-time workers. Local operations offshore are less structured and more dependent on flexible employment, primarily because they

---

[3] The relationship between women and technology in female oriented clerical tasks shapes the production and, therefore, the location of these types of economic activity; for example, Andolsen (1989), Carter (1987), Lowe (1987), and Barker and Downing (1985).

operate by contract and do not have the guarantees of constant work held by subsidiaries. It is difficult to estimate the global scale of offshore offices due to the informal structure of many of the contract operations. General estimates emerging from field research show over 100 back office operations in the Caribbean (7,000-10,000 workers) and over a dozen in Ireland (2,000-3,000 workers). Data on back offices in Asia are particularly difficult to obtain, with an estimate of 10,000-20,000 workers based on the number of US firms using Asian operations.

The operation of offshore back offices is similar for most firms in the industry. Materials, usually in the form of documents or magnetic tapes, are sent by air from the United States, Canada, and Europe to processing facilities offshore. Processing usually takes the form of data entry, statistical analysis, or information processing that involves decision making by trained employees. After processing, results are returned to originating data processing locations by courier, air freight, dedicated line, satellite, or telephone/modem. The turnaround time for offshore offices varies from several days to weeks, depending on the urgency of the work. Security or time sensitive material continues to be processed domestically, but many of the fully integrated subsidiaries can process documents as quickly as a domestic facility. The operational scale of offshore back offices is substantial:

New York Life insurance clients mail a health insurance claim form to Kennedy Airport in New York. The claim is sent overnight to Shannon (Ireland) airport and then by courier to the NYLERIN processing center in Castleisland, which is approximately 60 miles (100km) south west of the airport. After processing, the claim is returned by dedicated line to the firm's data processing center in New Jersey, and a check or response mailed to the client.

American Airlines assembles accounting material and ticket coupons in Dallas for transport on its own scheduled flights to Barbados for processing by its offshore subsidiary AMRIS (AMR Information Services/Caribbean Data Services). In Barbados, details of 800,000 American Airlines tickets are entered daily on a computer system and the data returned by satellite to its data center in Tulsa.

Data entry for the white pages telephone directory for Montreal was handled on a contract basis in Asia using labor intensive double entry with two workers entering data and then checking for errors by electronic comparison of files.

3. Services, Specialization, and Location

Back office services are labor intensive and increasingly technology intensive inputs to the production of many goods and services. Enhanced productivity and cost savings are derived in two ways, from changing the ways that the service is produced, and from relocation or outsourcing to less costly areas. Service tasks are simplified and made routine so that less skilled and costly labor can be used or the process becomes a candidate for automation. The routinization of service production often allows previously bundled operations to be broken into simpler functions. Instead of needing workers with a range of abilities to work on multiple purpose tasks, simplification establishes mass production of services with each worker focussing on one specific task. The unbundling of tasks also means that functions historically carried out in one place or division can be moved elsewhere. One incentive to simplify and rationalize services production is the ability to use communications technology to relocate activities away from head office or downtown to less costly suburbs, small towns, or offshore.

Location theory assumes that firms are structured to maximize profits in terms of both production and location, which takes into account production costs as well as market access and pricing.[4] The cost of inputs frequently varies spatially, which in turn influences the location of production. Changes to the organization of production that require different types and levels of inputs may also dictate a change in location. For overall firm operations location is addressed in terms of profit maximization, but the location of intermediate inputs tends to be seen from the cost side alone. The concern for the firm is the least cost source of intermediate services, such as back office activities, and their delivery to production centers. Least-cost location theory has been attacked for its abstraction and limitations due to its assumption of delivery of inputs to one point in space. For intermediate services, however, this constraint need not apply, as data and information processing inputs are delivered through communications and computer networks to one point in space - the firm's

---

[4] Common to location theory as detailed by Isard (1968) and Smith (1981) is the central motivation of the firm to maximize profit, minimize costs, or maximize market area. Offshore back offices seek to minimize costs to serve internal demand within the firm.

computer system. The ability to deliver all production to one point frees firms to produce or purchase inputs at the least-cost location, which communications allows to be as much abroad as in the United States.

The location of back office functions also represents two observations on recent trends in location noted by Storper and Walker (1989). First, that location theory assumes a passive firm choosing from a set of pre-existing conditions when, in fact, firms are increasingly able to demand concessions from government or parallel location by suppliers. The economic power of many factories and facilities allows the creation of advantageous economic space where none existed before. While parallel location by suppliers is unlikely for back office functions, back offices offshore often are able to extract valuable concessions from governments eager for the many entry level jobs they provide.

The second observation is the significance of the social division of labor as a way for firms to obtain economic advantage. Location theory has long seen labor as wages or costs alone, but additional factors of growing importance are the flexibility of the workforce and its acceptance of the rewriting of social contracts. The heterogeneity of workers' ability makes supervision and management essential to quality control for many back office services. One way control of work and wages is gained is through unpopular and disruptive restructuring of wages or defiance of strikes, but this result can also be achieved by relocation to areas with fewer restrictions on labor practices. This trend can be seen by the popularity among employers of right to work states, and locations with low rates of unionization and peaceful industrial relations. The flexible production manufacturing has achieved through capital intensive systems is harder to achieve for labor intensive services. Despite limitations, back offices are showing some hallmarks of flexibility such as the shifting of risk away from firms and preferences for unregulated or minimally regulated labor markets.

Until recently, spatial restructuring of services presented two spatial dimensions: suburbanization and decentralization. Firms commonly relocate back offices to suburban areas using communications to link with management and planning functions maintained in more costly central locations [Daniels (1987), Marshall (1988)]. Suburban locations offer access to less costly and often better educated part-time workers with greater productivity for repetitive tasks [Metzger and Von Glinow (1988), Nelson (1986), Baran (1985)]. At the national level, firms also use communications to produce services at low cost locations, such as airline and hotel reservation services. Warf (1989) provides the example of American Express, which reduced costs by relocating its credit card processing facilities to Florida and Arizona from New York, and Posthuma's (1987) example of Citibank's shift of data processing activities from New York to South Dakota. Metropolitan Life Insurance, which has an offshore facility in Ireland, also has data processing centers in Greenville SC, Scranton PA, and Wichita KS [Moss and Dunau (1987)]. These cases emphasize the ability of firms to divorce back office service functions from other firm activities, and relocation to utilize nonunionized and often temporary or part-time workers. [5]

The third dimension of back office production is the shift offshore, continuing the spatial decentralization of services already evident for suburbs and regions in the United States. Analysis of offshore back offices shows three sets of factors as primary location determinants: communications and transportation; labor requirements; and public policy. Firms routinize production to use less skilled labor and further minimize costs by using communications to access less expensive offshore workers. An additional incentive to relocate offshore comes from host nations with public policy designed to reduce local production costs for foreign firms. Each of these influences will be discussed in turn.

4. Communications: Erasing the Friction of Distance

Offshore back offices rely on both aviation and telecommunications in order to function. Documents are sent by air cargo and express delivery services, causing Kuzela (1987) to term these back offices "air intensive" data entry. Finished material is returned by air, or increasingly, electronically. The sophistication and relatively low cost of telecommunications allows firms to connect operations in many locations and countries without a significant financial impact. The primary factor in the establishment of offshore back offices is that international transport and communications costs are now sufficiently low to make access to low cost labor abroad competitive with domestic operations. Posthuma (1987) shows the annual real cost of a telephone circuit moving from $22,000 in 1965, to $800 in 1980, and $30 in 1985, with transmission capacity by satellite up to 6.3 million bits per second. Many back office operations find that their communications costs are less than 5% of total operating costs. The key issue for back offices is not the cost of communications but access to high quality infrastructure. Telephone, satellite, and data transfer systems that encouraged spatial restructuring in the United States are now sufficiently advanced in many countries to support the cost effective international transmission of material. Rather than one factor, it is the transport and

---

[5] For a discussion of the domestic back office location and public policy issues see Glasmeier and Borchard (1989) and Dickstein (1991).

communications infrastructure as a whole that allows offshore services to operate.

Heavy investments in communications technology by many Caribbean and Asian nations and Ireland has produced sophisticated systems that rival those in advanced economies. Barbados has a digitalized communications system offering direct international dialling for telephone/fax and satellite based high speed data transmission capacity. Barbados External Telecommunications provides leased lines to North America at 56Kbps and to Europe at 64Kbps, and capacity up to 2Mbps also available. Jamaica is expanding its communications capacity through digitalized systems, while the Jamaica Digiport earth station in Montego Bay has capacity of 20,000 lines and transmission speeds of 56Kbps to 1.5Mbps that allow both real time and batch processing by back offices. The implications for back offices are evident from the way Jamaica Digiport views itself, as an extension of AT&T's domestic American network. Ireland's decision in the early 1980s to upgrade telecommunications to international standards made possible the back office development that followed. Ireland offers 64kpbs and 2 Mbps trans Atlantic private circuits as well as a domestic special data services network. Telecom Ireland has further recognized the importance of global business demand with the 1991 opening of a US office to serve American users of its system.

Another consideration for the location of back offices is the efficiency of interaction between offshore location and firm headquarters and offices, with time zones being commonly noted. Operations in the Caribbean are not affected because they share North American time zones. Firms in Ireland are occasionally inconvenienced by the five hour advance on their primary facilities on US eastern time, but a number of firms see this as an advantage as it allows them access to US computer facilities at off-peak times, enabling increased utilization and reduced computer costs.

5. Labor: Wages, Benefits, and Culture

The primary motivation for offshore relocation or outsourcing is access to low cost labor. Labor cost for office work is not wages alone, but a variety of other factors that influence worker productivity and employer expenses. In addition to wages, labor costs are affected by productivity and worker turnover, worker availability, benefit packages, occupational safety and health considerations, and cultural and social influences. Labor intensive office work in the United States faces wage and cost pressures from declining numbers of young workers and increasing insurance and benefit costs that are not evident in many offshore locations. The resulting high wages and expectations of future wage growth has made low cost labor the central issue for back office operations.

United States' firms pay wages of $7-10 per hour plus benefits for basic office and information processing work. In addition to these costs, firms face high rates of worker turnover due to the repetitive nature of routinized office work and the availability of more attractive opportunities in many regions of the country. Firms are increasingly finding that they cannot attract workers at prevailing wage rates. One of the primary motivations for the establishment of a subsidiary of American Airlines to process data in Barbados was the shortage of labor in Tulsa, its information processing center. Offshore offices are attracted to countries with well trained and educated workers, and high levels of population growth and unemployment, such as Ireland and Jamaica, which can equal the skill needs for back office work without the supply constraints of the US workforce.

Another labor consideration is the growing impact on US costs and benefits of repetitive motion injuries. In addition to increased insurance premiums for workers, firms also face the need to consider the occupational safety of their employees internally or through regulation. Recent legislation to regulate use of workplace video display terminals in San Francisco improves the quality of work life for employees but also increases production costs. Firms must provide additional lighting and adjustable furniture as well as provide 15 minute breaks after two hours work on a terminal [Pollack 1990]. US employers are concerned about labor shortages and escalating costs, and anticipating additional expenses as improved health conditions are required for the workplace.

By locating back offices offshore firms can avoid paying health benefits or pay far less than in the US. In Ireland, occupational safety regulations for back office work is similar to the US, although less stringent than legislation pending in a number of cities and states. In addition, Irish workers pay for a national health system through taxation on their income, rather than through insurance paid by their employers. In Barbados and Jamaica, the cost of health insurance contributions is far lower than in the costly medical environment of the United States. The move offshore allows firms to employ workers with a lower benefit package cost in the Caribbean, or shift responsibility for benefits from the firm to the worker, as in Ireland.

Offshore wages, productivity, and work practices lead to labor costs of one-half to two thirds of the US rate. Labor cost and quality offshore vary with location. Ireland's labor market is cited by most firms operating there as the main reason for their Irish operations, with well educated workers and wages over one-third lower than in the United States. Workers are well educated and trained, so that school leavers can be employed for work that in the US is usually carried out by those with some post-secondary training. In several locations, firms rely on schools and vocational training centers to guarantee availability of trained workers. Firms carefully place facilities within Ireland to maintain low labor costs by locating in small towns with limited employment opportunities and high levels of unemployment: in Castleisland, New York Life received 600 applications for its first 25 positions. Back offices become major employers of high school leavers without competing with similar firms, thereby reducing pressures on wages and affording influence in local labor markets.

In the Caribbean, Barbados has relatively more skilled workers and higher wages than other islands, such as Jamaica. Data entry workers in Barbados earn US$2-3 per hour, with trainees earning less (US$1.50 per hour), and supervisors more (US$4-6). In addition, employers must share with the employee the cost of the National Insurance and Social Security Scheme to cover pensions, sickness, invalidity, maternity, and unemployment benefits. Pressures on wages in Barbados are low due to high rates of unemployment (10-20%) in a highly literate workforce. Workers have the right to unionize, but there are no unions in back offices as the data processing industry actively discourages unionization. Posthuma (1987) reports that one firm used the threat of relocation to another low wage Caribbean nation to prevent unionization.

Jamaican wages are lower than in Barbados, often with less formal employment arrangements. Wages range from 50 cents to $1 per hour with benefits of uniform, lunch, and transport allowances costing 30-50% of the base wage. The industry in Jamaica relies on female high school graduates, many of whom receive data processing training in schools through the Human Employment and Resources Training (HEART) program. The availability of trained workers and unemployment rates of up to 25%, with even higher rates for women [Bourne (1988)], exert downward pressure on wages for most industries in Jamaica. Anderson and Gordon (1989) find that the prime age cohort (25-39 years) has the best employment opportunities in Jamaica, with younger workers likely to find only secondary or informal jobs. It is this younger population that is often found in contract back office work. The informal organization of much of the industry in Jamaica produces a labor market providing new entrants with limited security or advancement. Despite these conditions, deteriorating economic circumstances maintain labor supplies for back office work.

Asian data entry operations commonly quote wage rates of $1-2 per hour. In these countries the benefits available to workers are considerably reduced in comparison to the United States, with few benefits and no unionization. Asian data entry focuses on basic tasks with language no barrier for numerical material. One firm even noted that data entry of text was better if workers did not know English as workers were not distracted by the content of their work. Back offices tend to be found in major cities with inexpensive labor and good communications and transportation service, such as Manila, Madras, and Seoul. Unlike Caribbean and Irish back offices, operations in China and the Philippines have been disrupted by political instability. With many competing offshore locations, these two countries face significant problems in the re-establishment of confidence in their back office functions.

Common to offshore back offices is their location in labor markets where cultural and social attitudes to work and its organization are different to conditions in the United States. For example, back offices are placed in high unemployment areas with few alternative sources of employment, conferring both employment opportunity and labor market power on employers. In many locations, family ties mean that workers are reluctant to leave to find permanent work and are willing to accept relatively low wages in order to remain near their family and community. Locations in nonmetropolitan areas often also carry lower living costs, resulting in lower wages than urban areas. These forces are evident in western Ireland, where few urban centers and high rates of unemployment often mean the only opportunities available for young workers are in Dublin, Britain and the European Community, or the United States. In this environment, back office firms find strong local support and an eager supply of well trained workers.

Local attitudes to work are important factors for the location of back offices offshore. Firms often noted the desirability of workers with a "positive" approach, which can be interpreted widely from loyalty to subservience. In Ireland, FAS (Industrial Training Authority) is concerned to instill in workers a positive attitude to employment and then work with firms and schools to develop specific skills rather than general education. Several back offices in Jamaica were concerned about the preparation and attitudes to work of their employees. Another dimension of the role of culture emerges in Furnham's (1991) study of the Protestant Work Ethic (PWE) in Barbados, finding that PWE tends to be higher for females than males, and that adolescents tended to have higher PWE scores than similar groups in more advanced countries. In Barbados, back office work carries a higher status than it would in the US as it is seen as desirable work with computers in air conditioned surroundings, hallmarks of high status employment. Offshore locations are frequently sought because their societies represent different interpretations of work that rewrite the social contract by US standards.

Having noted the greater flexibility and market power possible in offshore offices it is important to state that many locations have benefitted from the employment generated by offshore offices. In some areas hundreds of entry level jobs have been created that, while low paid, offer greater security than previously possible. The generally positive employment experiences of Ireland and Barbados, however, are balanced by concern for worker exploitation in Jamaica. Antrobus (1989) cites poor working practices and anti-union pressures as the basis for exploitation of primarily female labor in Jamaica. Despite the rhetoric on both sides of such development debates it is important to remember that back offices are relatively mobile and willing to find new areas if economic conditions are attractive. It is instructive that when Caribbean Data Services expanded operations it chose not to enlarge its Barbados facility but to establish a second operation in the Dominican Republic where wages were half the rate in Barbados.

6. Public Policy: Entrepreneurial Islands

Public policy influences production costs to attract offshore services that contribute to local employment and economic growth. Over the past decade, poor and deteriorating economic conditions for most Caribbean nations and slow growth in Ireland made active employment policies essential for government. The desirability of labor intensive service employment has led to strong government support for this activity, even to the point where attraction costs may equal or exceed benefits. Offshore offices are able to benefit from the financial incentives offered by foreign government, and often able to share risk by using government owned facilities or through partnerships. The costs and risks associated with a back office are partially shifted from the firm to the taxpayers in the host country. Public policy designed specifically for back office development is most advanced in Ireland and the Caribbean, particularly Jamaica and Barbados.

Ireland's economic development oriented policies provide overseas firms with financial, labor, and location benefits. Offshore back office operations pay corporate taxes at a rate of up to 10% compared to the standard rate of 43%; a benefit recently extended from 2000 to 2010. Corporate tax abatements are used to attract firms to Ireland, while differentials in local taxes are used to influence internal location to areas most in need, usually counties outside Dublin.

Remission of taxes by local authorities in designated areas can reach two-thirds for up to ten years, depending on local needs for development. Firms are also able to easily repatriate profits, and face few restrictions on capital flows. Training funds are also provided, with one firm received 3200 pounds per employee in training grants. The Irish government prefers firms to bring training programs and instructors from the US to Ireland, but will also pay for Irish employees to train in the United States. Assistance is also offered for construction of facilities, and the purchase of computers, office equipment and furniture. European Community rules allow Ireland to offer more benefits than competing locations due to its need for development and to overcome its peripheral location in Europe. For example, Ireland can offer grants of up to 75% of a new investment while potential competitor, Scotland, can offer only up to 40%.

Barbados offers low tax rates to offshore service firms, with no withholding tax on dividends, interest, and royalties. Firms pay income tax at the rate of 2.5%, are exempt from exchange controls and import duties, and do not require any licensing or local incorporation in order to operate. In addition to fiscal incentives, the Barbados Industrial Development Corporation actively seeks relocating firms, and offers established offices and industrial estates at advantageous rents. Back offices are recognized as desirable policy targets with services included in development oriented legislation over the past decade.

Jamaica also encourages offshore development, principally through incentives and the establishment of free trade zones. Firms locating in free trade zones must operate for export and not local trade, and transact all business in US dollars. While originally oriented to manufacturing, the zones also legally recognize services such as banking, insurance, and professional services. Approved firms receive 100% holiday on taxation of profits, in perpetuity, compared to the normal rate of 33.5%, as well as repatriation of profits and duty free importation of equipment. Pantin (1990) traces financial incentives to government schemes in the 1950s, which were often designed for all firms, but International Monetary Fund pressure for budget austerity during the 1980s meant that financial benefits now are often only available to foreign firms. One concern among Jamaican firms is that foreign facilities receive more benefits than local entrepreneur because of external pressure to expand exports industries.

Another dimension of the policy issue is the longevity of attracted firms, as offshore office investments tend to be relatively small, and certainly more mobile than manufacturing capital. Offshore offices can consist of rented space with highly portable personal computers as the major capital asset: a form of investment that can be easily moved to another location should conditions change. Only Ireland's industrial policy has clawback language to require the return of funds if firms do not deliver the scale of operation promised, although to date this option has not been exercised.

The attraction of basic service employment is appealing to many governments, especially those facing high rates of unemployment and slow rates of growth. While public policy is commonly used to attract firms it is important to note that the large number of potential sites for offshore offices means that many countries could be competing with each other to attract firms. In fact, the International Monetary Fund is actively encouraging Caribbean nations to develop their services exports through incentives to foreign firms. This produces the potential for strong competition for offshore offices by many countries, which erodes the net benefit to the successful location. The desirability of service employment is often gained only through the expenditure of taxpayer revenue on enhanced infrastructure and forgone tax revenue on back office operations. Such policies represent a shift of resources from local workers to foreign firms, which, in moderation can greatly assist an economy, but when excessive can be costly and inequitable.

7 . Other Factors: Corporate Culture, Political Environment, and Exchange Rates

The existence of a global system that allows offshore back offices to develop and expand does not automatically mean that this option will be exercised by all firms. That firms are able to shift some operations offshore does not mean that all will. So far, attention has focussed on the firms that have developed offshore offices, but a number of factors may inhibit this phenomenon. The economic ability to relocate may not overcome the social and political forces that influence offshore relocation, such as corporate culture; political environment; and international financial conditions.

Firms may not develop offshore facilities because of cultural aspects affecting corporate decision making. Perceptions of risks and benefits vary among firms, with some organizations preferring not to entertain the potential costs of a failed offshore operation. The information problems that led to the growth of intermediaries for back office work also apply to firms. It is instructive that the first firms to locate facilities in Ireland did so because of the actions of executives with considerable local knowledge; once several insurance firms established operations the uncertainty about such a move was reduced and other firms followed. Firms also may be concerned about long distance management of offshore facilities, and prefer local operations that allow frequent face to face contact with back office managers. The need to maintain the security of back office work also led some firms to keep operations in the United States rather than make the move offshore.

One factor that many firms cite as important is the political stability of countries housing their back office functions. Moving operations offshore immediately introduces the possible disruption of services due to political and social upheaval in the host country. The countries commonly housing multinational back offices are recognized for their political stability, such as Ireland, Barbados, and Jamaica. A number of firms found their operations in China and the Philippines disrupted during the 1980s, and this experience has sensitized the industry to the potential problems associated with offshore locations facing political and social problems. The changing political and social environments in Eastern Europe, Caribbean nations such as Trinidad and Haiti, and India and Korea, mean that these potentially desirable locations for back office work may not be sought out until domestic conditions offer some guarantees for future stability.

Another dimension of the political environment is domestic policy in the United States. US policy supporting free trade and transborder data flows allows the US to be the leading source of offshore back office trade, while the Caribbean may be an even more desirable location if included in the North American Free Trade Agreement. But policy may also limit offshore relocation. If political leadership condemns US firms moving production abroad, or limits movement through policy measures, the offshore option will be less attractive. Cushman (1992) notes that the Clinton administration may influence firm behavior by removing tax benefits for firms that move production offshore. At this stage, specific industrial policies have not been identified by the Clinton administration.

The financial determinants of offshore production are subject to exchange rate fluctuations, with unstable currencies offering little support for long term arrangements. Fluctuations may not affect local firms as much as multinationals as they can focus on short term contracts in US dollar denominated amounts. US firms with offshore investments must carry their investment when exchange rates deteriorate for the United States, and offshore production costs increase. Fluctuating exchange rates add instability to calculations of costs and pricing. Even when the fluctuations are downward, as in the case of the Jamaican dollar in 1990-2, there is the price of uncertainty about costs to consider. Even more problematic is the appreciation of the currency of the offshore host, which is the case for Ireland. The increasing value of the Irish pound, and fluctuations associated with its membership in the European Monetary System have reduced the cost savings possible for US firms with established back offices in Ireland. Wide ranging fluctuations in exchange rates for potential offshore sites increases the risk associated with that location and reduces the potential savings from offshore production.

Offshore back offices are a new trend in the production of services that illustrate the ability to use communications to access low cost labor overseas to produce intermediate inputs to the production of domestic goods and services. While currently a small and relatively specialized phenomenon, offshore offices are instructive because they indicate the potential future for services as a global production system. Offshore back offices connect to many issues not directly addressed here due to space limitations, such as trade in services and the international political environment for GATT discussions; international competition in the communications industry; the threat of importation of offshore work practices to gain concessions from workers; and regulatory issues associated with transborder data flows and the legal state of information as a commodity. The themes that have emerged as significant in this analysis reflect the location determinants of services; the social division of labor and the use of location to obtain a favorable contract between employer and employee; the role of the state as a force in location decisions; and the potential for international competition among countries for back office facilities.

The future potential for offshore offices is not yet clear. On one hand, technological advances can erase many of the tasks now carried out overseas. Some tasks initially undertaken offshore have returned to the United States for more efficient electronic processing. For example, Mead Data Central no longer processes documents in Asia for its on-line data bases as it relies on tapes purchased directly from newspapers and printers. Within a decade, technological advances in scanning equipment may make unnecessary many basic data entry tasks. On the other hand, Ireland represents the most advanced form of offshore office, with more than just routine data entry. Information processing for the insurance industry requires educated workers with decision making functions, which suggests that even more advanced tasks can be performed offshore, such as legal and financial services. Perhaps the most important lesson for services from analysis of offshore back offices is that they may have the same potential as manufacturing for production internationalization, and the structural, spatial, and social change experienced as a result.

References

Anderson, P., and Gordon, D. (1989). "Labor and mobility patterns - the impact of the crisis," in *Development in Suspense,* ed. P. Anderson (Association of Caribbean Economists, Kingston), 174-196.

Andolsen, B.H. (1989). *Good Work at the Video Display Terminal* (University of Tennessee Press, Knoxville, TN).

Antrobus, P. (1989). "Gender implications of the development crisis," in *Development in Suspense*, ed. P. Anderson (Association of Caribbean Economists, Kingston), 145-160.

Baran, B. (1985). "The technological transformation of white-collar work: a case study of the insurance industry," in H.I. Hartmann, R.E. Kraut, and L.A. Tilly (eds.), *Computer Chips and Paper Clips* (National Academy Press, Washington, DC).

Barker, J., and H. Downing (1985). "Word-processing and the transformation of patriarchal relations of control in the office," in D. MacKenzie and J. Wajcman (eds.), *The Social Shaping of Technology* (Open University, Milton Keynes, UK).

Bourne, C. (1988). *Caribbean Development to the Year 2000* (Commonwealth Secretariat/Caribbean Community Secretariat, London/Georgetown).

Carter, V. (1987). "Office technology and relations of control in clerical work organization," in *Women, Work, and Technology: Transformations* ed. B.D. Wright (University of Michigan Press, Ann Arbor, MI).

Coffey, W., and A. Bailly (1991). "Producer services and flexible production: an exploratory analysis," *Growth and Change* 22(4), 95-117.

Cushman, J.H., Jr. (1992). "Tax breaks ahead, but how big and for whom" *The New York Times* (December 14, 1992), C1.

Daniels, P.W. (1987). "Technology and metropolitan office location," *Service Industries Journal* 7, 274-291.

Dickstein, C. (1991). *Offshore Competition for Back Offices: Policy Implications for Promotion of Back Offices in West Virginia,* Report to the Institute for Public Affairs, West Virginia University.

Downes, A.S. (1991). "Economic growth and stabilization in Barbados," *Datapac* 11(2), 11-17.

Furnham, A. (1991). "The Protestant Work Ethic in Barbados" *Journal of Social Psychology* 131(1), 29-43.

Glasmeier, A., and G. Borchard (1989). "From branch plants to back offices: prospects for rural services growth" *Environment and Planning A* 21(12), 1565-1583.

Isard, W. (1968). *Location and Space Economy* (MIT Press, Cambridge).

Kuzela, L. (1987). "New Jamaican teleport to serve US business" *Industry Week* (October).

Lowe, G.S. (1987). *Women in the Administrative Revolution: The Feminization of Clerical Work* (University of Toronto Press, Toronto).

Marshall, J.N. (1988). *Services and Uneven Development* (Oxford University Press, Oxford, UK).

Massey, D. (1984). *Spatial Dimensions of Labor* (Methuen, New York, NY).

Metzger, R.O., and M. Von Glinow (1988). "Offsite workers: at home and abroad" *California Management Review* 30(3), 101-111.

Moss, M.L., and A. Dunau (1987). "Will the cities lose their back offices?" *Real Estate Review* 17(1), 62-68.

Nelson, K. (1986). "Labor demand, labor supply, and the suburbanization of low wage office work," in *Production, Work, Territory* eds. A.J. Scott and M. Storper (Allen & Unwin, Boston, MA).

Pantin, D.A. (1990). "Prospects for the FDI export model in Jamaica and the Caribbean," *Latin American Perspectives* 17(1), 55-72.

Pollack, A. (1990). "Board in San Francisco passes VDT ordinance," *New York Times* (December 18, 1990), A18.

Postuma, A. (1987). *The Internationalization of Clerical Work: A Study of Offshore Office Services in the Caribbean* Science Policy Research Unit Paper 24. University of Sussex (Brighton, UK).

Smith, D. (1981). *Industrial Location: An Economic Geographical Analysis* (Wiley, New York, NY).

Storper, M. and R. Walker, (1989). *The Capitalist Imperative* (Basil Blackwell, New York, NY).

U.S. Bureau of Labor Statistics (1992a). *Employment and Earnings* 39(1), Table 20.

U.S. Bureau of Labor Statistics (1992b) *Employment and Earnings* 39(4), Table B2.

Warf, B. (1989) "Telecommunications and the globalization of financial services," *Professional Geographer* 41(3), 257-271.

Wilson, M. (1992a). "Spatial and structural change in the production of services: the offshore back office," paper, Institute for Public Policy and Social Research, Michigan State University, East Lansing, MI.

Wilson, M. (1992b). "Office politics: the political economy of the Caribbean back office," paper presented at conference, the Association of American Geographers, San Diego, CA.

Wilson, M. and S. Bagchi-Sen (1990). "The determinants and consequences of the offshore location of services," paper presented at conference, Regional Science Association, Boston, MA.

Woodward, P. (1990). "Getting a start in data entry," *China Business Review* (January/February), 20-23.

Chapter 8   The Economics of Customer Lock-In and Market Power in Services

Severin Borenstein, Jeffrey K. MacKie-Mason and Janet S. Netz[1]

1.   Introduction

Many service businesses provide aftermarket services, which may include parts, maintenance, consulting, upgrades and modifications to durable consumer and business equipment. A diverse group of products, such as dishwashers, automobiles, and highly complex electronic equipment (computers, telephone switches, medical imaging devices, etc.), spawn service markets. Typically, the first firm offering service to owners of durable equipment is the original equipment manufacturer (OEM) itself; after all, it already has parts and expertise. Often, the *only* service provider is the manufacturer. The broad question in this paper is the effect on the manufacturer and on consumers if a manufacturer is the only service provider for equipment it sells.

For a manufacturer the benefits of a monopoly over service are obvious. However, the manager must compare these benefits to the costs of maintaining the monopoly, which may be quite high. After any initial advantages have diminished, the manufacturer may have to invest in further entry barriers. Alternatively, the costs of monopoly may be felt in declining market share for

---

[1]MacKie-Mason has testified as an expert witness for the plaintiffs in some of the cases cited below.

P. T. Harker (ed.), The Service Productivity and Quality Challenge, 225–250.
© *1995 Kluwer Academic Publishers. Printed in the Netherlands.*

the original equipment sales.[2] Finally, as we shall see below, there may be substantial legal costs and risks from attempting to maintain a monopoly for service on one's own products. Our analysis explores when a manufacturer will find it profitable to exploit a service monopoly that it has obtained.

While the manufacturer usually will have an initial service advantage due to its knowledge of the workings of the equipment, for durable equipment that advantage can quickly depreciate. Within a year or so of model introduction, independent service technicians can master new auto engine designs, VCR circuitry, even complex computer components. In addition, engineers trained by the manufacturer will leave—often involuntarily given the rapid restructuring of many equipment manufacturing industries in recent years—and these engineers often start or join independent service operations.

Besides the initial knowledge advantage, how can a manufacturer maintain a service monopoly on its own products? Often ongoing service will require one or more *proprietary* components, such as patented parts or copyrighted diagnostic software. The equipment's value to the consumer often depends on these ancillary, proprietary materials. A manufacturer might use its control over the proprietary components to maintain a monopoly over the provision of all aftermarket service by, for example, conditioning access to the proprietary materials on simultaneous purchase of the manufacturer's service.[3]

A manufacturer's proprietary rights over essential service components or ancillary products might seem to provide a costless device for perpetuating a service monopoly. In fact, as with second-sourcing, customer preferences may make the monopoly strategy too costly to be worthwhile. The manufacturer's problem is the possible availability of alternate sources for the original equipment. Although durable equipment generally differs by brand, many

---

[2] Even if a manufacturer does not exploit its monopoly over service, customers might try to shift to other equipment manufacturers if they have a strong preference for second sourcing on service (that is, they value the option of obtaining service from more than one vendor). We are unaware of any research on second-sourcing for services (this issue is beyond our scope) but there is a relevant literature on second-sourcing for manufactured products (Shepard (1987); Riordan and Sappington (1989)).

[3] Of course, in the extreme the manufacturer might condition the initial equipment sale on the simultaneous purchase of a lifetime service contract. Although this seems quite rare, in fact leasing is an example of this, since manufacturer service is usually required. However, one almost always has the choice of buying the equipment without mandatory service.

customers (perhaps most) will find that another brand offers an attractive alternative given a sufficient price difference. If a manufacturer *exploits* a service monopoly by charging above-competitive prices, equipment buyers may simply choose a different equipment brand in the first place.[4] If the equipment sales loss were large enough it might not pay to monopolize service.

On the other hand, the manufacturer may have some power to exploit in the aftermarket. The critical issue is the extent to which customers are "locked-in" to the manufacturer of the original equipment. There are often high costs of switching to another brand of equipment. A consumer must balance the switching costs with the benefit of saving money in a competitor's aftermarket. Switching costs are particularly important for complicated electronic equipment. For example, custom software may have to be rewritten, and data archives converted; switching a large enterprise computer may take years and cost millions of dollars. Costs of switching once committed to a particular brand may provide the manufacturer with room to raise service prices above cost, and to collect some monopoly rents on the provision of service.

In fact, over the past decade independent service firms have initiated some twenty-odd antitrust suits against manufacturers such as Kodak, Prime Computer, Data General, Northern Telecom, Picker, Unisys, Xerox, and Siemens, alleging that these manufacturers are behaving anticompetitively in aftermarkets. In these cases, the manufacturer sells one brand of complex equipment in a market that may be competitive (*e.g.*, the market for minicomputers), and aftermarket service products to customers who purchased the original equipment. The services include hardware maintenance, spare parts, and software upgrades and revisions. Due to proprietary rights, the original manufacturer is often the exclusive seller of at least one aftermarket product, such as upgrades to the operating system software. Plaintiffs charge that the manufacturer exploits its special position in the proprietary product in violation of the antitrust laws.

The central economic dispute in these cases is whether the manufacturer *profitably* can exploit its proprietary advantage over the service products. For example, according to the Supreme Court, "Kodak [states] that even if it

---

[4]If, for example, Maytag monopolized Maytag service through a restrictive parts policy, and started charging monopoly service prices, it might not be long before Maytag lost substantial market share to Kitchen Aid and General Electric, *et al.*

concedes monopoly *share* of the relevant parts market, it cannot actually exercise the necessary market *power* for a Sherman Act violation. This is so, according to Kodak, because competition exists in the equipment market" (*Kodak*, Supreme Court 90-1029 at 11; emphasis in original).   The question becomes whether competition in the upstream market prevents anticompetitive behavior in downstream markets.   For instance, Kodak argued to the Supreme Court that "equipment competition *precludes* any finding of monopoly power in the derivative aftermarkets" (emphasis added; *Kodak*, S. Ct. 90-1029 at 12).[5] The manufacturer might appear to have an opportunity to exploit its economic power over service customers, but the attempt might be unprofitable (at least in the long run) because of customers lost in the equipment market, as explained above. Indeed, if the manufacturer is no longer able to sell any equipment, it eventually will have no service customers to exploit.

Along these lines, a "starving monopolist" paradox appears in many recent cases. Wang Laboratories has stopped manufacturing equipment, and has entered Chapter 11 reorganization proceedings. Prime Computer has liquidated its equipment manufacturing operations, and reorganized as Computervision. Data General and Unisys have suffered repeated years of massive losses, and have drastically declined in size. If these are monopolists exploiting their market power over service customers, where are all the profits?

In this paper, we address the following questions: Can economic power over locked-in service customers be profitably exploited if the original equipment market is competitive? If so, under what circumstances? What happens when there is product differentiation and imperfect competition in the original equipment market? Among other things, our answers to these questions show that there *is* a role for antitrust enforcement in service aftermarkets. We also resolve the "starving monopolist" paradox.

We first review the recent legal history, emphasizing how the central economic questions have emerged from the facts of the cases. We then describe some simple theoretical models to answer the questions. Analysis of these markets in a free-entry competitive market reveals an important flaw in the common argument that competitive equipment markets lead to efficient pricing of the aftermarket product for locked-in customers: competition will eventually drive profits from *any* pricing strategy to zero. If reputation is not a factor, then

---

[5]The *Kodak* case concerned a motion for summary judgment before discovery was complete.

the firm charges monopoly service prices and below-cost equipment prices. The firm earns zero profits overall but unambiguously lowers output and makes consumers worse off. If a firm follows a "reputation" strategy it can raise profits by exploiting its reputation in the short run (*i.e.*, raising service prices *despite* a low-price reputation) and then exiting the market or reverting to a pricing strategy that requires no reputation.

Those who believe that service pricing will be competitive emphasize reputation as the key element in ensuring competitive service pricing. Since reputation is ineffective in our analysis of a free-entry, perfectly competitive equipment market, we next consider an imperfectly competitive equipment market. We find that reputation does have some value in a model with imperfect competition and that firms will price service below its locked-in monopoly level. We also find, however, that they will always price above cost for the aftermarket product. The degree to which they exploit locked-in consumers by pricing the aftermarket product above cost will depend on the discount rate and the nature of demand for the aftermarket product. But surprisingly, as the equipment market becomes more competitive, the price of service does not approach cost.

We show that in general the presumption should be that an equipment manufacturer with a dominant position in a service aftermarket *can* profitably exploit its position despite competition in the equipment market.[6] It is worth emphasizing that our results assume throughout that consumers are fully informed and have perfect foresight about changes in costs, technology and demand. In practice complete information is very costly and long-run forecasts of high-technology markets are rarely accurate. In practice these imperfections provide the manufacturer with even greater opportunities to exploit its economic power over service customers than we show below.

Our results have several implications for managers. Controlling the service market for one's own manufactured products may be a profitable strategic objective. But there are several problems that may eradicate profitability. In particular, it will generally be necessary to have some long-term intellectual property advantage to prevent independent service organizations from gaining a nearly equal competitive footing. But even with such a proprietary advantage, service monopolization may not be particularly attractive. If there is active competition between alternatives for the original equipment, the firm may find

---

[6]This is consistent with the Supreme Court ruling in *Kodak*.

itself making profits on service but dissipating those profits through equipment discounts to maintain market share. Further, when manufacturers have the needed intellectual property to dominate the service market, if they do so it now appears that they may run afoul of the antitrust laws.[7]

2. Aftermarket Economic Power in the Courts

There are many cases before the federal courts that involve claims of antitrust violations in aftermarkets for service products. Two, both concerning alleged tie-ins, have recently reached the Supreme Court. The Court ruled on the *Kodak* case in June 1992. Firms selling service for Kodak micrographic equipment alleged that Kodak adopted a restrictive policy on the availability of spare parts, including tying the sales of spare parts to the purchase of other maintenance services from Kodak. The Court upheld the Circuit Court's denial of Kodak's motion for summary judgement, concluding that "it is clearly reasonable to infer that Kodak has market power to raise prices and drive out competition in the aftermarkets . . . [and] to infer that Kodak chose to gain immediate profits by exerting that market power where locked-in customers, high information costs, and discriminatory pricing limited and perhaps eliminated any long-term loss" (*Kodak*, S. Ct. 90-1029 at 24).[8] Kodak, and the United States as *amicus curiae*, argued that as a matter of economic theory competition in the equipment market prevents manufacturers from exercising market power in the service market in all circumstances. The Supreme Court rejected the idea that Kodak's theory *must* hold. Rather, the Court argued that while Kodak's theory is *plausible*, whether it actually holds will depend on the particular circumstances of each case.

In October 1992 the Supreme Court ruled on an appeal in the *Prime Computer* case. An independent service company alleged and won a unanimous jury verdict that Prime (now Computervision) illegally tied software support and upgrades to the purchase of hardware maintenance from Prime. Prime appealed

---

[7]Klein (1993) argues that the problem of aftermarket exploitation should be a problem for contract law, not antitrust law. His argument is strong, but abstracts from the fact that the Supreme Court has stated that power in service aftermarkets *is* a proper matter for antitrust consideration.

[8]This is not a final determination in the case, but merely a decision that the case can go forward to trial.

and the Sixth Circuit reversed the jury verdict. In its appeals, Prime argued that it could not take advantage of its locked-in customers because of competition for new equipment sales (see, e.g., Prime's Brief for Judgment N.O.V., E.D. Mich., Case 89-CV-71762, 29 November 1990, at p. 7). The Supreme Court vacated and remanded the Circuit Court decision for reconsideration in light of *Kodak*.

Nearly all of the service aftermarket cases in the courts include a claim of tying. Tying is a popular business strategy that under some restrictive circumstances can be illegal. A tie requires customers to purchase one good or service (the tied product) if they wish to purchase a second good or service (the tying good). Not all ties are illegal; it is perfectly permissible for General Motors to require you to buy tires from them when you buy a new car. Whether a particular tying strategy is illegal is largely an economic question. A tie is illegal if the tying firm has sufficient economic power over the tying product to adversely affect competition in the market for the tied product.[9] We might announce, for example, that you can buy pencils from us only if you also send your children to Davis, Michigan, or Purdue and pay our salaries to teach them. Since you can easily buy pencils elsewhere, we have no power over you, and this tie will harm the price, quantity or quality of university education. But if we were the exclusive sellers of a cancer cure rather than a competitive seller of pencils, we might well be able to raise tuition at our schools and force many people to attend unwillingly. Thus the issue largely depends on whether the seller has market power in the tying good which she is trying to extend to the tied good market.[10]

The many service industry tying suits in the past decade introduce a new wrinkle. There are usually at least *three* products or services that are relevant. The firm imposes a tie between one aftermarket service product and another (such as spare parts and equipment maintenance in the *Kodak* case). But the defense relies on claims that competition in a *third* market--for original equipment sales-- prevents them from having any economic power to exploit with the tie in the service aftermarkets.

---

[9]This criterion was first established in *International Salt v. U.S.*, 332 U.S. 392 (1947), and has been recently restated and somewhat clarified in *Jefferson Parish Hospital District No. 2 v. Hyde*, 466 U.S. 2 (1984).

[10]This point was made, for example, in *Carbice Corp. of America v. American Patent Development Corp*, 283 U.S. 27 (1941), in which the Supreme Court decided against allowing the owner of a patent to "secure a partial monopoly on the unpatented supplies consumed in its operation."

In *Kodak* the Supreme Court ruled that while original equipment competition may enforce competitive behavior in the service aftermarkets, competition is not assured. The theory's applicability must be analyzed on a case by case basis.   As the Court of Appeals stated in *Kodak*, "market imperfections can keep economic theories about how consumers will act from mirroring reality" (*Kodak*, 903 F.2d 612 at 617).

Ties are not the only way that an equipment manufacturer can affect competition in the service markets. In several cases, manufacturers allegedly monopolize the market for equipment maintenance on their brand of equipment, in violation Section II of the Sherman Act. (See, for example, *Grumman v. Data General*, *Datasat v. Unisys*, *Comm-Tract v. Northern Telecom*, and others.)[11] To prevail in a monopolization claim in a service aftermarket, the plaintiff must show that the manufacturer has substantial economic power in the aftermarket and is exploiting that power.

Thus, whether the allegations are tying (Section I) or monopolization (Section II), the crucial question at issue is whether a manufacturer that faces competition in the original equipment market can have sufficient economic power over customers for the aftermarket service product to profitably raise service prices or otherwise burden the customers.

In the remainder of this section we examine how three parts of the central economic question have emerged in the recent cases: the role of customer "lock-in" in establishing economic power; the paradox that failing or low-profit businesses are so often the subject of service antitrust suits; and the extent to which reputation can prevent manufacturers from profitably exploiting whatever economic power they have in service aftermarkets.

2.1   Customer   lock-in.   The   manufacturer's   ability   to   charge above-competitive prices for its aftermarket service product depends largely on the availability of substitutes to the customer.   For example, an existing customer could sell or scrap the used equipment and purchase anew from a different manufacturer if the original seller raises the service price enough. A

---

[11]As another example, Dimidowich filed a case quite similar to the Kodak case, though under California's Cartwright Law, not under the Sherman Act. Dimidowich was a third-party maintainer of Bell and Howell micrographic equipment, who accused Bell and Howell of conspiring to restrain trade by refusing to sell parts to Dimidowich. There was evidence that Bell and Howell became concerned with increasing competition in the market for service of their equipment and hence instituted the policy in order to reduce competition.

central issue in the cases has been the extent to which the opportunity for customers to switch constrains the manufacturer to price service competitively.

Once a customer purchases a piece of complex durable equipment, she may find that switching to another brand is costly. There can be significant costs for retraining personnel, converting data files, rewriting critical software programs, and so forth. The higher the costs of switching, the more the customer is "locked-in" to the original manufacturer's brand of equipment. Thus, for these customers the manufacturer may be able to substantially raise service prices without fear of significant switching.[12]

A distinguishing feature of most of the recent service antitrust cases is that the equipment involved is complex and proprietary. The products include minicomputers, hospital CT scanners, telephone PBX switches, and micrographic reproduction equipment. In every case, users and experts have testified to the high costs of switching.[13] Evidence introduced in the *Wang* case showed that typically about 80 percent of minicomputer consumers buy the same brand when they replace their equipment, suggesting a low degree of switching between minicomputer brands.

Switching costs must also be weighed against the amount that supracompetitive pricing increases the lifetime cost of owning the machine. A five percent increase in the price of service can be enough to trigger antitrust concern,[14] yet may only raise the present value of lifetime costs on the

---

[12]This point was emphasized by the Supreme Court in *Kodak*: "If the cost of switching is high, consumers who already have purchased the equipment, and are thus 'locked-in,' will tolerate some level of service-price increases before changing equipment brands" (*Kodak*, S. Ct. 90-1029 at 23).

[13]For example, a senior design systems manager for Ford Motor Co. testifying on behalf of Prime stated that if forced to switch quickly from Prime minicomputers to another brand Ford could not "stay a competitive auto manufacturer in the world market," *Virtual*, Plaintiff's Response Brief on Appeal. See also, *Kodak*, S. Ct. 90-1029 at p. 23.

[14]U.S. Department of Justice Merger Guidelines (1992 rev.).

equipment by half a percent.[15] With significant switching costs, even sizable increases in the cost of service may not induce customers to switch brands.

Several authors show how lock-in can create market power.[16] But these studies all examine a single market where the customer becomes locked-in for repeat purchases. There has been little attention to a firm with locked-in service customers that faces competition in the upstream market for the initial sale of the equipment. When there are two interrelated markets the central question becomes the ability of the manufacturer to exploit economic power in one market without a larger adverse impact on profits in the other market.[17] In section 3 we explicitly incorporate lock-in in our discussions of competition and market power in equipment markets and service aftermarkets.

2.2 The "starving monopolist." One peculiarity in this area of the law is that so many of the antitrust cases have been against low-profit and failing firms. Prime has gone out of business; Wang (subject of two suits) has stopped producing equipment and is in bankruptcy proceedings; Data General (two suits) experienced 16 straight quarters of losses and has downsized considerably; Unisys (two suits) has been struggling. Other defendants have low profit margins and do not appear to be classic monopolists: Northern Telecom, Hewlett-Packard, Siemens, Picker, etc.

If manufacturers are monopolistically exploiting locked-in service customers, where are all the profits? We provide an answer to the "starving monopolist" paradox in section 3, below. In short, while firms may obtain above-normal service profits, they may dissipate these profits through

---

[15]For example, an independent study in 1989 by the Sierra Group estimates that the hardware maintenance costs represent 11.9% of the five-year life-cycle total costs for a Data General MV/1000 DC system. A 5% increase in hardware maintenance prices would thus increase total five-year system costs by only 0.6%. Memorandum in Support of a Motion for Summary Judgment on Grumman's Antitrust Concerns, Exhibit 6, 23 March 1990, U.S. District (Mass.) No. 88-0033-S.

[16]See, for example, Beggs and Klemperer (1992), Farrell and Shapiro (1988), and Klemperer (1987).

[17]This is of course the fundamental question of market definition and economic power in antitrust analysis, thrown into a new light because of the derivative, or aftermarket, status of the service products in question.

competition in the equipment market to "buy market share." This market share provides locked-in customers to exploit.[18]

Oddly, *both* the defendant and the United States (filing as *amicus curiae* in *Kodak* on behalf of Kodak) argued along these lines. Even if firms were charging supracompetitive prices in service aftermarkets, they wrote, that might be part of an overall pricing strategy in combination with subcompetitive prices for the original equipment (see *Kodak*, S. Ct. 90-1029 at 18). They then asserted that such a strategy is "competitive." In fact, such pricing is not as efficient as competitive pricing in both markets, as we show below. Consumers are harmed, and it is appropriate to invoke the antitrust laws, even if the monopolist appears to be, or is, starving.

2.3   Reputation and imperfect competition. A manufacturer faces two types of customers: those who already own the manufacturer's equipment and those who do not.[19] Although customers with equipment may face significant costs of switching brands and thus provide the manufacturer with an opportunity to price supracompetitively, *de novo* customers do not. Is it possible that competing for potential new customers provides sufficient discipline that manufacturers will not exploit their economic power over aftermarket service products?

The claim that potential new customers provide the competitive discipline in the service market is central to the position taken by defendants in the recent cases. Kodak, for instance, argued that "there will be some large-volume, sophisticated purchasers who will undertake the comparative studies and . . . hold down the package price for all other customers" (*Kodak*, S. Ct. 90-1029 at 22).

---

[18]The Supreme Court dissolved a merger between Ford Motor and Autolite in part because Autolite's practice of selling original spark plugs at below cost was evidence that Autolite was exploiting customers for replacement Autolite spark plugs. (*Ford Motor v. U.S. et al.*, 405 US 562 (1971)). In this case customer lock-in to Autolite for replacement spark plugs was important, even though that lock-in was more psychological than technologically or economically necessary.
[19]The distinction between customers who own another brand already and customers who are making their first purchase is not important for our point in this section.

Prime argued that

> The quality and price of post-sale service are critical to the competitiveness of each firm's computer systems. No firm has the power or incentive to take advantage of its current system users by lowering the quality or raising the price of such service. Any firm attempting to do so would quickly lose future system sales and place its entire business at risk (Prime's Brief for Judgment N.O.V., E.D. Mich., Case 89-CV-71762, 29 November 1990, at p. 7).

The argument depends on reputation effects. The manufacturer claims it cannot afford to exploit locked-in service customers because the information will become widespread and new consumers will purchase other brands. That is, a reputation for exploiting locked-in customers will result in a loss of equipment sales.

The tradeoff between profits from aftermarket service and from original equipment sales causes confusion in the courts. The appellate court in *Virtual* argued that "lock-in theory is viable only when the producer can charge its customer monopoly prices without fear of being replaced by competitors due to the customer's substantial investments" *(Virtual,* 957 F.2d 1318 at 1328). However, it is not necessary to charge full monopoly prices for service in order to exploit economic power, nor does the loss of *some* customers for new equipment necessarily offset the profits from service. The Supreme Court observed in *Kodak* that even monopolists have to give up sales when they raise prices, yet they find it profitable to charge higher than competitive prices (S. Ct. 90-1029 at 17). Short of charging the full monopoly price for service, "there could be a middle, optimum price at which the increased revenues from the higher-priced sales of service and parts would more than compensate for the lower revenues from lost equipment sales" *(id.).*[20] The proper question, then, is the extent to which monopolistic behavior in the service aftermarket reduces profits in the equipment market.

If a manufacturer can establish a credible reputation for low service prices, then it might be able to charge higher equipment prices than its competitors and earn some profits in the equipment market. This strategy is sensible if the profit

---

[20]Notice that the Supreme Court here is assuming that firms want to maximize total revenues, not profits. Most evidence indicates that firm behavior is generally more consistent with profit than revenue maximization. But the Court's point is valid if "revenues" is replaced with "profits."

potential in the equipment market is greater than the profits foregone on service. However, since there is a tradeoff, this doesn't mean that service prices will be lowered all the way to the competitive level (at which price equals cost).

To have an incentive to invest in a reputation, the manufacturer must anticipate the possibility of earning above-normal profits. Thus, there must be some product differentiation or other source of profits in the equipment market. To address the role of reputation we need to consider that the equipment market is not perfectly competitive.

Vigorous but imperfect competition in the equipment market is a reasonable characterization for most of the cases. Complex, high-technology products tend to be differentiated, even if they are similar enough that customers can consider them as partial substitutes. For example, Wang minicomputers might be favored by customers who need strong document and image processing capabilities; DEC computers by scientific and engineering users; and IBM minicomputers by those with significant data processing needs. Northern Telecom designs PBX telephone switches to maintain complete "upward" compatibility so that customers can expand and upgrade their system without replacing it. ATT, on the other hand, produces different lines of switches that are not all upward compatible, but provide other advantages. With imperfect competition manufacturers may earn above normal returns or quasi-rents on their new equipment business and thus face the profit tradeoff described above.

Curiously, the proponents of the reputation defense never identify the source of the excess profits that manufacturers are so anxious to protect by establishing low-service-price reputations. Rather, they emphasize strong competition in the equipment market and the availability of good substitutes for the consumer. This suggests there should be no excess profits in the equipment market to protect.

The recent cases raise interesting legal and economic issues. The following sections discuss the economic issues. In particular, we address the strong theoretical claim that it is impossible for a competitive equipment firm to profitably exploit the aftermarkets. We analyze a theory of power in the aftermarkets that is motivated by the descriptive features of equipment and service markets, in particular including switching costs. We find that the theoretical presumption should run in the other direction: equipment market competition in general will not prevent exploitation of economic power in service markets.

3. A Competitive Equipment Market and a Non-Competitive Service Aftermarket

To think through the economics of competition in service aftermarkets, we begin with a very simple case.[21] Consider a market in which original equipment sales are perfectly competitive, but the brand manufacturer monopolizes aftermarket service of the brand. What possibility is there for a manufacturer to exploit market power in the service market?

Suppose that the equipment has a two-period life-cycle. In the first period a customer decides whether to buy a unit of equipment. If she buys, then in the second period the customer can: (1) use the depreciated equipment as is; (2) buy some service from the original manufacturer to enhance the equipment; or, (3) reenter the market to purchase new equipment. To keep things simple, we assume that all firms can produce equipment and service (on their own equipment) at the same cost, and that these costs are constant for each unit produced.

We also assume that all consumers are identical. In the spirit of a free-entry, perfectly competitive equipment market, consumers consider equipment brands to be homogeneous. That is, at a given price they do not care from which producer they purchase. This ensures that if one producer cuts price a small amount below the price of other producers, all consumers will buy that low-priced brand. Similarly, we assume that each unit of service on a machine is equally valuable to a consumer, whatever the brand of equipment. That is, the value of the enhanced equipment to a consumer with brand X equipment and one unit of service is the same as the value to a consumer with brand Y equipment and one unit of service.

These assumptions grant the benefit of the doubt to the arguments of the defendant, such as espoused by Kodak and the U.S. Solicitor General in that case. The model assumes the equipment market is competitive with consumers who respond instantaneously and completely to price differences. This is the most likely setting in which competition in the equipment market can prevent manufacturers from exploiting their market power in service markets. However, we shall see that to get a completely efficient outcome--in which firms price both equipment and service at cost--requires that firms can credibly commit to

[21]This section is based in part on technical results derived in Borenstein, MacKie-Mason, and Netz (1994).

charging a low service price. As discussed below, this assumption is generally implausible.

To ensure that a service market can exist, we assume that if equipment and service are priced at cost the consumer would have a higher net benefit from keeping and buying service for old equipment than if she sold the used equipment and purchased new equipment. We also assume that the purchase of a small amount of service yields a benefit to the consumer worth more than the cost of producing that service. Together, the two assumptions imply that the socially most efficient outcome in these markets is for producers to charge prices equal to cost, and for consumers to use each unit of the equipment for two periods and to purchase some positive quantity of service in the second period.

3.1   Forward-looking customers but no reputation effects. We first consider the manufacturer's profit-maximizing strategy if the decision horizon is two periods long, and if no new customers enter after the first period.[22] With no new customers, and no future equipment purchases by the original customers, there is no role for reputation.[23] We do assume, however, that customers look ahead and correctly anticipate the manufacturer's service pricing decisions. This setting allows us to show the generic inefficiencies that can result from the absence of competition in the service aftermarket.

To solve for profit-maximizing strategies, we follow the standard method of backward induction for a finite decision horizon. That is, we first consider what the producer does in the second (last) period, given past history. Then, with the producer knowing its optimal second-period pricing strategy, we step back and solve for the optimal first-period pricing strategy.

In the second period, each firm decides what price to charge for service. At this point its customers are locked-in: everyone made their brand choice in the first period, and only the manufacturer can offer service for its proprietary equipment. That does not mean the firm can charge any price it wishes. If it sets the service price too high customers will abandon the used equipment and

---

[22]The assumption that there are no new consumers of equipment in the second period may seem extreme, but relaxing this assumption in the context of a two-period model does not change our results. If consumers purchase equipment in the second, final period, there is no period in which they can purchase service, and hence service prices will be irrelevant to their purchasing decision.

[23]We introduce reputation effects in section 4, below.

purchase new equipment from another vendor to use during period two.[24] We call the price at which customers abandon their used equipment the "switch price." The firm must choose a monopoly price to maximize service profits, subject to the constraint that price can be no higher than the switch price that induces customers to leave. If the unconstrained monopoly price is above the switch price, the producer should charge the switch price.

Why isn't the switch price equal to cost? That is, why don't customers switch brands in the second-period if the producer charges a price for service that is higher than cost? This is where lock-in is crucial. We assumed that the customer's net benefit from keeping the used equipment and buying some service at cost is *greater than* the net benefit from selling the used equipment and switching to a different brand of new equipment. This assumption will typically be true for some equipment (*e.g.*, computers, telecommunications switches, imaging equipment) because there are significant costs of switching, as we discussed earlier. The switching costs provide the firm with some room to charge more than cost for service; the user's switching costs determine the maximum price the firm can charge (the switch price). It is the switching costs that create lock-in, and lock-in that allows the firm to earn above-competitive profits in the service market.

If consumers know that a manufacturer is going to charge them above-competitive prices for service in period two, why don't they prevent this by buying their equipment from a different manufacturer in period one? This is the crux of the issue: can competition in the equipment market prevent the exploitation of market power in the service aftermarket? The problem is that when period two arrives, if a firm has any customers at all it will maximize profits by charging the constrained monopoly price. This is true for *all* firms. Thus, in period one the customer can know that the manufacturer will charge her above-competitive prices, but she has nowhere to turn.

What, then, happens in period one? Each of the perfectly competitive sellers realizes that in period two it can earn above-competitive profits on servicing each unit of equipment sold in period one. Thus, there is a premium on attracting equipment customers. The sellers enter a classic battle for market share by cutting equipment prices to attract customers who can be profitably exploited in the next period. With free entry and exit into the market, price-cutting will continue until the firms in the market break even overall.

[24]Our results are unchanged if there is a market for used equipment so that the customer can sell rather than scrap her equipment.

Thus, the equilibrium price for equipment will be equal to the equipment's production cost less the discounted future service profits. That is, each customer obtained in period one is worth $X in discounted period two profits, so the manufacturer breaks even if it charges $(C - X)$ for equipment, where C is the cost of producing one unit of the equipment.

The result of this analysis is that even when (a) the equipment market is perfectly competitive, (b) customers correctly anticipate future service prices, and (c) firms earn zero excess profits, there is still above-competitive pricing for service and below-competitive pricing for the equipment. This outcome resolves the "starving monopolist" paradox mentioned in the first section. Above-competitive prices in the service market combined with below cost equipment prices provide the firm with zero total profits.

For producers the profits in the service market are equal to the losses in the equipment market, leaving producer welfare unchanged from efficient, cost-based prices. However, below-cost pricing in the equipment market does not offset the loss to consumers from above-cost pricing in the service market. Thus, consumers are worse off than if both markets were competitive, and producers are no better off since they still earn zero economic profits.[25]

To see why this is so, recognize first that consumers will buy less service than they would if they faced a service price equal to cost. As usual in a monopoly situation, the consumer loss from high service prices is greater than the producers' extra profits, because consumers respond in part by reducing their purchases. The reduction in quantity represents a loss to consumers with no corresponding gain to producers, *i.e.,* a "deadweight loss."

Competition in the equipment market forces the firm to "give back" the service profits through below-cost prices on equipment. The equipment price is below cost by the amount of (discounted) profits earned on service, but the service profits are less than the consumer loss from above-cost service pricing. Thus, the discount on equipment does not fully compensate consumers for the loss of benefits in the service market. As a result, the combined package of equipment and service is less attractive, and fewer consumers choose to buy the equipment. This is precisely the outcome that the antitrust laws seek to prevent: higher prices and lower quantities that result in consumer losses.

---

[25]Thus societal welfare, the sum of producer and consumer welfare, falls relative to welfare under non-cost-based pricing, since producer welfare is the same and consumer welfare is decreased.

3.2 Pre-commitment. The strong result above holds because each firm's only rational pricing strategy in the second (and last) period is to charge a (constrained) monopoly price.[26] Customers can't buy first-period equipment only from firms that will charge competitive service prices because there aren't any. This may seem peculiar. If a firm could attract all the customers in the first period by promising to charge a price on service less than the monopoly level, why won't such a firm exist?

The problem is the credibility of such a promise. We assumed above that firms could not credibly commit to competitive service pricing. Once the second (final) period arrives, past behavior is irrelevant. A profit-maximizing firm will charge the price that maximizes second period profits whatever it promised in the first period. With no future sales to anyone, there is no cost to breaking a promise and charging the monopoly price. Since consumers anticipate this behavior, they will purchase equipment from whichever firm has the lowest equipment price since all firms will charge the monopoly service price.

If a firm *could* credibly commit to charging a low service price, then it would because it would want to try to attract all of the first-period equipment customers. Why is commitment impossible? In our simple abstract analysis it might seem trivial to write a legally-binding contract that guarantees that second period price would be set equal to cost. If and only if a credible commitment is possible, then equipment competition between firms offering credible contracts would lead to efficient pricing (equal to cost) for both equipment and service. To see this, start from the situation with competitive equipment prices and supracompetitive service prices. Each firm would try to undercut its competitors, up to the point where the service price is equal to the cost of service.

In fact, fully credible complete commitments are usually impossible. To begin with, they require low-cost external enforcement, presumably through the courts. But contracts predicating price on cost are almost impossible to enforce, because it is almost impossible to precisely measure unit cost in the real world. How much of the R&D department costs should be attributed to the unit cost of service? What about marketing and headquarters staff? In practice a manufacturer is selling several different types of service (including service for multiple varieties of hardware and software) with several different levels and qualities (e.g.,

---

[26]The results derived above hold so long as there is a finite horizon, regardless of whether the last period is after two periods or after twenty periods.

one-hour response, four-hour response, evening-and-weekend calls, etc.).
Enforcement would require the calculation of the cost of each type of service.

It is also impossible to write a complete contract, *i.e.*, one that covers all
possibilities. The constant and unpredictable changes in technology, service
needs and service offerings make it difficult to write contracts or offer price
guarantees much in advance. Equipment of the sort involved in the pending
antitrust suits often has a useful life of 10 years or more. It is infeasible for
customers and sellers to envision all possible contingencies and write those
explicitly into service contracts at the time of original purchase.

For example, in the *Virtual* case, Ford Motor Company committed its
engineering design software to run exclusively on Prime minicomputers several
years before Prime began tying software upgrades to hardware maintenance.
(*Virtual Maintenance v. Prime Computer*, Court of Appeals Appendix at
526-560.) To obtain a binding commitment from Prime that Prime would not
exploit service customers, Ford needed to anticipate Prime's policy when the
minicomputer industry was in its infancy, before there had been experience with
restrictive policies[27].

Thus, for a fully efficient outcome to occur with a perfectly competitive
equipment market and proprietary service, it is necessary that customers and
firms enter fully-specified contingency contracts. Such contracts must be
enforceable by courts, and prevent the firm from exploiting market power over
service customers for many years to come. Long-term contracts that control
service prices over the life of the equipment have been absent from the evidence
in the recent antitrust cases. In general we believe such contracts are infeasible.
In practice, of course, the existence of binding precommitments is a question of
fact, not theory. Since it is a question of fact, the economic theory again
supports the Supreme Court's conclusion in *Kodak*, *i.e.* precommitment must be
analyzed on a case by case basis.

3.3   Building a reputation. The problem with credible commitments we
described largely follows from assuming that there is a final period. What
happens in the situation where decisions are made over an infinite horizon?
Then firms may attract consumers by building a reputation for pricing service at
cost, or at least below the monopoly level. If consumers believe in the

---

[27]Likewise, most of the owners of Wang equipment at the time *Systemcare, Inc.
v. Wang Laboratories* was filed had purchased their equipment before Wang
introduced its policy of tying software support to hardware maintenance.

reputation, then reputation building and competition in the equipment market might achieve efficient pricing for both equipment and service.

We now go to the other extreme and assume the firm makes decisions over an infinite horizon, though it still discounts future cash flows using a positive interest rate. Machines continue to be useful for only two periods. Thus, in period t a consumer is only concerned about the price of service in period $t+1$. However, because firms make decisions over an infinite horizon, the service price in period $t+1$ depends on future periods. In the simple two-period approach—or in any finite-horizon model—consumers could form expectations of future service prices by solving backwards for the firm's optimal pricing strategy. In an infinite-horizon setting there is no "last period" to solve, and so no place to begin the backward induction. Therefore, we have to assume another method for consumers to set price expectations.

We assume that consumers believe that service prices will remain constant over time. That is, they forecast that tomorrow's service price will be the same as today's. This is plausible if we assume that real production costs are constant over time. Of course, assuming constant costs abstracts from the need to forecast changes in technology, which would clearly affect equipment and service prices. Testimony in many of the legal cases we discussed suggested that when consumers think ahead about service prices at all they make roughly this assumption. This also allows for maximal reputation-building. That is, consumers fully react to a firm's behavior in prior periods.

Now suppose firms are in the pricing equilibrium derived in the two-period model, charging monopoly prices for service and below-cost prices for equipment. How might a firm try to profit from building a reputation for lower service prices? The firm could lower its current service price, leading equipment buyers to believe that it will charge low service prices in the future. The firm will sacrifice some current profits on service, but the payoff to the firm is that it could then charge a higher price for equipment.[28] The firm will sacrifice the present discounted value of current and future service profits only if the present discounted value of future increased equipment profits is greater.

To learn how much profit reputation building yields, we need to know how quickly other firms will imitate the strategy of low-price service. Surely, in a free-entry competitive equipment market, if reputation-building turns out to be

---

[28]Alternatively, the manufacturer could charge the same equipment price but obtain a higher market share, which would increase profits if the equipment price is higher than cost.

profitable there will be quick imitation of this strategy by competitors. Other firms also price service at cost, driving the competitive price of equipment down to its production cost and eliminating profits on equipment sales. That is, if all firms are charging service at cost, the firm with the lowest equipment price attracts the customers. Thus firms will have an incentive to lower the price of equipment until it equals cost. Thus, building a reputation is worthwhile only if the short period of above-normal equipment profits exceeds (in present value) the loss of service profits while building the reputation.

Once competition between firms with low-service-price reputations sufficiently erodes profits, these firms will begin to exploit their reputations by suddenly reverting to a monopoly price for service. The switch does not raise firm profits in the long run, but it temporarily increases profits from the higher service price charged than buyers anticipated when they bought the equipment.

Clearly the speed of imitation by other firms is crucial. If other firms imitate the strategy of cost-based service pricing very quickly, profits from that strategy are zero. Then no firm will recoup the profits foregone to build the reputation for cost-based service pricing.

Thus, one plausible outcome is that firms will not attempt to build reputations, because the expected return does not reward the current loss in service profits. Alternatively there may be a series of cycles in which firms in the industry build reputations and then exploit their reputations by again raising service prices. Most important, however, there is a not a long-run equilibrium in which competitive, zero-profit firms all maintain a reputation for low service prices.

It is unlikely that a permanent reputation strategy would be optimal for a profit-maximizing firm for several other real-world considerations. For example, customers cannot easily observe service production costs. Thus they cannot easily distinguish between a firm that is deviating from cost-based service pricing and a firm experiencing an increase in costs. This uncertainty gives firms some room to raise their service prices without significantly harming their pricing reputation.

Perhaps the most serious drawback to the reputation theory is the infinite-horizon assumption. Business lives are short for many, perhaps most, firms in highly-complex equipment markets. Once a firm anticipates that it has a finite horizon, it becomes immediately profitable for that firm to revert to monopoly service pricing.[29] The firm increasingly obtains its revenue from service, rather than from new equipment sales. Accordingly, the firm's incentive to exploit its market power over its locked-in existing customers increases.[30]

Indeed, even ongoing firms may experience the finite-life-cycle constraint on the efficacy of reputation-building. The products at issue often have finite marketing lifetimes, even if the company continues. New product families replace old, often within just a few years. If the reputation effects do not carry over completely to the new product line there is another incentive to deviate from a low-service-pricing reputation.

For example, before 1980 IBM was viewed as a firm that sold large computers to large corporate customers through a direct sales force. After the introduction of the PC desktop computer, IBM very rapidly became a company with extensive sales to small end-users, often through distributed sales outlets. It is unlikely that IBM's prior reputation with its corporate mainframe customers would influence new customers without IBM experience, buying products radically different from the machines on which IBM built its reputation.

More recently, several defendant minicomputer companies have been either entirely replacing their existing product line, or completely dissolving. For example, Prime Computer liquidated (and reorganized its design software branch as Computervision) and Wang Laboratories has entered bankruptcy proceedings and stopped producing its own minicomputers. Data General has moved rapidly away from its proprietary MV line of minicomputers that are the subject of the suit by Grumman. It now focuses on entirely different open-architecture UNIX machines with the brand name Aviion.

4. Imperfect Competition in the Equipment Market

A central problem with the theories advanced by antitrust defendants in these cases is the following: If the equipment market is perfectly competitive, then

---

[29]We show this for the finite-horizon, N-period game in Borenstein, MacKie-Mason and Netz (1994). We are assuming that in the finite-horizon game, customers again form forward-looking rational expectations about future prices since they can solve the firm's optimal pricing problem backwards in time, as we did above.

[30]This may be precisely the case with Prime, which during the course of its lawsuit has abandoned manufacturing and changed its name to sell only software.

where are the profits that the manufacturers are afraid of losing if they exploit their locked-in customers for service? The hallmark of a fiercely competitive equipment market is the absence of excess profits. Yet, without excess profits in the equipment market, firms will prefer to charge monopoly service prices to make at least some profits.

We have shown the futility of a reputation strategy in a free-entry, zero-profit market. We now examine markets in which there is some opportunity for above-normal profits without entry driving them to zero. Such profits might be a return on a new technological innovation that differentiates one firm's equipment from another's. We show that the presence of an imperfectly competitive equipment market does not induce competitive pricing of service at cost in the aftermarket. However, firms now have an incentive to maintain a low-service-price [31] reputation.

In this environment, it is feasible and rational for a firm to maintain a reputation for pricing service below the monopoly level, but it is still not profit-maximizing to price service at cost. The firm will instead trade off current profits from high service prices for locked-in customers against future equipment profits that are possible with low service prices. The firm thus sets a service price between the monopoly price and the competitive price.

The most extreme form of imperfect competition—monopoly—illustrates the intuition for the result. Consider a new monopolist selling equipment and service, with no locked-in customers. She would maximize profits by pricing service at cost to maximize consumer benefits, while extracting those benefits through a high price for equipment. However, while pricing service at cost maximizes profits earned from all *new* generations of consumers, it is below the profit-maximizing price for already locked-in customers. Raising today's price of service slightly above cost raises profits earned from locked-in customers today, but lowers profits earned on all future generations of customers. For at least a small increase of price above cost, we can show that the increased profits from locked-in customers exceed the present value of decreased profits from future customer generations.[32] As the discount rate on future profits increases, so that

---

[31]This section is based in part on technical results derived in Borenstein, MacKie-Mason, and Netz (1994).

[32]In technical terms, the reason that this is true is that the loss in profits on new generations is second order when the price of service is raised slightly above cost and there is an associated profit-maximizing adjustment in equipment prices, but the gain in profits on locked-in customers is first order from this change.

future profits are less valuable today, the service price can profitably be raised further above cost. Pricing service at cost is profit maximizing only when the discount rate is zero (so that future profits are as valuable today as are current profits).

The opposite argument shows why the monopolist wouldn't set the price of service at the monopoly level. Monopoly prices maximize profits earned on the currently locked-in customers, but diminish profits earned on future generations of customers. Suppose the monopolist considers profits on both locked-in and future generations of customers, so that reputation has some value. Then we can show that for at least a small decrease in service price below the monopoly level (with an associated increase in the price of equipment), the profit gains from future customers are greater than the profit losses from currently locked-in customers. As the discount rate on future profits decreases, the price of service can be lowered further below the monopoly level and still improve the present value of profits. Only with an infinite discount rate is the present value of all profits maximized by setting the price of service at the monopoly level.

The reasoning that applies to a monopolist holds equally well for imperfectly competitive firms, whose entry does not drive profits to zero. Faced with the actions of competitors that produce imperfect substitutes for its own products, a firm still faces downward sloping demand for both equipment and service. It must still make pricing decisions in which it is trading off current profits from locked-in customers against future profits from new customers.

In fact, greater competition among existing firms—which would occur if the firms' products were better substitutes for one another—may not move service prices closer to cost. High service prices would cause the loss of more future business when there is a close substitute product. However, the profits from that future business are small to begin with due to the more intense competition. This is the same effect that discouraged reputation formation in the perfectly competitive market. In contrast, the presence of close substitutes in the equipment market does not reduce the profits from exploiting locked-in customers.[33] In our model of imperfect competition presented in Borenstein, MacKie-Mason, and Netz (1994), the degree of differentiation among equipment

---

[33]This is true so long as we maintain the assumption that no customer abandons her equipment "prematurely." To the extent that competition in the equipment market lowers the service price at which consumers will abandon their old machines, such equipment competition will have an indirect effect on profits from locked-in customers.

products does not affect the equilibrium markup on service. Each imperfect competition model relies on special assumptions, but clearly in general greater equipment market competition will not necessarily discipline prices in the service market.

5. Conclusion

The Kodak Co. recently sought summary judgement on antitrust charges of the sort discussed in this paper. Dismissal in summary judgement relies on theory rather than factual inquiry.   According to the U.S. Supreme Court, Kodak argued that "even if it concedes monopoly *share* of the relevant [replacement] parts market, it cannot actually exercise the necessary market *power* for a Sherman Act violation. This is so, according to Kodak, because competition exists in the [original] equipment market" (*Kodak*, Supreme Court 90-1029 at 11; emphasis in original). The Court recognized that "In the end, of course, Kodak's arguments may prove to be correct. It may be that its parts, service and equipment are components of one unified market, or that the equipment market does discipline the aftermarket so that all three are priced competitively overall" (*Kodak*, S. Ct. 90-1029 at 33). The Court believed, however, that imperfect information and other market conditions might prevent equipment market competition from fully protecting service customers. Thus, the Court decided that the charges were worthy of a factual inquiry.

     To our knowledge, there has not been previous economic research that supports either view. Our results, however, support the Supreme Court's conclusions in *Kodak* and go further. We find that equipment market competition does not prevent service market exploitation, even in theory. Our result holds even without imperfect information or other market barriers. The only exception we have found occurs when firms and customers sign fully-contingent, long-term contracts for service over the entire life of the equipment. Such contracts are not feasible, nor do we observe them in practice. Thus, it appears that theory compels us to presume that firms with a dominant position in a service aftermarket *can* profitably exploit their power despite competitive pressures from the equipment market.

References

Beggs, A., and P. Klemperer, (1992). "Multi-period competition with switching costs," *Econometrica* 60, 65-66.

Borenstein, S., J.K. MacKie-Mason, and J. S. Netz (1994). "Exercising market power in proprietary aftermarkets," Working Paper, University of Michigan (Ann Arbor, MI).

Farrell, J., and C. Shapiro (1987). "Dynamic competition with switching costs," *Rand Journal of Economics* 19, 123-37.

Klein, B. (1993). "Market power in antitrust economic analysis after *Kodak*," *Supreme Court Economic Review*.

Klemperer, P. (1987). "The competitiveness of markets with switching costs," *Rand Journal of Economics* 18, 138-50.

Riordan, M. H., and D.E.M. Sappington (1989). "Second sourcing," *Rand Journal of Economics* 20, 41-58.

Shepard, A. (1987). "Licensing to enhance demand for new technologies," *Rand Journal of Economics* 18, 360-368.

Chapter 9   **Information   Technology   and   Organizational Effectiveness**

Johannes M. Pennings[1]

1 . Introduction

Information technology (IT) has become a central feature of service firms. IT investments have profoundly altered the way service businesses operate. Perhaps, the inroads of IT are nowhere as visible as in the financial services sector. Its effect on measurable productivity as well as its impact on service quality and customer satisfaction are widely discussed. The arrival of IT is deemed crucial for maintaining efficiency and improving market penetration, or promoting organizational performance in general. Innovation is a panacea for lingering decline, or *the* factor for those who are in search of excellence.

IT is usually linked to innovation. IT represents a broad class of innovations that have primarily an internal role. Yet, IT can also have repercussions on the way services are perceived by the customer, and therefore also manifesting an external, marketing relevance. Likewise, we should recognize that performance is multi-dimensional with some aspects having an internal efficiency oriented

[1]This research has been supported by the Jones Center, the Fishman-Davidson Center at the University of Pennsylvania, and by a National Science Foundation grant #SES 8909674. Joseph Barber and Leah Guttierez provided research assistance in data management and data analysis. Eric Abrahamson, Deborah Dougherty and Joe Harder provided helpful comments on the manuscript, but any errors remain my responsibility.

P. T. Harker (ed.), The Service Productivity and Quality Challenge, 251–280.
© 1995 *Kluwer Academic Publishers. Printed in the Netherlands.*

meaning, while others are germane to external performance issues. Secondly, we believe that the underlying motives for information technology should be described. Presumably, innovations are adopted in anticipation of some economic return, but in many instances adoption is simply the result of firms jumping on the bandwagon. Finally, IT takes place in a context. Adoptions do take on different forms in different industries (e.g., Pavitt, 1991). As a minimum we should realize that IT-based innovations in manufacturing and service might have different implications. These are some of the considerations that triggered the present research.

In this paper, we investigate an organization's performance in relation to the adoption of different manifestations of information technology. We will differentiate both innovation and performance into distinct categories. Some IT adoptions remain largely restricted to the process for producing outputs, while others involve the very outputs themselves. Performance criteria can also vary, because some pertain more to internal indicators of efficiency and productivity, while others mirror a firm's success in the market place (compare Goodman and Pennings, 1977). We can relate all kinds of innovations to a wide range of performance indicators; yet, it is plausible to expect that process innovations are more germane to internal and product innovations to external effectiveness criteria.

The motives for adoption vary and appear to depend on the conceptual orientation of researchers. Economists assume some rational cost benefit analysis (e.g., Phillips, 1985), while sociologists start often from the assumption that organizational behavior is largely conditioned by institutionalized practice: organizations run with the pack (e.g., Scott, 1986). Naturally, it may be cost effective to conform to institutional practices because this allows a firm to maintain legitimacy, but a systematic and analytical justification for adoption is usually lacking. Indeed, several studies indicate that early adopters "need" the innovations they adopt, while later adopters may not (Abrahamson, 1991).The timing of an adoption relative to that of other firms is probably a good indication of innovation being rational or "boundedly" rational. Whereas rational and mimicking behavior are useful concepts for articulating alternative motivations to adopt, we believe that later adopters will face significant disadvantages compared to the first movers (compare Williamson, 1975). Late adopters are likely to be more governed by institutional pressures than are early adopters. The implication is that we need to consider the timing and diffusion levels of innovations.

Much of the innovation research has treated innovation as a dependent or left-hand-side variable, particularly in marketing (see Mahajan, Muller and Bass, 1990). Innovation as adoption can and should also be examined as an antecedent; hence, innovation is treated as an independent variable in its own right. The research reported here is also quite distinct on other accounts, since we explore issues in a sample of service organizations, i.e., financial institutions. Much of the innovation research has covered manufacturing organizations, and it is this sector on which virtually all of our diffusion knowledge is based. Industrial firms provide much of the metaphors about work organizations--whether in textbooks, academic journals, or educational cases, even though fewer than 20% of the U.S. labor force is currently employed in manufacturing, and even though the service sectors embody a vast and growing component in the U.S. and other "industrialized" nations alike. Technology represents also a production factor in many service sectors, where innovations abound in many areas and insights in the performance consequences of innovations will add major value to our stock of knowledge.

In the present research we describe findings from longitudinal data of service organizations that shed some new light on innovation and performance. First, we provide additional details on IT as process-product innovation distinction. Next, we explore the rationale for an IT-performance relationship and contrast the above mentioned economic and imitation scenarios for innovation. Finally, we show findings on significant technological innovations in the banking industry as antecedents of performance attributes, as interpreted within the framework of an economic-institutional framework.

2. IT and Performance: A Rationale?

Adopting new technology may be disruptive in the short run, when organizations seek to incorporate new know-how into their current stock. However, adoption may eventually lead to increased levels of efficiency and productivity. The addition of new know-how permits the firm to maintain its hold on best practice or to preserve its competitive advantage. New technology can find its way in new production processes and equipment, or in the development and commercialization of new products. In the first case, new equipment replaces inferior equipment or substitutes for labor; in the second case, existing products make room for new ones, or entirely new products reach the market. Efficiency gains, productivity improvements, and enhanced returns are likely outcomes. True, innovations can have dysfunctional consequences, but more commonly they bring advantages.

Innovations can be classified into a variety of dimensions or types--e.g., "technical" and "administrative," incremental and radical, and "process" versus "product." This latter distinction (e.g., Abernathy and Utterback, 1987) is relevant for the present paper. Process innovations pertain to the change, refashioning, and automation of the technology that is required for the production of an output; product innovations to transformations or replacement of the old output by some novel one. Output involves either product or service.

Although this presumption needs to be developed further, we assert that the distinction between process and product innovations is useful for understanding their performance consequences. Process innovations are not readily visible to the external environment, may not impact a firm's competitive position, market penetration, or income stream but are prone to improve internal operations. Product innovations afford opportunities for exploiting market opportunities. Compared with the former, these innovations represent an outward manifestation of a firm's innovative activities. We should, however, examine the innovation-performance relationship more thoroughly.

2.1   Strands of innovation literature.   The rationale for attributing efficiency and effectiveness benefits to IT adoptions has been touched upon by many strands of literature. However, much of that literature is not organizational, because it addresses levels of analysis that exceed the firm level (e.g., industry or "technological trajectory") or examines lower or different levels of analysis (such as new products, projects, or new product attributes). Much of the research is anchored in economics and stresses the cost-benefit implications of innovative investments. There seems to be a widespread "pro-innovation bias," and IT is beneficial no matter what. Several traditions in innovation research mirror this bias.

A major tradition has dwelt on learning and views innovation as a never ending quest to fine tune the process and product routines that firms have accumulated (e.g., Arrow, 1962; Rosenberg, 1982). A second tradition links innovation to a firm's production function and examines how innovations substitute for labor or capital production factors (e.g., Davis, 1990; Mensch, 1975). This stream of work overlaps with efforts at examining the so called "hedonic price index." This index captures the changes in product quality relative to changes in price, with the understanding that price changes are more than off set by changes in the product's performance. The research by Chow (1967), for example, showed that the quality-adjusted price of computers as measured by multiplication time, retrieval time, and memory size (during 1960-1965) declined by about 21%.

Other studies try to capture the imminent benefits of innovation. Event studies have, for example, examined whether new product announcements have a discernible effect on changes in abnormal stock returns. The inference here being that the capital markets anticipate the future earnings potential of a new product line (Chaney, Devinney and Winer, 1989). In general, these studies do not examine firm, or firm attributes, as a context for innovation and performance.

2.2 Contributions from Industrial Economics. Among the studies that come closer to the present investigation is extant research on industrial economics and industrial organization, which includes a large body of research examining the performance consequences of R&D expenditures. R&D expenditures can be examined in their own right, or they can be traced as a matter of competitive conduct in which rivals mimic each others' innovative behavior (e.g. Mansfield, 1980; Scherer, 1978; Kamien and Schwartz, 1982; Ben-Zion, 1984). This is probably the most significant area of organizational innovation research to date. In general, the impact of R&D expenditures on subsequent performance is quite strong and clearly attests to the comparative advantage of firms that invest in R&D. The limitation of these studies, however, is that they are highly aggregative in the measurement of innovation, i.e., they typically equate R&D expenditures with innovation. This measurement problem does not only pertain to highly diversified firms, where R&D expenditures at the product line level are lacking. It also applies in highly specialized, single-product firms, where R&D expenditures include a myriad of projects, some of which never culminate in full commercial application. Furthermore, over time R&D expenditures cannot readily be tied to income streams if the lag is too short, or if the latency from expenditures to actual adoption is extensive. R&D expenditures are an input to new products or new production processes, not actual innovative outputs. Finally, much of the R&D expenditures is aimed at product innovations, and far less at process innovations. Both types of innovation may have performance advantages.

Nevertheless, the industrial organization research has informed us on important matters involving innovation, diffusion, and performance. Implicitly, or explicitly, R&D conduct mirrors shared norms among the members of an industry. R&D expenditures are not solely committed on an exclusive cost-benefit basis, but in fact are often competitively induced making the connection between rational premises and choice more tenuous. In fact, over time variations in R&D expenditures among firms can be analyzed with oligopoly models in which firms make conjectures about each others' actions and restrain themselves to preserve competitive equilibria (Pennings, 1981). The saliency of industry norms around R&D should be particularly strong in the domain of new products and services, because innovations may destroy the prevailing order among the members of the industry. Oligopolists observe each others' decisions, and respond to changes that are initiated by a market leader (e.g., Grabowsky and Baxter, 1973). Equilibrium levels signal commonly agreed norms about strategic behavior.

The so called structure-conduct-performance paradigm (e.g., Scherer, 1970), which examines industry norms and coordination among strategically interdependent organizations, has yielded a significant body of findings. This strand of work clearly attests to the importance of collectively defined norms about competitive behavior, including R&D and new product development among rivals. It overlaps considerably with the institutional view of organizations (DiMaggio and Powell, 1983; Zucker, 1985), to which we alluded before, and is suggested as a useful complement to these economic contributions.

2.3   Innovation as institutionalization. Unlike   industrial economic treatments with a strong rational slant, institutional theory assumes that relevant behaviors (pricing, hiring practices, collective bargaining, and last but not least innovations) trigger a flurry of interfirm reactions that eventually evolve into some established pattern of behavior to which most firms conform. Performance issues enter into the argument here. Non-conformity endangers a firm's legitimacy, jeopardizes a firm's reputation, deprives it from sharing in the industry's growth and can even result in bankruptcy. When the conduct involves innovation, this applies specifically to uncertain periods during which initial adopters have set the tone for the remaining members of the pack.

Innovative conformity is probably even more likely in service sectors with high levels of inter-organizational interdependence, mutual coordination, ease of imitation, and low thresholds of competitive reactions. Airlines, telephone companies, and financial institutions have to manage their strategic and operational interdependence. Changes in service delivery, such as airline reservations and electronic fund transfers might even necessitate collective effort before such changes can be presumed to be implemented.

Interdependent service organizations have created various forms of interfirm coordination systems and display high levels of networking. The emergence of industry norms, particularly around new service delivery methods, is therefore highly probable. One might also state that "mimetic isomorphism" (DiMaggio and Powell, 1983) is much more rampant in densely networked industries.

Institutional theory provides insights here that might not be obtained under any other paradigm. As applied to IT investments, the theory would hold that firms adopt certain innovations when uncertainty prevails. Firms seek to eliminate or reduce uncertainty, and by mimicking each others' conduct they enjoy the illusion of infallibility, particularly when the majority of their peer organizations have already innovated (compare DiMaggio and Powell, 1983). Conformity to industry norms also provides a stamp of legitimacy. This sociological interpretation supplements the earlier economic views on IT, in that rational motivations are followed by more "intuitive" reasons to jump on the bandwagon.

Abrahamson and Rosenkopf (1991) have suggested an important synthesis here. Early adopters are guided by rational expectations that the innovative investment will generate maximum returns. Later adopters, in contrast, are guided by the desire to avoid a worst case scenario that non-adoption might be a disastrous decision--even if the information at the time of adoption was too scant and ambiguous to make a full-fledged cost benefit analysis. In the absence of pertinent net present value data, the magnitude of the diffusion in the industry becomes a decisional inducement: somewhere during the ramp-up toward the inflection point, more firms start to run with the pack.

A major shortcoming of institutional theory is the lack of empirical corroboration. Compared to industrial-economic studies, we simply do not have an unequivocal test (Scott, 1988; Tolbert and Zucker, 1983) that informs us about the difference in motivation between early adopters and later adopters. It is possible, however, to assume that later adopters have exploited fewer learning opportunities, and pay dearly for it. Not only have they been guided by incomplete justification, but they have also been travelling shorter on the learning curve.

Early adopters can be described as "lead users" (Urban and von Hippel, 1989). Lead users typically have articulated their needs better, are strongly motivated to find solutions to those needs, and have a greater capacity to absorb those solutions. In fact, lead users are often seen as the source of new process and product innovations. Laggards are less cognizant of new developments, and their learning might be qualitatively different. They engage not as much in "re-invention," (Rogers, 1983) or "learning by using" (Rosenberg, 1982) and therefore enjoy fewer innovation benefits. If the innovation was worth adopting, non-adopters face the worst prospects since they do not engage in any kind of beneficial learning.

2.4 Significance of this study. To summarize, a number of research traditions have examined the benefits of innovation in general and IT adoptions in particular, and generally found justification for a "pro-innovation bias." While there is a disparate set of research traditions on innovation and performance, both individually and jointly, many of these strands have an overly rationalistic conceptualization of innovation. They need to be complemented by paradigms that consider choices as being both rational and mimetic to answer a number of questions. These questions include the relative significance of process and product innovations, the impact of innovations themselves as opposed to R&D expenditures (which are really inputs to innovations as outputs); the implications of innovation for organizational performance, rather than "average" or aggregate performance on the level of process or product (Grilliches, 1984); and the longer term implications of innovations as distinct from the immediate, very short-term consequences. In short, we believe that industrial organization and institutional theory provide the most useful perspective on the innovation's performance effects.

While many studies inform us on the virtues of innovation and strongly endorse the expectation that innovation will improve organizational performance, the application of IT to new products or processes can be disastrous for individual firms (Braun and McDonald, 1982; Henderson and Clark, 1990; Hannan and Freeman, 1984). IT investments may be highly detrimental to a particular firm, if the adoption is overdue and others have reaped most of the benefits, or if IT is implemented with a great deal of reluctance. Non-adoption can also occur when IT is inharmonious with the firm's existing routines, making it difficult to integrate new ideas into the firm's existing repertoire (Nelson and Winter, 1982). If IT diffusion is widespread, the aberrant (i.e., non-adopting) firm will be penalized for its non-conformance.

In this paper we will, therefore, attempt to provide an additional contribution to institutional research on IT and performance. First, we will deal with the IT effects at the organizational level of analysis, rather than product, market, technology, or society level. Second, we will focus on IT as outcomes, or adoption events rather than on inputs such as R&D expenditures. Third, we will explore the differential effects of more than one form of IT on multiple performance indicators. Fourth, the effects are examined longitudinally, as well as cross-sectionally by considering the timing of a firm's adoption relative to that of competing firms as a precursor to changes in performance.

The last aspect forms the cornerstone of the present study and its institutional framework. We view IT adoption events over time as being motivated not only by what happens internally, but also by the activities of peer organizations. Organizations pioneer a given IT or they lag behind, but may eventually join the bandwagon, which is triggered by those innovative pacesetters. Organizations cannot remain idle when "first movers" expand their

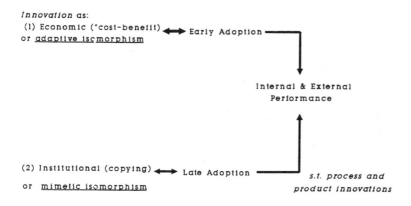

Figure 1. Relationship between Incidence and Timing of Innovation and Organizational Performance

product offerings; provided they observe it, they have to reciprocate their rivals' behavior. Convergence of behavior approximates the above mentioned emergence of industry norms about firm conduct. Hence we may describe this study as an effort to examine IT adoptions as an institutional phenomenon, with the performance benefits being contingent upon the actual adoption and the timing of adoption.

In general, we *hypothesize that IT activities enhance performance.* Secondly, we expect that *earlier adopters enjoy performance advantages over later adopters and non-adopters, although the advantages may vary depending on whether the adoption involves IT-based process or product innovations, and we consider internal versus external as well as general performance.* This hypothesis is further outlined in Figure 1.

Figure 1 gives a schematic representation of our argument and its derivative hypotheses. It indicates that we distinguish innovation in terms of its timing and suggest that early adoptions can be construed as more "rational" and late adoptions as more "mimetic." The adoption and its timing have performance implications, subject to two aspects: (1) process versus product based IT innovation and (2) leaders in front of the pack versus members of the pack. IT as product innovation is more germane to external, and IT as process innovation to internal performance. The rational-mimetic hypothesis is more compatible with and has a greater force for explaining the effects of product innovations. We assume that the institutional hypothesis fits better with visible, outward manifestations of organizational innovation, which is what product innovations represent. Later adopters will face disproportionate performance disadvantages due to delayed legitimization. The delay is due to their reluctance to move earlier. Pioneers, adopting visible innovations might enjoy superior goodwill and are more likely to become a "most admired company" as reported by magazines like *Fortune.* The early and late adopter distinction is probably less pertinent for process innovations.

3. Performance and Banking Innovations

In the present study these issues are examined with respect to the banking industry in the United States. It is particularly in this sector that we witness the simultaneous rather than sequential occurrence of gigantic IT investments. IT pervades both the processing of transaction activities as well as the creation of new services. True, there are still product innovations whose adoption did not require process innovations, or vice versa. For example, banks have refashioned check clearing procedures to reduce their lost availability (i.e., the opportunity costs associated with the "float" whenever checks against other banks are not processed sooner). Likewise, numerous product innovations among banks have been extensive; they range from asset management, NOW accounts, small gifts as inducements, and certificates of deposit. Similarly, decentralization and automation of backroom operations amount to significant process innovations that in themselves had no direct connection with product innovations. All telematic innovations that are discernable in the banking industry strengthen the notion that contemporary banks are increasingly "information banks."

Information technology innovations in banking have been phenomenal (e.g., *The Economist*, 1989). Mohr (1987) refers to a micro-electronic "sweep." Information technology innovations comprise both process and product innovations. Compare automated data processing and video banking respectively. However, as we have argued before, in a service sector like banking the distinction between the two types might not be as sharp as in manufacturing organizations. Product innovations drawing from information technology know-how can have major repercussions on how transactions are processed. Consider for example automated teller machines (ATM) or smart cards, which could be labeled as product innovations, yet these very adoptions do not exclusively represent opportunities for product differentiation, increased customer deposits, or occasions for cross selling. Indeed, these innovations eliminate paper work, data entry, and data retrieval and potentially embody major improvements in efficiency. Obviously, computer based information and telecommunication technologies have been major ingredients of a bank's ability to significantly expand the scope and the competitiveness of its services. However, these very same innovations also provide many opportunities for process improvements as indicated by the time reduction for processing a transaction, by diminishing the number of transactional errors, or by the abatement of slack human resources.

The empirical findings will be presented now. The findings involve product and process innovations. We treat the adoption and expansion of automated teller machines (ATMs) as primarily a service innovation, while the investment in computer hardware and software (HW/SW) can be construed as leaning toward process innovations. While both forms of IT impact efficiency and effectiveness, it is assumed that ATM is more salient from an external, market standpoint, while computers have a greater internal effectiveness relevance. We treat ATM and computer HW/SW as separate innovations, although the former assumes the presence of the latter (Harianto and Pennings, 1989).

Given the more pronounced external visibility of ATMs, the adoption of this innovation should be more congruent with the institutional hypothesis than the adoption of computer HW/SW. The institutional manifestation of innovation effects are further amplified by the widespread interfirm networking which ATM brings about. Computer HW/SW represents largely a stand alone adoption that organizations can accomplish without having to engage in interfirm communication.

In the testing of the hypothesis we need therefore to not only examine the entire banking sample, but also perform an examination of its subgroups. Specifically, the hypothesized relationship may be idiosyncratic to the types of banks involved. Retail banks, for example, are much more sensitive to certain product innovations which incorporate routine banking services, and require a great deal of interfirm coordination. Commercial banks, or wholesale banks, are less concerned with interfirm networking of service delivery, but stress customization of output to their corporate and commercial clients. Interfirm interdependence of innovation implementation is largely absent. McKinsey (1989) showed, for example, that investment in micro-electronics is disproportionately highly profitable for such banks. The distinction between process and product innovation as illustrated by investment in data processing capabilities may be more tenuous for this subgroup. For these banks, the institutional argument is therefore less likely to aid in the interpretation of empirical results.

4.   Methodology

4.1 The sample. The hypotheses were tested with a set of 107 banks, drawn from a list of approximately 250 banks as reported by *The American Banker*. This listing included most of the larger banks, many of which have both consumer and commercial banking operations. The loss of observations was due to several factors. Since the data window comprised eleven years, several banks disappeared from the listing as a result of mergers, acquisitions, and death. Others were deleted due to lack of data. The sampling proceeded retroactively with as many banks with complete data as possible being sampled; the primary consideration was non-missing information with respect to the variables of interest. Some reduction in loss of data was accomplished by interpolation of missing firm years--provided not more than one firm year was missing.

The data covered the period 1977-1987 and originated from various sources. They include *Predicast Index*, *The American Banker*, *FDIC Directories*, *Moody's Financial Directories*, Annual Reports, *Electronic Fund Transfer Directories*, complemented with telephone interviews among about 30% of the firms involved. Additional information on data collection, triangulation, and sampling is reported in Pennings and Harianto (1992).

4.2 The variables. Table 1 presents a listing of the variables, their measurement, and their source. We distinguish between two cost categories and overall cost category to measure efficiency as *internal* performance measures. The other set of dependent variables comprises non-interest income, which was selected from a set of possible *external* performance measures. Finally, we include a *general* performance indicator: cash flow. The independent variables include the two innovation variables (for which we use the metaphorical description of process and product innovation) as well as several control variables.

The innovation represented adoptions of either of the two types, i.e., process (computer SW/HW) or "product" (ATM) innovations. In the present study, two different variable construction approaches were undertaken. They both are aimed at testing the hypotheses, but do so in alternative ways. We constructed innovation variables as (1) "cumulative share" and (2) discrete adoption decisions. The cum-ulative share idea led to the construction of innovation variables in terms of a firm's increment, if any, in its cumulative share of technology stock that was currently present in the banking industry.

$$I = \sum_{t=1}^{11} \frac{\sum_{j=1}^{t} innovation_i^t}{\sum_{j=1}^{t} \sum_{k=1}^{i} innovation_k^j} \tag{1}$$

where I stands for cumulative innovative share of firm i in year t. We might think in terms of the banking industry accumulating a stock of technology that is shared by some of its firms. At any time any firm might increase its share in that stock by adding chunks to that stock--hence its "cumulative share."

Table 1. Listing of Variables and their Measurement

NAME	*SOURCE*
Computer Hardware	Adoptions listed and Software by Predicast (1977-87)
ATM	Adoptions listed by <u>Predicast</u> (1977-87)
Region(WEST)	AZ,CA,NV,WA,OR
Region (NO-EAST)	CO, ID, IL, IN, IA, KS, KY, MI, MN, MO, MT, NB, ND, OH, SD, UT, WI, WY
Region (NO-EAST)	CT, DE, DC, ME, WD, MA, NH, NJ, NY, PA, RI, VT
Region (SO-WEST)	AL, FL, GA, MS, NC, PR, SC, TN, VA, WV
Commercial Loans	Annual Report
Consumer Loans	Annual Report
Real Estate Loans	Annual Report
Total Domestic Loans	Annual Report
Personnel Expenses	Personnel/Assets
Other Expenses	All Expenses, Exclusive of Personnel Expenses, from Annual Report / Assets
Efficiency	(Salary + Equipment + Personnel + Interest + Other + Prms) / Assets, from Annual Report
Other Income	Other Income / Assets, from Annual Report
Cashflow	(Net Income Before Taxes + Loss Provisions + Depreciation) / Assets, from Annual Report
Assets	Annual Report

During the eleven year window a bank may adopt one or more IT in any of two technology categories. For example, ATM can begin with a single cash machine and culminate in the joining of a regional, national, or even an international electronic network. Likewise, banks follow a learning curve in computer hardware and software in which they continuously add new systems to their existing repertoire of systems and programs. Note the difference with R&D expenditures, which is a commonly used innovation measure in industrial economics. Innovation as measured here is not an input, but amounts to one or more events that can be viewed as output.

The rationale for constructing IT innovations as "cumulative share" was predicated on the earlier mentioned institutional paradigm and the associated assumption that performance benefits of IT accrue more to early adopters than to those who refrain from adoption or join the bandwagon at a later point in time. Furthermore, this innovation measure captures both the firm and industry level of analysis. It acknowledges that innovation may be either an "efficient choice" or a "fad" (Abrahamson, 1991). The technological innovation index was constructed for both automated teller machines and computer hardware and software. Note that innovation adoption need not be a single event within the eleven year window; for example, initially a bank may have installed its own rudimentary cash machine, and later have expanded the technology to include other services such as account information retrieval, the joining of a regional or national ATM network, and the formation of electronic clearing houses. The ATM technology stock continues to expand by virtue of the initiatives of various banks, by so called "network externalities," but also, of course, by new technological developments. Consistent with the earlier reasoning, we assumed that the computer HW/SW was more predictive of internal performance aspects, while ATM was more susceptible to competitive mimicking and should therefore be more relevant for external performance considerations.

The cumulative share index captures IT investments as either "rational" or "mimetic." The variable has the effect of giving rather low weight to firms which are in the rear of the pack (i.e., late adopters) or to innovations that are adopted rather late. Therefore, we added a second analysis strategy, by simply taking the technological innovations, and complementing them with a dummy variable: 1 for innovations that are adopted during the early years of our window, and 0 otherwise. Note that the window 1977-1987 was a crucial period for the US banking industry because it was in this period that investments in computer hardware exploded, and the growth of automated teller machines expanded each year exponentially.

In addition to the IT variables, the models included regional dummy variables and loan portfolio variables to adjust for strategic differences. In our model, we employed therefore nine right-hand-side variables, including the two innovation variables. Since the statistical procedure adjusts for heteroskedasticity, size as an independent variable was not included in the model.

The dependent variables were obtained from the banks' annual reports. Internal performance measures include "other" expenses, efficiency, and personnel expenses. "Other expenses" seems like a rest category, but actually covers mostly expenses in "plant and equipment." External performance includes non-interest or "other" income. Finally, cash flow is a generic performance index; unlike RoI it is immune to extensive depreciations of non-performing assets, particularly those involving Latin American countries. We chose cash flow rather than profitability since the latter indicator is highly sensitive to provisions for loan losses. A bank's income comprises both interest and non-interest income, but for the present study we focus on the latter.

4.3   The design. Pooled, cross-sectional time series regression analysis, employing the so called Parks method, was conducted. The method is described in the SUGI Supplementary Library User's Guide manual(SAS, 1986). In this method, the error is assumed to be heteroskedastic and is taken into account in the estimation process. The intercept term was not suppressed. All variables were standardized with a mean of zero and a standard deviation of 1. Furthermore, this method lags the dependent variable by one year. More formally, the model is as follows:

$$Y_{ij} = \sum_{k=9}^{11} X_{ijk}\beta_k + e_{ik} + \varepsilon_{jk} \qquad (2)$$

In this estimation procedure, the effects of nine independent variables (X_{ijk}) on performance (Y_{ij}) are examined. Both the dependent and independent variables have a time (e_{ik}) and a cross-sectional (ε_{jk}) error component. The error term can be decomposed accordingly. We are particularly interested in the two innovation variables; the remaining seven variables are largely control variables.

The pooled, cross sectional time series regression analysis examines the effects of independent variables over time (Sayrs, 1989). Unlike a single time series where one would examine the evolution within one case, we compared here a large number of cases over eleven years. In the procedure, the model assumed is first-order autoregressive, with contemporaneous correlation between the cross sections. The covariance matrix for the vector of random errors follows through two stages. (1) From ordinary least squares regression, beta is estimated to obtain the fitted residuals in order to compute the first order autoregressive parameter; the autoregressive nature of the data can be removed by the transformation of taking weighted differences. (2) The second step in estimating the covariance matrix of error terms consists then of applying ordinary least squares to the transformed data before the generalized least squares analysis can proceed. Further details are furnished by Zellner (1962).

While the models were equivalent for internal ("efficiency") and external ("effectiveness") measures, it was surmised that compared with ATM, computer HW/SW innovations were not as sensitive to mimetic isomorphism. Accordingly, we expected the former variable to have a stronger effect on non-financial performance indices such as income derived from fees, and the latter a stronger effect on internal performance measures. Product innovations were more conspicuous or ostentatious and not only benefit "lead users," but also conferred legitimacy, albeit diminished, to tardy adopters when the innovation became widely dispersed. Such legitimacy considerations were less applicable to imperceptible innovations like investments in data processing equipment. We also assumed that the effects would be stronger for banks strongly committed to retail banking since the labor for automation substitution benefits were more likely in those banks that processed large volumes of information. We expected ATM also to be more germane to those banks which had a comparatively large volume of retail operations.

5. Results

Table 2 presents the results involving internal, external, and general performance indicators. The main concern is with the two innovation variables. Both have effects in the hypothesized direction: ATM and computer HW/SW reduce "other" expenses and personnel expenses, while improving cash flow and "other" income. Consistent with the hypotheses the effect on "other" expenses is stronger for the computer investments ($\beta = -.023$; $t = -103.91$) than for the ATM investments ($\beta = -.008$; t -7.59). There is a slight tendency for the former to have a stronger effect on internal performance, and for the latter to have a stronger effect on external performance, although computer investments have larger though less significant consequences. Computer HW/SW enables banks to market and to license software to peer institutions and other customers, thus generating substantial amounts of non-interest income (compare $\beta = 0.03$; $t = 3.25$). Furthermore, banks that have heavily invested in computer HW/SW can deliver extensive data processing services for both banks and non-banks, thereby generating substantial non-interest revenues. Those information technology based assets are more lucrative than assets aimed at interest income (McKinsey, 1989).

The timing of adoption of computer HW/SW relative to the timing adoption of competing organizations has therefore important efficiency and effectiveness implications. The analysis involving "overall" efficiency remains inconclusive: the results show a negligible effect of both innovation measures on the banks' overall efficiency ($\beta = .021$ and $-.014$ respectively). Naturally, this efficiency measure involves *all* expense categories, including those for generating interest income and non-interest income, so this finding might not be as robust.

The effect of the regional dummies shows that southern banks are comparatively less efficient. Finally, consumer loans make for lower efficiency levels. Overall, it should also be noted that the effects reported in Table 2 are stronger compared to the analysis in which the dependent variables were not lagged (results not reported). The implication is that there exists some latency for the innovation variables to have their hypothesized effect.

Table 3 presents results on *internal*, and Table 4 on *external* performance, but now the analysis involves a sub-group analysis for banks that are either strongly or mildly committed to retail banking. We anticipate that the product innovation effects stand out more among retail oriented banks. We continue to expect the two innovation variables to have a divergent impact on the two classes of performance variables, but in this sub-group analysis, the effects' bifurcations should be even more pronounced. ATMs are primarily devices for delivering retail banking services. Computer HW/SW is more inconspicuous.

Table 3 shows that computer HW/SW has major effects on "other" and personnel expenses, particularly for banks emphasizing retail banking, although the group of banks on the left hand side of this table also witnessed reductions in personnel expenses. Table 4 shows that the effect of ATM adoptions on external performance is significant for retail banking but not for other types of banks (compare β coefficients of $.0014$ (t=5.01) and $.019$ (t= 2.81) versus $.0025$(NS) and $.0056$(NS) respectively). In contrast, computer HW/SW effects do not conform to the hypothesized bifurcation of the effects. In fact, banks de-

Table 2. Time Series Cross-Section Regression: Analysis of Performance and Technological Innovation.*

	Internal Performance			External Performance	"General" Performance
	"Other" Expenses	Efficiency	Personnel Expenses	"Other" Income	Cashflow
Intercept	0.324	0.097	0.799	0.041	-0.062
	7.01	2.75	1.37	0.42	-4.28
ATM	-0.008	0.021	-0.002	0.022	0.004
	-7.59	1.4	.28	1.46	3.56
Computer HW/SW	-0.023	-0.014	0.011	0.03	0.02
	-103.91	-1.45	-4.28	3.25	2.7
Northeast	-0.371	-0.137	0.634	-0.463	0.014
	-3.91	-1.56	1.57	-4.29	1.67
South	0.139	0.386	1.27	-0.033	1.05
	0.86	2.34	7.00	-0.14	5.72
Midwest	-0.483	-0.117	0.850	-0.374	-0.0079
	-6.99	-2.75	1.46	-1.68	-0.07
Loan (Commercial)	-0.241	-0.171	-0.103	0.055	0.457
	-15.75	-5.89	-5.87	0.42	9.23
Loan (Consumer)	0.284	-0.0045	0.045	0.165	0.135
	53.65	-0.65	19.44	2.09	8.86
Loan (Real Estate)	-0.101	-0.111	-0.092	-0.025	0.142
	-19.06	-4.63	-6.83	-0.27	4.71
Loan (Domestic)	-0.023	0.266	0.131	-0.032	-0.78
	-1.40	8.48	4.53	-0.16	-8.90
No. of observations	1177	1177	1144	1177	1177

Note: Values under the coefficients are t-values
*The first entry in each column represents standardized regression coefficients.

Table 3.   Time Series Cross-Section Regression Analysis of "Internal" Performance Subgroup Analysis Based on Degree of Consumer Banking

	Banks Emphasizing Retail Banking			Banks De-emphasizing Retail Banking		
	"Other" Expenses	Efficiency	Personnel Expenses	"Other" Expenses	Efficiency	Personnel Expenses
Intercept	0.437	-0.016	-0.308	0.015	-0.019	0.330
	13.69	-0.14	-3.08	0.44	-0.15	0.93
ATM	-0.004	0.009	-.007	0.001	0.005	0.003
	-1.13	0.41	-3.24	0.05	0.43	0.27
Computer HW/SW	-0.012	-0.011	0.007	0.021	0.008	-0.001
	-3.78	-1.10	3.7	1.83	0.39	-0.18
Northeast	-0.408	0.121	0.047	-0.255	-0.168	-0.444
	-5.88	1.08	1.16	-3.37	-1.50	-.88
South	-0.611	-0.055	0.418	-0.128	1.74	0.384
	-5.44	-0.39	1.08	-0.12	1.48	0.489
Midwest	-0.662	-0.063	-0.201	-0.323	-0.097	-10.49
	-10.25	-0.84	-2.27	-2.26	-1.29	-0.42
Loan (Commercial)	-1.421	-0.233	-0.171	-0.024	0.008	-0.157
	-28.66	-1.68	-10.41	-1.08	0.14	-6.81
Loan (Consumer)	0.305	-0.012	0.021	0.25	0.026	0.072
	52.59	-0.26	2.82	10.28	0.70	5.27
Loan (Real Estate)	-0.823	-0.162	-0.104	0.065	-0.023	-0.123
	-37.54	-2.10	-11.84	2.55	-0.54	-4.04
Loan (Domestic)	1.699	0.408	0.205	-0.307	0.03	0.138
	28.19	2.57	12.78	-6.15	0.36	3.67
No. of observations	539	539	528	638	638	616

Note: Values under the coefficients are t-values
        *The first entry in each column represents standardized regression coefficients.

Table 4.   Time Series Cross-Section Regression Analysis of "External Performance Subgroup Analysis Based on Degree of Consumer Banking.*

	Banks With Retail Emphasis		Banks De-emphasizing Retail Banking	
	Cashflow	"Other" Income	Cashflow	"Other" Income
Intercept	-0.034	0.103	-0.035	-0.105
	-6.93	1.07	-9.97	-0.98
ATM	0.0027	0.019	0.0025	0.0056
	5.01	2.81	1.75	1.14
Computer HW/SW	0.0014	0.003	0.029	0.036
	2.75	0.49	5.14	7.17
Northeast	-0.008	-0.45	-0.007	-0.287
	-0.38	-7.64	-0.44	-3.52
South	0.025	-0.166	1.352	0.791
	2.91	-0.96	5.73	1.14
Midwest	0.01	-0.117	0.025	-0.216
	2.06	-1.11	4.13	-4.14
Loan (Commercial)	0.0027	0.203	0.757	0.059
	0.52	2.25	43.93	5.65
Loan (Consumer)	0.0087	0.089	0.211	0.189
	4.22	1.32	27.68	16.00
Loan (Real Estate)	0.0084	-0.01	0.258	-0.0035
	1.75	-0.13	31.78	-0.31
Loan (Domestic)	-0.015	-0.063	-1.23	-0.137
	-1.62	-0.28	-37.18	-5.33
No. of observations	539	539	638	638

Note: Values under the coefficients are t-values
*The first entry in each column represents standardized regression coefficients.

emphasizing retail banking enjoy greater amounts of non-interest income (compare ß = .003 (NS) and ß = .036 (t== 7.17) respectively) per unit of invested computer HW/SW. They appear to reap more income from their involvement in information technology. Nevertheless, Tables 3 and 4 combined reveal that these IT adoptions have performance effects that are contingent on the strategic orientation of the banks of this study.

Finally, a subgroup analysis was conducted in which the sample of firms was partitioned into those that did not adopt ATM or computer HW/SW technology during the period 1977-1982 versus those that did. Problems of multi-collinearity and small numbers render the documentation of results somewhat inconclusive. This analysis yielded mixed support for the hypothesis. For example, the ATM effect on salary expenses was - 658.04 (t=-4.66) for late adopters, but 59.49 (t=7.09) for early adopters. Late adopters show also better cash flow but not better streams of non-interest income.

6.   Discussion

This paper has attempted to identify the performance impact of two types of innovations in the financial services sector. Computer HW/SW and ATM were viewed as manifestations of process and product based IT innovation respectively, and organizational performance was partitioned into internal and external criteria. The results show that both computer HW/SW and ATM innovations have a positive effect on efficiency and effectiveness indicators. There is also a tendency for computer innovations to have a stronger effect on internal performance, and ATM on external performance. Yet some findings, contrary to the hypothesis, suggest that not all IT investors get "bank for the buck." Furthermore, the analysis yielded additional insights when we contrasted banks which differ in their emphasis on retail banking.

The paper followed an economic-institutional argument, with the implication that innovation may be adopted on seemingly sub-rational grounds. Although we hypothesized ATM to have a stronger external performance effect, the results indicated that computer HW/SW has also strong external performance considerations. The strong effect of computer HW/SW is consistent with the findings of management consultants; McKinsey (1989) had already revealed that software sales and consulting yield far greater returns per invested dollar, or per one unit of asset, than did expansion of traditional financial services. This paper echoes the McKinsey publication and shows that successful banks are increasingly those that fit the label "information banks." Unfortunately, the IT measures are categorical variables, precluding logarithmic transformation and therefore preventing a simple production function test.

It has been assumed in this study that IT adoptions are not solely implemented for their expected operational or marketing benefits. Banks are highly interdependent in the providing of services. Many banking services have near-commodity like qualities, such that banks should conform strongly to prevailing industry norms. These norms include the automation of service delivery, with ATMs as the most visible manifestation. The pioneers, which have left the pack, might have been motivated by cost-benefit consideration, i.e., what DiMaggio and Powell (1983) have called "adaptive isomorphisms." The members of the increasingly shrinking pack of non-adopters will experience growing pressures to jump on the bandwagon, their motivations being "mimetic" rather than "adaptive" (DiMaggio and Powell, 1983; Abrahamson and Rosenkopf, 1991). From the results presented here, it would appear that mimetic adopters enjoy fewer performance advantages than their innovating competitors who left the pack early. Of course, those firms which stay on the side line have even fewer benefits.

The emergence of industry practices has been of interest to many industrial economists. Such practices are often inferred from statistical moments (e.g., mean level of R&D or advertising expenditures). In longitudinal studies on R&D investments, it has been shown that leading firms are mimicked by laggards (e.g., Grabowsky and Baxter, 1973). Other manufacturing industries may show similar patterns. However, what sets a service industry like banking apart is the presence of network externalities. Banks are mutually dependent on the delivery of financial services, and any IT investment will reverberate throughout their network. Diffusion of innovations having a normative character is more likely. We should therefore expect that in such industries firms have less discretion as to whether they jump on the bandwagon. The results in this study show that non-involvement or delayed adoption puts them at a disadvantage.

It would be interesting to examine the interaction effects between the process and administrative innovations, particularly because this would furnish a more robust test of what Damanpour, Szabat and Evan (1989) call "technological lag." Likewise, more understanding about the interplay between process and product innovations is desirable.

In their developmental framework, Abernathy and Utterback (1987) represent process and product innovations with learning effects that evolve as successive movements around musical chairs. The process and product "S curves" succeed each other. When the process improvements are increasingly smaller, there is a growing likelihood for substitutes of the existing product design to emerge, one of which eventually might replace the old design. The new product will receive growing market acceptance and culminate into a dominant design, but will initially remain quite expensive and saddled with design flaws. The new product will diffuse until it begins to taper off, after which process improvements and associated efficiency gains permit price reductions. These price reductions stimulate additional demand until the market begins to saturate. Only those firms which then establish cost leadership by rationalizing and innovating in their production efforts can continue to compete. A well know example is Ford's Model T, a major automotive product innovation, followed by the introduction of the assembly line, illustrating a significant process innovation. Subsequently we have witnessed additional innovations in the automobile industry, up to the recent process innovations such as Just In Time inventory, group technology, and robotics that have been developed by Japanese firms (e.g., Clark and Fujimoto, 1991). Other examples can be found in the semiconductor, ship building, and home construction industries.

The process-product distinction may be overstated, however. Product changes often necessitate process redesign (Henderson and Clark, 1991) and numerous process innovations facilitate product innovations (e.g., Sanderson and Uzumuri, 1989). It may be more appropriate to examine whether the process-product innovation distinction is more germane to specific industries--for example, capital intensive versus labor intensive ones, or manufacturing versus service sectors, and to specific performance indicators. Various industries such as health care, transportation, telecommunication, and last but not least banking, have witnessed an information technology sweep (Mohr, 1987) that has not only affected their internal operations, but has also altered the service delivery system and the role that the client plays in producing the service. The results reported here are germane to other types of service organizations as well as manufacturing organizations. More research is needed however, to substantiate this claim.

6.1   Service versus manufacturing. The saliency of the distinction between process and product innovation may be greater in manufacturing than in a service industry like banking. In many manufacturing firms, the production process is sharply segregated from the recipients of outputs. Except for some industrial customer-producer relationships, the customer has little awareness of the technology required to produce the output. In contrast, the customer of a service organization is often intimately exposed to the rendering of outputs and is often an active contributor. The immediate exposure to the "production process" renders the process-product distinction therefore less adequate. Many service firms typically integrate the customer into the service rendering and delivery process (compare Normann, 1985).

Consider some examples. In libraries the customer takes the book from the shelf and checks it out, in medical centers he interacts with physicians and nurses in order to receive medical care, and when visiting a bank branch he communicates with officers to process a loan or to research the balance of his account. Innovations in these sectors often impart a blend of process and product transformations. Thus, in libraries the customer can benefit from computerized, on line, real time retrieval systems; in health care the patient can purchase pregnancy, cholesterol, and other detection kits. Many banks have introduced electronic fund transfer and smart cards, again illustrating innovations that embrace both the production of a service and the use function for its customer. The role of the recipient can vary on dimensions such as amount of contact with the organization, degree of delegation of service production, or the amount of time the customer is included in the organization. Yet the attributes of these product innovations are very much conditioned by the process through which they are generated.

Unlike manufacturing innovations, many service innovations can be copied over night, affording pioneer limited, first mover advantages. The rapid diffusion of innovations such as Individual Retirement Account, Electronic Tax Filing, and Frequent Flyer Discounts illustrate the comparative ease of mimicking competitors' moves. Institutional arguments might therefore be more applicable to banking and other service industries and provide a better setting for treating innovation as an institutional phenomenon.

Some service innovations, however, are anchored in capital intensive systems, necessitating process innovations. In banking, we need only to mention "trivial" IT applications such as "900 numbers," which simply bills the caller for a service received, or "debit card" which debits a card user's checking account. Such innovation implementation calls for extensive interfirm networking. Ease of copying and interfirm delivery arrangements in the service sector point to the importance of a firm's institutional environment in shaping its adoption decisions, and should furnish us with a better account of the innovation-performance relationship.

The paper is limited to financial returns, not so called "social" returns which are probably significant (Mansfield, 1977). Social returns include improved quality of service, customer satisfaction, or cost and time savings due to automation of information processing. In view of the earlier distinction between product and process innovation and the associated role of being a producer or user of innovation, it would be most desirable to determine these social returns.

These returns might be at variance with the firms' financial returns. This is because, as we have seen, the diffusion of micro-electric technology may eventually amount to substantial customer savings which occur at the expense of their banks (e.g., because of the float elimination).

The strong effect of IT on measurable productivity indices suggests that there are considerable competitive advantages for banks in adopting new technology. Many banks have been laggards, postponing the acquisition of hardware and software. As the popular business press (e.g., *The Economist*, 1989) has pointed out, banks have little choice in whether or not to adopt such new technology—they must. It is equally clear that new technology has generated surplus benefits for banks which do. This new technology provides not only private returns to a bank, but also enhances the firm's ability to differentiate its products. While these externalities were not included in the examination of technological innovations, it is plausible to assume that they are prevalent.

IT adoption may not always yield the immediate returns that were expected. As the results indicated, it takes time for organizations to absorb the new technology. While learning "by using" the new technology, they may in fact encounter decline in productivity and income--a decline which is sometimes called the innovation's "productivity paradox" (Davis, 1990).

Underlying these speculations is the view that in a service sector like banking, competitive mimicking is widespread and imperative. Banks display dense levels of interfirm networking, they depend on each other for service delivery, and are governed by extensive governmental regulation. Firms in this sector have very little room to deviate from industry standards. Any innovative activity that acquires some momentum creates strong inducements to participate in fads and fashion. Even if the immediate cost-benefit implications of IT remain ambiguous, banks are still pressured to join the bandwagon since doing so furnishes a stamp of legitimacy. That stamp may have performance implications in its own right as the results of this study suggest.

References

Abernathy,W., and J. Utterback (1987). "Patterns of technological innovation," *Technology Review* 80, 40-47.

Abrahamson, E. (1991). "Managerial fads and fashions: the diffusion and rejection of innovations," *Academy of Management Review* 16, 586-612.

Abrahamson, E., and L. Rosenkopf (1991). "When do bandwagon diffusions roll? How far do they go? And when do they roll backwards: a computer simulation," *Academy of Management Best Paper Proceedings*.

American Banker (1977-1988). *Annual Survey* (The American Banker, Washington DC).

Arrow, K. (1962). "The economic implications of learning by doing," *Review of Economic Studies* 29, 155-173.

Braun, E., and S. McDonald (1982). *Revolution in Miniature: The History and Impact of Semiconductor Electronics*. 2d ed. (Cambridge University Press, New York, NY).

Ben-Zion, U. (1984). "The R&D and investment decision and its relationship to the firm's market value: some preliminary results," in Z. Sos (ed.), *R&D, Patents and Productivity* (University of Chicago Press, Chicago, IL), 299-312.

Chaney, P.K., T.M. Devinney and R.S. Winer (1989). "The impact of new product introductions on the market value of the firms," Working Paper, Marketing Science Institute, Cambridge, MA.

Chow, G.C. (1967). "Technological change and the demand for computers," American Economic Review, 57: 1117-1130.

Clark, K. B., and T. Fujimoto (1991). *Product Development Performance* (Harvard Business School Press, Boston MA).

DiMaggio, P., and W.W. Powell (1983). "The iron-cage revisited: institutional isomorphism and collective rationality in organizational fields," *American Sociological Review* 48, 147-160.

Damanpour, F., K.A. Szabat, and W.M. Evan (1989). "The relationship between types of innovation and organizational performance," *Journal of Management Studies* 26, 587-601.

Davis, P.A. (1990). "The dynamo and the computer: an historical perspective on the modern productivity paradox," *American Economic Review* 80, 355-361.

Directory of Electronic Fund Transfer (1986). *Directory of Electronic Fund Transfer* (EFT, New York, NY).

The Economist (1989). "Metamorphosis: a survey of international banking," (March 25, 1989).

Federal Deposit and Insurance Commission (1976-1983). *Bank Operating Statistics*. (FDIC, Washington, DC).

------- (1985-1987). *Statistics on Banking* (FDIC, Washington, DC).

Goodman, P.S., and J.M. Pennings (1977). *New Perspectives in Organizational Effectiveness* (Jossey Bass, San Francisco).

Grabowsky, H.G., and N.D. Baxter (1973). "Rivalry in industrial research and development: an empirical study," *Journal of Industrial Economics* 21, 209-235.

Grilliches, Z. (1984). *R&D, Patents and Productivity* (University of Chicago Press, Chicago).

Hannan, M.T., and J. Freeman (1984). "Structural inertia and organizational change," *American Sociological Review* 49, 149-164.

Harianto, F., and J.M. Pennings (1989). "Technological innovations through interfirm linkages," in L. Gomes and M. L. Lawless (eds.), *Managing the High-Technology Firm* (JAI Press, Greenwich, CT).

Henderson, R.M., and K.B. Clark (1990). "Architectural innovation: the reconfiguration of existing product technologies and the failure of established firms," *Administrative Science Quarterly* 35, 9-30.

Kamien, M.I., and N.L. Schwartz (1982). *Market Structure and Innovation* (Cambridge University Press, New York, NY).

Mahajan,V., E. Muller, and F.M. Bass (1990). "New product diffusion models in marketing: a review and directions for research," *Journal of Marketing* 54, 1-26.

Mansfield, E. (1980). "Basic research and productivity increase in manufacturing," *American Economic Review* 70, 863-873.

Mansfield, E. (1977). "Social and private rates of return from industrial innovations," in E. Mansfield (ed.), *The Production nd Appropriation of New Industrial Technology* (Norton,New York), 144-166.

McKinsey (1989). "Electronic returns in banking," cited by *The Economist*, "Metamorphosis: a survey on international banking."

Mensch, G. (1975). *Stalemate in Technology* (Ballinger, Cambridge, MA).

Mohr, L.B. (1987). "Innovation from the vantage point of new electronic technology in organizations," in J.M. Pennings and A. Buitendam (eds.), *New Technology as Organizational Innovation* (Ballinger, Cambridge, MA), 13-34.

Moody (1978-1988). *Manual for Banking and Finance* (Moody, New York, NY).

Normann, R. (1985). *Service Management: Strategy and Leadership* (Wiley, New York, NY).

Nelson, R.R., and S.G. Winter (1982). *An Evolutionary Theory of Economic Change* (Harvard University Press, Cambridge, MA).

Pavitt, K. (1991). "Key characteristics of large innovating firms," *British Journal of Management* 2, 41-50.

Pennings, J.M. (1981). "Strategically interdependent organizations," in P.C. Nystrom and W.H. Starbuck (eds.), *Handbook of Organization Design* (Oxford University Press, New York, NY).

Pennings, J.M. and F. Harianto (1992). "Technological networking and innovation implementation," *Organization Science* 3, forthcoming.

Phillips, A. (1985). "Changing technology and future financial activity," in R.C. Aspinwaa and R.A. Eisenbeis (eds.), *Handbook of Banking Strategy* (Wiley, New York, NY), 125-148.

Predicast (1978-1988). *Index of American Business* (Predicast, New York, NY).

Rogers, E.M. (1983). *Diffusion of Innovations*. 3d ed., (Free Press, New York:, NY).

Rosenberg, N. (1982). *Inside the Black Box: Technology and Economics* (Cambridge University Press, New York, NY).

Sanderson, S. W., and V. Uzumuri (1989). "Strategies for new product development and renewal: design based incrementalism," Working Paper, Center for Science and Technology Policy, Rensselear Polytechnic Institute.

Sayrs, L.W. (1989). *Pooled Time Series Analysis* (Sage, Newbury Park, CA).

SAS (1986). *SUGI Supplementary Library User's Manual*. version5 ed., (SAS Institute, Cary, NC).

Scherer, F.M. (1970). *Industrial Market Structure and Economic Performance* (Rand McNally, Chicago, IL).

___ (1982). "Firm size, market structure, opportunity and the output of patented inventions," *American Economic Review* 68, 1097-1125

Scott, W.R. (1988). "The adolescence of institutional theory," *Administrative Science Quarterly* 31, 493-511.

Tolbert, P.S., and L. G. Zucker (1983). "Institutional sources of change in the formal structure of organizations: the diffusion of civil service reform, 1880-1935," *Administrative Science Quarterly* 28, 22-39.

Urban, G.L., and E. von Hippel (1989). "Lead user analysis for the development of new industrial products," *Management Science* 34, 569-582.

Williamson, O.E. (1975). *Markets and Hierarchies* (Free Press, New York, NY).

Zellner, A. (1962). "An efficient method for estimating seemingly unrelated regressions and test for aggregation bias," *Journal of the American Statistical Association* 57, 348-368.

Zucker, L. (1985). "Organizations as institutions," in S.B. Bacharach (ed.), *Research in the Sociology of Organizations* (JAI Press, Greenwich,CT), 1-47.

Chapter 10   Improving Claims Operations: A Model-Based Approach

Uday M. Apte, Richard A. Cavaliere and G. G. Hegde

1. Introduction

The insurance business requires an insurance company to pay the insured in the event of a loss in return for the insured's payment of the premium to the insurance company. In case of a loss, the insured files a claim with the insurance company, which then moves on to perform the necessary investigation and evaluation of the claim before making the appropriate payment to the insured. The process of claims investigation, evaluation and payment is known as the claims handling or claims adjustment process and is one of the most essential and basic functions of an insurance company.

The claims handling process has a significant impact on the profitability of a property and casualty (P&C) insurance company.[1] A poor performance in claims handling can lead to excessively large loss payments in some cases and unfairly low payments in others, leading to both low profitability and unhappy customers. In fact, arriving at a loss payment that is fair, i.e., neither more nor less than what the insured deserves, is a fundamental responsibility of an insurance company. In addition, the claimant is also interested in receiving the payment in a timely manner. Hence, an efficient and effective management of

---

[1]The property and casualty insurance companies sell insurance products such as automobile, home owners, product liability and workers compensation. The P&C insurance companies represented about $200 billion in premiums out of a total of $500 billion for the total insurance industry.

P. T. Harker (ed.), The Service Productivity and Quality Challenge, 281–310.

claims handling process, from both time and cost perspectives, is considered a critical success factor for the insurance industry.

The P&C insurance industry's profitability is cyclical in nature with alternating periods of profits and losses. During the period of losses, a natural managerial tendency is to cut costs by reducing staff including that in the claims department. The claims handling workload, however, remains high as it is determined by the number of policies sold in the previous profitable years. Mismatch of increased workload and reduced staff results in overloaded claims analysts and increased backlog of unsettled claims (Martin, 1986). The resultant need to reduce backlog puts pressure on some analysts to settle claims, on an average, for amounts larger than warranted (Stevenson, 1988). The profitability, consequently, suffers even further. A key component in managing claims operation, therefore, is to maintain an adequate claims handling capacity. A claims manager is, at present, somewhat handicapped at making this medium-term capacity planning decision, since, neither the insurance nor the operations management literature contains models suitable for this task. A claims manager is also faced with other important day-to-day operational decisions such as assignment of claims to analysts, choice of claims handling method, and involvement of an attorney. In this paper, we propose model based approaches for addressing both of these needs of a claims operations manager.

A review of insurance literature shows that a vast body of material, mainly in the realm of actuarial and underwriting sciences, is available concerning the financial aspects of claims handling where the size and distribution of loss payments are analyzed. See, for example, Cummins and Harrington (1984) on forecasting of auto paid-claims cost, Hogg and Klugman (1984) on mathematics of loss distributions, Peterson (1981) on loss reserving and Paulson and Faris (1984) on measuring distribution of total annual claims.

In comparison, however, only a small body of literature is available concerning the operational aspects of the claims handling process. Moreover, the available literature on claims operations, except perhaps the paper by Apte and Cavaliere (1993) which lays foundation for some of the work presented here, is mostly descriptive in nature. For example, refer to Cissley (1980), Crane (1984), Magarick (1989) or Webb, et al. (1981).

In this paper, we address the need for analytical approaches for improving the management of claims handling operation by proposing two specific model-based prescriptive approaches. First, we present a capacity planning model for claims handling process (CHP) and illustrate its use through a numerical example. Second, we discuss the results of the empirical study conducted at a large P&C insurance company involving about 20,000 "automobile bodily injury" claims. The purpose of this study was to identify important attributes that drive the cost and time performance of claims handling process, and to understand the implications of such analysis for helping claims operations managers deal with day-to-day operational decisions.

The paper is organized in five sections including this introductory section. In the next section, we present an overview of the claims handling process and discuss the important medium-term and operational decisions faced by a claims operations manager. In the third section, we develop a capacity planning model of claims handling process, and illustrate its use through an example. In the fourth section, we discuss the results of the empirical study on development of decision rules to aid operational decisions. We conclude the paper in the fifth section by discussing managerial implications of these analytical approaches to claims handling operation.

2. Claims   Handling   Operation: Process   Overview   and   Managerial Decisions

The claims handling process begins in the mail room where the mail clerks separate new claims by lines-of-business (LOB) such as automobile, property and liability. This mail is distributed to a "set-up" committee consisting of LOB and other managers. The set-up committee performs a preliminary review of the claim file to judge the complexity of the claim, and assigns it to a suitable claims representative (or rep for short).

After making a determination that the said loss is covered under the insurance contract, a claims rep begins the process of investigation, documentation and evaluation (i.e., estimation of the size of fair payment) of the claim. After completing these, negotiations with the insured or claimant or their representatives are started. When all parties are in agreement, the claim is finally settled by the claims rep by authorizing a loss payment and writing the final report for closing the claim file.

In the case of a simple automobile accident claim, a claims rep may need to perform about four to six hours of claims adjustment work. The total time that a claim may spend in the system, however, is significantly longer since the process of gathering information depends on parties external to the system. During this time, a claims rep continues to work in parallel on other claims. In practice, a claims rep's diary, at any given time, typically contains two hundred or more claims.

A claims office handles several classes of claims based on the line of business and complexity. This diversity of claims is handled by specialization of claims reps.

2.1   Medium-term decisions. The decisions faced by a claims operations manager can be divided in two categories: medium-term decisions and short-term, or day-to-day operational decisions. Inadequate capacity can lead to insufficient investigation and evaluation of claims due to overload of handling work on claims reps. This, in turn, can lead to both low profitability and unhappy customers as mentioned earlier. Hence, making sure that the claims handling capacity is adequate for dealing with the expected volume of claims is an important medium-term managerial responsibility.

2.2   Short-term decisions. An ongoing task, related to the above responsibility, for an operations manager is the monitoring of operating characteristics of the CHP system, and taking corrective actions if necessary. For example, an increase in the level of pending claims or the closing age of claims may indicate inadequate claims handling capacity. In this case, management may choose to increase the number of claims reps. Similarly, if the proportion of older claims in pending claims is increasing relative to the proportion of younger claims, then management may instruct claims reps to spend relatively more time on older claims as compared to the younger claims. These actions, changing capacity or distribution of handling work, are two important control levers available to management for achieving the desired operating characteristics.

The earlier description of claims handling process also allows us to identify the day-to-day responsibilities of a claims operations manager:

1. Given certain preliminary information on a claim, estimating the expected loss payments and settlement time.
2. Based on the above estimates, judge the complexity of a claim, which is further used in making assignment of claims to reps.
3. Choosing the method of investigation, "on-site" or "inside office," to be used by a rep.
4. Deciding whether or not to involve an attorney.

An overriding consideration in making these operational decisions is the time and cost implications of these decisions. We will present the claims handling process model in the next section. The empirical work pertaining to understanding of cost and time drivers and the development of decision rules for operational decisions is presented in the fourth section.

3. Claims Handling Process Model

The proposed claims handling process (CHP) model is deterministic in nature. The CHP model assumes that a claims rep needs to perform a certain amount of claims adjustment work on each claim before it is settled. As a new claim enters the system, a rep begins to perform adjustment work on that claim. The claim is settled and closed when the total adjustment work performed on it reaches the required level.

By keeping track of the amount of adjustment work being performed on claims, the CHP model analyzes and estimates the various operating characteristics of the system such as the number of pending claims in the system, the closing rate of claims, the closing age of claims, the number of claims reps employed in the CHP system, and the average caseload of claims reps, i.e., the number of claims per claims rep.

The CHP model also assumes a homogeneous body of claims, with each claim requiring an identical amount of adjustment work for settlement. This is not an overly restrictive assumption, since a diverse body of claims can be divided into multiple segments where each segment is reasonably homogeneous. The CHP model can then be applied to each segment, and through a suitable aggregation procedure, the operating characteristics of the entire body of claims can be estimated.

As mentioned earlier, a claims manager has two control opportunities to maintain the operating characteristics of the CHP system within the desirable range: adjustment of staffing level and the distribution of adjustment work across the claims portfolio. The proposed CHP model explicitly allows management to predict the impact of these two control opportunities on various operating characteristics, and thereby improve his/her medium-term decisions.

3.1 Variable input CHP model. We now develop a variable input CHP model (see Apte and Cavaliere (1993) for detailed exposition). We present in

Table 1, all the variables and parameters used in the model. At any point in time there exist claims of all ages in the body of pending claims, from age zero to whatever the closing age is for a claim at that point in time. If we plot the amount of adjustment work performed on a claim versus the age of a claim, over a period of time, we obtain the work function surface, w(a,t) represented in Figure 1.

Table 1.		Definition of Parameters and Variables Used in CHP Model
		Parameters
R	=	Number of claims reps available. R will be a controlparameter in that it may be altered, at discrete intervals, by management to achieve desired operating characteristics.
H	=	The number of hours per year a claims rep works.
W	=	The number of hours of adjustment work required to close a claim.
N(t)	=	Arrival rate of claims (claims/year). Note that the arrival rate of claims of age a at time t is given by N(t-a).
		Variables
A(t)	=	The age of a claim that closes at time t.
P(t)	=	The number of claims pending at time t.
w(a,t)	=	The total amount of work (hours) performed on a claim that has age a at time t. The work function surface, w(a,t), for claims in the CHP system is given in Figure 1.
f(a,t)	=	N(t-a)Æw(a,t) = Total hours per year of work done on all claims of age a at time t. f(a,t) is useful in that for a fixed value of t, the area under the curve f(a,t) represents the total amount of work in the system at time t (see Figure 2).

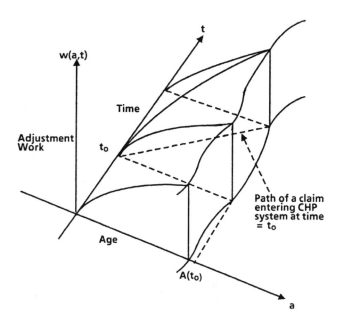

Figure 1. Adjustment Work Surface.

A cross section of the work function surface, at a fixed point t_0 in time, gives the work function, $w(a,t_0)$, with the following features: (1) $w(a,t_0)$ is nondecreasing, which reflects the fact that older claims have received more work than younger ones; (2) the graph of $w(a,t_0)$ ends when the level of adjustment work reaches the fixed value W, at which point the claims are closed and leave the system. It should also be noted that the path of a claim through the CHP lies on a line inclined at $45°$ to the time axis starting at the entry time of the claim.

We can plot the total adjustment work in system, $f(a,t)$, versus the time and age of the system to get the Figure 2.

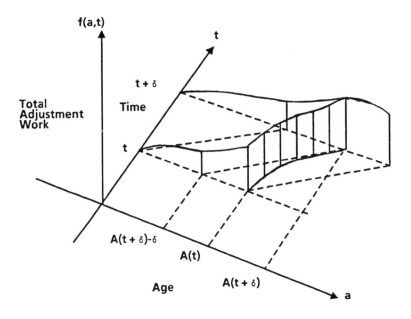

Figure 2. Adjustment Work Surface: Variable Input Case.

We use the principle of conservation of work over the time interval [t,t+δ]. The amount of work added to the system during the interval [t,t+δ is distributed to three distinct claim groups:

G_1: New Claims - claims in the system at time t+δ which were not present at time t.

G_2: Continuing Claims - claims which were present at time t and remain open at time t +δ.

G_3: Closed Claims - claims which have closed during the interval [t,t +δ].

The work added to the system (R·H· δ) must equal the sum of the net change in the work for each of these claim groups. Since work in the system at time t is represented in Figure 2 by the area under the slice curve at time t, the change in work from t to t + δ is the difference in area between two slices at t and t + δ. We use the integral representation of area to find,

Net change in work for G_1: $\int_0^\delta f(a,t+\delta)\,da - 0$

Net change in work for G_2: $\int_\delta^{A(t+\delta)} f(a,t+\delta)\,da - \int_0^{A(t+\delta)-\delta} f(a,t)\,da$

Net change in work for G_3: $\int_{A(t+\delta)-\delta}^{A(t)} W \cdot N(t-a)\,da - \int_{A(t+\delta)-\delta}^{A(t)} f(a,t)\,da$

Hence, with an obvious change of variable, we obtain,

$$R \cdot H \cdot \delta = \int_0^\delta f(a,t+\delta)\,da + \int_0^{A(t+\delta)-\delta} \{f(a+\delta,\, t+\delta) - f(a,t)\}\,da$$
$$+ \int_{A(t+\delta)-\delta}^{A(t)} \{W \cdot N(t-a) - f(a,t)\}\,da \qquad (3.1)$$

Dividing by δ we find that,

$$R \cdot H = I_1 + I_2 + I_3 \qquad (3.2)$$

where

$$I_1 = \frac{1}{\delta} \int_0^\delta f(a,t+\delta)\,da$$

$$I_2 = \int_0^{A(t+\delta)-\delta} \frac{f(a+\delta,\, t+\delta) - f(a,t)}{\delta}\,da$$

$$I_3 = \frac{1}{\delta} \int_{A(t+\delta)-\delta}^{A(t)} \{W \cdot N(t-a) - f(a,t)\}\,da$$

Equation (3.2) must hold for all δ, and thus in the limit as δ approaches 0. I_2 will provide the main term since,

$$\lim_{\delta \to 0} I_1 = \lim_{\delta \to 0} I_3 = 0$$

and with some manipulation we find that,

$$\lim_{\delta \to 0} I_2 = \int_0^{A(t)} \{ f_a(a,t) + f_t(a,t) \} da$$

   The evaluation of the limit can be justified by an appeal to the Dominated Convergence Theorem. (Refer to Apostol (1974).) Equation (3.2) becomes

$$R \cdot H = \int_0^{A(t)} \{ f_a(a,t) + f_t(a,t) \} da \qquad (3.3)$$

Equation (3.3) can be interpreted as follows:

$$f_a(a,t) + f_t(a,t) = N(t-a) \cdot \{ w_a(a,t) + w_t(a,t) \} = N(t-a) \cdot w'((a,t);(1,1))$$

where $w'((a,t);(1,1))$ is the rate of work done on a claim of age a at time t. This directional derivative is necessary since the paths of claims through the system lie on diagonal $45°$ lines in the domain plane. Multiplication by N(t-a) gives the total rate of work done on all claims of age a at time t. Hence, (3.3) expresses the equality of the total rate of work (R·H) with the sum of rates of work for claims of all ages. Equation (3.3) can be viewed as a "system" equation since it uses rates of work for claims of all ages. We may derive a "claim" equation by observing that the difference in height between two points on the work function surface, w(a,t), is equal to the line integral of the directional derivative over a path connecting the points. Our path will be the claim path, and the direction of the derivative will be the path direction. We find that,

$$w(a,t) = \int_{t-a}^{t} \{ w_a(\tau - t + a, \tau) + w_t(\tau - t + a, \tau) \} d\tau \qquad (3.4)$$

which, when a = A(t), becomes

$$W = \int_{t-A(t)}^{t} \{ w_a(\tau - t + A(t), \tau) + w_t(\tau - t + A(t), \tau) \} d\tau \qquad (3.5)$$

The claims closed during the interval $[t, t + \delta]$ are precisely those claims which, at time t, have ages in the interval $[A(t + \delta) - \delta, A(t)]$. The number of such claims, $C_{[t,t+\delta]}$, is therefore found by integrating the arrival rate over this interval:

$$C_{[t,t+\delta]} = \int_{A(t+\delta)-\delta}^{A(t)} N(t-a)\,da \qquad (3.6)$$

The claims pending in the system at time t must have ages in the interval $[0,A(t)]$. Integrating the arrival rate of claims over this interval establishes the pending claims volume:

$$P(t) = \int_{0}^{A(t)} N(t-a)\,da \qquad (3.7)$$

This completes the variable input CHP model development. We have a total of four equations:

$$R \cdot H = \int_{0}^{A(t)} \{ f_a(a,t) + f_t(a,t) \}\,da \qquad (3.8)$$

$$W = \int_{t-A(t)}^{t} \{ w_a(\tau-t+A(t),\tau) + w_t(\tau-t+A(t),\tau) \}\,d\tau \qquad (3.9)$$

$$P(t) = \int_{0}^{A(t)} N(t-a)\,da \qquad (3.10)$$

$$C_{[t,t+\delta]} = \int_{A(t+\delta)-\delta}^{A(t)} N(t-a)\,da \qquad (3.11)$$

In order to permit applications outside the current context, the claims handling process, we have imposed as few conditions as possible on the work function $w(a,t)$. Given this lack of restriction on $w(a,t)$, it should come as no surprise that there exist infinitely many functions, $w(a,t)$, which satisfy equations (3.8) and (3.9). There is a need for more information concerning $w(a,t)$ so that a solution is determined. Indeed, by specifying the distribution of a claim rep's work to his/her portfolio, management can influence the directional derivative of $w(a,t)$. This additional "first order" information together with initial conditions will yield the work function $w(a,t)$. With $w(a,t)$ known, $A(t)$ can be computed by recalling that $A(t)$ is the level curve $w(a,t) = W$. Equations (3.10) and (3.11) are then purely computational in nature.

3.2   Model implementation.   In this sub-section we will discuss the procedure for implementing the CHP model for use in planning claims operations. As discussed earlier, establishment of suitable staffing level is a key managerial decision.   By using the CHP model as a simulation tool, management can determine the appropriate staffing level to achieve the desired levels of operating characteristics.

In simulating the CHP, trial values for R and the work distribution are selected as initial values. The resultant operational characteristics are computed using the variable input model and compared with the desired levels of these characteristics. If the operating characteristics are not satisfactory, then the trial values of R and/or work distribution are suitably updated and the simulation is performed again.

Simulating the CHP system involves solving the variable input CHP model to "build up" the work function surface $w(a,t)$ one slice at a time. We will uniformly partition the time axis: $0 = t_0 < t_1 < t_2 < ... < t_n = 1$ year. Given the function $w(a,t_0)$ as the initial slice, we proceed inductively to compute $w(a,t_1)$, $w(a,t_2)$, ... $w(a,t_n)$. $A(t_k)$ can be computed by solving $w(a,t_k) = W$. Hence, pending claims volumes and closing claims volumes will be known, from (3.10) and (3.11), at each of the partition points. The inductive step requires specification of a directional derivative of $w(a,t)$ along the slice $w(a,t_k)$ and then uses the tangent line approximation to obtain $w(a,t_{k+1})$. A conservation of work equation is checked to verify results at each stage.

In the next section we discuss the procedure for estimating $w(a,t_1)$ using $w(a,t_0)$. The procedure involves using trial values for the number of claims reps and work distribution in solving the CHP model. Subsequent slices $w(a,t_k)$ are derived by a repetition of this procedure. A numerical example is given illustrating the simulation procedure.

3.3   Construction of the work function surface.   We must specify the distribution of work over claims of various ages at time t=0. This distribution will reflect the way a claims rep apportions work to his/her portfolio of claims. For example, management can insist that half of the time spent on a rep's portfolio be devoted to the youngest quarter of the claims in that portfolio. More generally, reps can be instructed to spend σ of their time on the youngest λ part of the claims in their portfolio, where σ and λ are the control parameters, whose values lie in the open unit interval. Management may alter the values of these control parameters to produce the desired results as predicted by the model. It should be noted that σ and λ are controlled by the management in an indirect manner, through defining suitable handling procedures and training programs. Initially, $t_0 = 0$, and we define

$S_0(a)$ = the fraction of work done by a rep on claims younger than age a,

a_λ = the age for which λ of the portfolio is younger.

$S_0(a)$ should interpolate the points $(0,0)$, (a_λ,s) and $(A(0),1)$ (see Figure 3).

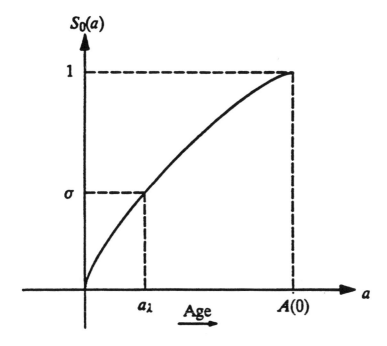

Figure 3. Distribution of Adjustment Work to Claims.

We observe that a_λ is found by solving

$$\int_0^a N\left(t_0 - x\right) dx = \lambda \cdot \int_0^{A(t_0)} N\left(t_0 - x\right) dx = \lambda \cdot P(t_0) \qquad (3.12)$$

for a. Since claims move through the domain of w(a,t) along lines inclined at 45° to the t-axis, our directional derivative, d(a), will be in the direction of the vector (1,1) (i.e., along the claim path). Now

$R \cdot H \cdot S_0'(a)$ the rate at which work is being performed on all claims of age a.

However, this rate should be equal to the rate at which work is done on a single claim, d(a), times the arrival rate of such claims. Thus

$$d(a) = \frac{R \cdot H \cdot S_0'(a)}{N\left(t_0 - a\right)}$$

Using d(a) as our derivative in the tangent line approximation, we obtain the next slice:

$$w\left(a, t_1\right) = w\left(a - \delta, t_0\right) + d\left(a - \delta\right) \cdot \delta \cdot \sqrt{2}$$

Here δ is width of the subinterval t_1-t_0. The closing age $A(t_1)$ is found by solving $w(a,t_1)=W$. Unaltered, the above procedure introduces an error by relying on the tangent line approximation. This error will propagate upon iteration and must be removed. The principle of conservation of work provides a method of correction. Recalling the incremental analysis discussed earlier, we find that:

$$\int_0^{A(t_0)} f\left(a, t_0\right) da \quad = \text{work in the system at time } t_0$$

$$R \cdot H \cdot \delta \quad\quad\quad\quad = \text{work added during the time interval } [t_0, t_1]$$

$$\int_0^{A(t_1)} f\left(a, t_1\right) da \quad = \text{work in the system at time } t_1$$

$$W \cdot \int_{A(t_1)-\delta}^{A(t_0)} N\left(t_0-a\right) da \qquad = \text{work leaving the system as closed claims}$$

Conservation of work requires

$$\int_0^{A(t_0)} f\left(a,t_0\right) da + R \cdot H \cdot \delta = \int_0^{A(t_0)} f\left(a,t_1\right) da + W \cdot \int_{A(t_1)-\delta}^{A(t_0)} N\left(t_0-a\right) da \qquad (3.13)$$

Equation (3.13) must be satisfied, and so the value of $A(t_1)$ must be considered a trial value which will be accepted if the right and left sides of (3.13) are sufficiently close. If not, their ratio r is computed, d(a) is replaced by rd(a), and a new trial value of $A(t_1)$ is found. This process is continued until the right and left sides of (3.13) are sufficiently close. Having determined $A(t_1)$, we may now compute the pending claims volume and the closing rate using (3.10) and (3.11). This entire process is repeated, effectively yielding slices of the work function surface at the partition points t_k on the t-axis.

3.4   Numerical example. Let us consider a hypothetical ABC Insurance Company and its staffing problem. We use as given the following parameters and starting conditions:

   N = 40,000 claims/yr   H = 1600 hours/yr.rep   W = 4 hours/claim

   R = 100 reps   P = 20,000 claims   A = 0.5 years

Under the homogeneity of claims assumption, the value of W will remain constant during the simulation. Since the number of hours per year that a claims rep can work does not depend on time, H also remains fixed during the simulation. The value of R is usually constant but may be adjusted by management to obtain the desired results as predicted by the model during simulation. In fact, the different simulations presented are a result of discrete changes in R timed so as to maintain certain operating characteristics within management imposed tolerances. All other quantities will depend on time. After an initialization, the simulation is performed and a plot of the operating characteristics is obtained indicating the behavior of closing age, pending volume and closing rate throughout the year.

Our planning horizon is one year. Since the arrival rate of claims experiences seasonal fluctuations, we choose as our arrival rate function N(t), a function whose average value during the planning horizon is the benchmark value of 40,000 claims/year:

$$N(t) = 40,000 + 4000 \sin(\pi t) \qquad (3.14)$$

A choice of $\delta = 1/20$ yr. $= 2.6$ weeks was deemed fine enough for practical purposes. In other words, knowledge of the operating characteristics of the system at approximately two and a half week intervals throughout the year is sufficient for planning the operations of a claims department. The simulation requires the specification of an initial work function $w(a,0)$. This initial work function reflects the initial status of the claims body and thus depends upon the particular situation. We choose $A(0) = 0.5$, the benchmark value, and select

$$w(a,0) = \frac{c_1 a}{a + c_2} \qquad (3.15)$$

as our initial work function "slice." The constants are chosen so that $w(0,0)=0$, $w(0.5,0)=4$ and $w(a,t)$ satisfies the smoothness conditions given in the remarks following Figure 1. A typical distribution of work over a claims rep's portfolio is found, from practice, to be $\sigma = 1/2$ and $\lambda = 1/4$. The simulation, as described above, was performed using Macsyma on a MicroVax II. The resulting operating characteristics are plotted in Figure 4. It can be observed that the pending claims volume peaks at almost 15% above the benchmark value, a level management may find unacceptable given that the arrival rate fluctuates by no more than 10%. The total adjustment work performed in this scenario is 100 rep-years. If the simulation is run again but with R=102 for the first .6 year and R=96 for the remaining part of the year, the results are given in Figure 5. The pending volume as well as the closing age is now well within 10% of the benchmark value and the total adjustment work performed is only 99.6 rep-years. Given the customary high turnover rate among reps, the necessary downward adjustment is easily achieved by simply not hiring replacements.

This example illustrates the most important use of the CHP model - planning for the required staffing level of a claims department given the expected level of claims arrival rate and the desired range of operating characteristics of the claims handling system.

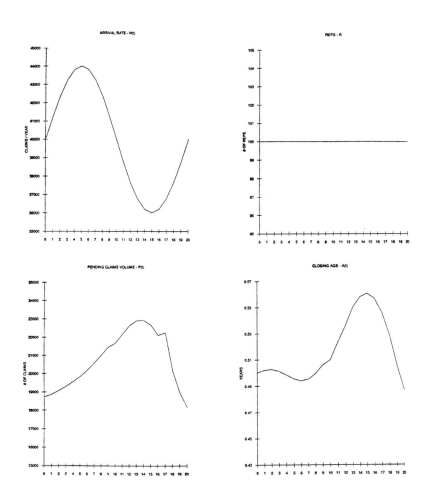

Figure 4.   Operating Characteristics of the Claims System (Constant Number
              of Reps)

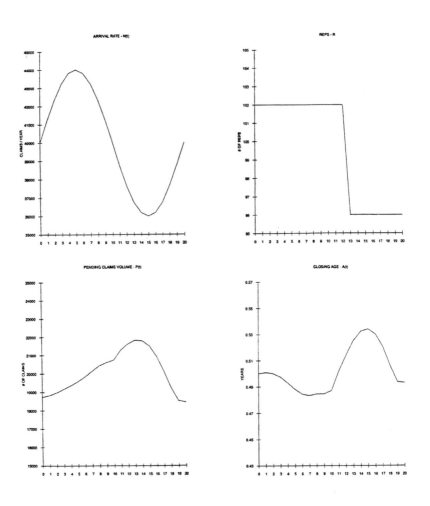

Figure 5.   Operating Characteristics of the Claims System (Variable Number
             of Reps)

4. Supporting Operational Decisions: An Empirical Study

As discussed earlier a claims manager is faced with a number of operational decisions including assignment of claims to reps, choice of a claims handling method, and involvement of an attorney. The second analytical approach, the details of which we discuss in this section, involves understanding the time and cost drivers of claims settlement for improving these operational decisions. To this end, we conducted an empirical study at a large P&C insurance company (see Apte and Hegde (1991) for a preliminary analysis). Records pertaining to automobile bodily injury claims settled in 1989 were collected. We collected data on a large number of operations variables and accumulated a data base of 20,000 observations. This data was analyzed to determine relationships between time, cost, and the claims operations variables.

4.1   Data collection and variable description. For each claim, we collected about 30 data elements. We summarize that information below by stating the logical groupings of data. The definitions of variables used in the statistical analysis are given in Table 2.

- *Claim Identification Data*:   These data elements provide a unique identification of each claim, the branch office where the claim was handled, the marketing division that sold the underlying insurance policy, the line-of-business, the state where the claim was filed, and whether the claim was generated by a personal or commercial policy.
- *Claim Event, Notice, Close Dates*: Note that the notice date of a claim may be, and it is usually, different than the event date of a claim.
- *Accident and Injury Type Codes*: Indicate the type of accident, the underlying reasons for the accident, and the nature of the injury.
- *Method*:   Claim handling method code that denotes whether the investigation was performed on-site or inside office.
- *Attorney Number*: Indicates whether an attorney was used; and if so, whether an in-house or an outside attorney was used.
- *Expense and Reserve Information*: Information on various types of expenses and reserves is given here.
  - Non-legal loss adjustment expenses
  - Legal expenses for outside attorney or house counsel
  - Gross Reserve set for the claim
  - Amount paid for settlement to claimant, i.e., the loss payment.

Table 2. Definitions of Variables Used in the Statistical Analysis

SYST	=	Total time spent in claims handling; a measure of response time. Given by the difference of claim close date and claim notice date.
	=	CLOSE - NOTICE
NLAE	=	Non-legal claims adjustment expenses
LPAY	=	Loss Payment to the claimant
TEXP	=	Total of Loss Adjustment Expenses and Loss Payments
GRSRV	=	Gross Reserve
ATTDUM	=	1 if attorney is assigned
	=	0 otherwise
PERCOM	=	1 if the claim is commercial
	=	0 otherwise
ACCDCODE	=	1 if the claim is 'regular auto'
	=	0 otherwise
INJCODE	=	0, 1, 2, 3, 4, or 5, depending on the nature of the injury with increasing value indicating increasing severity. (e.g., INJCODE = 0 indicates a minor injury, and INJCODE = 5 indicates very severe injury (such as a head injury)).
METHODUM	=	1 if the claim is handled by on-site investigation
		0 if the claim is handled by inside investigation
ATTYxINJ	=	ATTYDUM x INJCODE
COMPLEX	=	1 if the claim is deemed complex, given the criteria defined by the claims division
	=	0 otherwise

4.2 Empirical analysis and results. Experience indicates that the amount of time a claim spends on the service floor is a good proxy for the complexity and severity of the claim. Hence, in making assignment decisions, managers can use an estimate of expected time to be spent in the system. We define:

System time (SYST) = Close Date - Notice Date = CLOSE - NOTICE.

The system time is a sum of claims handling time and waiting time. The handling time, however, is negligible compared to the system time, and hence the system time is almost equal to the waiting time, which must be reduced in any operating system. Preliminary analysis showed that the distribution of SYST was skewed to the right. Managers clarified that these extreme delays are invariably caused by reasons which are not under any operations personnel's control, and hence, it would be misleading to include these observations in the analysis. After eliminating the extreme observations, we were left with 10,391 observations. The average system time for the sample is 326 days and the standard deviation of system time is 256 days. The summary measures are presented in Table 3.

Table 3. Summary Statistics

Variables	Mean	Std. Deviation
SYST	345	266
LPAY	6083	18371
GRSRV	9426	31611

Discussions with claims reps and managers indicated that the delay on the service floor is closely linked to the nature of the injury, and the method used to handle the claims. This delay is also observed in claims for which an outside attorney is used. A major concern of our empirical study was precisely to understand such impact of these operational decisions. Therefore, we decided to systematically investigate the positive and the negative effect of various operational decisions on different performance measures. Accordingly, we formulated the following hypotheses,

H$_1$: The involvement of an outside attorney is accompanied by a delay in the service completion time.

H$_2$: On-site investigation expedites the settlement of claims.

To test these hypotheses, we modeled system time as a function of: (i) the method of handling claim, (ii) the nature of injury, (iii) the attorney's involvement. The sample data was analyzed using SAS. As a result of multiple regression, the following empirical model was estimated.

Model 1: (The numbers in parenthesis are standard errors)

SYST = 355.0 + 656.9 ATTDUM - 60.0 PERCOM - 56.3 METHODUM
       (9.08)   (10.6)   (6.87)   (21.14)

       - 53.0 ACCDCODE +   14.1 INJCODE   ($R^2 = 0.24$)
       (6.8)   (2.1)

Several insights can be developed using this simple model. The claims managers had generally believed that the commercial policies take longer time for settlement. The model, however, reveals that this belief is not true. In fact, after controlling for other factors, it is seen that the commercial policies require 60 days less in the CHP system.

Concerning the hypotheses defined earlier, the model shows that use of attorneys and/or inside investigation is accompanied by a delay in claims handling. Thus, both the hypotheses H$_1$ and H$_2$ cannot be rejected. This also provides a clear evidence to the claims management that on-site investigation is generally a preferred method for handling of claims.

We also note in Model 1 that the claims which are handled by attorneys do require a longer settlement period.[2] This is expected since the very severe injury

---

[2]We also presented a model with a separate dummy for in-house and outside attorneys. The coefficients of both the dummies were significant and outside attorneys did take a longer time.

cases that typically take longer time to settle are generally assigned to attorneys. The issue to be investigated here is: given that there is a delay, how does the presence of an attorney affect the system time for cases with severe injury? To answer this question, we developed and estimated the model given below using an interaction term for the presence of an attorney and the severity level of injury.

Model 2:

$$SYST = 355 \quad + 652 \text{ ATTDUM} \quad - 6 \text{ PERCOM} \quad - 56 \text{ METHODUM}$$
$$\quad (9.1) \quad\quad (12.5) \quad\quad\quad (6.8) \quad\quad\quad\quad (21.0)$$

$$\quad - 14 \text{ ATTxINJ} \quad - 55 \text{ ACCDCODE} \quad +14.1 \text{ INJCODE} \quad\quad (R^2 = 0.28)$$
$$\quad (1.8) \quad\quad\quad\quad (7.9) \quad\quad\quad\quad (2.1)$$

This model shows that attorneys are able to reduce delay for severe injury cases. Thus, the attorneys are best used in cases with severe injury.

4.3   Total paid and total cost of claims adjustment.   The corporation is also interested in estimating the total amount to be paid to a claimant and the corresponding gross reserve amount. A comparison of gross reserve and total paid revealed that the gross reserve is significantly higher than the amount paid in total. The average of ratio of TPAID to GRSRV, in fact, was only 0.54. The correct estimation of GRSRV is evidently crucial for accuracy in predicting the financial performance of the corporation. To help decide the amount of GRSRV, we estimated the loss payment as a function of claim characteristics.

The discussions with the management revealed that the loss payment is dependent upon the severity of the injury. To derive meaningful results, separate analyses were done for different severity codes. The qualitative nature of results, and corresponding discussions, are similar for these different codes. Hence, we present below the discussion for one category of code.

The loss payment can be estimated from the following model:

Model 3:

$$LPAY = 3118 \quad +17222 \text{ ATTDUM} \quad +1937 \text{ METHODUM} \quad (R^2 = 0.13)$$
$$\quad (395) \quad\quad (1592) \quad\quad\quad\quad (95)$$

The positive coefficient of ATTDUM was expected, since the more expensive, severe-injury cases were generally handled by attorneys. The positive coefficient of METHODUM was also expected since the complex cases were usually handled by making an on-site investigation. Further, the following model helps understand the relationship between loss adjustment expenses (legal and non-legal adjustment expenses) and the operations decision variables.

Model 4:

$$LAE = 11.9 + 2251 \text{ ATTDUM} + 261 \text{ METHODUM} \quad (R^2 = 0.25)$$
$$\quad (4.18) \quad (119) \quad\quad\quad (82.6)$$

This model is useful for estimating the Loss Adjustment Expenses.

4.4   Cost of claims adjustment. The total claims handling and settlement cost is sum of (i) legal expenses, (ii) non-legal adjustment expenses, and (iii) the amount paid to claimant. As Stevenson (1988) asserts, the ever increasing levels of loss payments is at least partly caused by short-sighted budget cutting of claims handling expenses. To reduce loss adjustment expenses, insurance companies, in recent years, have resorted to conducting more inside investigation than the on-site investigation. This is being "penny wise and pound foolish." The small saving in loss adjustment expenses is dwarfed by unnecessarily higher loss payments which could be lowered, or even avoided, if the claims reps gather more accurate and timely information through on-site investigation.

To ascertain if the insurance industry is really suffering due to myopic budget cutting in claims adjustment expenses, we analyzed the relationship between loss payment and different categories of loss adjustment expenses. In specific, we tested the following hypothesis:

H_3: There is no relationship between Loss Payment and the Loss Adjustment Expenses.

Relating loss payment directly to loss adjustment expense may give misleading results since levels of both are driven by the severity of claim.

Hence, we relate the loss payment to the fraction of total expenses that was spent for loss adjustment. Accordingly, we defined

$$REXP = \frac{LAE}{TEXP}$$

and estimated the following equation:

Model 5:

LPAY   = 10733   - 10921 REXP $(R^2 = 0.06)$
            (236.3)   (1294)

We note that the hypothesis H_3 is rejected. Moreover, the negative coefficient of REXP indicates that a higher ratio of loss adjustment expenses does indeed lower the loss payment amount. The analysis indicates that the loss incurred due to "penny wise pound foolish" policy is likely to be quite significant.

4.5 Decision support system. The above analysis of the time and cost drivers of claims settlement was helpful in predicting the expected system time, and expected expenses. It is also useful for understanding the impact of different operations variables on the system performance. As a decision support tool, what managers needed was rule/s for "scheduling and assignment", which will help them make decisions such as whether to assign an in-house attorney or an outside attorney. For this purpose, we conducted a simple discriminant analysis. A sample output is presented in Table 4. Thus, given the characteristic of a claim, a manager would be able to decide, with the help of this discriminant function, whether to use attorneys or not, or whether to use an inside investigation or an on-site investigation. This would amount to an 'artificial intelligence' type system, the usefulness of which was immediately recognized by the senior management.

Table 4. Discriminant Analysis Results: Attorney Classification

Number of Observations (Percent) Classified into ATTDUM

		0	1	Total %
From ATTDUM	0	4995 (63)	2900 (37)	100
	1	262 (40)	393 (60)	100
	Total %	61	39	

To elaborate, how such a system works, we illustrate through an example that is based on a subset of data. The discriminant function coefficients obtained for using an attorney versus using no attorneys are:

	Constant	PERCOM	COMPLEX	ACCD-CODE	INJCODE
No Attorney	-41.5	3.47	0.37	1.41	.94
Attorney	-49.7	3.2	1.21	0.94	1.06

Now, suppose that a claim with characteristics, PERCOM = 1, COMPLEX = 0, ACCDCODE = 1, INJCODE = 2 is to be adjusted. We note then that score for using an "attorney" is higher than that for "no attorney" and thus, the claim should be handled with the help of an attorney.

5. Managerial Implications and Future Research

In this paper, we proposed two model-based approaches for improving claims handling operation. The first approach, involving the CHP model, is useful for the medium-term capacity planning and for the control of claim handling operation. The proposed CHP model captures the relationship between the management controlled parameters such as number of claims representatives and distribution of adjustment work among claims, and the operating characteristics of the system such as closing rate of claims, level of pending claims, caseload of claims reps, average age of claims at closing, and so forth.

The first important use of the proposed CHP model is in planning for the required staffing level of a claims department. Given the expected level of the new claims arrival rate and the desired operating characteristics, such as the target pending claims level or the caseload of claims reps, we can use the CHP model to determine the required number of claims reps. If the current pending claims volume is larger than the target pending level, some additional staff could be kept on board until such a time as the target pending level is achieved. Thereafter, the number of reps should be gradually adjusted downwards to the level suggested by target caseload. Thus, the variable input CHP model is useful for developing a detailed staffing plan.

The second important use of the CHP model is in using certain characteristics, such as the closing rate, the caseload for claims reps, and closing age of claims, for controlling the claims department operation. For example, caseload of claims reps can be predicted and compared to the desired caseload to determine whether or not there is a need to hire additional claims reps.

Given the probabilistic nature of a number of elements in the system, the deterministic CHP model presented in this paper, although useful and appropriate for a medium-term capacity planning decision, must be considered as an approximation of the reality. A stochastic model of CHP would certainly be a more realistic representation. Therefore, development of such a model would be a very important and useful enhancement. Development of a stochastic model using a Poisson process for claims arrival within bulk queues is an attractive possibility. The authors are currently working on this development.

The second analytical approach presented in the paper consisted of understanding the causes of delays and drivers of cost on the service floor, and thereby helping to improve the operational decision.

The empirical study allowed the managers to understand the drivers of the causes of delay and total settlement cost of claims. The process of identifying the drivers, consisting of our statistical analysis of historical data aided by management's intuition and experience, helped in determining the impact of different operations policies on the performance of claims operation. For instance, although it was known that outside attorneys took a longer time, the quantification of this impact uncovered the benefit of using attorneys for more severe claims. The analysis also uncovered a significant improvement potential for reducing the total amount of time a claim needs to spend in the CHP system. The key here is to use on-site investigation for severe claims. Finally, the analysis indicated that spending more money for claims handling is likely to be beneficial for reducing loss payments. This last conclusion, however, should be evaluated further through additional analytical studies and controlled experiments. In such a study, it would also be interesting to determine the optimal balance between loss adjustment expense and loss payment to minimize the total expense.

Although a vast amount of data is being gathered routinely in corporations, very little is known about the use of this historical information in improving decision making. It is now well understood that reducing cycle time is a key factor in sustaining competitive advantage (Stalk and Hout (1990), Hegde, Kekre and Kekre (1992)). However, there is little research done on "how" one may reduce the cycle time, especially in the service sector.

Our study indicates that understanding the "drivers" of cost and cycle time should be the first step in improving any process. In these efforts, one needs to carefully identify the process features which affect the system performance. Thereafter, one can reengineer the process and decision rules for improving the process. In this study, we have outlined a detailed procedure of identifying variables that drive cost and cycle time, and quantified the interaction that exists among the features of the process. We hope that, after conducting sufficient studies of this nature, for different corporations and in different industries, we will be in a better position to generalize and build theoretical models to understand tradeoffs that underlie the efforts towards reducing both cycle time and the cost of operations.

References

Apostol, T.M. (1974). *Mathematical Analysis* (Addison-Wesley Publishing Company, Reading, MA), 270-274.

Apte, U.M., and R.A. Cavaliere (1993). "A capacity planning model for the claims handling process," *Mathematical and Computer Modelling* 17(3), 67-82.

Apte, U.M., and G.G. Hegde (1991). "Cycle time improvement in service industry: Field study in insurance claims operation," Working Paper, Cox School of Business, Southern Methodist University (Dallas, TX).

Cissley, C.H. (1980). *Claim Administration: Principles and Practice* (International Claim Association, Cincinnati, OH).

Crane, F.G. (1984). *Insurance Principles and Practices* (J. Wiley & Sons, New York, NY).

Cummins, J.D., and S.E. Harrington (1984). "Econometric forecasting of automobile insurance paid-claims cost," in J.D. Cummins (ed.), *Strategic Planning and Modeling in Property and Casualty Insurance* (Kluwer-Nijhoff Publishers, Boston, MA).

Hegde, G.G., S. Kekre, and S. Kekre (1991). "Engineering changes and time delays: A field investigation," *Journal of Manufacturing and Operations Management,* forthcoming.

Hogg, R.W., and S.A. Klugman (1984). *Loss Distributions* (J. Wiley & Sons, New York, NY).

Magarick, P. (1989). *Casualty Insurance Claims: Coverage, Investigation, Law* (3rd ed.), (Clark Boardman Company Ltd., New York, NY).

Martin, F.H. (1986). "Claims investigations - Are they going out of style?" *CPCU Journal* 39(2),.

Paulson, A. S. and N.J. Faris (1984). "A practical approach to measuring the distribution of total annual claims," in J.D. Cummins (ed.), *Strategic Planning and Modeling in Property and Casualty Insurance* (Kluwer-Nijhoff Publishers, Boston, MA).

Peterson, T.M. (1981). *Loss Reserving: Property/Casualty Insurance* (Ernst & Whinney, New York).

Stalk, G., Jr., and T.M. Hout (1990). *Competing Against Time* (The Free Press, New York, NY).

Stevenson, D.F. (1988). "Is it short-sighted budgeting to reduce defense costs," *Claims* (February 16, 1988).

Webb, B.L., J.J. Launie, W.P. Rokes, and N.A. Baglini (1981). *Insurance Company Operations*, vol. 2, (2nd ed.) (American Institute for Property and Liability Underwriters, Malvern, PA).

Chapter 11   A Model For Analyzing Quality in the Service
Delivery Process

Pamela K. Armstrong

1 . Introduction

Deming (1986) maintains that improvements in quality also result in increased
productivity. This occurs because costs are reduced as rework, mistakes, and
delays in the process decrease due to quality improvement efforts. Time and
materials that were formerly wasted also become available for productive use,
thus improving productivity. While these results were first noted in a
manufacturing environment, they also hold true for service operations. The
converse, however, is not necessarily true: increasing productivity may actually
reduce quality. For example, pressure to increase output per unit time may
result in more mistakes as workers rush to complete each item or transaction. In
manufacturing, these defects can be detected and corrected before they reach the
consumer. Service firms, however, do not have this option since the consumer
often sees and participates in the production of service. If a mistake is made, the
consumer knows it.   This is a critical distinction between quality in
manufacturing, where quality is assessed on the production outcome, and quality
in services, where quality is largely based on consumers' perceptions of the
service experience as well as its outcome. For example, consider a bank
customer who experiences service in which the teller initially makes a mistake
but then corrects it. The outcome of the service is normal, but the customer
will perceive diminished service quality because of the way the service was

P. T. Harker (ed.), The Service Productivity and Quality Challenge, 311–342.
© 1995 *Kluwer Academic Publishers. Printed in the Netherlands.*

delivered. Thus, it is important for service managers to consider both the quantitative (e.g., cost savings) and the qualitative aspects (i.e., how the consumer perceives these changes) of proposed process enhancements to effectively improve quality and productivity. In this paper, we develop and test a method for evaluating the impact that various process improvements have on the consumer's evaluation of service quality, and for identifying which process changes improve perceived service quality the most.

Before proceeding, we need to establish a more precise definition of service quality. The term has different meaning in different fields. In marketing, service quality means understanding the customer's needs and identifying ways to meet or exceed them. It is sometimes equated with customer satisfaction, or the difference between the customer's perceptions and expectations of a service transaction. This type of service quality is evaluated using surveys, interviews, and focus groups. In operations, service quality is defined as conformance to operating specifications. Performance measures such as waiting times, error rates in transactions, and processing times are used to determine whether the process is in or out of control. In this paper, we focus on service quality from the consumer's perspective. Formally, it is defined as follows:

> "Service quality is a measure of how well the service level delivered matches customer expectations. Delivering quality service means conforming to customer expectations on a consistent basis." (Lewis and Booms, 1983)

In order to improve the consumer's assessment of service quality, we must first understand how the underlying perceptions are affected by the service delivery process. The implications of the service delivery process on perceived quality will obviously be greater for services that require a high level of interaction with the customer. The model developed in this paper describes the link between operations and consumer perceptions in services with a high level of customer involvement. For example, the following perceptions of bank service quality may be related to specific process attributes:

Perception	Process Attribute
Dependable	Accurate records kept, Open during stated hours
Responsive	Enough tellers so there is not a long queue
Understanding	Provides individual attention
Competent	No errors made in transaction
Good Facilities	Bank is Clean, well lighted

This paper describes the first step in a larger study on service quality, whose goal is to identify methods for managing quality in the service sector. The methods developed in this study can provide managers with useful information about the process. As a diagnostic tool, this technique can provide insights into inefficiencies in the system, and suggest opportunities for process improvements. The analysis can also highlight server behaviors that are associated with high perceived quality. Once these are identified, management can effect these behaviors using human resource management techniques. The results also provide management with a better sense of what their customers expect and suggest means for improving perceptions via operations. It can help the firm to assess "where we stand today" and "what might we do better," which is very useful information in the early stages of a quality improvement program. We might also discover important relationships using this approach that could easily be missed with simpler methods.

In this study, we view the service delivery process as a system, which is shown in Figure 1.

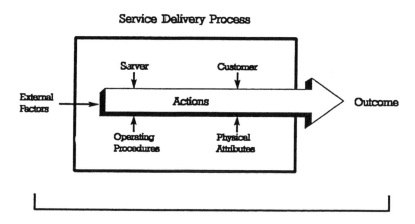

Figure 1. Model framework.

This system includes the following elements:
- the consumer, who has certain service expectations and requirements;
- the server, who interacts with the consumer to produce the service;
- operating procedures, which are specified by management and prescribe how the service is to be produced;
- physical attributes, such as the facility layout, resource availability, and the minimum time required to generate the service.

Within this system, the server and consumer perform a sequence of actions to produce the service. These actions can be affected by each of the elements in the system. In addition, external factors may be present that can also affect the service. These factors cannot be controlled by management and may include the weather (especially in the case of airlines), and supplier problems (e.g., computer services not available). Together, these actions determine the outcome of the service. The consumer then evaluates service quality based on his or her perceptions of the process and service outcome.

Once we have a model that links operations, perceptions and quality, we can use customer satisfaction survey results with the model to identify which parts of the process need to be changed to improve quality. For example, say that a bank is getting low scores for responsiveness. From the example above, we know that the number of servers available is linked to responsiveness, so we can use the model to determine the appropriate number of servers to add in order to improve perceived responsiveness.

The paper is organized as follows: the next section reviews related service quality research. The details of the methodology used are then discussed, and a test example is described. We conclude by discussing the usefulness of such models for managerial decision making.

2. Service Quality Research

To date, the methods for examining service quality have focused mainly upon techniques for monitoring operations to ensure conformance to specifications (operations perspective) and methods for measuring customer satisfaction (marketing perspective). Numerous books (for example, see Rosander 1985) extend the traditional statistical quality control tools to the service environment. An inherent problem with applying these methods to services is that they all deal with keeping variation within specific conformance standards; however, variation is often desired in delivering services, particularly ones that are "customized".

From the marketing perspective, service quality is often quite subjective, since it relies heavily on the consumer's perception of service in relation to his or her expectations of service. The most well-known work in this area is by Parasuraman, Zeithaml, and Berry (1985, 1988). They have developed a tool call SERVQUAL for evaluating consumers' assessments of service quality. SERVQUAL consists of survey questions about each of the following generic service quality attributes: tangibles, reliability, responsiveness, assurance (competence, credibility), and empathy (caring, individualized attention). For each of these attributes, SERVQUAL measures the service expectations of the consumer and his or her perceptions of the service received. The difference between these two measures is then assessed and used as an indication of service quality. The service delivery process itself is not evaluated in SERVQUAL; service quality is based solely on the consumer's feedback.

Another marketing study on the consumer's perception of service quality does consider the performance of certain aspects of the service. The authors (Bolton and Drew 1991) develop linear structural models to describe the consumer's assessment of service performance, quality, and value. Here again, only survey data (respondents' perceptions of performance) were used - no actual measures of operations were included.

Collier (1991) comes closest to linking the service delivery process with the consumer's evaluation of service quality. He quantifies the relationship between customer evaluations of specific quality attributes (e.g., customer service responsiveness) and the performance criteria of service operations (customer service should be responsive within a specified number of seconds) using recursive path analysis and other simple linear models. His hypothesized model relies on management's understanding of which operational activities affect the customer's perceptions of service. This assumes that management has a clear understanding of the consumer's expectations, which, as Parasuraman, Zeithaml, and Berry (1985) found, is not always the case. Collier illustrates and summarizes these relationships using what he calls a "service quality process map," which essentially indicates the correlation between the various operations and marketing measures. The measures used in his study were averages and, in some cases, aggregate performance measures; they do not consider the details of individual service encounters.

The problem with average performance measures is that they can only identify average effects. Extreme values are canceled out by these measures, thus hiding information about the process and perceptions. Aggregate performance measures represent a variety of activities. The problem with these measures is that, unless information is also available for each of its components, it is difficult to determine which elements are responsible for changes in such a measure. For example, consider an aggregate measure of customer service responsiveness that includes answering questions, handling customer complaints, and dealing with special requests. Without data that describes the number of each type of inquiry received, this aggregate measure cannot give clues to the causes for changes in this measure. For these reasons, we must examine individual service instances in which the consumer's perceptions are matched with data describing the service they received in order to fully understand the linkage between operations and perceptions.

We can also determine which process factors are most critical to perceived quality by examining the process as a system. By identifying the forces in the system that are working for and against quality, we can then determine methods for controlling these forces to improve total service quality. To date, such a comprehensive study of the service delivery process has not been performed.

3 . Methodology

In the SERVQUAL model (Parasuraman, Zeithaml and Berry 1988), quality is defined as a weighted average of the quality determinants. The weights used in this model are defined by the consumer as the relative importance of each quality attribute. However, there may be other factors that affect quality which are not included in the SERVQUAL model, and the way in which the attributes are combined may not be linear. To get a better understanding of how these perceptions affect quality, we need to define the relationship

$$Quality = h(p_1, p_2, ..., p_N)$$

where h is a general function, and pn represents the perception of the nth dimension of service quality. Such a function could be used by managers to determine which factors are important to consumers. For this information to be more useful, we need to understand what shapes these perceptions. To determine the degree to which operational procedures, physical attributes and external factors influence perceptions, we model each perception as a function of the components of the service delivery process:

$$P_n = g_n(x_1,...,x_I;y_1,....,y_j;s_1,....,s_k;c_1,....,c_L), \quad n = 1,....,N$$

where

- g_n is a general functional relationship for the nth dimension of quality;
- x_i, $i = 1,...,I$ are variables that describe the service delivery process (e.g., service time at step 1);
- y_j, $j = 1,...J$ are external factors, such as environmental factors or suppliers;
- s_k, $k = 1,...K$, are server description variables;
- c_l, $l = 1,...,L$ are variables that describe the customer in the service delivery process.

Together, these equations can be used to describe how the process affects service quality. There are a couple of reasons for using this two-step approach. First, by understanding the importance of each perception to quality, management can identify new ways of delivering the service that will improve these perceptions which, in turn, will improve quality. Second, the way in which certain process attributes affect service quality may not be clear from a model of quality as a function of operations; the intermediate role of perceptions can help to explain the effects of various operational activities on quality evaluations.

Approaches such as conjoint and path analysis were not used in this study for the following reasons. Conjoint was ruled out since it focuses primarily upon the physical features of the service, which is why it is generally used as a design tool for services (see Wind et al. (1989) for a service design application). It also relies on verbal descriptions of alternative services, for which it is more difficult for consumers to accurately describe their reactions (we are interested in studying how actual operations affect service quality). We are also interested in many more design variables than could be adequately judged by only a verbal description. Path analysis was not used since this is an exploratory study -- we do not know which factors impact which perceptions beforehand, so we cannot build the necessary structural models.

3.1   Model estimation. To estimate the relationships specified above, we must collect data for each variable specified in each equation. Since there is no underlying theory on the functional forms of g_n and h, we assume general nonlinear functions.   To avoid having to specify functional forms, we experimented with two flexible, nonparametric estimation techniques (neural networks and multivariate adaptive regression splines (MARS)) to model these relationships For an overview of neural networks, see Rumelhart, Hinton and Williams (1986); MARS is described in Friedman (1991). These are flexible models that are quite good at modeling complex relationships. In fact, Hornik, Stichcombe and White (1989) have recently demonstrated that neural networks can approximate any measurable function to any accuracy. We also compared the performance of these methods to linear models, since research on the judgment process has generally found linear models to produce strong statistical fits.

3.2   Model development. Once the equations for perceptions and quality have been estimated, they can be used to predict consumers' reactions to various changes in the process variables. To ensure that these changes are feasible, we also need to consider the physical aspects of the system, such as the relationship between waiting time and the number of servers. This can be done by adding equations (that describe the system) to the estimated models of perception and quality. For instance, the "physics" of the process can be represented using balance equations or standard queuing relations. Similarly, constraints may be needed to describe facility or resource limitations. We can also include operating specifications to assure conformance to a specified level of service. Together, these equations form a descriptive model of the consumer's perceptions and the service delivery system.

This system of equations can then be solved using optimization techniques to determine the process changes that will produce the greatest improvements in perceived quality. Greater insight can be gained by performing sensitivity analysis to see how perceived quality changes as operations change. This is accomplished by running the model many times using different settings for certain operations variables (e.g., the service capacity of the system, or the budget available for quality improvement). These results provide managers with useful information about the behavior of quality relative to system variables that they can control. The model will show the tradeoffs that exist for making various process changes. With this knowledge, managers can implement operations changes that improve quality the most while still meeting the firm's requirements. The results should also be useful for developing operating policies for providing consistently good service for a variety of customers and for a range of conditions. This model may also be used to address questions such as:

- How can the best level of service quality be achieved for the least cost?
- How does each step in the process contribute to overall quality?
- Where are the likely "quality failure points" or "quality bottlenecks"?
- Which parts of the process hold the greatest potential for improving service quality?
- Where in the process is high quality the most critical? the least critical?

4. Test Example: University Health Services

To test this methodology, we used the following example based on the Harvard Business School case "University Health Services: Walk-In Clinic" (case #9-681-061). This case describes changes made to service operations in an attempt to reduce the waiting time required for patients to receive medical attention. It was chosen as a test example because it provides a detailed description of an actual service delivery process.

4.1 Walk-in clinic service delivery process. The service delivery system described in this case and assumed for our study is illustrated in Figure 2. This service delivery process has five major steps which each patient experiences:
1. Filling out the patient data form
2. Waiting for record retrieval and to see the triage nurse
3. Triage (determines which provider the patient shall see)
4. Waiting to see the health care provider (nurse, doctor, or specific practitioner)
5. Medical examination by the health care provider.

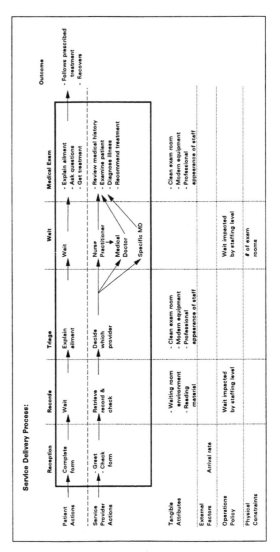

Figure 2: Walk-In Clinic Service Delivery Process

The actions performed by the patient and the server in each step are outlined in Figure 2, along with other factors that might affect the process (e.g., external factors, physical constraints).

If a patient has not come to see a specific health care provider, the triage nurse determines whether the patient can be seen by a nurse practitioner (NP) or if an examination by a medical doctor (MD) is required. Sometimes, a nurse practitioner requests that the patient see a doctor for a second opinion or further treatment. Since these patients must then endure a third waiting period (which administrators believe has a major impact on service quality), the goal of triage is to minimize these occurrences by making appropriate decisions regarding the care required by a patient.

4.2 Data used. The case provides data on the patient population, the reasons for patient visits, waiting time distributions for each of the waiting periods, and service distributions for the different types of care providers. The average time to perform each step of the process is also provided.

The case only deals with one dimension of service quality: waiting time (it explores ways to reduce customer complaints of excessive waiting times). It does not specify all of the quality attributes for the clinic. To define these attributes, we referred to a study by Reidenbach and Sandifer-Smallwood (1990) which used a SERVQUAL-like survey to capture patients' perceptions of inpatient, outpatient, and emergency room services. These authors used factor analysis to identify seven main perceptual factors for describing the service. Of these, the following are applicable to the walk-in clinic:

- Patient confidence, especially in the diagnosis and outcome of the care received;
- Waiting time;
- Empathy, which describes how well the staff tried to understand the patient's individual needs;
- Treatment quality, which involves the competence and credibility of the clinic personnel;
- Physical appearances, which includes perceptions of the staff and care facilities.

We estimated a model for each of the perceptions listed above. To model the relationships between these perceptions and the service delivery process, we needed data that matched the description of an individual's service encounter to his or her perceptions of that encounter. For this example, we used synthetic data which was generated based on data from the case and the perceptions study. To describe each service encounter, a program assigned values to each variable based on the value of a random number in [0,1] and the cumulative distribution function of the variable (from the case study). For example, wait(NP) was assigned the value x minutes when $P(wait(NP) \leq x) \leq random\ number$. Variables that describe the roles of the patients and providers were evenly distributed. The values for perception variables were determined using highly nonlinear functions of the operational variables found to be significant in the perceptions study (Reidenbach and Sandifer-Smallwood 1990). The variables used to describe the encounter are defined in Table 1. Variables that are real-valued have a domain denoted by [a,b]; integer-valued variables have domains denoted by 1,2,...n. The variables that represent the consumer's perceptions and quality assessment assume values in the range [0,1]. These values are based on a rating scale where 0.0 corresponds to "well below expectations", 0.5 corresponds to "as expected", and 1.0 corresponds to "much better than expected". Perceived service attributes, such as friendliness of the provider, use of medical history, and tangibles are evaluated using a similar rating scale, where 0.0 is "poor" and 1.0 is "excellent".

4.3 Model estimation. This section outlines our procedure for estimating the functional relationships defined in the methodology section. A data set (consisting of 300 data points) was generated and used to estimate the following relationships:

Quality = h(Diagnosis, WaitTime, KnowCustomer, Competence, Tangibles)

Diagnosis = g_1(MDexam, NPexam, patient type, provider, numqstns, explain,
        reason, Mhistory)

WaitTime = g_2(wait(records), wait(triage), numwait, wait(NP), wait(MD),
        Wcondn, patient type, reason, AVFqstns, AVFcheck,
        RecdChk, NPdiag, provider)

KnowCustomer = g_3(greet, triage, NPexam, NPdiag, MDexam, friendly,
        MHistory, reason, patient type, provider)

Competence = g_4(NPexam, NPdiag, MDexam, Mhistory, explain, patient type,
        reason, numqstns)

Tangibles = g_5(Clean facilities, reading materials, equipment, professional
        appearance of staff)

Table 1. Variables for the walk-in clinic models.

Variable	Definition	Domain
	Service Delivery Variables	
Greet	Was patient greeted by the receptionist?	0 or 1
AVFqstns	Number of questions completed on the patient data form	5,6,...,10
AVFcheck	How well was the patient data form checked?	[0,1]
Wait(record)	Time to retrieve patient record (minutes)	[11,16]
RecdChk	How well the record was checked for completeness	[0,1]
Wait(triage)	Waiting time to see triage (minutes)	[3,6]
Numwait	Number of patients waiting to see triage nurse	2,3,...,10
Triage	Time spent with triage nurse (minutes)	[3,5]
Wait(NP)	Waiting time to see nurse practitioner (minutes)	[0,52]
NPexam	Time for examination by an NP (minutes)	[28,37]
NPdiag	Was NP able to diagnose problem?	0 or 1
Wait(MD)	Waiting time to see a medical doctor (minutes)	[0,52]
MDexam	Time for examination by an MD (minutes)	[15,24]
Wait(SP)	Waiting time to see a specific provider	[20,52]
SPexam	Time for examination by a SP (minutes)	[15,24]
Friendly	Friendliness of provider	[0,1]
MHistory	Degree to which NP or MD considers patient's history	[0,1]
Numqstns	Number of questions asked by patient	2,3,...,8
Explain	How well patient explained symptoms	[0,1]
	Tangible Variables	
Wclean	Cleanliness of the waiting room	[0,1]
Wread	Variety of reading materials in waiting room	[0,1]
Wcondn	Waiting room environment (e.g., temperature, noise)	[0,1]
Tclean	Cleanliness of triage room	[0,1]
Tcondn	Triage room environment (e.g., temperature)	[0,1]
Teqmt	Availability of modern medical equipment in triage	[0,1]
Tprfl	Professional appearance of triage nurse	[0,1]
Eclean	Cleanliness of examination room	[0,1]
Econdn	Examination room environment (e.g., temperature)	[0,1]
Eeqmt	Availability of modern medical equipment for exam	[0,1]
Eprfl	Professional appearance of care provider	[0,1]
	Reason for Patient Visit	
Emrgcy	Emergency	0 or 1
Medical	Medical problem	0 or 1
Surgical	Visit related to surgery	0 or 1
SP	Patient requests to see a specific provider	0 or 1
Other	Other reason	0 or 1
	Patient Characteristics	
Age	Patient age	[18,72]
Sex	Male or female	0 or 1
Student	Patient is a student	0 or 1
Staff	Patient is on university staff	0 or 1
Medicare	Medicare patient from the community	0 or 1
Numvisit	Number of times patient has visited clinic	1,2,...,5
	Perceptions	
Diagnosis	Patient confidence in diagnosis	[0,1]
WaitTime	Waiting time (inverse relationship)	[0,1]
KnowCustomer	Degree of individual attention received by patient	[0,1]
Competence	Competence and credibility of clinic staff	[0,1]
Tangibles	Physical attractiveness of the service facilities, staff	[0,1]
Quality	Evaluation of perceptions relative to expectations	[0,1]

Each function was estimated using neural networks, MARS, and linear regression. The variables listed in Table 2 were found to be significant by all three estimation techniques. Since the remaining variables did not add much to the performance of these models, only the significant variables were kept in the estimated equations.

To test the fit of the resulting models, five test data sets were generated and each model was tested using all five data sets. The results of these tests appear in Figures 3 and 4. The MARS models for Know Customer and Competence were the only models that outperformed their linear counterparts. We see from this figure that, in general, the linear model was competitive with the nonlinear, nonparametric methods. This result agrees with decision processes research which finds that linear models of clinical judgment provide very good statistical fits. For example, studies by Slovic and Lichtenstein (1971) and Einhorn, Kleinmuntz and Kleinmuntz (1979) found that simple linear models were excellent predictors of judge's decisions.

Table 2. Significant variables for all models.

DIAGNOSIS:	Patient type Provider Exam duration Number of questions	COMPETENCE:	Medical history Number of questions Patient type Exam duration
WAIT:	Triage wait Exam wait Patient type Reason Provider	TANGIBLE:	Clean Condition Equipment Staff appearance
KNOW CUTOMER:	Friendly Exam duration Provider Medical history Reason	QUALITY:	Diagnosis Waiting time Know customer Tangibles

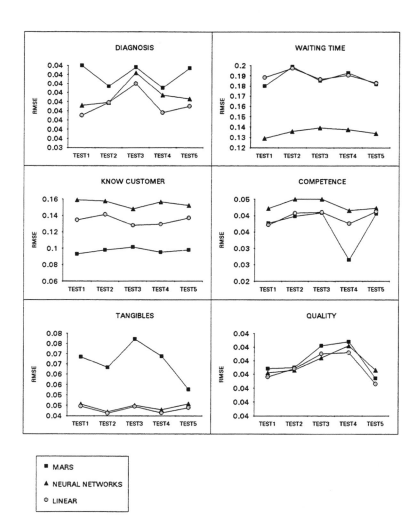

Figure 3. Comparison of model performance: root mean square error.

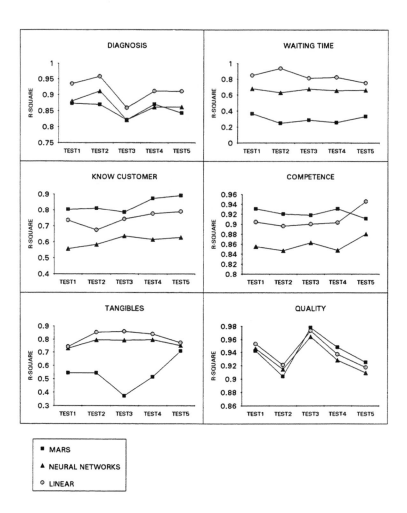

Figure 4. Comparison of model performance: R-squared.

We examined the performance of these models further by analyzing the error for each model for the five test data sets. To do this, we found the range of the error, the first quartile, the median, the third quartile, the mean and the standard deviation. The box plots shown in Figure 5 summarize these statistics for each perception model for the first validation set. These plots are very useful for revealing the central tendency and spread behavior of the models. In general, the errors for all three models cluster in a similar range about zero. It is interesting to note that both MARS and the linear model for Waiting Time often underpredicted. This result may have been caused by the distribution of the response variable, which in this case spans the entire range (from 0 to 1), with most instances occurring at the lower end (0.2 to 0.4). The neural network model also underpredicted when the sigmoid transfer function was used; we were able to model both ends of the scale more accurately by switching to the hyperbolic tangent function (see the neural network box plot for Waiting Time).

For the models labeled Diagnosis, Tangibles and Know Customer, note that most of the errors for MARS are tightly clustered. This indicates a very good fit for most of the data points. However, there are certain data instances that MARS does not fit well at all, which is indicated by the relatively high RMSE for the MARS models for Diagnosis and Tangibles.

From this analysis, we see that linear models produced estimates that were comparable to those generated using neural networks and MARS. However, linear models are much easier to use and interpret than the other models. For these reasons, we decided to use linear models for the subsequent analysis of the service delivery process.

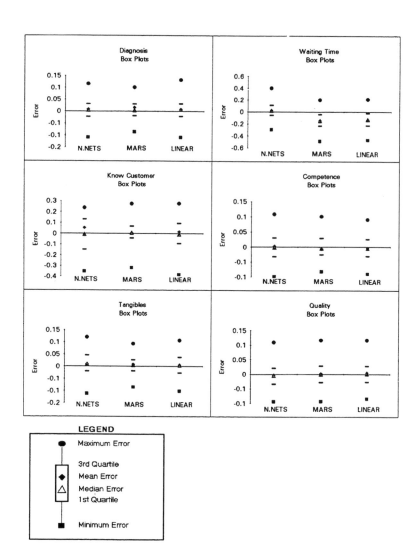

Figure 5. Box plots of the errors.

4.4 Optimization models and results. The resulting linear models can then used to identify where and how to improve quality in the process. We can also examine the tradeoffs involved in making various quality improvements, such as how increasing the amount of time spent with each patient impacts the perceptions of "knowing the customer" versus "waiting time." To ensure feasibility, constraints are added that describe the physical flow of the process. These constraints also relate the process variables to factors under management's control, such as the number of NPs and MDs scheduled to work in the clinic. If we assume that the model is steady state, and we know the distributions of the arrival and service times, then we can use standard queuing relationships to represent the process. For this example, if we assume that each step of the process is an $M/M/m$ queue, then we can use Burke's Theorem to model this network of queues (Burke's Theorem states that the output process of an $M/M/m$ queue is a Poisson process with rate λ if $\lambda < m\,\mu$ see, for example, Ross (1983, p.157)). Then we can describe the waiting times at each step k in the clinic (k = records, triage, NP, MD) as a function of the arrival rate at each step (λ_k), the service rate (μ_k), and the number of servers (m_k):

$$\text{Waiting time at step } k = P_0 = \frac{\rho_k \left(\lambda_k / \mu_k\right)^{m_k}}{m_k! \left(1 - \rho_k\right)^2 \lambda_k}$$

$$\text{where } P_0 = \left[\sum_{n=0}^{m_k - 1} \frac{\left(\lambda_k / \mu_k\right)^n}{n!} + \frac{\left(\lambda_k / \mu_k\right)^{m_k}}{m_k!} \frac{1}{1 - \rho_k} \right]^{-1} \text{ and } \rho_k = \frac{\lambda_k}{m_k \mu_k}$$

Since this relation only holds for $\lambda_k < m_k\,\mu_k$, we need to add restrictions on the values that m_k can assume.

We also need to add constraints to describe limited resources in the system. For instance, the number of examination rooms in the clinic is limited to 4 rooms for NPs and 9 rooms for MDs. The budget for improving quality is also limited, so a constraint is included that computes the additional expenditure necessary to improve quality. Operating specifications such as the desired capacity of the system may also be included. For the clinic, management may want to determine how to staff in order to handle a specific number of patients per day. We also must include the minimum amount of time required for medical examinations. Here, the minimum examination time was determined using a 25% increase in the number of patients seen per hour by NPs and a 10% increase for MDs (the smaller increase for MDs reflects the higher level of efficiency that the MDs have already achieved).

The remaining constraints hold the variables in the estimated models within the ranges used during estimation. For example, the variables that describe tangibles in the process must remain in [0,1]. The estimated equations, combined with these constraints, form a descriptive model of perceived service quality in the service delivery process.

Quality $= -0.39 + (0.44 * \text{Diagnosis}) + (0.54 * \text{WaitTime})$
$+ (0.32 * \text{KnowCustomer}) + (0.31 * \text{Tangibles})$

Diagnosis $= 0.74 + (0.012 * \text{MDexam}) - (0.22 * \text{student}) - (0.019 * \text{staff})$
$- (0.0006 * \text{numqstns})$

WaitTime $= 1.76 - (0.02 * \text{wait(records)}) - (0.007 * \text{triage})) - (0.02 * \text{numwait}$
$- (0.03 * \text{wait(NP)}) - (0.04 * \text{wait(MD)}) + (0.046 * \text{SP}) - (0.13 * \text{stu}$
$- (0.015 * \text{staff}) - (0.73 * \text{NPdiag})$

where numwait $= (\text{wait(triage)} * \lambda(\text{triage}))$

KnowCustomer $= -0.79 + (0.002 * \text{NPexam}) + (0.85 * \text{NPdiag}) + (0.01 * \text{MDexam})$
$+ (0.42 * \text{friendly}) + (0.34 * \text{Mhistory}) - (0/05 * \text{medical}) - (0.03 * \text{s}$

Tangibles $= 0.069 + (0.17 * \text{Wclean}) + ().25 * \text{Wread}) + (0.18 * \text{Wcondn})$
$+ (0.06 * \text{Eeqmt}) + (0.24 * \text{Eprfl})$

$$\text{Wait (k)} = \frac{P_0 \left(\lambda_k / \mu_k\right)^{m_k} \left(\lambda_k / \left(m_k \mu_k\right)\right)}{m_k! \left(1 - \left(\lambda_k / \left(m_k \mu_k\right)\right)\right)^2 \lambda_k} \quad , \; k = \text{records, triage, NP, MD}$$

$$\text{where } P_0 = \left[\sum_{n=0}^{m_k - 1} \frac{\left(\lambda_k / \mu_k\right)^n}{n!} + \frac{\left(\lambda_k / \mu_k\right)^{m_k}}{m_k!} \; \frac{1}{\left(1 - \left(\lambda_k / m_k \mu_k\right)\right)} \right]^{-1}$$

$$\text{Throughput} = \frac{\#\text{patients}}{\text{day}} \leq \text{Capacity}$$

$$\text{where Capacity} = \left(480\frac{\text{minutes}}{\text{day}} * (\text{m}(\text{NP}) + \text{m}(\text{MD}))\right)\Big/\left(\frac{\text{NPexam}}{3} + \frac{2*\text{MDexam}}{3}\right)$$

$$\text{Qualcost} \geq \left(\frac{\$1.50}{\text{day}} * (\text{Wclean} - 0.726)\right) + \left(\frac{\$2}{\text{day}} * (\text{Wread} - 0.654)\right)$$

$$+ \left(\frac{\$100}{\text{day}} * (\text{Eeqmt} - 0.606)\right) + \left(\frac{\$200}{\text{day}} * (\text{Wcondn} - 0.654)\right)$$

$$+ \left(\frac{\$14.51}{\text{hour}} * \frac{8\text{hours}}{\text{day}} * (\text{m}(\text{NP}) - 3.687)\right)$$

$$+ \left(\frac{\$28.98}{\text{hour}} * \frac{8\text{hours}}{\text{day}} * (\text{m}(\text{MD}) - 3.563)\right)$$

$$+ \left(\frac{\$14.51}{\text{hour}} * \frac{8\text{hours}}{\text{day}} * (\text{m}(\text{triage}) - 2)\right)$$

$$+ \left(\frac{\$8.30}{\text{hour}} * \frac{8\text{hours}}{\text{day}} * (\text{m}(\text{records}) - 4)\right)$$

Room Limits: $m(NP \leq 4)$

$\qquad m(MD) \leq 9$

Limits: $\lambda_k/\mu_k < m_k$, $k = $ records, triage, NP, MD

$\qquad 26.2 \leq NPexam \leq 40$ minutes

$\qquad 15.8 \leq MDexam \leq 30$ minutes

$\qquad 0 \leq friendly \leq 1.0$

$\qquad 0 \leq Mhistory \leq 1.0$

$\qquad 0.726 \leq Wclean \leq 1.0$

$\qquad 0.654 \leq Wread \leq 1.0$

$\qquad 0.654 \leq Wcondn \leq 1.0$

$\qquad 0.606 \leq Eeqmt \leq 1.0$

$\qquad 0.691 \leq Eprfl \leq 1.0$

$\qquad Diagnosis \leq 1.0$

$\qquad WaitTime \leq 1.0$

$\qquad KnowCustomer \leq 1.0$

$\qquad Tangibles \leq 1.0$

The decision variables for this model are listed in Table 3 along with their baseline values which describe current operations (the current level of each perception and overall quality was determined by plugging the values for current operations into the estimated model). These values were used in the cost equation to determine the amount of *additional* spending required per day to move beyond the baseline values of the decision variables. Note that this cost can be negative if the model suggests values that are less than the baseline levels.

These equations were formulated into optimization problems to answer the following questions:

- What is the maximum level of quality that can be attained at no extra cost?
- (Maximize {*Quality : Qualcost $\leq$ 0*, remaining constraints})
- What is the smallest investment required to achieve a specific quality level?
- (Minimize {*Qualcost: Quality $\geq Q$*, remaining constraints})

Table 3: Results for Several Quality Levels

	Current Value	Maximize Quality	Minimize Cost			
Quality	0.35	0.61	0.70	0.80	0.90	1.00
Cost	0.00	0.00	47.24	119.18	232.96	717.88
Diagnosis	0.76	0.74	0.74	0.74	0.74	0.84
Waiting Time	0.22	0.48	0.64	0.82	1.00	1.00
Know Customer	0.24	0.46	0.46	0.46	0.46	0.58
Tangibles	0.68	0.88	0.88	0.88	0.90	0.95
Records Staff	4.00	4.53	4.63	4.79	5.04	5.10
Triage Nurses	2.00	1.22	1.26	1.31	1.39	1.41
NPs	3.69	3.47	3.61	3.81	4.00	4.00
MDs	3.56	3.91	4.00	4.13	4.34	6.18
Wait: records	15.22	7.57	6.78	5.40	3.93	3.67
Wait: triage	5.21	8.14	7.05	5.78	4.41	4.17
Wait: NP	15.59	11.63	9.69	7.46	5.88	5.89
Wait: MD	15.15	13.96	11.94	9.61	7.10	7.33
Total Wait: NP	36.68	27.74	23.51	18.64	14.22	13.72
Total Wait: MD	36.24	30.06	25.76	20.78	15.44	15.17
NP exam time	32.80	26.20	26.20	26.20	26.20	26.20
MD exam time	19.40	17.59	17.59	17.59	17.59	26.52
Cleanliness	0.73	1.00	1.00	1.00	1.00	1.00
Reading Material	0.65	1.00	1.00	1.00	1.00	1.00
Waiting Rm Condtion	0.65	0.65	0.65	0.65	0.74	1.00
Equipment	0.61	0.61	0.61	0.61	0.61	0.61
Prof'l Appearance	0.69	1.00	1.00	1.00	1.00	1.00
Friendliness	0.68	1.00	1.00	1.00	1.00	1.00
Medical History	0.66	1.00	1.00	1.00	1.00	1.00

If we consider *Quality* to be a production function, then *Qualcost* is its dual. The purpose of the first question is to determine how current operations should be modified in order to put them on the efficient frontier; the second question explores means for improving perceived quality to various levels by investing in operations. These problems were solved using GAMS, a modeling system for solving mathematical programming problems. The equations *Wait(k)* make these nonlinear programs. To solve these models, we used the NLP option of GAMS which calls the nonlinear program solver MINOS. To solve nonlinear programs, MINOS computes derivatives; however, it cannot take the derivative of $m_k!$ which appears in equations $Wait(k)$. Therefore, we substituted Stirling's equation $\left(\sqrt{2\pi}\ m_k^{m_k+0.5}\ e^{-m_k}\right)$ for $mk!$. The summation $\Sigma_{n=0}^{m_k-1}\left(\lambda_k/\mu_k\right)^n/n!$ presents a similar problem. This was approximated using

$(e^{(\lambda_k/\mu_k)}-(\lambda_k/\mu_k))$ for $\left(\lambda_k/\mu_k\right)\leq 2.5$ and $(e^{(\lambda_k/\mu_k)}-(\lambda_k/\mu_k)^2)$ otherwise.

We did not require m_k to be integer-valued since we were interested in the average number of staff members available per day. The parameters in the model were defined as the expected values given in the case. For example, the value for "student" is set at 0.67, since this is the proportion of patients which are students. The solutions for these problems are summarized in Table 3. Note that because these models are based on estimations, we should regard the results as relative guidelines rather than absolute solutions.

To improve quality at no additional cost, the model suggests increasing the number of MDs and records workers, and reducing the average number of triage nurses and NPs. By doing this, the clinic could reduce waiting times for record retrieval by over 50%, and would reduce the total time to see a triage nurse by almost 5 minutes. The waiting time to see an NP would also be reduced, which results from a 25% increase in the NP's service rate, which translates into spending 6.5 fewer minutes with each patient. The results are similar for MDs, who would improve their service rate by 10% and thus reduce the waiting time involved. This shift in staffing would provide a small net savings, which could be applied towards improving the tangible aspects of the service. The model recommends purchasing additional janitorial services, ordering additional reading materials for the waiting room, and assuring that the staff look professional. These changes would increase every perception except for "confidence in diagnosis," which is slightly lower due to shorter examination times.

Once we know how to improve current operations by shifting resources, we now want to understand what it will take to increase perceived quality up to its maximum level. To do this, the minimum cost model was run for a series of different quality levels and for the two throughput levels: the average number of patients served per day (143), and the maximum number of patients per day (163). The results for this model are shown in Table 3 and in Figure 6. Each column under Minimize Cost in Table 3 lists the solution values of the decision variables that resulted from running the model with a different quality setting, which is given at the top of each column. The corresponding cost to improve to this level of quality is given in the next row. The first column shows the current values for these decision variables which serve as a baseline.

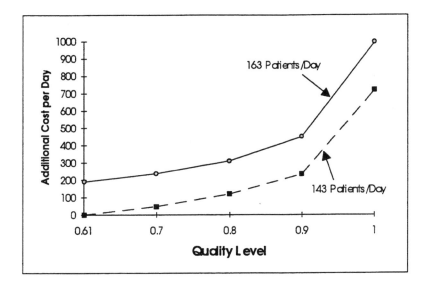

Figure 6: Summary of Model Results

In general, the model specifies that the maximum amount of all "free variables" be used. It also recommends that only the least expensive changes be made to the tangible attributes. The remaining costs are labor costs associated with adding MDs and records staff. Figure 7 shows the allocation of quality costs for various levels of quality. We see from this figure that the increased spending for MDs is greatly offset by reducing the average number of triage nurses working each day. This figure also suggests that the number of MDs available is the driving factor for increasing quality, since this value is increased even though they are the most expensive resource in a minimum cost problem. It also shows that spending on tangibles only becomes significant once quality reaches about 0.9.

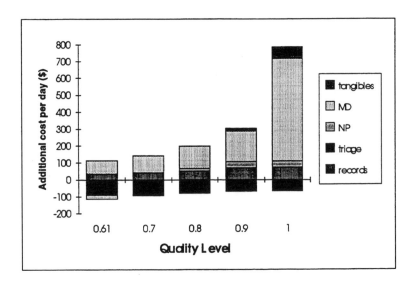

Figure 7. Allocation of Quality Costs

To see why this is, it is useful to look at the relative contribution of each perception to quality (see Figure 8). By comparing the first two levels of quality (the current level (0.35) and 0.61), we see that the reallocation of staff increases the perceptions of "waiting time" and "knowing the customer." These results are mainly due to more productive medical providers; examination times were reduced, which in turn, reduced the amount of time spent waiting. The perception "knowing the customer" improved due to increases in friendliness and the use of the patient's medical history.

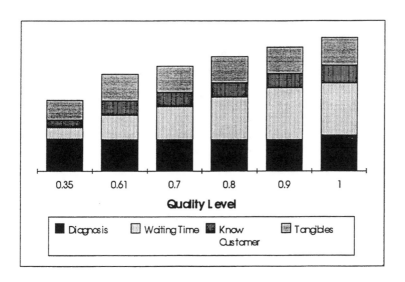

Figure 8: Contribution of Each Perception to Quality

This figure also shows that gains in quality up to 0.9 come from improving perceived waiting times, which is accomplished by adding staff. If we look at the level of the underlying perceptions at this quality level, we see that "WaitTime" has reached its maximum value of 1. To make up the remaining quality gains, further investment in tangibles (i.e., the condition of the waiting room) is needed. However, once this reaches its maximum perceived level, management must resort to increasing the amount of examination time by MDs (which requires a substantial increase in the average number of MDs (from 4.3 to 6.2)) to make the last improvement in quality from 0.9 to 1.0. This is why the marginal cost of quality in this range is so high.

This analysis indicates that tradeoffs exist when developing quality improvement strategies. For example, in order to increase the quality to 0.61 the model recommends reducing the time spent with patients (which will reduce

"Confidence in the Diagnosis") in order to achieve greater gains in the other perceptions that determine quality.

We can also use these results to answer the questions posed in the methodology section. The answer to the first question (how can the best level of quality be achieved for the least cost?) is given in Table 3. To address the remaining questions, we substitute the perceptions equations into the quality equation so that we now have quality as a function of process variables. Since this is a linear equation, we can rearrange the terms so that the variables are grouped according to process step. Variables that pertain to more than one step are assigned in proportion to the appropriate steps (records, triage, NP, and MD). Variables that describe the consumer are grouped separately. This gives us the following relation of quality as a function of each process step and consumer attributes:

Quality = α + Step(records) + Step(triage) + Step(NP) + Step(MD) +
   Consumer

where
- α *is a constant*
- *Step(record) = G_1(Wait(records),Wclean,Wread,Wcondn);*
- *Step(triage) = G_2(Wait(triage),Triage,Wclean,Wread,Wcondn);*
- *Step(NP) = G_3(Wait(NP),NPexam,NPdiag,Friendly,Mhistory,*
   Wclean,Wread,Wcondn,Eeqmt, Eprfl);
- *Step(MD)= G_4(Wait(MD),MDexam,Friendly,Mhistory,*
   Wclean,Wread,Wcondn,Eeqmt,Eprfl);
- *Consumer = G_5(Student,Staff,Medical,Numqstns).*

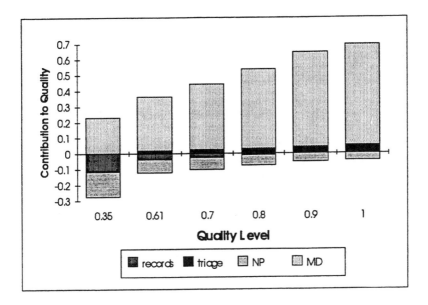

Figure 9: Contribution of Each Step to Quality

The functions G_k are all linear relationships.

Using this equation for quality and the variable values from Table 3, we can determine the contribution of each step to perceived quality. These results appear in Figure 9. The consumer's contribution to the quality equation is not shown in this figure since it remains about the same (-0.16) for each quality level. We see that under current operations, only the MD part of the process has a positive influence on quality. To improve quality from 0.35 to 0.61, these positive effects are further leveraged and the negative impact from the other steps were reduced. The time required for records retrieval is gradually reduced so that this step has a minimal impact on quality. By making the staffing adjustments discussed earlier, the MD step can have a significant positive effect on service quality. This suggests that the MD examination is a quality bottleneck, since overall quality will not change much without changes to this step. It also holds the greatest potential for improving service quality. Within this step, the driving factors appear to be the length of time spent waiting to see a provider, friendliness of the provider, and taking more time to understand the patient's needs (when sufficient capacity exists).

5.   Conclusions

In this paper, we described a method for developing a better understanding of the links between operations, perceptions and service quality. By modeling the delivery process as a system, we were able to identify many possible sources of quality problems. In estimating the perceptions models, we found that linear models provided better statistical fits than more flexible nonlinear methods. This is consistent with the decision processes literature. We also found that, by modeling the underlying perceptions of service quality, we gained a better understanding of why perceived quality changes as a result of operational changes.

The usefulness of the approach presented in this paper was demonstrated using the walk-in clinic example. The results of the optimization models identified key tradeoffs for improving quality in the process. For example, we saw that although the examination time had a positive effect on service quality, it should not be increased until other parts of the service delivery process have been improved. The model also indicated that by improving quality, we could gain service capacity, since the means for increasing quality was to increase the number of MDs, thereby making more doctors available to handle heavy patient traffic should it occur. In this way, quality builds flexibility into this service.

The results of this test example suggest that this approach is quite useful for identifying potential quality problems and areas to focus improvement efforts. By considering many elements of the system, this method also allows management to define and weigh the tradeoffs involved in quality management decisions. However, this model is limited in several ways. Since it is based on empirically estimated functions, the results cannot be interpreted in absolute terms; rather, they provide insight into the qualitative relationships between the variables. Also, the steady state queuing assumptions may not be appropriate in services that experience very uneven traffic flows. The most significant limitation of this approach, however, is that it can only deal with changes to variables that describe the existing service delivery process; it cannot consider the impact of redesigning the service delivery process. Finally, the model only considers perceived quality at a snapshot in time; i.e., it does not account for changes in consumers' expectations over time.

The next step is to verify these results by building such a model for actual service operations. This application will be discussed in a future paper. A related question to be explored is how should management allocate incentives for employees who work at various steps in the service delivery process so that these employees will work in a way that is best for total system quality.

References

Bolton, R.N., and J.H. Drew (1991). "A multistage model of customers' assessments of service quality and value," *Journal of Consumer Research* 19, 375-384.

Collier, D.C. (1991). "The service quality process map for credit card processing," *Decision Sciences* 22, 406-420.

Deming, W.E. (1986). *Out of the Crisis*. (MIT Center for Advanced Engineering Study, Cambridge, MA).

Doyle, S., R. Pigneri, and D.H. Maister (1981). "University health services: walk-in clinic," Case Study #9-681-061 (Harvard Business School, Boston, MA).

Einhorn, H.J., D.N. Kleinmuntz, and B. Kleinmuntz (1979). "Linear regression and process tracing models of judgment," *Psychological Review* 86, 465-485.

Friedman, J.H. (1991). "Multivariate adaptive regression splines," *The Annals of Statistics* 19, 1-141.

Hornik, K., M. Stinchcombe, and H. White (1989). "Multilayer feedforward networks are universal approximators," *Neural Networks* 2, 359-366.

Lewis, R.C., and B.H. Booms (1983). "The marketing aspects of quality," in L. Berry, G. Shostack, and G. Upah, (eds.), *Emerging Perspectives on Service Marketing* (American Marketing Association, Chicago, IL), 99-107.

Parasuraman, A., V.A. Zeithaml, and L.L. Berry (1985). "A conceptual model of service quality and its implications for future research," *Journal of Marketing* 49, (Fall) 41-50.

Parasuraman, A., V.A. Zeithaml, and L.L. Berry (1988). "SERVQUAL: a multiple-item scale for measuring customer perceptions of service quality," *Journal of Retailing* 64, 13-37.

Reidenbach, R.E., and B. Sandifer-Smallwood (1990). "Exploring perceptions of hospital operations by a modified SERVQUAL approach," *Journal of Health Care Marketing* 10, 47-55.

Rosander, A.C. (1985). *Applications of Quality Control in Service Industries* (ASQC Press, Milwaukee, WI).

Ross, S.M. (1983). *Stochastic Processes* (John Wiley and Sons, New York, NY).

Rumelhart, D.E., G.E. Hinton, and R.J. Williams (1986). "Learning internal representations by error propagation," in D.E. Rumelhart and J.L. McClelland, (eds.) *Parallel Distributed Processing: Explorations in the Microstructure of Cognition - Volume 1: Foundations* (MIT Press, Cambridge, MA), 318-364.

Slovic, P., and S. Lichtenstein (1971). "Comparison of Bayesian and regression approaches to the study of information processing in judgment," *Organizational Behavior and Human Performance* 6, 649-744.

Wind, J., P. Green, D. Shifflet, and M. Scarborough (1989). "Courtyard by Marriott: designing a hotel facility with a consumer-based marketing model," *Interfaces* 19, 25-47.

Chapter 12   Hotel Sales and Reservations Planning

Gabriel R. Bitran, Stephen M. Gilbert, and Thin-Yin Leong

1. Introduction

The management of a hotel reservation system involves repeated resource allocation decisions under uncertainty. The objective of these decisions is to maximize the expected profit of the hotel by allocating reservations to different types of customers. Since both the demand for reservations and the rate at which customers fail to show up are uncertain, the decision problems are inherently difficult. Historically, reservations were accepted in an ad hoc basis and managers were evaluated on the basis of the average utilization of capacity. However, as data collection methods become increasingly sophisticated, there is an opportunity to take advantage of formal modeling techniques to maximize revenues and improve productivity in the hotel industry.

In the reservations planning problem, a hotel manager must allocate inventories of reservations for particular target dates to several different types of customers. The customers may be differentiated by room type (eg. single vs. double, economy vs. luxury), price, or duration of stay. Additionally, different types of customers may book further in advance or fail to show with different probabilities than others. Once a reservation is issued to a customer, he is guaranteed a room on a particular date or set of dates. Although customers can usually cancel without penalty at any time prior to the targeted check-in date, the hotel must pay a stiff penalty if it is unable to honor its part of the contract by providing a room. The penalty generally includes the price of finding the

343

P. T. Harker (ed.), The Service Productivity and Quality Challenge, 343–363.
© 1995 Kluwer Academic Publishers. Printed in the Netherlands.

customer a comparable (or better) room at another hotel plus the intangible cost of goodwill.

We model the reservations planning problem in terms of perishable inventories of multiple types of reservations. Management controls these inventories by limiting the number of each type of reservation that it will issue. Since the reservations can be cancelled at any time, the inventories are subject to uncertain perishability. The objective of our model is to maximize expected revenues subject to a service level constraint, i.e. a constraint on the probability of being unable to honor a customer's reservation. Since the variable cost of assigning a customer to a room does not differ among the various customer classes, maximizing revenues is equivalent to maximizing profit.

In section 2, we discuss the various approaches that have been taken to the reservations problem in the literature. In section 3, we discuss the specifics of our model. In section 4 we present computational results. In section 5, we discuss directions for future research.

2. Literature Review

A number of authors have studied reservations planning problems in either the hotel, airline, or equipment rental industries. Most of the work falls into one of the following categories:
-    Allocation of a fixed resource to multiple classes of demand.
-    Dynamic control of a Markovian reservation process.
-    Detailed models of the arrival of different customer types to the facility.
In the airline industry, the cost of a denied boarding tends to be low. If the number of customers who show up for a flight exceeds the number of seats on the plane, it is usually possible to find a passenger who will gladly give up his seat in exchange for a free ticket. Since these free tickets are usually used for incremental discretionary travel, and restrictions prevent them from being used on crowded flights, the marginal cost to the airline for issuing them is small. In contrast, the cost of an empty seat tends to be high, it is equal to the revenue that could have been earned if the seat had been filled. Because of this cost structure, a simple heuristic which allows ticket sales to exceed seat capacity by a certain percentage is a reasonable method for accounting for uncertain no-shows. Thus most of the models of airline reservation systems have focused on allocating a fixed number of tickets to a variety of fare classes.

Rothstein (1985) and Belobaba (1987) provide detailed reviews of mathematical approaches which have been taken to the problem of maximizing the expected revenue associated with a given flight in which capacity is fixed. The work of Belobaba (1989) is representative. He has taken a marginal pricing approach in what he calls the Expected Marginal Seat Revenue (EMSR) model. In this model, he assumes that lower fare classes purchase before high ones. He shows that for each fare class i, seats should be "protected" or withheld in such a way that the marginal revenue (with respect to the number of seats withheld) from sales to higher paying classes is exactly equal to the fare for class i. Although he extends this work to account for "no shows", the emphasis is placed upon the allocation of a fixed number of tickets to different fare categories.

For cases in which low fares do not necessarily book first, a variety of Markovian sequential decision models have been proposed. The focus of these models is upon how to adjust booking limits on one or more types of reservations at various decision points leading up to a target date. Requests for reservations, cancellations, and show rates are all sources of uncertainty. Rothstein (1974) provided the first such model for a hotel with only one type of room and single night stays.

Ladany (1976) proposes another dynamic decision model for a hotel with both single and double rooms. In each stage of his dynamic program, a random number of reservation requests and cancellations are received. The controls are the limits on the number of each type of reservation to accept. Ladany provides a concise dynamic programming formulation of the problem.

Alstrup et. al. (1986) consider a similar model in an application to airlines with two types of seats. However, because of the computational effort required to solve the dynamic program for an airplane with 110 seats, they suggest that an approximation problem be solved instead. In the approximation model, passengers are treated as groups rather than individually. That is, the limits on ticket sales can only be set at multiples of the group size. They show that it is possible to obtain accurate results using a group size of 5 or fewer.

Liberman and Yechiali(1978) propose another dynamic decision model. Although they consider only one type of room, they assume that in addition to limiting the number of reservations to accept, management can either cancel previously confirmed reservations, or acquire additional bookings at some specified cost. They show that the optimal strategy is a 3-region policy. In each period, upper and lower limits on reservation inventory create three regions.

The optimal action depends only upon where the current reservation inventory lies within these regions.

The third approach to the reservations planning problem is to focus on the details surrounding the arrival of customers at the hotel. Williams (1977) models a particular date that represents a peak in demand. He assumes that demand for rooms on this date comes from three sources, listed in decreasing order of priority: (1) stayovers - guests occupying rooms on the day preceding the critical date. (2) reservations - guests arriving on the critical date with reservations. (3) walk-ins - guests arriving without reservations. He further assumes that the occupancy of the hotel on the day before the critical one is known with certainty, and calculates the expected costs of forgone revenues and overbooking that are associated with various numbers of reservations. Although Williams' suggests methods of designing decision aids, his model is concerned more with estimating the costs of specific policies than with optimization.

Bitran and Gilbert (1994) model the allocation of rooms to customers as they arrive throughout a given check-in day. They assume that different types of customers arrive during different periods of the day. In particular they assume that customers who have not guaranteed their reservations with a credit card arrive prior to those who have. They explain that, in practice, reservations which have not been guaranteed expire at a certain time, usually around 6 p.m. Given a set of guaranteed and non-guaranteed reservations, management must decide if and when to begin "walking" customers. When a customer is "walked", the hotel is obligated to pay for him to stay in a room of at least comparable quality to the one he had reserved. The cost of doing this increases with time at which the "walk" is performed. Not only does the customer's perception of the inconvenience increase later in the evening, it may become increasingly difficult for the hotel to find a comparable room in which to put him. In practice, hotels often "walk" customers while they still have rooms available in order to avoid having to walk customers very late in the evening. Bitran and Gilbert derive optimal policies for allocating rooms to customers and motivate heuristics for issuing reservations.

3.1 Problem description. Many large urban hotels offer a variety of room types: suites, doubles, singles, etc. Although reservations specify a given type of room, some substitution is generally possible. For example, a customer with a reservation for a single will gladly accept a double if no singles are available. In addition, because of corporate discounts, travel agency commissions, etc., the hotel may earn different revenues from different customer types for the same room. Hotel management attempts to respond to requests for a variety of types of reservations in order to maximize expected revenues subject to a constraint on the probability of being able to honor a given reservation, i.e. service level. Let us make the following assumptions:

1. There is a set $S=[1,...,m]$ of room types, indexed according to level of luxury, such that a room of type $i \in S$ can be substituted for a room of type j if $j \geq i$.
2. There is a set $A=[1,...,n]$ of reservation types. The relationship between reservation and room types is shown in Figure 1. Let $a(s)$, $s=1,...,m$ be the indices of classes such that $1=a(1) < a(2),...,a(m) \leq n$ and a guest i $\in [a(s),....,a(s+1) - 1]$ requests room type s.
3. A guest in class i pays c_i per room per night of occupancy and $c_i \geq c_j$ for i $\leq$j.
4. Reservations for multiple-day stays are treated as a series of independent single day reservations.
5. Walk-in customers arrive at the hotel after customers with reservations.

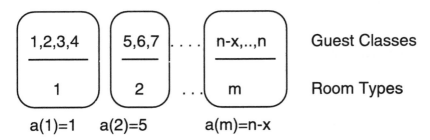

Figure 1. Guest Classes and Room Types

Assumption 1 specifies that there exists a preference ranking of rooms that is shared by all customers. In practice hotels tend to have large numbers of standard rooms, and a few special purpose rooms such as luxury suites.
Assumption 2 has the following interpretation: If $a(s) = k$, then k is the lowest indexed guest class that requests room type s. In practice, the same room may

be rented for a variety of prices because there are a variety of distribution channels such as travel agents, corporate discounts, government employee rates, etc. Assumption 3 requires that customer classes be indexed according to the rental fee that they are charged, and that no customer requesting a reservation for a given type of room will pay more than any other customer who requests a better room. Assumption 4 results from the fact that, at the hotel that we studied, the reservation system accepts multiple day reservations as a series of independent single day reservations. Thus, the only way to find out about scheduled stayovers is to check whether the same customer has a reservation on consecutive days. Assumption 5 is valid in hotels which are able to enforce a policy in which customers are billed for reservations which are not cancelled prior to some deadline, usually no later than the afternoon of the date of the reservation. When such a policy is in place, it is common for management to delay the admission of walk-ins until after the cancellation deadline. Let us introduce the following notation:

Parameters:

C_s:	The number of type s rooms available.
$A(s)$:	The set of all guest classes for room type s.
$AU(s)$:	The set of guest classes for room type s or higher.
c_i:	The revenue collected from a customer of class i.

Decision Variables:

N_i:	The booking limit for class i reservations.
M_i:	The number of rooms allocated to guest class i after the demand for reservations has been realized but prior to to the arrival of the guests to the hotel.
Y_i:	The number of class i walk-ins who are assigned to rooms.

Random Variables:

q_i:	The fraction of class i reservation customers who show up.
NS_i:	The number of requests for class i reservations.
$NS_i(N_i)$:	The number of class i reservations that are booked, i.e. the

minimum of the booking limit N_i and the number requests, NS_i.

R_i: The number of class i reservations that arrive and are given rooms,
$R_i = \text{Min}\{q_i \cdot NS_i(N_i), M_i\}$.

YS_i: The number of class i walk-in customers.

Other notation:

$E_x[\bullet]$: The expectation function over the random variable x.

Consider the following model of the hotel reservations problem, which we will refer to as problem (S):

$$Z_S = \underset{N_1,\ldots,N_n}{\text{Max}}\left\{E_{NS}\left[\underset{M_1,\ldots,M_n}{\text{Max}}\left\{E_q\left[\sum_{i=1}^{n} c_i \cdot R_i + \underset{Y_1,\ldots,Y_n}{\text{Max}}\left\{E_{YS}\left[\sum_{i=1}^{n} c_i \cdot Y_i\right]\right\}\right]\right\}\right]\right\}$$

(1)

subject to:

$$\sum_{i=1}^{a(s+1)-1} (Y_i + R_i) \leq \sum_{j=1}^{s} C_j, \text{ for } s = 1,\ldots,m$$

(2)

$$0 \leq Y_i \leq YS_i, \text{ for } i = 1,\ldots,n$$

(3)

$$R_i = \text{Min}\{q_i \cdot NS_i(N_i), M_i\}, \text{ for } i = 1,\ldots,n$$

(4)

$$\text{Prob}[q_i \cdot NS_i(N_i) \leq M_i] \geq \alpha, \text{ for } i = 1,\ldots,n$$

(5)

$$\sum_{i=1}^{a(s+1)-1} M_i \leq \sum_{j=1}^{s} C_j, \text{ for } s = 1,\ldots,m, \text{ where } a(m+1) = n+1.$$

(6)

$$N_i \geq 0, \text{ for } i = 1,\ldots,n$$

(7)

$$M_i \geq 0, \quad \text{for } i = 1,\ldots,n \tag{8}$$

Where NS, YS, and q are n-dimensional vectors of the random variables NS_i, YS_i, and q_i respectively, and:

$$NS_i(y) = NS_i \text{ for } NS_i \leq y \text{ and } NS_i(y) = y \text{ otherwise,}$$

The objective of problem (S) is to maximize the expected revenue by allocating first reservations, and subsequently rooms, to various classes of customers. The first term in the objective function represents the expected revenues that will be derived from reservations customers, and the second term represents the revenue that will be derived from walk-ins. Constraints (2) and (3) represent the limitations on the hotel's ability to accommodate walk-ins. Constraint (2) says that the hotel can accept walk-ins only up to the number of rooms that were not taken by reservation customers. Constraint (3) says that the hotel cannot accept walk-ins in excess of the number of requests that they receive. Constraint (4) represents the fact that R_i, the number of class i reservation customers who are given rooms, is equal to the minimum of the number who show up, $q_i \cdot N\Sigma_i(N_i)$, or the number of rooms M_i which were allocated to them. Note that the allocation of rooms to customer classes is done after the demand for reservations has been realized but prior to the arrival (for failure to show) of the customers to the hotel. Constraint 5 requires that the hotel maintain a service level of α for each guest class, where α is a parameter between zero and one, usually between .9 and .95. The interpretation of this constraint is that, when a class i customer arrives with a reservation, the hotel must be able to give him a room of as good or better quality than he reserved at least α percent of the time. Constraint 6 represents the fact that, the total number of allocations of room types with an index of s or lower cannot exceed the number of those rooms that are available.

Note that the above model represents three sequential decisions. The first decision is to determine the N_i, the booking limits for guest classes i=1,...,n. This decision is made some time prior to the target date. After the requests for reservations have been realized and bookings have been made, it is necessary to determine the number of rooms M_i to allocate to each guest class i in anticipation of the arrival of customers with reservations. When the customers arrive on the target date, R_i the number of class i reservations that can be honored is equal to either $q_i \cdot N\Sigma_i(N_i)$, the number who show-up, or M_i, the number of rooms allocated to them. The final decision is the walk-in room allocation problem. After the reservation customers have either arrived or failed to show-up, the remaining rooms can be allocated to customers who do not have reservations.

Clearly, the three decisions are highly interdependent. The decisions about booking limits affect the alternatives that will be available when it comes time to allocate rooms to reservation customers. In turn, the decisions about allocating rooms to reservation customers affect the walk-in allocation problem. We propose to develop insights into how the decisions about booking limits are affected by these interdependencies by approximating the original problem with a concave stochastic program. The following two propositions are necessary:

Proposition 1: The solution to walk-in room allocation sub-problem is the following:

$$Y_i^* = \text{Min}\left\{ \sum_{s:\, a(s) \leq i} I_s - \sum_{j=1}^{i-1} Y_j^*, \; YS_i \right\}, \text{ for } i = 1,...,n,$$

where $I_s = \text{Max}\left\{ \left(\sum_{k=s}^{m} C_k - \sum_{j=a(s)}^{n} R_j \right), 0 \right\}$, for $s = 1,...,m$

Proof: The walk-in allocation sub-problem is the following linear program:

$$\underset{Y_1,...,Y_n}{\text{Max}} \left\{ E_{YS}\left[\sum_{i=1}^{n} c_i \cdot Y_i \right] \right\}$$

subject to:

$$\sum_{i=1}^{a(s+1)-1} Y_i \leq \sum_{j=1}^{s} C_j - \sum_{i=1}^{a(s+1)-1} R_i, \text{ for } s = 1,...,m \qquad (9)$$

$$0 \le Y_i \le YS_i, \quad \text{for } i = 1,...,n \qquad (10)$$

Suppose that $Y \ne Y^*$ is a feasible solution to this problem. From the definition of Y^*, for any $s \in (1,...,m)$, either: $Y_i^* = YS_i$ for all $i \in (a(s),...,a(s+1)-1)$, or: there exists an index k such that:

$Y_{i^*} = YS_i$ for $i \in (a(s),...,k)$,,
$Y_{i^*} \le YS_i$ for $i = k$,
and $Y_{i^*} = 0$ for $i \in (k,....,a(s+1)-1)$

Since Y is feasible, it satisfies constraints (2) and (3), and:

$$\sum_{i=1}^{j} Y_i^* \ge \sum_{i=1}^{j} Y_i, \text{ for all } j \in (1,...,n), \text{ and } \sum_{i=1}^{j} Y_i^* > \sum_{i=1}^{j} Y_i \text{ for at least one } j \in (1,...,n)$$

Since $c_i \ge c_j$ if $i < j$, we have that: $\sum_{i=1}^{n} c_i \cdot Y_i^* \ge \sum_{i=1}^{n} c_i \cdot Y_i$.

QED

Proposition 1 has a simple intuitive explanation: After the reservation guests have arrived, the hotel is left with inventories, I_s, of the various room types s = 1,...,m. The hotel must respond to limited numbers of requests for rooms from walk-ins from classes i = 1,...,n. The proposition says that the hotel should give priority to the lowest indexed, i.e. highest priced, guest classes. For example, suppose that I_s rooms of type s remain unfilled after the arrival of the reservation customers. The hotel should first try to fill those rooms with walk-ins of class a(s). If there are still unfilled rooms after all of the requests from class a(s) have been accommodated, then they should begin responding to requests from classes a(s)+1, a(s)+2, etc.

Proposition 2: The walk-in allocation sub-problem is concave in N_j.

Proof: The walk-in allocation problem is a linear program in which N_j appears only as a parameter in the right hand side. Note that $R_i = \text{Min}\{q_i \cdot NS_i(N_i), M_i\}$ is a concave function of N_j. The result follows from the fact that a linear maximization program is concave in its right hand side, and a concave function of a concave function is also concave.   QED

Using the result of proposition 1, let us define $Y(R)$ to be the solution to the following set of equations:

$$Y_i(R) = \text{Min}\left\{\sum_{s:\ a(s)\le i} I_s - \sum_{j=1}^{i-1} Y_j(R),\ YS_i\right\},\ \text{for } i = 1,...,n,$$

where $I_s = \text{Max}\left\{\left(\sum_{k=s}^{m} C_k - \sum_{j=a(s)}^{n} R_j\right),\ 0\right\}$, for $s = 1,...,m$

Note that, because this system of equations depends upon the random vectors NS, YS and q, $Y(R)$ is a random vector. We can now introduce a modified version of our original model, which we refer to as (SA):

$$Z_{SA} = \underset{N_1,...,N_n}{\text{Max}} \left\{ E_q\left[E_{NS}\left[\sum_{i=1}^{n} c_i \cdot q_i \cdot NS_i(N_i) + E_{YS}\left[\sum_{i=1}^{n} c_i \cdot Y_i(R)\right]\right]\right]\right\} \tag{11}$$

subject to:

$$\text{Prob}\left[\sum_{j=1}^{i} q_j \cdot NS_j(N_j) \le \sum_{s:a(s)\le i} C_s\right] \ge \alpha,\ \text{for } i = 1,...,n \tag{12}$$

$$N_i \ge 0,\ \text{for } i = 1,...,n \tag{13}$$

From Propositions 1 and 2, we see that the objective function of problem (SA) is concave in N_i. Observe that problem (SA) does not contain the decision variables, M_i, which represent the allocation of rooms to customers with reservations. In contrast to the original model, the objective function in (SA) includes the revenues associated with all of the reservations customers who show-up, instead of only those who are given rooms. Thus, (SA) is only an approximation to the original model. Although the optimal solution value for

(SA) will tend to over-estimate the value of an optimal solution to problem (S), the error tends to be small if the service level α is high, i.e. close to 1.

3.2   Solving the reservations problem. Using procedures developed in Bitran and Leong (1989), it is possible to obtain a deterministic version of (SA) by linearizing the probabilistic constraints. By creating a large number of linear constraints, we can obtain a deterministic math program that is an arbitrarily close approximation to problem (SA). This program can then be solved using traditional mathematical programming techniques.

The value of the deterministic version of (SA) is that its solution provides insight which motivates a heuristic procedure for solving the original problem (S). We have developed a straight-forward heuristic for allocating reservation booking limits to the various classes in a manner which mimics the form of the solution to the deterministic version of approximation problem (SA). To facilitate the explanation of the heuristic, let us define the following additional notation:

$F_X^c(x)$:   The probability that a given realization of random variable X is greater than or equal to the value x, i.e. the complement of the cumulative distribution function.

$F_\alpha^{-1}(X)$:   The a fractile of random variable X.

W: The set of reservation classes which are candidates for receiving increased allocations.

The heuristic, which we refer to as H1, works as follows:

H1:

INITIALIZE: Set $\Omega = \{1,...,n\}$, $N = Y = 0$.

ITERATE: While $\Omega \neq \{ \}$:

STEP 1:

Choose $i \in \Omega$ such that: $c_i \cdot F_{NS}^c\left(\sum_{j=1}^{i} N_j\right) = \max_{i \in \Omega}\left\{c_i \cdot F_{NS}^c\left(\sum_{j=1}^{i} N_j\right)\right\}$

STEP 2:

Let $k = \max_{k=1,...,m} \{k: a(k) \leq i\}$

STEP 3:

For $j = a(k),..., n$:

If $c_j \cdot F_{YS}^c \left(\sum_{l=1}^{j} Y_l \right) \geq c_i$, then increment Y_j

STEP 4:

If STEP 3 did not result in any Y_j increments, then increment N_i

STEP 5:

For $i = 1,...,n$:

If $\frac{1}{i} \cdot F_{\alpha}^{-1} \left(\sum_{j=1}^{i} q_j \right) \cdot \sum_{j=1}^{i} N_j + \sum_{j=1}^{i} Y_j \geq \sum_{s=1}^{k} C_s$, then delete $\{1,...,i\}$ from Ω

The basic idea is to allocate the capacity of the hotel to the various classes of walk-ins and reservations based on the maximum "marginal" expected revenue. In each iteration, a customer class is selected, and increment is made to either the booking limit or the walk-in allocation for that class. The selection of the customer class and the type of increment is based on the marginal effect upon expected revenues.

At the start of each iteration, there is an allocation $(N_1,...,N_n)$ of booking limits for the various customer classes. In step 1, we identify the customer class for which the marginal expected revenue from increasing its booking limit is the greatest. The expected marginal revenue associated with increasing the reservation allocation to class i is calculated by multiplying the price c_i by the probability that there will be at least $N_1 + ...+ N_i$ requests from class i or lower. In step 2, we identify k, the highest index of room type (i.e. lowest level of luxury) that will satisfy a customer of class i. In step 3, we determine the marginal revenue associated with increasing the number of type k rooms which are set aside for walk-ins of classes indexed by a(k) or higher. Recall that a room of type k can be rented to reservation or walk-in customers of classes $a(k),...,n$.

The marginal revenue associated with increasing the walk-in allocation to class j can be calculated by multiplying the price c_j by the probability that there will be at least $Y_1 + ... + Y_j$ walk-ins from class i or lower. If we are able to identify an index=j such that the marginal revenue associated with increasing the walk-in allocation to class j exceeds the price paid by a reservation customer of class i, then we increment the walk-in allocation to j. In step 4, we increment the booking limit for class i only if we failed to identify a walk-in class to increment in step 3. In step 5, we test whether the service level constraints would be violated if we 1) book the maximum numbers of reservations allowed by the booking limits, and 2) reduce the capacity of each room type by the number of rooms that are set aside for walk-ins. If the current booking limits and walk-in allocations would violate the service level constraint for some customer class i, then we would not consider any more increments to classes j=1,...,i. Any further increments to these booking limits classes would only decrease the likelihood that we would be able to honor all of the reservations. Although the tests in Step 5 of the heuristic are not quite equivalent to the service level constraints, it is easy to show that:

$$\frac{1}{i} \cdot F_\alpha^{-1}\left(\sum_{j=1}^{i} q_j\right) \cdot \sum_{j=1}^{i} N_j \le F_\alpha^{-1}\left(\sum_{j=1}^{i} q_j \cdot N_j\right), \quad \text{for } i = 1,...,n$$

Thus, step 5 is a conservative test of the service level constraints.

4. Computational Results

The model that is described in this paper was validated with data that was collected from a major hotel in Singapore which belongs to an international chain. During a period of nineteen days, a total of 2,504 transactions were tracked. The first use of the data was to validate the assumption that the distribution of the fraction of reservations that show-up does not depend upon the number of reservations. Figure 2 contains a scatter plot of the show-rate against

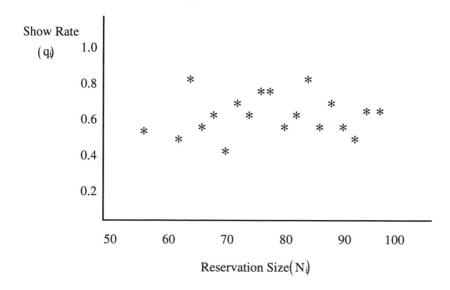

Figure 2: Show Rate Versus Reservation Size

the total number of reservations. The absence of any significant pattern confirms our assumption.

The second use of the data was to fit distributions in order to perform simulation experiments. Gamma distributions provide reasonable fits to the distributions of walk-in demand. Unfortunately, the hotel keeps track of only the number of reservations that are booked, not the total number of requests that are made for reservations. Thus, we could not confirm whether the distribution of reservation requests can also be fitted to a Gamma distribution. However, based upon the distribution of walk-in demand, and the plots in Williams (1977), this assumption seems reasonable. Beta distributions provided good fits to the distribution of show-rate.

We performed a series of simulation experiments to test the heuristic H1 against the rule that is currently used to set booking limits. The current rule allows reservations to be accepted up to 110% of the available capacity. For example, suppose that the hotel has C_1, ...,C_m rooms of the various types, and they receive a reservation request from a class j customer where $j \in (a(k),...,a(k+1)-1)$ for some $k \in (1,...,m)$. This request would be denied only if

the current number of bookings from classes a(k),...,a(k+1)-1 was already at least
110% ·C_k.

For the purpose of our simulation experiments, we assumed that a 95%
service level was desired for each guest class. This was consistent with the goals
of the management of the hotel with which we were involved. We assumed that
there were four guest classes, a number that is not uncommon among large
hotels. Finally, we assumed that there was only one class of room. Clearly the
hotel has much more flexibility when there is only one room type than if certain
rooms can only be used for certain classes of customers. Thus, this case
represents the most difficult decision problem.

Since different types of hotels face a wide variety of types of demand, we
attempted to test our heuristic under a variety of distributional assumptions. The
management of the hotel with which we were working described several possible
scenarios. Based on their descriptions, we tested nine different probability
distributions for the number of reservation requests, demand for walk-ins, and
show-up rate for each of the four customer classes. As shown in Table 1, the
mean number of reservation requests ranged from 30 to 70; the mean demand
from walk-ins ranged from 5 to 19; and the mean show-rate ranged from .6 to
.9. For each of these means, we tested the coefficients of variation at three
levels, .2, .5, and .7.

Table 1: Mean Values for Simulation Experiments

	Reservation Demand	Walk-in Demand	Show-Up Rate
LOW	30	5	0.6
MED	50	10	0.75
HIGH	70	19	0.9

By varying the means and coefficients of variation at three different levels for
reservations demand, walk-in demand, and show rate for each of the four
customer classes, we obtained a total of 1458 different scenarios.

In the simulation experiments, we assumed that the hotel could delay the assignment of rooms to reservations and walk-ins until after the requests for reservations, no-shows, and demand for walk-ins were observed. The reservations heuristics (H1 and the 110% rule) were used only for the purpose of setting booking limits, not for allocating rooms to customers who actually show-up.

The results of the simulation experiments are presented in Figure 3. The figure shows how the expected revenues from using our proposed heuristic compare to those from using the 110% rule that is currently being used. Each point in these figures corresponds to a particular combination of distributional parameters. Points above the 45 degree line represent situations in which our heuristics outperform the current rule. The average improvement in expected revenues over the 110% rule is 9.8%. The heuristic has the additional advantage of being faithful to the α service level constraint. The 110% rule is not.

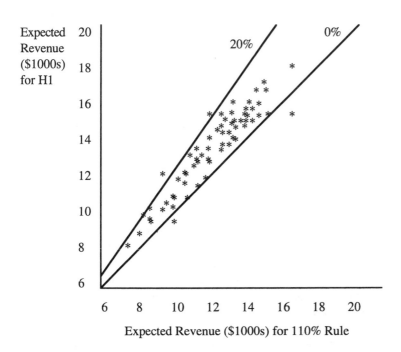

Figure 3: Expected Revenue of H1 vs. the 110% Rule

5. Summary and Conclusions

The primary contribution of our paper is the development of a model which captures many of the trade-offs that are present in hotel reservation systems in practice. These trade-offs include:

1. If the hotel accepts too many requests for reservations from low priced customer classes it incurs the risk that it will have to refuse later requests for reservations or walk-ins from higher priced classes.
2. If the hotel accepts too many total reservations it increases the likelihood that it will not be able to provide rooms for all of the customers who show-up on the date of their reservations.
3. If the hotel turns away too many requests for reservations they incur the risk that not all of their rooms will be rented.

These trade-offs are complicated by the fact that certain room types cannot be used to satisfy certain customer classes.

The objective of our model is to set booking limits for the various customer classes in order to maximize the expected revenues for some targeted date. Although no explicit cost is associated with failing to honor reservations, we have assumed that, for each guest class, the hotel strives to honor all of the reservations with probability equal to α. Since many of the costs associated with overbooking, i.e. "walking customers", are intangible, this assumption is consistent with industry practice.

Based on the solutions to a mathematical model of the problem, we have developed a heuristic, H1. In simulation experiments, the heuristic performs favorably with respect to the rule that is commonly used in practice.

The model proposed in this paper should be regarded as a first step in improving the management of hotel reservations systems. Although the simulation results indicate that our heuristic outperforms a rule that is commonly used in practice, further tests need to be performed in order to assess whether our heuristic performs better in some situations than in others. It would also be desirable to compare the performance of our heuristic to a bound on the value of an optimal solution to the problem.

Several directions appear promising for future research: One direction is to consider multiple day reservations. Although the current computer system records these as series of single day reservations, it is likely that the probability that a customer shows up for the ith day of his reservation depends upon whether he showed up for the (i-1)th day. If the system were given the capability to track multiple day reservations, this information could be used to develop policies for giving preference to requests for multiple day reservations.

Another direction for future research is to consider the control problem of allocating rooms to customers as they arrive at the hotel on the target day. Recall that the simulation experiments were based on the assumption that hotel management can delay the assignment of rooms to customers until after they have observed the number of each customer class that show-up. In practice, hotels do not have this luxury. In contrast to the airline ticket problem, where all of the passengers of a given flight are boarded simultaneously, the arrivals of customers to a hotel are spread out over about twelve hours. Thus, the hotel must begin allocating rooms to customers before they have complete information about the number of no-shows and cancellations.

Once models of the room allocation control problem are developed, it would be desirable to link them to decisions about reservations limits. Since the dynamics of the room allocation problem depend upon the numbers and types of reservations that are accepted, decisions about booking limits need to consider the way in which later, recourse decisions will be made. Similarly, booking limit decisions should be able take into account the fact that there may be opportunities to revise them after observing some of the demand for reservations. For example, we may tend to set lower limits on booking limits for low fare guest classes if we know that we can increase them later if demand from the higher fare classes does not materialize.

Another direction for research is to study the implications of performance measures. In practice, hotel managers are frequently evaluated on the basis of the average fraction of rooms that are rented. More sophisticated measures create incentives to obtain the highest possible rental rates for rooms. However, few of these performance measurement systems take the service rate into account. When a hotel overbooks, it simultaneously increases its expected revenues and costs of "walking" customers. Although the individual hotel derives all of the benefits from increased expected revenues, it shares the intangible costs of "walking" customers with the other hotels in the organization. When a customer's reservation is not honored by the XYZ Hotel in New York, he may be reluctant to make a reservation at the XYZ Hotel in Los Angeles. Thus, performance measures should create incentives for hotel managers to strive for service levels that are consistent with maximizing the overall profits of the organization.

References

Allen, F.M., R. Braswell, and P. Rao, (1974). "Distribution-free approximations for chance-constraints," *Operations Research* 22, 610-621.

Alstrup, J., S. Boas, O.B.G. Madsen, and R.V. Valqui (1986). "Booking policy for flights with two types of passengers," *European Journal of Operations Research* 27, 274-288.

Belobaba, P. (1987). "Airline yield management - an overview of seat inventory control," *Transportation Science* 21, 63-73.

Belobaba, P. (1989). "Application of a probabilistic decision model to airline seat inventory control," *OR Practice* 37(2), 183-197.

Baker, K.R., M.J. Magazine, and H.L.W. Nuttle (1986). "The effect of commonality on safety stock in a simple inventory model," *Management Science* 32(8), 982-988.

Bitran, G.R. and T.Y. Leong (1992). "Deterministic approximations to co-production problems with service constraints," *Management Science* 38(5), 724-742.

Bitran, G.R., and S.M. Gilbert (1994). "Managing hotel reservations with uncertain arrivals," *Operations Research*, forthcoming.

Birge, J.R. (1982). "The value of the stochastic solution in stochastic linear programs with fixed recourse," *Mathematical Programming* 24, 314-325.

Drake, A.W. (1967). *Fundamentals of Applied Probability Theory* (McGraw-Hill, New York, NY).

Glover, F., R. Glover, J. Lorenzo, and C. McMillan (1982). "The passenger-mix problem in the scheduled airlines," *Interfaces* 12(3), 507-520.

Ladany, S. (1976). "Dynamic operating rules for motel reservations," *Decision Sciences* 7, 829-840.

Liberman, V., and U. Yechiali (1978). "On the hotel overbooking problem: an inventory system with stochastic cancellations," *Management Science* 24(11), 1117-1126.

Png, G.T. (1991). *Hotel Reservation Planning: An Evaluation of Overbooking Models*, Unpublished Undergraduate Honours Year Academic Exercise, Faculty of Business Administration, National University of Singapore.

Rothstein, M. (1974). "Hotel overbooking as a Markovian sequential decision process," *Decision Sciences* 5, 389-404.

Rothstein, M. (1985). "OR and the airline overbooking problem," *OR Forum* 33(2), 237-248.

Shlifer, E. and Y. Vardi (1975). "An airline overbooking policy," *Transportation Science* 9, 101-114.

Symonds, G.H. (1977). "Deterministic solutions for a class of chance constrained programming problems," *Operations Research* 15, 495-512.

Williams, F.E. (1977). "Decision theory and the innkeeper: an approach for setting hotel reservation policy," *Interfaces* 7(4), 18-31.

Chapter 13   Service Productivity in U.S. Credit Unions

Harold O. Fried, C.A. Knox Lovell and Philippe Vanden Eeckaut[1]

1. Introduction

Credit unions play an important role in the financial intermediation segment of the service sector of the U.S. economy. Most credit unions are minuscule relative to the commercial banks and other financial institutions with which they compete, yet in 1990 over 14,000 credit unions provided deposit and loan services to some 61 million members. Their significance stems not from their diminutive size, however, but from their organizational structure and their legal status. They are not-for-profit cooperative enterprises, pursuing different objectives than other financial intermediaries, under different legal and institutional constraints. Since credit unions serve so many members, many of whom have little or no contact with other financial intermediaries, their competitive viability is a matter of no small import. The financial condition of credit unions is monitored by the industry's main regulatory body, the National Credit Union Administration (NCUA). The NCUA uses as its criteria various financial ratios, and has the objective of ensuring the financial safety and soundness of the industry. The industry's trade association, the Credit Union

---

[1]We would like to thank Dr. Albert Burger, Director, Center for Credit Union Research, School of Business, University of Wisconsin-Madison, and Dr. Robert Hoel, Director, Filene Research Institute, for their guidance and support through the duration of this project.

P. T. Harker (ed.), The Service Productivity and Quality Challenge, 365–390.

National Association (CUNA), is currently seeking a way of monitoring the industry's performance on a different set of criteria: the ability of credit unions to provide their membership with a range of services that is of sufficient quantity and quality to ensure the continued competitive viability of the industry. Thus while NCUA's orientation is toward financial soundness, CUNA's orientation is toward service provision. The purpose of this paper is to suggest a service-oriented performance evaluation methodology that might serve the needs of CUNA. The methodology we propose incorporates the quality, as well as the quantity, of the services credit unions provide their members. It also acknowledges the unique objectives and constraints of credit unions, without losing sight of the fact that credit unions must still compete with other more conventionally structured financial intermediaries.

The key to our performance evaluation methodology lies in the way we define the services a credit union provides its membership. In contrast to much of the banking literature, in which the services of a bank are typically restricted to the number or the value of various types of account, we treat credit union accounts as being multidimensional in nature. Accounts have a quantity dimension, as is customary, but they also have a quality dimension, which is somewhat novel. The quality dimension has two components, a price indicator and a variety indicator. Thus one important characteristic of both deposit accounts and loan accounts is the interest rates attached to them. A second important characteristic of deposit accounts and loan accounts is the range, or variety, of services offered within each type of account. Thus the deposit and loan services a credit union provides its membership each have a quantity dimension, a price dimension, and a variety dimension. An increases in any dimension is interpreted as an improvement in the service productivity of the credit union.

In Section 2 we analyze the credit union as a not-for-profit cooperative financial intermediary. This sets the stage for the creation in Section 3 of a set of variables with which to measure the performance of credit unions. These variables describe the resources credit unions employ, the services they provide, and the environment in which they operate. They are constructed from information provided annually by all active credit unions to the two national supervisory bodies, NCUA and CUNA. In Section 4 we outline the analytical technique we use to measure the performance of credit unions.[2] The technique is similar to the data envelopment analysis (DEA) technique that has been widely and successfully applied in the management science field, in that it is both nonparametric and nonstochastic, but it differs from DEA in one very useful respect. This difference allows us to evaluate performance in terms of productive efficiency, as in DEA, and also in terms of dominance. Whereas efficiency describes proximity to best practice operation, dominance provides a count of the number of other credit unions that perform better than, or worse than, the credit union being evaluated. The two criteria of dominance and efficiency provide independent, complementary information on the performance of a credit union.

In Section 5 we present our empirical results. We begin by summarizing results for the entire sample, roughly two-thirds of all credit unions active in 1990, that are discussed in greater detail in Fried, Lovell and Vanden Eeckaut (1993). However, the focus of the analysis is on the performance of a single, arbitrarily selected credit union. This enables us to concentrate on the managerial implications of our analysis. We are able to show which credit unions dominate the credit union under evaluation, by how much, and in which service and resource dimensions. This provides a set of role models this credit union can emulate in an effort to improve its performance relative to other credit unions, and to enhance its competitive viability relative to the larger financial intermediation sector. We also provide information on a list of exogenous variables that characterize the structure and the business practices of the credit union under evaluation, and of those that dominate it. These variables serve two purposes. They are first used as independent variables in a regression analysis designed to explain the inferior performance of the dominated credit union under evaluation. To the extent that performance of the credit union being evaluated is sensitive to these exogenous variables, this information is next used to adjust the performance evaluation to obtain a more accurate picture of its actual performance in the environment in which it operates. These variables also provide a set of tools which management (of the credit union under evaluation, or of the national leadership) may employ in an effort to improve the perfor-

---

[2]The methodology we employ to evaluate credit union performance is nonparametric and nonstochastic, and goes by the name Free Disposal Hull (FDH) analysis. It was developed by Deprins, Simar and Tulkens (1984). A detailed description of the technique is provided by Tulkens and Vanden Eeckaut (1993), and its relationship to Data Envelopment Analysis (DEA) is described in Lovell and Vanden Eeckaut (1993).

mance of this (or any other) credit union. If, for example, performance is adversely affected by the presence of branch offices, the national leadership may wish to discourage branching as a means of growth.

Concluding observations are contained in Section 6.

2. The Organization and Objectives of Credit Unions

Credit unions are not-for-profit cooperative financial intermediaries operated by, and for the benefit of, their members. The fact that they are financial intermediaries means that they do not operate in a vacuum. They compete with commercial banks, finance companies and savings and loans, and any effort to analyze the performance of credit unions must acknowledge the competitive pressure that originates in these other segments of the industry.

The not-for-profit feature of credit unions means that many commonly used performance measures--profitability, cost efficiency, etc.--are inappropriate for credit union performance evaluation. Performance evaluation must be based on criteria specifically tailored to the special features of credit unions, without losing sight of the competitive pressures emanating from outside the credit union segment of the industry. Thus not-for-profit status notwithstanding, we cannot completely ignore factors that contribute to the competitive viability of the credit union movement. These two features of credit unions, their not-for-profit status and the competition they face from proprietary institutions, influence the variables we use and the way we model credit union performance.

The cooperative nature of credit unions is important because the size and diversity of the cooperative is limited by the common bond of association, occupation or residence that characterizes the cooperative membership. Generally speaking, to become a member of a credit union requires that one belong to the association, occupation or region which sponsors the credit union, and a credit union cannot accept deposits from, or make loans to, non-members. The field of membership sometimes extends to relatives of members, but in either event the potential market facing most credit unions is severely restricted by its common bond. This limit to growth and diversity may restrict the ability of credit unions to exploit the cost-reducing effects of scale and scope economies, but it has the countervailing benefit of reducing uncertainty about the credit-worthiness of member borrowers, which in turn reduces all sorts of operating expenses associated with the processing of loans.

The members of the cooperative are both lenders and borrowers, making credit unions simultaneously producer cooperatives and consumer cooperatives, or "pure" cooperatives in industry parlance. This distinguishes them from most other cooperatives, and creates an inherent conflict of interest between lender-members and borrower-members. Lender-members want high deposit rates, which in a not-for-profit environment requires high loan rates, while borrower-members want low loan rates, which require low deposit rates. This has led to much debate about whether or not credit unions can be identified as being lender-oriented or borrower-oriented, and if so, what effect such orientation may have on performance.[3] At the very least it suggests that modelling credit unions in the conventional economic manner, as seeking to maximize a single well-defined objective subject to a similarly well-defined set of constraints, is apt to be a fruitless task. It is difficult at best, and if done wrong is apt to produce misleading or possibly erroneous results.

In light of these difficulties, we think it best to avoid analyzing the performance of credit unions on the basis of conventional constrained optimization models of producer behavior. Instead, we evaluate performance on the basis of a model that is in part much more general than conventional models of producer behavior, and in part very idiosyncratic, and tailored to the special features of credit unions.

We treat credit unions as seeking to maximize benefits of membership in a credit union. Maximum benefit is expressed as maximum service provision, subject to resource availability. Since this framework involves only the "production" aspect of credit union operation, it is more basic than, and hence more general than, any behavioral model of the credit union. What remains is to specify the services credit unions provide, and the resources they employ, and their structural characteristics. It is this specification of variables representing services, resources, and structural characteristics that makes our performance evaluation model idiosyncratic.

Credit unions use four types of resource: human resources, other variable operating expenditures, volunteer labor and sponsor-donated resources. The first two are paid for, reported on an annual basis, and relatively easy to measure with some degree of accuracy. The last two are not paid for, not systematically reported, and almost impossible to measure accurately.[4]

---

[3]Flannery (1974) and Smith (1984, 1986) have attempted to model and test empirically the orientation of credit unions. A survey of these and other models of credit union behavior is provided by Overstreet and Rubin (1991).

[4]The Yearbook includes information on the number of volunteers, including board and committees, at the end of the year. Whether this provides useful information on the amount of volunteer labor input used during the course of the

The services credit unions provide their members can be classified as services provided to lenders and services provided to borrowers. Within each classification we specify three types of service. They include the number of deposit and loan accounts, the interest rates paid on deposit accounts and charged on loan accounts, and the variety or convenience features of deposit accounts and loan accounts. The numbers of accounts capture the quantity dimension of service provision, while the interest rate and variety indicators characterize the quality dimensions of service provision.

Credit unions differ in more ways than just the resources they use and the services they provide. They can also be characterized in terms of their structural features, such as their common bond and their field of membership, the nature of their charter, their branching structure, and their loan practices. Most of these features, which we call environmental variables because they are neither resources nor services in our model specification, are susceptible to influence by management, if not at the individual credit union level than at the national leadership level. To the extent that we are able to relate these environmental variables to performance, we can then provide guidance to management on how to improve performance.

Thus our performance evaluation is based on a view of credit unions as using two resources to provide six services, given their structural characteristics, in an effort to serve their membership. This view is reasonably consistent with the stated objective of the Federal Credit Union Act, to "...promote thrift among its members and create a source of credit for provident and productive purposes." (cited in Overstreet and Rubin (1991:4)). It is also cognizant of the realities of life in a partly deregulated, increasingly competitive environment, since it recognizes the quality indicators of price, variety and convenience as competitive tools.

3. Data Sources and Variable Construction[5]

All data used in this study come from two primary sources. One is the NCUA Supervisors Year-end Call Report for the year 1990. The other is the CUNA Yearbook Questionnaire, also for the year 1990. The Call Report is a statement of financial condition as of the end of the year. It includes information on assets

year is uncertain. Wolken and Navratil (1984) report subsidies in kind on the order of 6% of reported operating costs in 1975, with the impact being substantially larger for small credit unions.

[5]This section is adapted from Fried, Lovell and Vanden Eeckaut (1993).

(mainly loans and investments), and liabilities and equity (mainly shares/deposits). It also contains information on operating income (mainly interest on loans and investments), and operating expenses (split fairly evenly between employee expenses and office expenses). These two types of information are used to construct the resource variables and service variables that are used to measure performance. The Call Report also contains information on the number of employees, and on a small number of environmental variables that might help explain measured performance. The Yearbook provides information on several environmental variables, and is the principal source of information on the variety and convenience features of loan and deposit services offered by credit unions. Finally, a small number of variables (e.g., the number of full-time employees and the number of members) appear in both data sources, and this provides a useful consistency check.

Two variable inputs are identified. The labor input is defined as the number of full-time employees plus half the number of part-time employees. Other operating expense is defined as the sum of travel and conference expense, office occupancy expense, office operations expense, educational and promotional expenses, loan servicing expense, professional and outside services, operating fees, and miscellaneous operating expenses. Other operating expense is equal to total operating expense, less employee compensation and benefits, and less provision for loan losses, provision for investment losses, and member insurance.

We have created six output variables, three designed to characterize loan services and three designed to characterize deposit services. One pair of variables measures quantity, the second pair measures price, and the third pair measures variety. The second and third pairs characterize the quality of service provided by credit unions.

A loan quantity index is constructed as the total number of outstanding loans of all types, excluding loans to other credit unions because they provide no direct service to the borrower-members of the credit union making the loan.

A loan price index is constructed in three steps. First, interest on loans less interest refunded yields net interest on loans. Second, dividing net interest on loans by the value of all outstanding loans gives a loan price. However since the service a credit union provides its borrower members is a low interest rate on loans, the third step is to take the reciprocal of the loan price. This creates a loan price index that achieves its minimum value for the credit union having the highest loan price, and that increases in value as loan prices decline, i.e., as this service dimension increases.

The Yearbook lists 36 different types of loan and insurance services that a credit union might offer. These include various types of vehicle loans, mortgage loans, unsecured loans, miscellaneous loans, variable rate loans, insurance services and other services. A loan variety index is created by weighing whether or not a credit union offers a loan type by the proportion of all credit unions in its class that do offer the service, dividing this weighted (0,1) variable by the maximum value observed in its class, and summing over all 36 loan types. The purpose of confining the comparison to a credit union's class is to avoid comparing small, narrowly focused credit unions with large, full-service financial institutions. A credit union's class is determined by its asset size and its common bond category, defined below.[6]

A deposit quantity index is constructed as the total number of share and deposit accounts.

---

[6]Somewhat more formally, the loan variety index is constructed as follows:

$$\text{Loan variety index} = \alpha \frac{\sum_{j=1}^{J} S_j^i \, SM_j(k)}{\text{Max}_j \sum_{j=1}^{J} S_j^i \, SM_j(k)} + \beta \frac{\sum_{j=1}^{J} S_j^i \, SM_j(l)}{\text{Max}_j \sum_{j=1}^{J} S_j^i \, SM_j(l)}$$

$i = \{1,...,I\}$	number of credit unions (I = 8,947)
$j = \{1,...,J\}$	number of loan services (J = 36)
$k = \{1,...,K\}$	asset size classes (K = 5)
$l = \{1,...,L\}$	common bond categories (L = 3)
$S_j^i \in \{0,1\}$	categorical variable taking on the value 1 if credit union i offers loan service j, and taking on the value 0 otherwise
$SM_j(h)$	proportion of credit unions in category h offering loan service j, h = k, l
$\alpha, \beta =$ (0.75, 0.25)	Weights assigned to asset size class and common bond category.

A deposit price index is constructed in two steps. First, net interest paid is constructed as the sum of dividends on shares, interest on deposits and accrued dividend and interest. Second, the deposit price index is constructed by dividing net interest paid by the value of all share and deposit accounts.

The Yearbook lists 40 different types of deposit and related services that a credit union might offer its members. These include various types of deposit accounts, credit card services, share draft (checking) services, direct deposit and payroll deduction, transaction services, and other services. A deposit variety index is constructed in exactly the same way the loan variety index is constructed. The index rewards a credit union for offering a wide range of deposit services relative to other credit unions in its asset size class and common bond category.

Summary statistics for the two resource indicators and the six service indicators appear in Table 1.[7]

The Call Report and the Yearbook contain data that allow the construction of several exogenous variables that characterize the structure and business practices of a credit union. These variables may account for observed performance variation among credit unions, and they may be manipulated by credit union management or the national leadership to enhance performance.

The Call Report and the Yearbook both contain information on the year-end value of current assets, from which five asset size class categories are defined. These are below $1 million, between $1 million and $5 million, between $5 million and $20 million, between $20 million and $100 million, and above $100 million. Nearly 83% of the credit unions in our sample are in the three smallest asset size classes. The purpose of this variable is to provide a test of the hypothesis that (this indicator of) size influences performance, since most other financial intermediaries are so much larger than most credit unions.

---

[7]The reciprocal of the mean loan price variable, multiplied by 10,000, generates a mean interest rate charged on loans of 11.75%. The mean deposit price variable divided by 100 generates a mean interest rate paid on deposits of 6.25%. The two variety variables are pure numbers scaled on (0,1000).

Table 1. Summary Statistics for Variables

	Variables	Mean	Std. Dev.	min	max
Labor	x_1	10.2	32.3	0	1,730
Operating expenses	x_2	251,541.8	740,207.	0	127,359,345
Loan Quantity	y_1	2,451.3	7,115.2	1	254,457
Loan Price	y_2	851.0	107.8	316	1,992
Loan Variety	y_3	684.4	88.4	0	1,000
Deposit Quantity	y_4	7,124.6	19,508.0	1	591,840
Deposit Price	y_5	624.6	114.6	251	1,468
Deposit	y_6	708.9	118.6	7	1,000

The Yearbook lists the common bond of a credit union at the time of its formation. On this basis a credit union is assigned to one of three common bond categories: associational, occupational and residential. The occupational common bond category is by far the most popular, accounting for 82% of the credit unions in our sample. The purpose of this variable is to enable us to investigate the impact of a credit union's common bond on its performance.

A credit union typically receives some sort of support from its sponsor, the association or organization with which it is allied, in the form of donated resources that are not systematically reported in either the Call Report or the Yearbook. Although existence of subsidy can be difficult to determine, and extent of subsidy impossible to determine, the Call Report does contain sufficient information to permit the construction of a subsidy indicator. A binary (0,1) variable identifies a credit union as being subsidized if any one of the following variables is zero: employee compensation and benefits, office occupancy expense, and office operations expense. On this criterion one-third of the credit unions in our sample show evidence of being subsidized. This indicator undoubtedly understates both the number of subsidized credit unions, and the extent of subsidization for most, if not all, credit unions. However at the present time it is the best indicator we can construct. The purpose of this variable is not to test the hypothesis that subsidies affect performance, which they evidently do in a positive way, but to quantify the impact of subsidies.

Asset size class and common bond category are used in the construction of the two service variety variables, and in the second stage explanation of the observed pattern of credit union performance. Sponsor subsidies are is used only in the second stage. So are several other environmental variables, which are created from information provided by the Call Report and the Yearbook. They include:

1) the number of members
2) the ratio of the number of members to the number of potential members[8]
3) the type of charter (1 if state, 0 if federal)[9]
4) the age of the credit union ("new" if organized since 1987, "recent" if organized 1970-86, "old" otherwise)
5) branching (1 if at least one branch, 0 if no branches)
6) geographic location
   Northeast (CT, MA, ME, NH, NJ, NY, PE, RI, VT)
   Atlantic (DC, DE, MD, VA, WV)
   South (AL, AR, FL, GA, KY, LA, MS, NC, SC, TN)
   Lake   (IL, IN, MI, MO, OH, WI)
   Central (AZ, CO, IA, KS, MN, ND, NE, NM, OK, SD, TX, UT, WY)

[8]Some credit unions have a narrowly defined field of membership that makes ineligible for membership relatives of members, other unrelated groups, and former members. Others have a more broadly defined field of membership. The ratio of actual to potential members thus serves as a capacity utilization indicator that imposes a constraint on growth.

[9]State charters place more or less stringent constraints on credit union operations than does a federal charter. Restrictive charters presumably limit risk taking, which may inhibit or enhance performance.

Pacific (AK, CA, HI, ID, MT, NV, OR, WA)

7) asset size group (1 if asset size class is above $100 million, 0 otherwise)
8) loan size (the ratio of the value of loans to the number of loans)
9) saving size (the ratio of the value of deposits to the number of deposit accounts)
10) delinquency (the ratio of the number of delinquent loans to the number of loans)
11) investment (the ratio of the value of investments to the value of loans)
12) real estate (the ratio of the value of real estate loans to the value of loans)

The variables we have created represent our best effort to model credit unions as providing multidimensional deposit and loan services to their members. The three deposit services, and the three loan services as well, are constructed so as to capture the quantity and quality (price and variety) components of deposit and loan services that members desire. Finally, the environmental variables we have constructed should go a long way toward explaining performance variation. Many of them are useful as well as informative, since they can be influenced by credit union managers and movement leaders.

4. The Performance Evaluation Methodology

In keeping with our analysis of credit union behavior in Section 2, we treat credit unions as seeking to provide maximum service to their members, given their resource base and their structural characteristics. In keeping with our data construction effort in Section 3, we assume that credit unions use two resources to provide six services in an environment characterized by a number of more or less exogenous variables.

Performance is evaluated in terms of dominance and efficiency. Dominance is measured by simple counts of the number of credit unions providing no less of each service with no more of each resource, and of the number of credit unions providing no more of each service with no less of each resource. Being undominated is associated with best practice operation, while being dominated implies the existence of at least one better performing credit union that can serve as a role model. In each case the number of dominating or dominated credit unions provides an important component of our performance evaluation.

The efficiency of a credit union is measured by its proximity to best practice operation, as defined by the resource usage and the service provision of the most dominant of the credit unions that dominate it. Efficiency quantifies the dominance relationship by showing how much improvement is feasible in each resource and service dimension.

Let the sample of credit unions be denoted by the set

$$T = \{(y^i, x^i), \quad i = 1, \dots, I\},$$

where credit union i uses resource vector $x^i = (x^i_j, \dots, x^i_n)$ to produce service vector $y^i = (y^i_1, \dots, y^i_m)$, and there are I credit unions in the sample. From this data set a set of feasible production activities is constructed as

$$\hat{T} = \left\{ \begin{pmatrix} x \\ y \end{pmatrix} \middle| \begin{pmatrix} x \\ y \end{pmatrix} = \begin{pmatrix} x^i \\ y^i \end{pmatrix} - \sum_{j=1}^{m} \mu_j \begin{pmatrix} 0 \\ e_j \end{pmatrix} + \sum_{j=1}^{n} \upsilon_j \begin{pmatrix} e_j \\ 0 \end{pmatrix}, \ (x^i, y^i) \in T \cup \begin{Bmatrix} 0 \\ 0 \end{Bmatrix}, \ \mu_j \geq 0, \ \upsilon_j \geq 0 \right\}$$

The set of feasible production activities consists of all possible production activities having resources no smaller than, and services no larger than, those of each credit union in the sample. $\hat{T}$ is in fact the free disposal hull of the observed data. It is the smallest possible set of feasible production activities that contains all observed data and satisfies the property of free disposability of resources and services.

The efficiency of every credit union in the sample can be obtained from the solution to a mixed integer programming problem. For credit union k the problem can be expressed

minimize Θ^k
subject to

$$\frac{y^k_j}{\Theta^k} \leq \sum_{i=1}^{I} \lambda^k_i y^i_j \qquad j = 1, \dots, m$$

$$\sum_{i=1}^{I} \lambda_i^k x_j^i \leqq x_j^k \quad j=1,\dots,n$$

$$\lambda_i^k \geq 0, \ \sum_{i=1}^{I} \lambda_i^k = 1, \quad \lambda_i^k \in \{0,1\}.$$

Here $\theta^k \leq 1$ is the radial component of the efficiency of credit union k. It measures the minimum proportion by which all services of credit union k could be deflated, or the reciprocal of the maximum proportion by which all services of credit union k could be expanded, and still not exceed those provided by the most dominant of the credit unions that dominate credit union k. However the dominance relationship is unlikely to be neutral, or equiproportionate, and slacks in both services and resources may remain after radial efficiency is measured. Slacks are inferred from the inequalities in the (m+n) functional constraints of the problem, with equality meaning no slack and inequality showing existence and magnitude of slack. The overall inefficiency of credit union k is measured by combining the radial component with the slack component. Since slacks cannot be aggregated across variables, overall inefficiency is reported separately for each resource used and each service provided. The constraints involving the intensity vector λ^k imply that (I-1) elements of this vector are zero, and the one non-zero element identifies the best practice credit union that most dominates credit union k, and against which the radial efficiency and slack of credit union k are measured.[10]

The mixed integer programming problem is solved using a simple two-step vector comparison algorithm. In the first step the set D(k) of credit unions that dominate credit union k is determined by finding the set of credit unions for which the vector inequality $(y, - x) \geqq (y^k, - x^k)$ holds. In the second step the first set of functional constraints in the programming problem is transformed to

---

[10]Deleting the constraint $\lambda_i^k \in \{0.1\}$ makes $\hat{T}$ a <u>convex</u> free disposal hull of the data set, and yields a feasible set that coincides with the Banker, Charnes and Cooper (1984) DEA model.

$$\theta^k \geq \frac{y_j^k}{\sum_{i=1}^{I} \lambda_i^k y_j^i} \qquad j=1,...,m,$$

from which it follows that

$$\theta^k \geq \underset{i \in D(k)}{\text{minimize}} \left\{ \underset{j=1,...,m}{\text{maximize}} \left\{ \frac{y_j^k}{y_j^i} \right\} \right\} \qquad k=1,...I.$$

This second step minimax algorithm generates a radial efficiency score θ^k for each credit union. It also identifies through the "minimize" part of the algorithm the most dominant credit union relative to credit union k under evaluation. Once this role model is identified, measurement of slacks is straightforward.

5. Empirical Analysis of Credit Union Performance

In this Section we report results of applying the analytical technique presented in Section 4 to the data generated in Section 3. We begin with a brief discussion of dominance and efficiency in the entire sample of 8,947 credit unions. This provides an overview of the performance of the credit union segment of the financial intermediation sector. Then we concentrate on a performance analysis of a single arbitrarily selected credit union. This provides insight into the managerial implications of the analysis.

Dominance results are summarized in Table 2. Roughly 78% of the 8,947 credit unions are dominated by at least one other credit union. Although it is not shown in the Table, there exist over 150,000 instances of dominance in the sample, and so each of the 6,946 dominated credit unions has on average 22 dominating credit unions to serve as role models. Among the 22% of credit unions that are undominated, 4% are efficient by default since, although they are undominated, they dominate no other credit union. Their unique size, service mix or resource mix makes them self-evaluators.

Asset Size Class and Common Bond Categories	[0,...1] Million	[1,...5] Million	[5,...20] Million	[20,...100] Million	[100,...[Million	ROW SUMS
Associational	451	389	193	81	7	1121
Dominated(#)	246	322	160	65	2	795
Undominated(#)	205	67	33	16	5	326
Efficient by default(#)	43	9	6	6	2	66
Occupational	1550	2589	1889	1035	280	7344
Dominated(#)	1075	2183	1639	757	115	5769
Undominated(#)	475	406	250	278	165	1574
Efficient by default(#)	67	30	33	72	73	275
Residential	90	125	134	111	23	483
Dominated(#)	56	110	124	80	12	382
Undominated(#)	34	15	10	31	11	101
Efficient by default(#)	10	1	2	10	8	31
COLUMN SUMS	2091	3103	2216	1227	310	8947
Dominated(#)	1377	2615	1923	902	129	6946
Undominated(#)	714	488	193	325	181	2001
Efficient by default(#)	120	40	41	88	83	372

Table 2. Dominance Relationships in the Sample

Table 3. Efficiency Results in the Sample

	Total Inefficiency (%)	Radial Inefficiency (%)	Nonradial Inefficiency (%)
x_1: Labor	0.2246	na	0.2246
x_2: Operating Expense	0.3046	na	0.3046
y_1: Loan Quantity	0.3257	0.0423	0.2835
y_2: Loan Price	0.1436	0.0818	0.0618
y_3: Loan Variety	0.1615	0.0800	0.0815
y_4: Deposit Quantity	0.2000	0.0513	0.1487
y_5: Deposit Price	0.1586	0.0782	0.0804
y_6: Deposit Variety	0.1454	0.0782	0.0673

na: not applicable

Efficiency results are summarized in Table 3. Since slacks cannot be aggregated across variables, efficiency scores are reported for each variable, and decomposed into radial and non-radial (= slack) components. On average, credit unions are 22% inefficient in their use of labor, and all of this inefficiency is slack. The figure for other operating expense is 30%. An unknown share of this measured resource use inefficiency is undoubtedly attributable to unmeasured variation in volunteer labor and sponsor-donated resources. Nonetheless, there still exists substantial inefficiency in the provision of services, which are measured fairly accurately. Under-provision relative to best practice ranges from 14% to 20%, with the exception of loan services, where under-provision averages 33%.

Three conclusions emerge, two related to credit unions and one concerning performance analysis in general. First, it appears that credit unions offer on average only about 80% of the services provided by best practice credit unions. [11]

---

[11]This figure of 80% efficiency is not out of line with results reported in banking by Ferrier and Lovell (1990), Berger and Humphrey (1991), Bauer, Berger and Humphrey (1993) and Berger (1993). There appears to be

This suggests that there exists a real need for an expansion of the advisory services currently provided by CUNA. Second, this figure varies considerably by type of service, there being much less inefficiency in the provision of the four quality components of service than in the two quantity components.[12] Third, much of the observed shortfall between average practice and best practice is attributable to slack. This suggests that reporting only the radial component of inefficiency may seriously understate the magnitude of inefficiency and must conceal the non-neutrality of inefficiency.

We now turn to an application of these techniques to the analysis of the performance of a single arbitrarily selected credit union to which we assign ID# AAAAA.[13] The purpose of the ensuing analysis is to show how information on dominance and efficiency can be used, together with supporting information on structural characteristics and business practices, to analyze the performance and the improvement potential of a specific credit union. The aggregative analysis of the entire sample enables us to conduct this micro-level analysis for each individual credit union in the sample. The first set of results for credit union AAAAA appears in Table 4. Credit union AAAAA has a radial efficiency score of 0.8847. It is therefore capable of a 13% expansion in its provision of all six services with no increase in its resource use, without exceeding best observed practice. It is dominated by five credit unions, three of which are undominated. Of the five role models for AAAAA, credit union BBBBB is most dominant, and it dominates 1,679 credit unions in all. Many other credit unions have higher radial efficiency scores than credit union AAAAA, but only these five credit unions dominate it because no other credit union provides no less of all six services with no more of the two resources. In turn, credit union AAAAA dominates six other credit unions. Similarly credit union AAAAA dominates no

---

considerable operating inefficiency in both segments of the financial intermediation sector.

[12]As Table 1 indicates, the coefficients of variation for the two service quantity indicators are much larger than those for the four other service indicators. Consequently greater proportionate slacks appear in the two quantity dimensions. A portion of the relatively small slacks in the two variety indicators is attributable to the way we have defined the variety indicators by narrowing the comparison sets, but this observation is not applicable to the two price indicators, which are defined using the entire sample as the comparison set.

[13]The actual ID# of this credit union, and those that dominate it and those it dominates, has been altered to preserve confidentiality.

other credit union in addition to these six, even those credit unions having lower efficiency scores, for the same reason.

Table 4 contains values of resource use and service provision for credit union AAAAA and all credit unions linked to it by a dominance relation. This enables the construction of total (radial plus slack) inefficiency in each of the eight variables for credit union AAAAA in comparison with the most dominant credit union BBBBB, or in comparison with any other dominating credit union if it is felt that some other less dominant credit union provides a more suitable role model for credit union AAAAA. This information can be used in either of two ways. It can be made available to the management of credit union AAAAA, with encouragement to contact management of dominating credit unions to see if they follow more productive business practices or if they have a more favorable operating environment. In this way this information provides an educational opportunity for the management of credit union AAAAA, and in a cooperative environment there is good reason to believe that such an opportunity will be exploited. Alternatively, this information can be used in a regression analysis based on similar information gathered from all credit unions. The objective is to determine the extent to which operating inefficiencies can be associated with business practices and environmental conditions. To the extent that such association can be established, resulting information on productive and unproductive practices can be disseminated throughout the movement, and information on favorable and unfavorable environmental characteristics can be used by the national leadership in their efforts to improve the environment in which credit unions operate. We now illustrate the second use of this information.

ID#	Radial Efficiency	x_1 Labor	x_2 Operating Expense	y_1 Loan Quantity	y_2 Loan Price	y_3 Loan Variety	y_4 Deposit Quantity	y_5 Deposit Price	y_6 Deposit Variety
BBBBB	1.000	20	31909	1862	1128	880	3677	700	893
CCCCC	1.000	25	58246	1815	1005	747	2882	796	840
DDDDD	1.000	25	41242	1099	825	778	3451	711	815
EEEEE	0.983	20	47588	1073	1053	865	2617	669	859
FFFFF	0.917	20	63238	1081	963	807	3267	623	796
AAAAA	0.885	25	64868	762	793	714	2389	543	790
GGGGG	0.860	35	80739	416	587	632	2114	488	768
HHHHH	0.788	30	89911	749	780	713	2260	493	625
IIIII	0.772	30	81197	309	577	679	1766	519	668
JJJJJ	0.740	40	135664	652	703	670	2059	537	581
KKKKK	0.726	35	71350	683	760	650	2204	492	611
LLLLL	0.719	60	94208	731	738	651	2229	518	596

Table 4

Resources and Services for Credit Union AAAAA

The performance of credit union AAAAA is below average. Its resource and service inefficiencies reported in Table 4 exceed the industry averages reported in column (1) of Table 3, in seven of eight dimensions. The next step in the analysis is to determine the extent to which the sub-par performance of credit union AAAAA can be associated with its structure and operating characteristics, and with the environment in which it operates. The following analysis enables us to "adjust" the performance of credit union AAAAA by accounting for its favorable and unfavorable managerial and environmental characteristics. The adjustment gives a different, and perhaps more accurate, picture of the true performance of the management of credit union AAAAA. The adjustment technique is similar in spirit, but much different in execution, to the use of DEA to isolate managerial efficiency from program efficiency proposed by Charnes, Cooper and Rhodes (1981).

We first use data from the entire sample of credit unions to estimate, by seemingly unrelated regression techniques, a system of eight equations of general form

$$(\text{inefficiency})_j^i = f^i(z_1^i,...,z_{20}^i,d_j^i;\beta), \quad i=1,...,8,947, \quad j=1,...,8,$$

where i indexes a credit union, j indexes the two resources and the six services, and the z_k's are the environmental variables described in Section 3.[14] The dependent variables in the system represent total (radial plus slack) inefficiency in the use of variable j by credit union i. The dummy variable dj takes on a value of one if credit union i has no inefficiency, radial or slack, in variable j, and takes on a value of zero otherwise. The parameter vector ß shows the effect of each of the independent variables in the system on total inefficiency in the use of each variable, for the sample as a whole. If $\beta_{kj} < 0$, the associated business

---

[14]The environmental variables are an associational common bond dummy, a residential common bond dummy, a subsidy dummy, the number of members, the ratio of actual to potential members, a state charter dummy, "recent" and "new" age dummies, a branching dummy, five regional dummies, a large asset size group dummy, average loan size, average deposit size, the delinquency ratio, the ratio of the value of investments to the value of loans, and the ratio of the value of real estate loans to the value of loans. The system $R^2 = 0.25$. Results of the estimation exercise are available on request.

practice or environmental characteristic tends to reduce inefficiency in activity j, while $\beta_{kj} > 0$ produces the opposite result.

The estimated parameters are used to predict inefficiency in credit union AAAAA by means of

$$(\text{predicted inefficiency})_j^{AAAAA} = \hat{f}^j(z_1^{AAAAA},...,z_{20}^{AAAAA},d_j^{AAAAA}\hat{\beta}), \quad j = 1,...,8.$$

The calculated inefficiencies for credit union AAAAA are thereby adjusted to account for the influence of the structural characteristics of credit union AAAAA and the business practices it follows in an effort to provide services to its membership. If these features are generally favorable, its predicted inefficiencies should decrease, while if they are detrimental to performance, its predicted inefficiencies should increase relative to its calculated inefficiencies. A comparison of calculated and predicted inefficiencies enables us to determine whether credit union AAAAA has performed better or worse than expected, under the circumstances described by its observed business practices and the features of its operating environment which we are able to measure.

Results of the adjustment exercise are reported in Table 5. On balance, credit union AAAAA performed somewhat worse than expected, since predicted inefficiencies declined in five of eight dimensions. Put another way, given its business practices and its operating environment, and given the effects these features have on credit union performance in general, credit union AAAAA should have experienced less inefficiency than it did in one resource dimension and in four service dimensions. The only two possible sources of these discrepancies are subpar managerial performance and environmental variables we have been unable to observe.[15]

---

[15]Two likely candidates we have been unable to measure are the incomes of a credit union's members, and the intensity of competition from other nearby financial intermediaries a credit union faces.

Table 5. Calculated and Predicted Inefficiencies in Credit Union AAAAA

Variable	Calculated Inefficiency (%)	Predicted Inefficiency (%)	% Change
x_1 Labor	+25.0	+163.1	+552.3
x_2 Operating Expenses	+103.3	+65.4	-36.7
y_1 Loan Quantity	-59.1	-53.7	-9.2
y_2 Loan Price	-29.7	-20.6	-30.7
y_3 Loan Variety	-18.9	-18.8	-0.6
y_4 Deposit Quantity	-35.0	-32.3	-7.9
y_5 Deposit Price	-22.4	-22.6	+0.9
y_6 Deposit Variety	-11.5	-15.9	+38.1

6. Summary and Conclusions

One way of assessing the competitive viability of the credit union segment of the financial intermediation sector is by monitoring the financial safety and soundness of individual credit unions. The NCUA does this, on a regular basis. Another way of assessing competitive viability is by evaluating the ability of individual credit unions to keep up with best practice credit unions in the provision of services to their members. The purpose of this study has been to conduct such an evaluation, paying particular attention to how the evaluation might be used to enhance the performance of dominated credit unions.

We found that, on average, dominated credit unions lag roughly 20% behind best practice credit unions in the provision of deposit and loan services to their members. The shortfall is not neutral, however, being much less pronounced in the quality dimensions than in the quantity dimensions. To the extent that quality is a better competitive tool than quantity, this finding is mildly encouraging. The finding of nonneutrality is also informative, for it points to areas in which remedial efforts are most likely to be productive. Thus, for example, efforts to control operating expense and to increase loans are apt to be more productive than similar efforts to improve loan and deposit rates, which are subject to the discipline of competition from other financial intermediaries.

Focusing our analysis on a single arbitrarily selected credit union has enabled us to explore the possible determinants of performance variation in some detail. The value of this exercise lies in the information it provides management at two levels: it may help management of individual credit unions improve their performance, and it may help the national leadership to formulate policies that enhance competitive viability of the credit union segment of the financial intermediation sector of the economy. We have found evidence of variables that may be of use to management at both levels in their effort to improve performance, but the majority of performance variation is left unexplained. This we attribute to uncaptured features of a credit union's operating environment, and to variation in managerial performance.

In this paper, and in somewhat more detail in our previous paper, we have shown how the service provision performance of individual credit unions may be evaluated, using regularly reported data. We have also shown how the performance evaluation can be interpreted in light of the business practices and environmental conditions of individual credit unions. Finally, we have shown how to identify, for each credit union, a list of dominating role model credit unions from which each credit union might learn how to improve its performance. We believe this feature of our work provides a prototype model that might be developed into a service that CUNA might provide to all credit unions on a regular basis. This would provide a service-oriented device that would complement the financial-oriented instrument already used by the NCUA. Together, the two devices would enhance the competitive viability of the credit union segment of the financial intermediation sector of the economy.

References

Banker, R.D., A. Charnes, and W.W. Cooper (1984). "Some models for estimating technical and scale inefficiencies in data envelopment analysis," *Management Science* 30(9) (September), 1078-92.

Bauer, P.W., A.N. Berger, and D.B. Humphrey (1993). "Efficiency and productivity growth in U.S. banking," in H.O. Fried, C.A.K. Lovell, and S.S. Schmidt (eds.), *The Measurement of Productive Efficiency: Techniques and Applications* (Oxford University Press, New York), 386-413.

Berger, A.N. (1993). "Distribution-free estimates of efficiency in the U.S. banking industry and tests of the standard distributional assumptions," *Journal of Productivity Analysis* 4(3) (September), 261-92.

Berger, A.N., and D.B. Humphrey (1991). "The dominance of inefficiencies over scale and product mix economies in banking," *Journal of Monetary Economics* 28 (August), 117-48.

Charnes, A., W.W. Cooper, and E. Rhodes (1981). "Evaluating program and managerial efficiency: an application of data envelopment analysis to program follow through," *Management Science* 27(6) (June), 668-97.

Deprins, D., L. Simar, and H. Tulkens (1984). "Measuring labor inefficiency in post offices," in M. Marchand, P. Pestieau, and H. Tulkens (eds.), *The Performance of Public Enterprises: Concepts and Measurements* (North-Holland, Amsterdam), 243-67.

Ferrier, G.D., and C.A.K. Lovell (1990). "Measuring cost efficiency in banking: econometric and linear programming evidence," *Journal of Econometrics* 46(1/2) (October/November), 229-45.

Flannery, M.J. (1974). *An Economic Evaluation of Credit Unions in the United States* (Federal Reserve Bank of Boston, Boston, MA).

Fried, H.O., C.A.K. Lovell, and P. Vanden Eeckaut (1993). "Evaluating the performance of U.S. credit unions," *Journal of Banking and Finance* 17, 251-65.

Lovell, C.A.K., and P. Vanden Eeckaut (1993). "Frontier tales: DEA and FDH," in W.E. Diewert, K. Spremann and F. Stehling (eds.), *Mathematical Modelling in Economics* (Springer-Verlag, Berlin and New York).

Overstreet, G., and G.M. Rubin (1991). *Blurred Vision: Challenges in Credit Union Research and Modelling* (The Filene Research Institute, Madison, WI).

Smith, D.J. (1984). "A theoretic framework of the analysis of credit union decision making," *Journal of Finance* 39, 1155-68.

_____ (1986). "A test for variant objective functions in credit unions," *Applied Economics* 18, 959-70.

Tulkens, H., and P. Vanden Eeckaut (1993). "Non-parametric efficiency, progress and regress measures for panel data: methodological aspects," CORE Discussion Paper 9316, Center for Operations Research and Econometrics, Université Catholique de Louvain (Louvain-la-Neuve, Belgium) and *European Journal of Operational Research* 1995.

Wolken, J.D., and F.J. Navratil (1984). "The valuation of subsidies in kind and their effects on costs," *Journal of Economics and Business* 36, 217-32.

**Chapter 14   Productivity   Growth   in   the   Telephone   Industry
Since 1984**

Robert W. Crandall and Jonathan Galst

Over the past ten years, the U.S. telephone industry has undergone a dramatic
transformation. Though not formally deregulated, the industry is no longer a
tightly regulated, protected set of monopolies dominated by the largest erstwhile
monopoly of them all, AT&T. Competition exists in long-distance services,
customer-premises equipment, Yellow Pages, switching and transmission
equipment, and -- to a lesser extent -- even at the local exchange.

When AT&T was forced to divest itself of its entire network of local
telephone companies, many feared that the U.S. had needlessly sacrificed its
efficient telephone monopoly in favor of a set of fragmented companies that
would not enjoy the economies of scale and scope of the erstwhile Bell system.
Moreover, there was a fear that the incompatibility of standards across so many
new players in the local and long-distance markets would further reduce
efficiency.

Others saw AT&T as a lethargic, protected monopoly that needed to be
invigorated by competition. As long as AT&T controlled the access to
customers through its local exchange companies, competition in equipment and
services would be impaired. If the AT&T divestiture was the price for making
competition work, the results might be worth the price.

More than ten years have now elapsed since the break-up of AT&T. It
should now be possible to compare the post-1984 performance of the industry
with the pre-1984 AT&T performance to determine who was right: those that

P. T. Harker (ed.), The Service Productivity and Quality Challenge, 391–405.

stressed the scale and scope economies or those opting for competition at the risk of sacrificing some static efficiencies.   In this paper, I provide at least preliminary evidence on the growth in total factor productivity in the post-1984 telephone industry.

1 . Divestiture and Competition

In 1984, AT&T was broken up into seven regional holding companies and one integrated long-distance company as part of a 1982 decree that settled a 1974 government antitrust suit against the company. This decree also required the divestiture of two partially-owned local-exchange companies. As a result of the decree, AT&T no longer participates in local telephone markets,[1] and its divested operating companies are no longer beholden to AT&T's manufacturing division for their capital equipment.

The AT&T break-up is premised on the theory that long-distance service and telephone equipment manufacture are potentially competitive industries that can be deregulated as long as they are not combined with local access/exchange service, which continues to be a regulated monopoly. As a result, the divested Bell Operating Companies (BOCs) are explicitly forbidden to enter manufacturing or long-distance service by the AT&T consent decree. Once local service is structurally competitive, these restrictions on the BOCs may be lifted and even local service could be deregulated by state government authorities.

The states have never been as comfortable with telephone-industry competition as the federal regulators or antitrust authorities have been. However, since 1984 even the states have begun to experiment with more flexible, incentive-compatible regulation while allowing competition to creep into intrastate markets.   Interstate service by "dominant carriers" remains regulated despite the theory that lies behind the settlement of the AT&T antitrust suit, but the Federal Communications Commission has substituted price-cap regulation for the more traditional rate-of-return regulation of AT&T and the interstate activities of local-exchange companies (*Report and Order and Second Further Notice of Proposed Rulemaking*, CC Docket No. 87-313, Federal

---

[1] It is now purchasing McCaw Cellular, a company that offers local service through a cellular technology. However, AT&T no longer operates traditional local telephone companies.

Communications Commission, April 17, 1989; *Second Report and Order*, CC Docket No. 87-313, Federal Communications Commission, October 4, 1990).

Customer premises equipment -- handsets, data terminals, and PBXs, for example -- are now completely deregulated. Switching and transmission equipment are available in a competitive world market. Long-distance competition has become quite spirited as AT&T's market share has now dipped below 65 percent, and unregulated carriers such as MCI, Sprint, and NTN grow rapidly. Even local access/exchange service is feeling the pressure of competition from cellular providers and large new Metropolitan Area Networks that utilize fiber optics to distribute signals in densely-populated large cities.

Competition has not yet replaced regulated monopoly in delivering telephone access service to small commercial and residential subscribers. Indeed, many states continue to resist the notion that competition could discipline the incumbent wire-based local carriers. State regulation of intrastate long-distance and local service has been designed to keep residential access rates low, particularly in less densely populated areas. As a result, intrastate toll rates and local business rates are used to cross subsidize these residential subscribers. State regulators are acutely aware that competition would surely undermine this politically-popular pricing policy.

The environment for many non-Bell local telephone companies has not changed as dramatically as have the markets for interstate telephone services and telephone equipment. Unlike the BOCs, the independent companies are generally not banned from long-distance services, information services, or equipment manufacture. State regulatory flexibility is spreading slowly and is far from revolutionary. FCC price caps for local exchange companies have only been in place for two years. Competition is much less vigorous in intrastate toll markets -- although it is increasing steadily -- than in interstate markets.

The divested Bell operating companies are much more constrained than their independent brethren. Besides being denied the right to engage in manufacturing and to participate in interstate long-distance markets, they were banned by the AT&T consent decree from offering content-based information services, such as electronic Yellow Pages, until a recent appellate court decision reversed the AT&T trial court's continued enforcement of this prohibition (*U.S. v. Western Electric Co.*, 767 F. Supp. 308 (D.D.C., 1991). However, there is considerable sentiment in the Congress -- due to aggressive lobbying from newspapers and other publishers -- to reimpose the information-services ban through legislation.

As the result of a 1984 amendment to the Federal Communications Act, all local telephone companies -- Bell and non-Bell -- are prohibited from offering (cable) television service in their own franchise areas. This prohibition has undoubtedly slowed the development of competition for cable television companies through broadband, fiber-optics facilities that telephone companies could potentially install.[2]

Thus, the changes in market environment have been most important for the long-distance segment of the telephone industry. The independent telephone companies have seen the least change, and the Bell operating companies have been most constrained in the post-1984 period. Given these developments, we should expect to see relatively little change in the efficiency of independent telephone companies, perhaps even a retrogression among the constrained Bell companies, but possibly major improvements in the efficiency of the long-distance carriers.

2. The Domain of This Study

Despite the fact that the telephone industry has been regulated in some fashion for about three quarters of a century, consistent data on inputs and outputs are not easily obtained. The FCC requires regulated carriers to report financial data and publishes summaries of these data for AT&T, all Regional Bell Operating Companies (RBOCs), and the larger independent carriers in its annual *Statistics of Communications Common Carriers*.

The United States Telephone Association provides a much more comprehensive summary of independent telephone company results, but its annual statistical report, *Statistics of Local Exchange Carriers*, was severely compressed in 1988. All subsequent reports provide only the most general information on revenues, costs, investment, and employment.

The new competitive long-distance carriers do not report operating data to the FCC. There are some data available for MCI and Sprint in public financial statements, but these statements do not allow one to estimate annual labor, material, or capital expenses or to separate interstate from intrastate revenues.

---

[2] A decision by the FCC to allow these companies to offer "video dial tone" has mitigated this restriction somewhat. In addition, the 1984 prohibition has been declared unconstitutional in two appellate courts.

As a result, this paper only examines the post-divestiture performance of AT&T, the Bell Operating Companies, and the independent telephone companies.

3. Measuring Performance -- Total Factor Productivity

There are many possible approaches to measuring the changes in productive efficiency among telephone companies over the past eight years. Econometric estimation of a translog production function is perhaps the most common approach in the literature (Waverman 1989). More recently, Charnes and others have used an operations-research methodology called "goal programming" to estimate the degree to which firms approach the efficiency frontier (Charnes et al. 1988).

Unfortunately, both the econometric production-function and operations-research approaches perform rather poorly when applied to an industry with rapidly-changing technology. Waverman shows that most such time-series exercises result in models that generate in-sample predictions of negative marginal costs for a substantial share of the observations (Waverman 1989).

An alternative approach is to measure total factor productivity directly in the manner developed by Jorgenson, Griliches, Christensen, and others (Jorgenson et al. 1967; Caves et al. 1980). By calculating Divisia-weighted indexes of inputs and outputs from published FCC and other financial data, one can obtain estimates of the rate of growth of output per unit input over a considerable period of time without worrying about the precise specification of the production function or the efficiency frontier.

Following Caves, Christensen, and Swanson (Caves et al. 1980), we can write the production function as:

(1) $F(Q;K,L,M;T) = 0$

where Q is the rate of output and K, L, and M are the rates of labor, capital, and materials services, respectively, and T is time. If there are no scale economies, the rate of total factor productivity (TFP) growth is simply $[(\partial F/\partial T)/F]$. However, with scale economies, $[(\partial F/\partial T)/F]$ overstates TFP growth by the quantity $(1-1/e)$ times the annual rate of growth in output, where e is the measure of returns to scale. Hence, if e is equal to 2 and output is growing by 4 percent per year, the degree of overstatement is 2 percent per year.

As Caves, Christensen, and Swanson show, $[(\partial F/\partial T)/F]$ is equal to the rate of change of the dual cost function to (1) or:

$$(2) \quad (\partial F/\partial T)/F = (\partial \ln C/\partial \ln Q)(d \ln Q/dT)$$
$$- [S_L (d \ln L/dT) + S_K (d \ln K/dT) + S_M(d \ln M/dT)]$$

Because there is no clear consensus about scale economies in telecommunications, particularly across different types of output, it is difficult to adjust estimates of $(\partial F/\partial T)/F$ in (2) for departures of $(\partial \ln C/\partial \ln Q)$ from unity. In the empirical section below, therefore, we display the results unadjusted for scale economies and for scale economies of 1.2 and 1.4.

4. The Data

As mentioned above, all data for this study are derived from public reports of the companies to the Federal Communications Commission or to USTA. Deflators for output are the Producer Price Indexes for telephone services. Capital-services deflators are the Bureau of Economic Analysis deflators for telephone and telegraph investment in equipment and structures.

The output series is a Divisia weighted index of eight categories of service -- local, switched interstate long-distance, switched intrastate long-distance, unidirectional interstate long-distance (WATS and 800), unidirectional intrastate long-distance, private-line and miscellaneous interstate toll, private and miscellaneous intrastate toll, and miscellaneous revenues (principally, Yellow Pages). Access charges are assigned to switched long-distance services; monthly "subscriber line charges" are assigned to local service. Wherever possible, the share of revenues accounted for by each service is estimated from FCC data in the *Statistics of Communications Common Carriers*, the underlying annual M-1 reports, or the December MR reports to the FCC.[3]

The Divisia weights for the output series are based on the nominal share of revenues for each service, the traditional approach in constructing such output series. However, this methodology requires that prices of all services be

[3] An alternative approach is to use physical measures of service, access lines, calls, or minutes of use, but these data fail to capture the potential role of new enhanced services, shifts in the average lengths of calls, or differences in the mix of switched and unswitched calls.

proportional to marginal costs. Given the distortions in telephone pricing, such an assumption is untenable. Therefore, the revenue weights are adjusted in an approximate fashion for shifts in "nontraffic-sensitive costs" from local service to long-distance service. Specifically, we assume that 20 percent of the revenue share for interstate and intrastate switched long-distance service should be assigned to local service.[4]

The input series are constructed in the standard fashion. Labor used in delivering telecommunications service is reported to the FCC annually. These labor hours have not been adjusted for potential improvements in relative human capital in the telecommunications sector because the data do not exist to make such an adjustment. Capital investment from 1960 to the present has been used to construct net and gross capital by the perpetual inventory method. Discards and depreciation rates are from BEA. Capital is constructed from two components -- equipment and structures. The division of AT&T capital stock in 1984 between AT&T and the regional Bell companies is based on FCC data on net and gross book value of capital. Capital services are assumed to be proportional to capital stock, which in turn is equal to 75 percent of gross stock and 25 percent of net stock per Denison's methodology (Denison 1979).

The third category of inputs is "materials," an admittedly unsatisfactory heterogeneous category of purchased inputs, including utilities, materials, energy, etc. This input category is equal to operating costs less capital charges (depreciation) and labor costs. The materials input purchases are deflated by the BEA GDP deflator.

The resulting Divisia indexes of inputs are based on weights derived from current-dollar cost shares from the FCC's *Statistics of Communications Common Carriers.*

5. The Results: 1984-1991

Because the breakup of AT&T resulted in substantial write-offs of obsolete assets and considerable transitional costs, it is somewhat problematical to

---

[4] This adjustment is rather arbitrary given the absence of precise data on the average share of costs that regulators have shifted from the local jurisdiction to interstate and intrastate toll. The repricing of service that has occurred in the 1980s has reduced this share substantially.

include 1984 in the analysis. However, we allow for AT&T's write-offs in the construction of the capital series, and begin nevertheless with 1984.

The simple, unadjusted estimates of TFP growth for each group -- AT&T, the RBOCs, and the Independents -- are reported in Table 1. Surprisingly, they show that the independent telephone companies enjoyed the greatest growth in output per unit input, followed by AT&T, and trailed by the RBOCs. The reasons for this relative performance is clear when one examines the rate of growth of output for the period (in column 2 of Table 1). The independents had easily the greatest output growth despite the fact that long-distance services grew most rapidly. AT&T was in the fastest-growing sector, but it was losing market share rapidly throughout the period.

Table 1. Average Annual Changes in Total Factor Productivity, Output and Input Use, 1985-91 (percent)

Companies	Total Factor Productivity	Output	Capital Input	Labor Input	Materials Input
AT&T	3.5	3.7	2.9	-5.8	2.2
RBOCs	3.1	2.1	0.9	-4.2	2.8
Independents	3.8	5.3	2.2	-1.9	0.8

Note: Output growth based on revenue weights.

Source: See text.

Before we turn to various adjustments of the TFP estimates for scale economies and rate distortions, it may be useful to examine the reasons why independent telephone companies grew more rapidly than the RBOCs. Table 2 provides some illuminating measures of the components of this output growth. Note that the independents had higher growth rates in each of the important categories -- local service, switched long-distance, WATS and 800, and even miscellaneous. Part of the reason was that independents had a higher rate of access-line growth, but they also had slower growth in revenues per line.

We next turn to adjusting the estimates in Table 1 for the distortions of using revenue weights in calculating output growth. In so doing, we provide estimates for the earlier periods, drawn from Crandall and Galst (1990), for the 1961-83 period. These earlier estimates utilize the methodology outlined above, but reflect a larger adjustment for rate distortions in the late 1970s and early 1980s because of the larger share of non-traffic-sensitive costs assigned to long-distance calls in this earlier period.

Table 2. Source of Growth-Regional Bell Operating Companies and Independent Telephone Companies

ANNUAL GROWTH RATES (percent)							
Companies	Access Lines	Total Output	Local Output	Interstate MTS	Intrastate MTS	WATS	Miscell- aneous
RBOCs	3.3	2.1	1.3	3.1	4.2	-4.0	0.6
Indepen- dents	4.3	5.3	2.0	7.8	5.4	6.7	12.0

NOMINAL REVENUES			
Companies	Average Annual Local Revenues per Line	Average Annual Toll & Access Revenues per Line	Average Annual Growth: Local Revenues per Line (%)	Average Annual Growth: Toll & Access Revenues per Line (%)
RBOCs	$322	$284	1.7	-3.7
Indepen- dents	$278	$390	1.4	-1.3

Source: See text.

Table 3. Total Factor Productivity Growth Using Cost Weights for Output (percent)

Companies	1961-70	1971-83	1985-91
Bell System	2.7	3.3	2.8 3.5 (AT&T) 2.6 (RBOC)
Independents	2.9	2.4	3.4 °

Source: See text; Crandall and Galst (1990).

The estimates of TFP growth using cost weights in constructing the output index, shown in Table 3, are obviously lower than those exhibited in Table 1. Of greater interest is the fact that the Bell System successors' (AT&T and the RBOCs) TFP growth appears to slow after the 1971-83 period while the independents' TFP accelerates substantially. This result, however, may be a reflection of the greater output growth in the independent sector than among the RBOCs and AT&T.

To demonstrate the potential effects of output growth on the estimates of TFP, we begin with the estimated output growth for each group of companies, utilizing the cost-weighted Divisia index of output. The effect of these rate-distortion adjustments on output growth are shown in Table 4. The "Bell" sector for 1985-91 is a weighted average of AT&T and the RBOCs, using weights of .25 and .75, respectively.[5] Note that there is a continuous reduction

[5] These weights reflect the approximate relative size of AT&T and the RBOCs at divestiture.

in output growth over the three periods shown, but that the deceleration is greater for the "Bell" companies than for the independents in the most recent period.

The decomposition of the TFP growth estimates into scale effects and those attributable to pure efficiency gains depends on the assumed scale elasticity in telecommunications. But any simple adjustment for scale economies is likely to be misleading. The growth in telecommunications output may reflect an extension of service into new areas and new exchanges, the filling of existing exchanges with incremental customers along an existing trunk line, the growth in long-distance services, or the emergence of new services, such as call-waiting, call-forwarding, voice messaging, or teleconferencing. No single parameter for "scale economies" can possibly reflect the effects of all of these disparate sources of growth on costs. Indeed, this is undoubtedly the reason that econometric estimates of these elasticities from time-series data are subject to so many problems.

Table 4. Estimated Output Growth, 1961-91, Using Revenue Weights and Cost Weights

	1961-70	1971-83	1985-91
Based on Revenue Weights			
Bell System (AT&T & RBOCs)	7.8	6.6	2.5
Independents	11.3	8.0	5.3
Based on Cost Weights			
Bell System (AT&T & RBOCs)	7.4	6.1	2.4
Independents	10.8	7.2	4.8

These difficulties not withstanding, it may be possible to gain some insights from the decomposition of the estimates in Table 3 into scale and efficiency effects. The adjustments are made for two assumed scale elasticity parameters, 1.2 and 1.4. The results appear in Table 5. Once again, the "Bell" estimate for 1985-91 reflects a 0.25 and 0.75 weighting of AT&T and the RBOCs, respectively.

The estimated growth in pure efficiency under both assumptions about scale economies now show that efficiency gains accelerated after the 1984 breakup of AT&T, but the acceleration is much greater for the independents than for the Bell successors. This result, if a reasonable approximation of reality, suggest that something other than the AT&T divestiture is propelling technical change or the reduction of x-inefficiency in the telecommunications sector. The enormous changes in technology that are being built into modern telephone systems, from sophisticated switching systems to fiber optics, would probably have occurred with or without the AT&T breakup. However, the increase in competition for equipment caused by the divorce of AT&T's Western Electric from its principal customers, the Bell Operating Companies, could be part of the explanation.

Table 5. Average Annual Growth in Total Factor Productivity Excluding Effects of Scale Economies (percent)

Companies	1961-70	1971-83	1985-91
Economies of Scale = 1.4			
Bell System (AT&T & RBOCs)	0.6	1.5	2.1
Independents	-0.2	0.3	2.0
Economies of Scale = 1.2			
Bell System (AT&T & RBOCs)	1.5	2.3	2.4
Independents	1.1	1.2	2.6

Note: Output growth based on cost weights.

Source: See text.

6. The Slowdown at the Bell Operating Companies

One of the clearest results that emerges from the above analysis is that the divested Bell Operating Companies have suffered a sharp deceleration in growth since 1984. By my calculations, they have grown at only 40 percent of the independents' growth rate. This difference in growth rates is partly attributable to slower access-line growth, but the growth in access lines is not the entire story. Revenues per line have grown more slowly for the Bell companies than for their independent brethren. Nor is the growth in access lines a totally exogenous magnitude, for it may reflect regulatory or internal pricing decisions.

The most obvious candidate for explaining the slow growth of the RBOCs is public policy. Given the size and sophistication of the Bell companies, one might expect them to develop new services and technologies more rapidly than the smaller, more fragmented independent sector. Indeed, the Bell companies have been in the forefront of providing new local switching systems, offering new central-office services, and moving to equal access for long-distance carriers. Throughout the 1984-91 period, however, the Bell companies have been constrained in developing new products by the ban on manufacturing in the AT&T decree and -- until recently -- by the information-services prohibition in this decree. In addition, all local-exchange companies have been prohibited from offering cable-television service in their own franchise areas by the 1984 amendment to the Communications Act.

Had there been no restrictions on Bell-company offerings of new services, their growth rate may have been substantially greater. The RBOCs would likely have been the first to move into fiber-optics delivery of television service to the household had such service been allowed and were it economical today -- which is far from clear. However, there is little evidence yet that the reversal of the information-services ban provision in the decree has unleashed a torrent of new services from the RBOCs. An equally likely explanation for the slow growth at the RBOCs is their greater participation in the large urban markets. These dense markets feature the greatest growth in new competition for the large business customers. In addition, these markets feature the greatest concentration of large business users who can build their own private networks. A more disaggregated investigation into the sources of growth across individual companies should provide at least some clue as to whether it is market forces, regulatory forces, or some combination of the two that has caused the slowdown among the RBOCs.

7. AT&T and Price Caps

In a recent paper, Schmalensee and Rohlfs (1992) find that AT&T's productivity growth accelerated after the imposition of price caps in 1989. It is difficult to compare their results with those in this paper because they only examine the rate of increase in AT&T's switched access minutes, not its entire output. Moreover, they adjust AT&T's capital for rapid obsolescence in a somewhat ad hoc fashion.[6] Finally, they do not report their results in terms of annual TFP growth, but rather assert that their results are the equivalent of a $1.8 billion cost savings in 1989-91 over the 1986-88 period.

By contrast, we find that AT&T's output growth decelerated markedly in the post-1989 period. AT&T's TFP growth in 1989-91 was below its 1984-88 average -- undoubtedly because of this decline in output. Thus, for all of AT&T, TFP does not rebound after the imposition of price caps.

8. Conclusion

This preliminary analysis of the performance of the telecommunications sector after the breakup of AT&T has shown that technical progress in the delivery of telephone service has accelerated -- after one accounts for the effects of putative scale economies. Absent scale economies, the rate of technical progress has not risen for the erstwhile "Bell companies" -- AT&T and the regional Bell operating companies -- but has accelerated for the independents. Regardless of the existence of scale economies it is clear that the Bell operating companies have grown much less rapidly than has the independent telephone sector. A closer analysis may find that this difference in growth is due to the restrictions on the BOCs in the AT&T consent decree. Whatever the cause, the BOCs have genuine cause for concern as new competitors nip at their heels in their largest markets.

---

[6] This is not to say that the consistent rates of depreciation used in the present paper are economically defensible. The rate of technical progress may have accelerated substantially in recent years, requiring more rapid rates of obsolescence in estimating the capital stock of telecommunications companies. It is simply unclear how to estimate this rate of obsolescence.

References

Caves, D.W., L.R. Christensen, and J.A. Swanson (1980). "Productivity in U.S. railroads, 1951-74," *The Bell Journal of Economics* 11(1) (Spring), 166-181.

Charnes, A., W.W. Cooper, and J. Sueyoshi (1988). "A goal programming/constrained regression review of the Bell System breakup," *Management Science* (January), 1-26.

Crandall, R.W., and J. Galst (1990). "Productivity growth in the U.S. telecommunications sector: the impact of the AT&T divestiture," unpublished ms.

Denison, E. (1979). *Accounting for Slower U.S.Economic Growth*. (The Brookings Institution, Washington, DC).

Jorgenson, D.W., and Z. Griliches (1967). "The explanation of productivity change," *Review of Economic Studies* (July), 249-83.

Schmalensee, R., and J.H. Rohlfs (1992). "Productivity gains resulting from interstate price caps," National Economic Research Associates, September 3, 1992. Paper prepared for AT&T.

Waverman, L. (1989). "U.S. interexchange competition," in R.W. Crandall and K. Flamm (eds.), *Changing the Rules: Technological Change, International Competition and Regulation in Communications* (The Brookings Institution, Washington, DC), 62-113.

Chapter 15   Improving Productivity in Intermodal Rail-Truck Transportation

Edward K. Morlok, John P. Sammon, Lazar N. Spasovic
and Linda K. Nozick[7]

1. Introduction

This paper has two purposes. One is to discuss and define the concepts of productivity and quality as they apply to transportation, particularly freight transportation, and to identify the similarities and differences with other service industries (e.g., banking and social services). The second purpose is to describe how productivity and quality improvements can be achieved in the trucking (or drayage) portion of intermodal rail-truck service, and the implications of these for market penetration.

---

[7]This work was completed while Drs. Spasovic and Nozick were in the Department of Systems at the University of Pennsylvania. The authors wish to acknowledge the assistance of John F. Betak and David M. Toth of Conrail in the conduct of this research. The University of Pennsylvania effort was supported by Conrail, The UPS Foundation, and The University Transportation Center Program of the U.S. Department of Transportation through the Mid-Atlantic Universities Transportation Center.

407

P. T. Harker (ed.), The Service Productivity and Quality Challenge, 407–434.
© 1995 *Kluwer Academic Publishers. Printed in the Netherlands.*

2. Productivity and Quality in Transportation

In order to understand how productivity and quality can be influenced and how they are related to one another in transportation, it is essential that these concepts be defined.

The concept of *productivity* as it applies to transportation refers to the ratio of transportation output to input, or more specifically, to the ratio of transportation output to the cost of the resources consumed in providing the transportation. The perspective taken is usually that of the transportation service provider, i.e., the carrier. The concept applies equally well to freight or passenger transportation, and also is applicable to private transportation-- transportation undertaken by the owner of goods moved or the traveler(s).

Output of a transportation service can be measured in a variety of ways. In freight transport, typical measures of output for an entire transportation system would be the total number of shipments delivered, the total ton-miles carried, etc. Inputs can be measured by total cost, although productivity terminology is usually applied to cases where inputs are measured in physical units rather than costs, e.g., vehicles, person hours of labor, etc. The concept of productivity can be applied to individual elements of the system, such as the vehicle fleet or terminal facilities, in which case the output and input measures would be correspondingly limited. Naturally higher values of productivity are preferred.

Quality is usually assessed from the standpoint of the user of the transportation system. In the case of freight transport this usually is the shipper, although in many situations the immediate transportation service buyer may be a representative or agent of the shipper (e.g., the U.S. Postal Service purchasing truck transport for parcel movements). In the parlance of the transportation field, *service quality* is usual referred to as *level of service*, and level of service refers to all of those attributes of the transportation service provided, except price, that affect the decisions of the shipper or user with respect to how much to ship, where to ship, and what modes, carriers and/or paths through the system to use. In the case of freight transport, typical service quality features are:

- door-to-door (or floor-to-floor) transit time;
- variability of transit time;
- promptness of pick-up or of provision of empty vehicle for loading;
- probability of loss and/or damage to the shipment enroute;

- ease of settling claims for loss and damage;
- ability to track shipment and re-route it if necessary;
- ease of doing business with the transportation carrier.

Obviously additional factors could be listed, but the above are indicative of the types of factors which freight service users consider.

It is customary to think of productivity and service quality as being in opposition to one another, in the sense that an improvement in one will typically result in degradation of the other. This is plausible for most productive activities, and the collective thinking in transportation appears to endorse it. This probably derives in part from the fact that major elements of transportation systems can be viewed as queuing systems, in which increasing throughput, or output, with a fixed facility (number and type of serving or processing channels), and hence fixed cost, can be achieved only with an increase in delay and hence a degradation of service quality. There certainly is an element of this involved in most transportation activities, but all transportation is not well represented by this type of model.

2.1 Improving productivity and quality. Considering a transportation system as a whole, in general it appears as though service quality can be enhanced while simultaneously enhancing productivity, at least over a certain range. By an entire system, we mean the collection of all facilities, equipment, personnel, procedures, etc., necessary to transport cargo from origin to destination. Thus a railroad, including tracks, trains, communications, yards, etc., would be such a complete system. In contrast, a truck line would not be a system, because it does not include the road network on which the trucks operate, traffic controls, and other essential elements. The relationship between productivity and quality can be seen easily by considering one of the most important aspects of service quality, transit time, and two of the most significant elements of cost for most transportation systems, the fleet and the labor used to operate it.

Consider the simplest system in which cargo is carried from a single origin to a single destination. If (a) the number of shipments per unit time is q, (b) one vehicle trip is required to deliver each shipment, and (c) the time required for each vehicle to complete delivery of a shipment is y (also known as the cycle time), then the number of vehicles required, n, is given by the following equation:

$$n = \langle qy \rangle \tag{1}$$

where $\langle \, \rangle$ indicates the smallest integer containing qy.

Thus as the cycle time is decreased, the number of vehicles required decreases as well. Fleet ownership and maintenance would also decrease. Assuming that the amount of labor required is proportional to the vehicles-hours operated (true if, for example, each employee worked a fixed number of hours operating vehicles each day), then labor costs would decline proportionally as well. This can be seen from the following equation in which h represents the total person hours that must be paid for.

$$h = yq \tag{2}$$

The implication of this for overall cost is that for most transportation systems there is an optimum speed at which the carrier's cost is minimized. This corresponds to an optimum travel time and hence round trip time for vehicles in any given market. This can be seen by reference to Figure 1. In the upper portion of that figure, the effect of speed on cost is portrayed. One element of these costs is the cost associated with fleet and operating labor which in general declines with increasing speed, as shown. Typically having the opposite effect on costs will be many other elements of cost, including the cost of energy or fuel to operate vehicles, which generally increases with increasing speed due to increasing resistance to motion (air resistance, mechanical friction), the cost of maintaining roadways or other vehicular facilities, and so on. Summing all costs together one typically finds a scalloped shaped curve, in which there is an optimum speed. Below this optimum, as speed is decreased, total cost will decrease, and above, as speed is further increased, costs will increase.

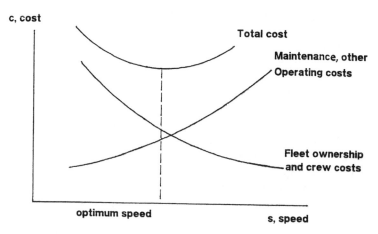

a. Total carrier cost vs. speed

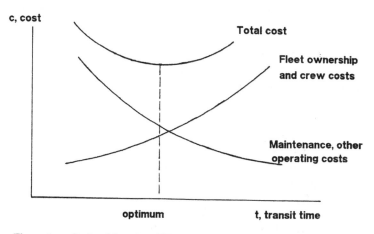

Figure 1.   Optimal Speed and Transit Time from Carrier's Perspective.

The same type of relationship can be drawn with respect to overall transit time--the time from pick up of the shipment to delivery to its destination, another measure of service quality. In the example system, transit time, t, would be related to speed as follows:

$$t = A + L/s \tag{3}$$

The constant A represents the time at the origin and the destination for vehicle loading and unloading and related activities, and also any intermediate terminal time which would not be affected by the operating speed of vehicles. The second term represents the speed of vehicle movement over the distance L between the origin and destination divided by the speed of the vehicle s.

While these relationships have been presented in a rather theoretical form here, it is important to note that such relationships have been developed for various transportation carriers and situations. While the optimum speed would depend upon the circumstances in any particular situation, that there is in fact a minimum cost speed is quite clear from the empirical evidence (see, for example, Morlok, 1979, 404-6, or Keaton, 1991).

2.2   The shipper's perspective. The shipper's perspective can also be added to this type of analysis. Shippers clearly have a preference in general for higher quality service, although presumably at some point there may be very diminishing returns to improved quality. Of particular importance is the effect of carrier service quality on inventory, and of course this is dramatically affected by overall transit time and the reliability (or variation) of that transit time, as numerous empirical studies have demonstrated (e.g., McGinnes, 1990). As transit time decreases, the inventory in transit is reduced at least proportionally in most situations, resulting in savings. Also, as transit time is reduced the timeliness of producer or seller response to customer needs may increase significantly, and this may be the basis for higher prices for the goods being realized in the market, or increased sales, or other benefits to the shipper. (Numerous examples are given in Davis and Davidson, 1991, 56-79.) Thus the effect of transit time on shipper costs would typically be as portrayed in Figure 2. If the shipper's cost is included with the carrier costs, then a new optimum travel time or speed is determined, and as can be readily seen, this will in general be at a higher service quality level than that which is optimum for the carrier's cost alone. This follows directly from the assumption of gains to the shipper from service quality improvements.

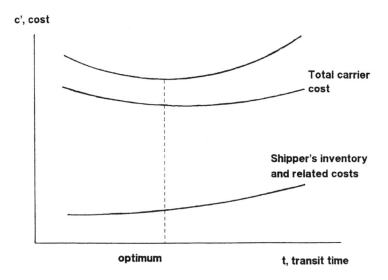

c', cost

Total carrier cost

Shipper's inventory and related costs

optimum   t, transit time

Figure 2.   Optimal Transit Time considering Carrier and Shipper Costs.

As the previous discussion suggests, the productivity concept is applicable to the customer or shipper, as well. From the shipper's standpoint the output is the movement of goods from origin to destination, and the input can be considered the inventory in transit, and other resources and costs associated with the movement. Thus as service quality improves and those inputs decline for any given quantity and spatial distribution of movement, then productivity is improved.

3. Intermodal Rail-Truck Service

As will be discussed below, intermodal rail-truck service suffers from serious problems in both productivity and service quality, in the drayage or trucking portion of that service. Unless drayage productivity is improved, this service will be limited to longer distance hauls and thus precluded from the higher volume shorter-haul domestic merchandise traffic markets. Without quality improvement, major inroads into over-the-road trucking will be impossible. After discussing these problems below, the results of a study to determine the feasibility of improvements in drayage productivity, with implications for service quality as well, will be described. We begin with a description of the intermodal system and the role of drayage.

The basic concept of intermodal rail-truck service is as shown in Figure 3. A tractor-trailer truck would be dispatched from the intermodal terminal to a shipper's location in order to pick up the cargo. The tractor and driver could wait with the trailer while the cargo is being loaded, in which case the loaded trailer would then be returned to the intermodal yard for the rail movement. This procedure is termed "stay with" drayage, drayage referring to the truck-on-road movement of the trailer by the tractor. Alternatively, the trailer might be left with the shipper for loading at a later time, the tractor then returning without the trailer to the intermodal yard. After the trailer has been loaded a tractor would be dispatched to pick up the trailer, and return with the loaded trailer to the inter-

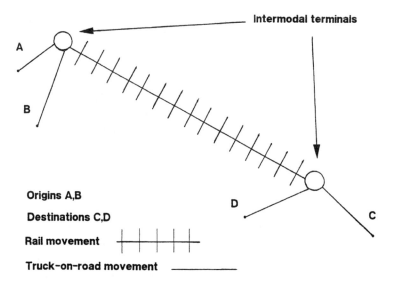

Figure 3.   Intermodal Rail-Truck Transportation.

modal terminal. This latter option is called the "drop and pick" procedure. At the terminal the loaded trailer would then be placed on a special railroad car designed for carrying trailers (termed "piggyback cars"), and then this car would be hauled in a train to the destination area intermodal terminal. At the destination end, the drayage operations would commence, with the trailer delivered to the recipient (consignee). After unloading, the empty trailer would be returned to a pool of empty trailers at the intermodal terminal. The delivery could use either the "stay with" or the "drop and pick" drayage procedure. (Separate from all of this are other variations due to the nature of the cargo being carried, e.g., parcels vs. full truckload shipments. In the former case a separate parcel pick-up and delivery operation is necessary, but this is distinct from the intercity operation.)

Thus intermodal service is essentially a substitute for over-the-road movement of the trailer. It is important to note that the trucking operation for which the rail movement is substituted is substantially simpler than the intermodal operation. The intermodal service requires coordination of the rail line haul with the drayage movements at both ends, and requires terminals for transfer of trailers. In contrast, over-the-road trucking simply operates directly to the destination once the trailer load has been picked up.

The rationale for the intermodal service is that in general long distance movement via rail is less expensive than parallel movement over the highway. The cost characteristics of intermodal service and trucking are quite different. This is illustrated in Figure 4, which portrays the cost as a function of distance. In the case of trucking, there is a small cost that is independent of distance, representing the cost of transactions associated with the movement (documentation, billing, etc.) and of the loading and unloading activity (truck time, etc). The cost of operating a truck (including ownership, maintenance, etc.) is essentially proportional to distance, and thus the total cost of truck shipment from the standpoint of the trucking company is as indicated. Typical values for the threshold cost are about $60 to $120 and the cost per unit distance is typically in the vicinity of $1 to $1.50 per loaded truck-mile, assuming about 80% of the total mileage is loaded (which is typical of the most efficient truck lines). The distance related cost could be increased proportionally to include the effect of greater empty mileage.

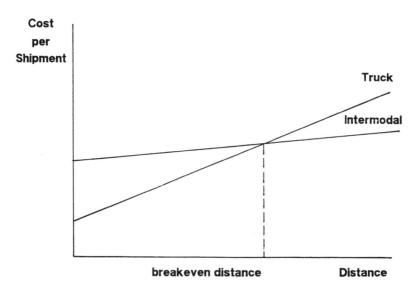

**Figure 4.   Breakeven Distance between Over-the-Road Truck
and Intermodal Rail-Truck Service.**

Source: Morlok and Sammon (1990), p.4.

Intermodal transport incurs a much higher threshold cost, including, in addition
to the transaction costs, the costs of providing the terminal facility, of loading
and unloading of the trailer, and of drayage at each end. Typical values for these
are $300 to $500. The cost per unit distance is in the vicinity of $.60 to $.80
per mile.

The net effect of the different cost structures is that there is a break-even
distance below which trucking is less costly and above which intermodal is less
costly, as indicated in Figure 4. Generally this is thought to be in the vicinity
of 500 to 700 miles for conditions in the U.S. at the present time. Of course,
local conditions, particularly the extent of adverse distance for drayage (i.e.,
drayage opposite to the direction of the destination), and the degree to which
equipment is fully utilized in both directions, will influence the break-even
distance.

While the preceding discussion has been in terms of the cost to the carrier, it is also important to consider the cost as perceived by the shipper. The shipper of course pays the carrier directly for the transportation service, but in addition incurs other costs associated with the movement. These include the cost of the cargo inventory while in transit, other inventory costs and possibly also production or distribution costs that vary with the mode, because of differences in travel time, reliability, and other level of service factors. While the effect of these other factors varies greatly among commodities and particular situations, these almost always increase the break-even distance between rail and truck, and usually it is thought to be in the vicinity of 700 to 1000 miles.

Using mid-range values for the costs of over-the-road truckload movement and intermodal movement, as presented earlier, a break-even distance of 809 miles is obtained. This is based upon inclusion of a penalty of 15% added to the intermodal carriers' costs to adjust for the service inferiority, the 15% representing a value often cited as representative of the value of this (e.g., Smith et al., 1989, 52). The truck cost would be, for a haul of x miles, $100 + 1.25x$, and the intermodal cost would be $1.15 ($400 + 0.70x$). Equating and solving for x yields

$$x = (1.15(400) - 100)/(1.25 - 1.15(0.70)) = 809 \text{ miles},$$

in the range of break-even distances given earlier.

When intermodal services were first initiated, the break-even distance was considerably less. Just prior to opening the Interstate System, many intermodal services were operated at distances as short as 200 miles. But the advent of the Interstate System, and concomitant advances in the design of trucks and trucking operations have worked to reduce the costs of trucking and simultaneously to improve service quality. While in the same period there have also been improvements to intermodal service, in general the gains in trucking have outpaced those in intermodal and as a result the break-even distance has increased to the values indicated previously.

3.1 Recent trends in technology and organization. In order to successfully compete with trucking over larger distances, there have been a number of changes to intermodal service in the last two decades; all have been significant.

One major change has been in the technology of rail equipment and track structure, motivated by a desire to improve ride quality, thus reducing loss and damage to cargo and also reducing the line-haul cost of rail movement. Specifically, in recent years railroads have placed in service equipment that is specifically designed for carrying truck trailers and containers. In most cases this equipment has been of the so-called articulated design, wherein adjacent platforms or rail cars are semi-permanently coupled together and share common wheel assemblies, reducing the weight and complexity of the units and also reducing the slack between cars which can be a source of jerking and banging, and hence of cargo damage, in train movement. This equipment is also less expensive to purchase and maintain, and reduces track wear and maintenance costs. Aerodynamic properties are also improved, reducing fuel and train operating costs.

Another major change has been to concentrate traffic at a fewer terminals and to operate dedicated intermodal trains between these. This densification of traffic has led to economies in terminal operation by virtue of enabling more highly automated equipment to be used. The use of dedicated trains has meant that the transit time of cars between terminals has been reduced, primarily because these trains make few if any intermediate stops. This has also reduced loss and damage to cargo since cars need not be removed or added to trains enroute, and thus intermodal trains avoid the classification yards used by regular freight trains. The use of dedicated trains has also facilitated their operation on a strict schedule, often rivaling or bettering that of passenger trains, improving both the overall travel time characteristics of intermodal and its reliability.

A third important change has been to reduce the costs of some of the very labor intensive portions of intermodal service by out-sourcing or contracting. Almost all railroads have turned over a sizeable portion of the sales or retailing effort for intermodal to third parties, termed intermodal retailers, who act as brokers in arranging for movements. While there are many pros and cons for this, primary motivations were to obtain nation-wide sales forces and also to obtain marketing services that were more responsive to the needs of shippers.

The other service that was out-sourced was that of the drayage or truck movement of trailers to and from the intermodal terminals, and this is now largely done by relatively small competitive trucking firms whose costs are considerably below the historic cost levels of railroad trucking (drayage) subsidiaries. These changes have resulted in a relationship between the railroad and the shipper which is at least one step removed, as shown in Figure 5.

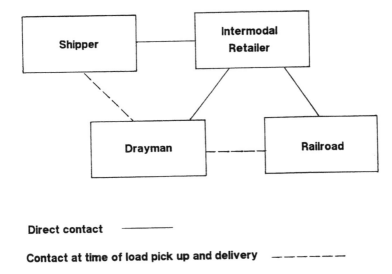

Direct contact ————————

Contact at time of load pick up and delivery — — — — — —

**Figure 5.   Relationship between Railroads, Shippers, Draymen,
and Retailers in Intermodal Service.**

While it has undoubtedly reduced the cost of these activities, this, along with the use of intermodal retailers, has two disadvantages. One is loss of contact with the shippers and consignees--the customers of the service. The second is fragmentation of responsibility for providing the service, this being split between the retailers, the draymen, and the railroads.

Despite the many trade-offs involved the net effect of all these changes has undoubtedly been positive. Unfortunately data on domestic intermodal trailer-on-flat-car (TOFC) and container-on-flat-car (COFC) services as a whole are not available, as this service is typically grouped with the carriage of international containers which are forwarded by rail to and from inland locations. Nevertheless, the data in Table 1 are indicative of the growth of intermodal, which as a whole has grown by a factor of over 100% in just the last decade.

Table 1. Growth of U.S. intermodal rail service.

Year	Total Trailers and Containers Carried (10^6)
1980	3.06
1981	3.15
1982	3.40
1983	4.09
1984	4.57
1985	4.59
1986	5.00
1987	5.50
1988	5.78
1989	5.99
1990	6.21

Source: Association of American Railroads (1992), 26.

3.2   Need for change. Despite the recent success of intermodal, there is ample evidence that there is considerable need for improvement if it is to capture a much larger share of freight movement. At present, it has been estimated that intermodal carries approximately 10% of the intercity merchandise cargo that is moving at distances over 500 miles (McKenzie, et al., 1989, 224). Thus its market share is very small in the high value cargo market for which it was intended.

There are numerous reasons for this that have been revealed by many recent studies probing shippers' views of intermodal. All seem to point to essentially the same features. Table 2 presents these, as they were described in a recent study survey of shippers undertaken by Temple, Barker and Sloane (1989). This table reports the percentage of shippers surveyed who cite each of the eleven reasons why they currently do not use intermodal.

Table 2. Reasons shippers cite for not using intermodal rail-truck service.

Reasons	% Shipper citing reason
1. Transit Time Not Competitive with Truck	62%
2. Service Not Available	45%
3. Fragmented Responsibility	43%
4. Undesirable Equipment	28%
5. Unreliable Equipment	25%
6. Lack of Information System	25%
7. Poor Customer Service	23%
8. Damage Problems	22%
9. Claims Problems	21%
10. Price To High	19%
11. Billing Problems	11%

Source: Temple, Barker, and Sloane (1989).

The most commonly cited reason is that intermodal transit time is not competitive with truck. This is not surprising given the typical intermodal service of one train per day in each direction (although over longer distances the higher cruise speed potential of rail could and sometimes does overcome this limitation). Another factor underlying this is the fragmentation of responsibility and control for intermodal movements described above. Compounding the effect of the fragmentation are the significant delays which are common between the time when the truck arrives at the destination terminal and when it is picked up by the draymen for delivery. The next most frequently cited reason is that the service is not available, and this reflects both the limited number of points between which intermodal service is operated and its absence from most shorter distance markets in which the majority of truck traffic moves. Interestingly, the third most frequently cited reason was the fragmented responsibility for the service. The difficulty associated with damage and loss problems was also cited, but less frequently. While fragmented responsibility is separately cited, it clearly is a major factor underlying items numbered 6 through 9 and item number 11 in the survey.

Cited by about a quarter of the shippers were undesirable equipment and unreliable equipment. This undoubtedly is partly due to many railroads' reluctance to invest in intermodal, traceable to a long-standing feeling by many analysts that intermodal profits have been low. Also, there is much uncertainty as to what particular equipment technologies will be desirable and needed in the future, a reflection of the fast pace of technological change. Interestingly about one fifth of the shippers indicated that the price of intermodal was too high. One interpretation of this is, of course, that the service disadvantages often found in intermodal are not sufficiently offset by price savings relative to trucking.

4. Analysis of Drayage System

The preceding discussion of shipper perceptions of intermodal service points rather clearly to drayage being a primary source of problems with the service quality of intermodal service. Given the reliable and fast dedicated train service, drayage is the primary source of both long transit times and transit time unreliability. Also, drayage accounts for a very disproportionate share of cost -- 36% on an 800 mile haul, using the values presented earlier, for example. Thus if the break-even distance with trucking is to be reduced, enabling intermodal to compete in the shorter distance markets where the largest truckload volumes are found, the cost of drayage must be reduced. This will also benefit all intermodal service by increasing profitability in the longer distance markets where most current traffic is located.

The question addressed in the analysis was whether or not drayage costs can be reduced while level of service can be improved. The basis for the expectation that this would be possible was that the current drayage operation is very fragmented. This can lead to a situation in which one draymen, working for one intermodal retailer, could be moving an empty trailer from the terminal to a shipper while at the same time another drayman is pulling an empty trailer back to the terminal from a consignee next door to that shipper. With typically a dozen or more retailers and an equal number of drayage companies serving each terminal, this is not surprising. As shown in Figure 6(a), if these movements were of the "stay-with" type, then this would result in almost twice as much tractor time (and mileage) as with an integrated operation in which the trailer emptied at consignee A is repositioned to shipper B, loaded, and then taken to the terminal. With "drop and pick" operation initially, for which a coordinated

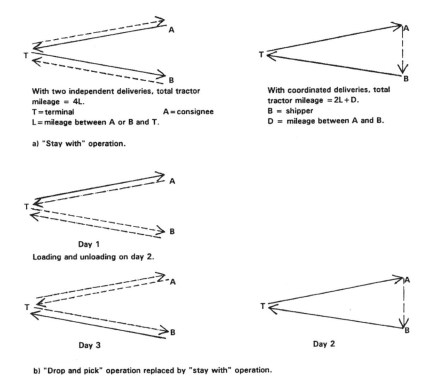

a) "Stay with" operation.

b) "Drop and pick" operation replaced by "stay with" operation.

Figure 6. Examples of Inefficient fragmented Operations and Gains
to be made from Coordination.

"stay with" operation is substituted, as in Figure 6(b), the gains can be even greater, a reduction from 8L tractor-miles to 2L+ D tractor-miles. The same gain could be achieved with a coordinated "drop and pick" operation, wherein trailers in addition to the two in the initial situation are moved by the tractors while the one(s) in this example are being loaded and unloaded. Thus even if each drayman or retailer tried to optimize its own operation--as they undoubtedly do--many if not most opportunities for improvement would not present themselves to the individual firm.

Improving this situation is essentially a problem in creating and using the right information and then changing the working relationship between the various actors so that the information can be acted upon. Specifically, the drayage associated with an entire terminal could be viewed as a system, and the drayage operation planned so as to meet the demands and service requirements at a minimum cost. While doing so the service requirements could be tightened so as to provide more truck-competitive service.

The basic idea, then, would be to ascertain each day the demands to be met in the form of loaded trailers to be moved, either to the terminal from shippers or from the terminal to consignees, and of empty trailers to be spotted for loading or to be removed after unloading. Tractors and drivers would be assigned to these tasks considering the totality of work to be done, so as to minimize total cost. Simultaneously the optimal movements of empty trailers, including repositioning from consignees to shippers, would be determined and tractors assigned. This would be done by bringing together data on all the demands to be met, and by applying an appropriate tractor-trailer scheduling procedure to the problem. Draymen would then follow this master plan in effecting the movements.

4.1 Modeling and analysis. The approach to answering the questions about the possible gains from centralized drayage operations planning was to model what would happen if this were done at one intermodal terminal in the Conrail system. The reasons for focusing on only one terminal was that obtaining information on the actual demands was difficult and time consuming, due to the fragmented nature of the industry. Furthermore, in the judgement of the management of Conrail, terminals are not so different that gains in one from the changes envisioned would be unexpected at other terminals.

The overall approach, then, is as shown in Figure 7. Both the cost of the current decentralized drayage and a centralized system would have to be estimated. Fortunately both the point-to-point rates charged currently by draymen and other costs are known.

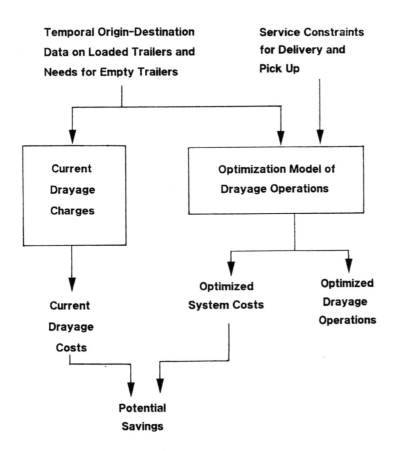

Figure 7.   Overall Approach to estimating the Gains from Centralized
             Drayage Operations Planning.

The case study used for the analysis was based on the actual drayage operation for the Conrail intermodal terminal in Morrisville, Pa., for the period February 26 through March 5, 1989. In this period 330 loaded trailers were moved between the terminal and consignees or shippers during the eight-day period. There was considerable directional imbalance of traffic: 215 trailer loads arrived by rail for delivery, but only 115 loads were to be picked up from shippers for outbound movement on rail. The relevant transportation, traffic volume and cost data were collected and used as the data input for the analysis.

The drayage transportation network consisted of 15 nodes, an intermodal terminal and 14 consignee/shipper areas. Each area represented a set of consignee/shipper zip code zones that were in close proximity to one another and had similar prices for drayage. Distances for drayage from or to the terminal ranged from a few miles to about 100 miles.

The cost of the current drayage operation was calculated based on current charges of draymen. Rates have been published, for specific cities, for both the "stay with" and "drop and pick" type of operations. However, these data did not cover all of the places in the demand set. Therefore we developed regression equations for estimating charges, based on mileage travelled, and these explained the price data very well. Therefore these were used to estimate current drayage prices to all places in our data set. The equations, along with the r^2 statistics on goodness of fit, are:

Stay with: $c = 103.1 + 1.215d, \ r^2 = .90$ (4)

Drop and pick: $c = 75.51 = 1.730d, \ r^2 = .86$ (5)

where c is drayage change and d is the distance between the terminal and the shipper or consignee.

With this we were then able to estimate the cost of drayage under the current system. This was from \$72,383 to \$78,604, the range reflecting the all "stay with" vs all "drop pick" movement. The actual value was between these, as there is an unknown mix of the two types of operations. A mid-range value of \$75,500 was used for later comparisons.

The cost of centralized drayage operations planning (CDOP) had to be approached in an entirely different way, although of course the demands (for loaded trailer movements) remain unchanged. This plan (CDOP) envisions that there is centralized control and management of the drayage operation wherein the trailers are moved according to an operating plan developed for the entire terminal service area. The draymen are paid for individual tractor and tractor-trailer activities, on a piece-work basis. The piece-work rates were based upon the "stay with" rates, and accounted for differences in the cost of different operations. For example, the rates for loaded movements are set at a higher level to account for the fact that more time is associated with moving a loaded trailer (i.e., additional time is spent handling documents). We assumed that the truckers are paid for:

- one-way loaded and empty trailer movements between the terminal and an area,
- tractor idling at areas during or between assignments,
- empty tractor-trailer repositioning, and
- tractor bob-tailing between areas.

Critical to costing this option is the determination of the specific tractor and trailer movements to be made each day. This was accomplished by use of an optimization model that determined these so as to minimize the drayage cost subject to meeting the demands and service requirements. The model is an integer linear programming model which has the major elements portrayed in Figure 8.

Minimize total drayage tractor ownership and operating costs, by selecting trailer movement times and locations and assigning tractors to those movements

Subject to:

Delivering all inbound loaded trailers from terminal to consignees within specified time constraints

Delivering empty trailers to shippers for loading within specified time constraints

Picking up outbound loaded trailers within specified time constraints and delivering to terminal

Repositioning trailers as they are emptied so as to avoid accumulation

---

Figure 8.   Structure of Integer Linear Programming Model for Optimizing Drayage Movements and Trailer Repositioning

The specific equations are not presented here, but can be found in Morlok, Hallowell, Spasovic and Sammon (1990, 12-30). Solving such a model is usually quite difficult, and this model was no exception. But since that aspect of the work is not germane to this presentation, it will not be covered here.

The model results were that the required drayage could be performed for $42,574, or about $43,000. This value assumes distance based payments to the drayman, following their current price levels. Thus the estimated overall cost is 43% less than the current operation.

Very stringent level of service requirement were applied, namely that each inbound loaded trailer had to be delivered within one day of arrival, and that each outbound shipment had to be picked up within one day of availability. These periods are much shorter than currently achieved. Data on actual operations revealed that inbound trailers remained at the terminal awaiting delivery for an average of 2.3 days, with a standard deviation of 1.8 days. Approximately 33% of those trailers were dispatched within 24 hours of arrival and 98% were removed within four days. Delivery to the consignee would normally be within a few hours of removal, given the distances involved. No similar data were available on pick-ups, but interviews with drayage companies revealed that most pick-ups were arranged one or more days in advance.

Considering the fact that any model is a simplification of reality, and that data limitations required many assumptions, it was concluded by a combination of Conrail and university personnel that a reasonable target would be a 30% reduction in drayage costs. The more important considerations were:

-   While the model imposes an overall level of service superior
    to that currently achieved, it assumes that, when stay-with
    drayage is used, the precise delivery time during the day can be
    negotiated with the customer. In reality some customers may
    require specific times that lead to less complete utilization of
    tractors. Of course, for drop and pick operation, the actual
    time of loading or unloading within the period when the trailer
    is on the customer's premises is irrelevant to the drayage
    operation.

-   Some customers, or third parties, might insist on being served
    by a particular drayage firm, or drayman, and thereby may
    preclude certain pairings of different drayage tasks.

- The model had perfect knowledge of the loaded trailer movements and empty trailer requests each day. For inbound loads the train consist (known at least 24 hours in advance) provides this, but only those outbound loads requiring placement of an empty trailer would necessarily yield many hours of advance notice.

4.2   Interpretation of model results. The gains estimated from CDOP arise from centralized operations planning that makes use of information that now exists but that is dispersed among many independent disconnected units

- the railroad, on trailer arrivals by rail
- the draymen, on the timing of movements and the location of trailers in the field
- the intermodal retailers, on shipper demands for empty trailers and time commitments for pick-ups and deliveries of loaded trailers.

To achieve the gains envisioned all this information must be brought together and operating decisions made considering all trailer movements that must be accomplished. This must be done on at least a daily basis.

The relationships envisioned between the parties are shown in Figure 9. The institutional home of the CDOP is deliberately not specified, as this could be an independent entity, a part of the railroad's intermodal organization, an undertaking of a consortium of retailers or drayman, or jointly by both, or done by a single retailer or drayman on behalf of the others. Obviously such a partnership will require a high level of compatibility of goals and ways of doing business among the parties, and a high degree of mutual trust.

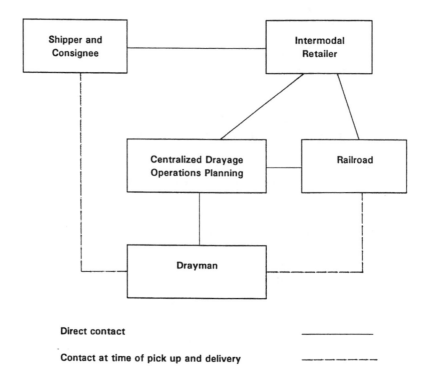

Direct contact

Contact at time of pick up and delivery

**Figure 9.   Revised Relationships among Parties with
                Centralized Drayage Operations Planning.**

Source: Morlok and Sammon (1990), p.5.

Numerous impediments to creating the type of system envisioned exist. One is the change in relationships between the parties, especially between the individual intermodal retailers (IMRs) and the draymen, who are now quite competitive within their respective groups. Also, the basis of payment for services provided will have to be rationalized. Presently there is considerable variation in the profitability of different drayage moves, those to some areas being highly desirable and profitable and other not so. This is due to such factors as payment essentially on a mileage basis even though costs are incurred largely on the basis of time expended, peculiarities of only partial reimbursement for tolls and other fees that vary with the specific move, hidden or only partly compensated movements in connection with some moves (e.g., the required return trip to pick-up the trailer in the case of a "drop and pick" assignment), among others. Now IMRs try to assign jobs so as to spread the desirable and undesirable movements among the drayage firms and drivers, mindful of seniority, cooperation shown, etc. All this must be changed in order to make the concept of centralized planning of drayage operations acceptable to the three parties involved in producing intermodal service.

However, the benefits from doing so are clearly substantial. Not only will this improve the service in the markets that intermodal now serves, but by reducing the threshold (not distance-related) cost of the service and improving its quality, the breakeven distance will be reduced substantially so that intermodal can compete in the largest truckload markets. To illustrate the leverage that reducing drayage costs and increasing service quality can have, consider their impact on the breakeven distance of 809 miles calculated earlier. If the drayage cost of $300 ($400 less typical values of $50 for sales and $50 for terminal activity) is reduced by 30%, it would be $310. If the improved quality reduced the service inferiority adjustment premium (.15) by half (to .075), then the breakeven distance is reduced to

$$(1.075(310) - 100)/(1.25 - (1.075)(0.70)) = 468 \text{ miles}$$

The breakeven distance is reduced to about half its previous value, more precisely, a reduction of 42%. While all the caveats mentioned earlier about the applicability of this to specific commodities and conditions still apply, it nevertheless indicates very persuasively the leverage of improvements in drayage have on the ability of intermodal to compete across major intercity trucking markets. A comparable reduction (30%) in any other costs element produces a much smaller reduction in the breakeven distance. Moreover, considering the improvements in cost or performance that have been made in the other major cost center (sales, terminals, and line haul), no means of creating a 30% cost reduction is foreseeable. Indeed, the only real prospect is the use of double-stack containers, and line haul savings of about 20% per container (load) have been reported, but against this must be weighed the cost of separate road chassis assemblies and the need for a unique fleet. But double-stack rates are typically less than trailer-on-flat-car rates, by 5 to 10% (Smith, 1990), reflecting differences such as lower capacities and more difficult loading. Incorporating both these adjustments leads to a breakeven distance of

$$((1.20(400) - 100)/(1.25 - (1.20)(0.70)(0.80)) = 657 \text{ miles}$$

only 19% less than the current estimate of 809 miles. Thus drayage improvements are clearly the key, substantially reducing the breakeven distance and thereby enlarging the intermodal market.

5. Conclusions

Intermodal service suffers from both productivity and quality problems, particularly in drayage. An especially promising approach to improvement is to reorganize the way the different players that combine to provide intermodal service relate to one another and perform various tasks. The potential exists for major and simultaneous improvements in both productivity and service quality in drayage, and hence in the overall intermodal transportation service. This is critical to intermodal becoming an effective alternative to over-the-road trucking over the spectrum of intercity markets.

References

Association of American Railroads (1992). *Railroad Facts* (A.A.R., Washington, D.C.).

Davis S., and B. Davidson (1991). *2020 Vision* (Simon & Schuster, New York, NY).

Keaton M.J. (1991). "Service-cost tradeoffs for carload freight traffic in the U.S. rail industry," Transportation Research, 25A(6), 363-374.

McGinnes M.A. (1990). "The relative importance of cost and service in freight transportation choice: before and after deregulation," Transportation Journal, 30(1), 12-19.

McKenzie D.R., M.C. North, and D.S. Smith (1989). *Intermodal Transportation-The Whole Story* (Simmons-Boardman, Omaha, NE).

Morlok, E.K. (1979). *Introduction to Transportation Engineering and Planning* (McGraw-Hill, New York, NY).

Morlok E.K., S.F. Hallowell, L.N. Spasovic, and J.P. Sammon (1990). *Studies in Intermodal Freight Transport Service Planning*, vol. 1. Final Report to U.S. Department of Transportation and Conrail, NTIS No. PB91-226993 (National Technical Information Services, Springfield, VA).

Morlok E.K., and J.P. Sammon (1990). "Summary of Results of University of Pennsylvania Research into Improving Service Quality and Reducing Costs in Intermodal Drayage Operations," University of Pennsylvania and Conrail (Philadelphia, PA).

Muller G. (1989). *Intermodal Freight Transportation* (Eno Foundation, Westport, CT).

Smith D.S., et al. (1988). *Double-Stack Container Systems: Implication for U.S. Railroads and Ports* Final Report to U.S. Department of Transportation by Manalytics, Inc. and others (San Francisco, CA).

Temple, Barker, and Sloane, Inc. (1989). "Shipper perceptions of intermodal," paper presented to the Intermodal Marketing Association, Maui, HI, February.

Chapter 16   Politics, Markets, and Equality in Schools

John E. Chubb and Terry M. Moe

American education can be said to have two basic problems. The first is that students generally achieve too little. According to the National Assessment of Educational Progress, the typical American high school student possesses only middle school knowledge and skills. According to the International Assessment of Educational Progress, the typical middle school student does not rank in the top ten in mathematics or science when compared with thirteen year olds around the world. This problem—call it a problem of efficiency—is compounded by a second problem, a problem of equality. Students differ too much in what they achieve, with poor, black and Hispanic students too often at the bottom. The United States sends a higher percentage of its students to college than most nations, and the best American students are as accomplished as any in the world. Yet, a fifth of all big city students fail to finish high school, roughly twice the national average. And despite considerable progress, black students trail white students by nearly 200 points on the SAT.

In a recent book, *Politics, Markets, and America's Schools* (Chubb and Moe, 1990), we proposed a reform to attack these problems fundamentally. We outlined a new system of public education based on market principles and implemented through a mechanism that is now usually called school choice. In essence, parents would be entitled to send their children to any school of their choice, at public expense, and schools would be encouraged to improve through competition with other schools for enrollment.

P. T. Harker (ed.), The Service Productivity and Quality Challenge, 435–469.

The reasoning behind this proposal was derived from our analysis of public and private education. Public schools are failing, we argued, because of the institutions that govern them. Driven by politics, institutions of direct democratic control—school boards and district offices, state legislatures, the U.S. Congress, and their respective education departments—work to overwhelm public schools with bureaucracy and rob public schools of the autonomy that is the foundation for effective organization and performance. Market institutions, which control private schools, do the opposite. Bureaucracy has little place in a competitive environment that places a premium on responding to family needs and organizing to produce superior educational results. If the United States wants different—and better—public schools, it will need to control them with different institutions. The institutions that control public schools today, directly and from the top down, should have their authority severely limited, and new institutions that would control schools indirectly and from the bottom up—market institutions of choice and competition—should operate in their place.

The benefits of institutional reform, we argued, would include not only greater effectiveness or efficiency but greater educational equality as well. Urban schools, attended disproportionately by poor and minority students and burdened disproportionately by politics and bureaucracy, are the schools most likely to change in an environment of school autonomy and parental choice. Flush with resources once consumed by oversized district offices and powers once exercised by unknowledgeable and distant authorities, urban schools should find their opportunities for innovation especially enhanced. Because of the density and diversity of city populations, urban families should find their selection of schools especially wide. Poor families would also gain effective access to a right—the right to choose their children's schools—that more affluent families have always exercised through residential decisions (or by opting for private schools) but that poor families have never been able to afford to use.

Still, we argued, equality requires more support than markets alone can provide. We therefore recommended an institutional structure in which market forces are carefully regulated. Our proposal, after all, was for a public system of educational choice—fully funded by the government and operated according to ground rules established by the government. Among them: Parents may not top off their public scholarship with private funds and thereby choose a more expensive education. Schools may not completely control their admissions, as every school is required to accept some students it would not admit voluntarily. And all parents, but especially poor parents, are to be assisted by public authorities in finding, evaluating, and applying to schools. We proposed, we thought, a system that would revolutionize public education and increase educational opportunity for all.

To judge from what our critics have said, however, our thinking was at least half wrong. Yes, a system of choice might reduce bureaucracy, enhance school autonomy, and strengthen the role of parents. It might even stimulate enough reorganization, innovation, and rededication within schools to nudge the average level of achievement across the nation upward. But whatever it might do in these regards, it would certainly do at too high a price, for it would certainly exacerbate inequality.

In a system of school choice, critics argue, some parents would inevitably be better choosers than others. Schools would inevitably prefer to admit the easy-to-educate over children who misbehave or have learning disabilities. Children with advantages, of parenting or of nature, would fill up the good schools while disadvantaged children would be left behind in bad schools made even worse by the departure of the ablest students. White families would, of course, flee black and Hispanic families, and some black families would choose Afrocentric schools with dubious academic curricula. The rich would get richer, the poor would get poorer, and the shameful days of school segregation would return.

Of course, we disagree with this assessment. But in fairness to our critics, we must admit that our book was principally about efficiency or effectiveness, about the roots of poor performance in schools. We were concerned with issues of equality too, and we tried to address them adequately. Still, our analysis focused on efficiency. It traced the effect of schools on children—all children—to school organization, to the administrative environment that shapes the organization, and finally, to the institutions that determine how schools will be administered or controlled. Our empirical analysis did not examine in any depth or detail the distribution of student achievement or the causes of inequality. Perhaps most importantly, our analysis did not compare educational equality under political and market conditions.

Now we would like to do just that. Specifically, we want to understand better what schools and school systems do to ameliorate inequality or to bring it about, and we want to consider whether political or market institutions are likely to differ on these scores. To help us, we have been analyzing a new longitudinal study of schools, students, and families—The National Educational Longitudinal Study, 1988 (or NELS:88)—which follows a national sample of approximately 25,000 students in roughly 1,000 schools from eighth grade in 1988 through tenth grade in 1990. The study uses many of the same survey items as High School and Beyond and the Administrator and Teacher Survey, which provided the data for *Politics, Markets and America's Schools*. NELS:88 is therefore especially appropriate for this follow-up research.

Here we want to summarize in a non-technical way the results of our first cut into these new data and our first effort to think comprehensively about educational equality. (The technical results, too extensive for this volume, are available on request.) We divide our discussion into two logical parts: equality within schools and equality between schools. When you get right down to it, educational inequality has two basic sources in schooling—the different treatment of children within schools and the different treatment of children by different schools. Either way, if the treatment differs in quality, educational inequality will be produced. Political and market institutions, we find, are not similarly prone to produce such differences. Suffice it to say that this analysis finds little evidence that political institutions are better at promoting educational equality than market institutions are. Indeed, our preliminary results go consistently the other way.

1 . Some Equality Standards

Before we consider how alternative institutions affect educational equality, we need to be clear what we mean by equality. We need to establish some equality standards against which institutions can be judged. Of course, this is no straightforward task. Equality can be defined in many different ways, and alternative conceptions of equality are regularly debated by democratic theorists, economists, and politicians—to name only some of the main contestants. We shall not venture any comprehensive definition of this complex concept but rather a set of standards that, taken together, form a loose hierarchy that builds from weaker forms of equality to stronger.

At the base of this hierarchy is the standard of non-discrimination: Students should not be denied access to schools or programs within schools because of their race, ethnic background, sex, or economic class. This does not mean that all schools and programs will have representative distributions of blacks and whites, rich and poor, and so forth. This is not a standard of affirmative action. The standard simply says that race, sex, and class shall not be explicit or—more likely—implicit criteria for access to education. For example, a black child might still be excluded from an accelerated math program because his test scores are low, but he would not be excluded because, regardless of test scores, schools believe black children do not excel at math: the latter would constitute discrimination. In the analysis that follows, we focus on race and class discrimination because these are the lines along which American society is most sharply and permanently divided educationally and, in some consequence, politically and economically. Of course, racial discrimination is also unconstitutional in all public schools and in all private schools that want tax-exempt status—which means all but a handful.

Next up the hierarchy is the standard of <u>separate but equal</u>. In a non-discriminating world, children of different racial, ethnic, and economic backgrounds are nevertheless going to end up in different schools and programs. Kids attend public schools in their neighborhoods and private schools of their choosing; they are not assigned to schools randomly. Within schools, kids choose different classes and programs. In addition, some kids qualify for gifted and talented programs, some for remedial programs, and some for nothing special at all. If children from different backgrounds are to have the chance to make equal educational gains, the disparate schools, programs, and classes in which they find themselves must provide equally good educational experiences. This means that the heavily minority urban school and the predominantly white suburban school must be places of similar quality, by whatever measures are relevant. It also means that the gifted and talented program, overpopulated with rich kids, and the remedial program, home to so many poor kids, must be equally well-suited to helping their respective groups of children work up to their potential.

A tougher standard than separate but equal is what we call <u>equal opportunity</u>. If we envision a society in which children from different racial and economic backgrounds do not differ radically in high school and college graduation rates or in academic achievement, it may be inadequate merely to accept well-qualified black children in college prep programs—for their test scores are too often too low—or to ensure that the remedial classes poor children take are truly excellent—for they will never be as good as the advanced placement classes rich children take. If we are serious about equalizing educational outcomes, it may be necessary to expand the availability of the best educational opportunities and to ensure maximum feasible participation in them. This means that more children, of all backgrounds, will take high level classes and follow the college track through high school. It also means that students of differing backgrounds—racial, economic, <u>and</u> academic—will attend classes together. Schools will be less likely to segregate kids by ability, since the opportunities are inherently limited for kids placed in slow groups. Schools will be more likely to operate heterogeneous classes where swifter and slower children work side by side or even together. This arrangement not only expands educational opportunity, it increases the interaction of children from different backgrounds. It satisfies a standard that might also be called equal, not separate.

Satisfying even a tough opportunity standard, however, does not guarantee any reduction in the education gap that divides American society. The next standard begins to. Following Amy Gutmann, we call it the quality threshold (Gutmann 1987). This standard of equality says that schools and school systems will ensure that the education of no child falls below a threshold necessary to participate effectively as a citizen. What this means precisely is open to debate. But what it means generally is that every child will leave school able to read, write, calculate, solve moderately complex problems, think about public affairs, and hold a job sufficient to avoid public dependence. It means at least a good high school education. This standard does not mean that there will not be huge gaps in ultimate educational attainment; some students will inevitably want more education than others—a Ph.D., an M.D., a J.D.—and not all students will be equally able at academics. But this standard is about more than opportunity. It judges schools by how its weakest or most disadvantaged students actually turn out.

The final and toughest standard is also about outcomes, but about outcomes for all. We call it equal outcomes. This standard says that if we are truly concerned about the wide disparity in academic achievement that follows class and racial lines, we ought to evaluate schools and school systems by the job they do in reducing this disparity. Take two schools that begin with similar distributions of children—equal numbers of slow, average, and bright children in each school. Then look at the distribution of academic achievement within each school when the children graduate. The school that is doing the better job for educational equality is the one with the tighter distribution, with the narrower gap between bright and slow. That school is providing more equal outcomes.

A school that provides equal outcomes, however, should not sacrifice educational excellence to do so. The education problems that the United States must address are twofold—problems of equality and of efficiency. A school that provides equal outcomes could conceivably do so by holding down the achievement of the brightest students. Its distribution of achievement might then be narrow, but its average level of achievement might be quite low. The same problem might occur if a school placed too many poorly prepared children in an advanced classroom; well-prepared students might be held back. In the analysis that follows we will be asking in various ways how schools measure up to our five standards of equality, but we will also be paying attention to their average level of performance—their effectiveness or efficiency.

2. Equality Within Schools

Critics of school choice have focused most of their attention on the disparities a marketplace might create from one school to the next. Yet critics of educational inequality more generally have focused as much or more attention on the disparities that exist within individual schools.[1] A school can create or exacerbate inequality in many ways. It can discriminate against children of certain races or ethnic backgrounds in assigning children to instructional groups or curriculum tracks. It can assign children to classes in a nondiscriminatory fashion—based on test scores, for example—yet provide instruction of widely varying quality to different tracks or groups. Even if organized objectively, groups or tracks may separate children of different class or racial backgrounds so thoroughly that a school can become effectively segregated internally. In addition, a school may so limit the size of its high group or college track, that all but the brightest children are denied educational opportunity.

Grouping and tracking are widespread practices in American education, so it is only reasonable to ask whether they contribute to the wide variation in student performance. As critics of these practices often point out, there is more variation in student achievement within American schools than there is on average between schools. It is no wonder, then, that the study of educational inequality has probably produced more research on grouping and tracking than on disparities between schools.[2] We, too, think that grouping and tracking practices deserve careful attention. But we think that existing research on the subject is deficient in one major respect. It has scarcely considered the roots of the practices to which so many critics strongly object. Could it be that the patterns of grouping and tracking found in public schools today are rooted in the institutional structure of which the schools are a part? Could it be that grouping and tracking, like other qualities of school organization that we have studied before, are institutionally determined?

[1]For a critical introduction to the literature on ability grouping and tracking, see Oakes (1985).
[2]For a brief review of the research literature on grouping and tracking, see Gamoran and DeMare (1989).

That is our suspicion. But existing research provides few clues whether we are right. The problem is that research into the effects of tracking and grouping looks mostly at public schools, which are all governed by institutions of the same basic form.[3] If we want to know whether these important organizational practices are influenced by how schools are governed or controlled, we must consider how schools that are controlled differently deal with student diversity, too. From an institutional standpoint, the schools that differ most from public schools are private schools. Despite their enormous diversity—from secular independent schools connected to no larger entity to religious schools sometimes part of sizable systems—private schools differ from public schools fundamentally: Private schools are not controlled directly, from the top down, by democratic authorities; they are controlled indirectly, from the bottom up, by market forces.

In the analysis that follows, we compare the grouping and tracking practices of public and private schools. Such a comparison cannot tell us everything we might need to know to predict how a system of school choice would affect inequality within schools. Private education today serves only 12 percent of America's children and provides only a quarter of the country's schools. If all children and schools participated in a public educational marketplace, matters might be somewhat different than they are in private education now. Nevertheless, the best evidence we can possibly have of how schools would manage student diversity in a marketplace is to compare schools that are doing so now to schools that are managing subject to political control.

2.1 Diversity within schools. Generally speaking, schools are more likely to separate children into ability groups or curriculum tracks if the children in the school differ substantially in their prior achievement or capacity to learn. Schools run a greater risk of reinforcing or worsening inequality if their students are unequal to begin with. It is generally easier for schools to integrate children if the differences among them are not large.

Public schools might be expected to face more student diversity than private schools do because public schools typically enroll all children in a neighborhood, regardless of background, while private schools enroll children interested in education of a particular type. This expectation must be tempered, however, by the fact that choice operates in the public sector, too. Families base their residential choices on, among other things, the quality of neighborhood public

[3]An important exception to this generalization is research into the egalitarian practices of Catholic schools, especially Coleman and Hoffer (1987), Lee and Bryk (1988), Bryk, Lee, and Holland (1993), and Camarena (1990).

schools and the cost of housing. This choice process sorts children into public schools by economic class and educational taste, much as an analogous choice process sorts children into private schools. It is an empirical question, then, whether public schools or private schools face more internal diversity.

In our analysis we measured the diversity that typical public schools and private schools must manage.[4] We calculated the average standard deviation of public and private eighth graders on a number of dimensions of educational inequality. What we found is that the average public school does face more diversity than the average private school, but not dramatically more. On average, student bodies are 10 to 15 percent less diverse in private schools than in public schools. This means, for example, that in a public school, a lower class student is somewhat more likely to be around a middle class student, or that a student living with two married parents is somewhat more likely to interact with a student living with a single mother. The biggest difference between public and private schools is in parent income, where there is 25 percent less diversity in private schools, presumably because most every parent in a private school must be able to afford the same tuition—high, low, or in between. A publicly funded system of school choice might reduce this source of homogeneity because ability-to-pay would not limit access to schools.

Interestingly, the dimension along which there is nearly the least difference between public and private schools is academic achievement. Students were given standardized tests in four subjects: reading, mathematics, history, and science. In our analysis we considered the average standard deviations within schools of math scores—because math is where ability grouping most often takes place—and combined scores. Basically, private schools are only slightly more homogeneous academically than public schools. Pending further analysis, we cannot say whether private schools have less internal inequality in student achievement because they admit slightly more homogeneous student bodies or because they better organize themselves to reduce academic inequality. The important point at this juncture is that private schools, by virtue of the control they exercise over admission, face less diversity than public schools face, but not dramatically less. Residential sorting in the public sector is evidently rather powerful because public and private schools have fairly similar student bodies, as measured by a number of gauges of diversity.

This similarity can be seen in yet another way. We examined the distribution of public and private schools by the percentage of black students in

[4] A data appendix describing the variables used in this paper is available from the authors, on request.

their eighth grades. What that examination revealed is that the overwhelming majority of public and private schools are almost completely white—only 0 to 2 percent black. There are more private schools than public schools in this category, to be sure. But when we consider schools that are not homogeneously white—say, enrolling 3 percent black or more—public and private schools are similarly distributed. In each sector such schools range fairly evenly from minority black to majority black enrollments.

2.2   Ability   grouping. The primary way by which schools have long managed student diversity is to group children homogeneously by ability. This practice is said to facilitate instruction, as teachers can concentrate on material at one level of difficulty without worrying that the material is too hard for some or too unchallenging for others. Homogeneous grouping is also criticized for locking kids into achievement tracks that diverge unnecessarily. Children in the slower groups in elementary school are said to never catch up with the children in the higher groups because the instruction in the slower groups is simply not as ambitious or effective as that in the higher groups. Children in the slower groups are said to feel stigmatized by their placement. Rarely, critics say, do these children ever escape their low groups and enter a college prep track in high school.[5]

Slower children are better off, critics of grouping argue, in heterogeneous classrooms and ability groups where they work side-by-side with swifter children on a common curriculum, only at a slightly slower pace. Instructional techniques such as "cooperative learning" are supposed to make it possible for slower children to succeed in heterogeneous groups and for swifter children to progress just as fast as they would in a homogeneous, accelerated group. Research on these claims is still far from definitive. And the effects of grouping, whether homogeneous or heterogeneous, depend on the particular ways in which grouping is implemented. For example, the inequality that homgeneous grouping may perpetuate can be overcome if group assignments are regularly reassessed and students reassigned. Nevertheless, research currently suggests that slower children are harmed by homogeneous grouping and that swifter children are served as well by heterogeneous groups as by homogeneous ones.[6] On grounds of equality then, and perhaps efficiency, it appears that heterogeneous grouping is a better instructional strategy.

---

[5]For critical views, see Oakes (1981) and Persell (1977).

[6] See, for example, research reviewed in Slavin (1990).

So, what is the preferred practice of American schools? In our analysis we estimated the percentage of eighth graders grouped homogeneously for mathematics. In public as well as private schools, the overwhelming majority of students are still taught in homogeneous ability groups. Most schools separate kids into groups of slow, medium, and swift learners and risk the inequality in learning that may result thereby. There is a sharp difference, however, between public and private schools in the use of grouping. Private schools place 15 percentage points more students in heterogeneous groups than public schools do. About 30 percent of all private school kids take math in heterogeneous groups; only 15 percent of all public school kids do.

This difference also appears to operate independent of objective reasons for grouping. Our analysis divided students into schools that are above and below the population median in socioeconomic diversity—because socioeconomic status is a strong predictor of academic success. Presumably, schools will separate kids into homogeneous groups less often as their student bodies decline in diversity: The more similar students are, the less the need to separate them. To a slight extent, this turns out to be true. But basically, public and private schools exhibit different propensities to group heterogeneously, regardless of student diversity. Public schools almost invariably sort and separate kids into homogeneous ability groups; private schools are more willing to keep different children together.

Is this really a basic difference between public and private schools? Or does the difference have other explanations? To try and find out, we considered a number of alternative explanations simultaneously. We estimated a probit model designed to predict a student's math group—that is, whether the group is homogeneous or heterogeneous. What we found is that the kind of group an eighth grader is in has many "causes," or at least is influenced in many ways. For example, a student is somewhat more likely to be placed in a homogeneous group (presumably a high one) if he comes from a family higher in socioeconomic status, has strong prior math grades, and is Asian. There is ever so slight evidence that black students are less likely to be grouped homogeneously.

But ultimately there are three strong influences on a student's group. First, the socioeconomic status of the school. Schools serving more affluent children are more likely to group homogeneously, presumably to provide high level groups. Second, schools that are internally diverse, with wide variations in math achievement, are more likely to group homogeneously—though this may be an effect as well as a cause. Finally, private schools. All things being equal, a child is much less likely to be grouped homogeneously—to be separated from children of different ability—in a private school than in a public school. For the average child the probability of being grouped homogeneously for math is .829 in public school but only .556 in private school.

Of course, private schools may be less able to group homogeneously because they are smaller and do not have enough students to offer more specialized classes. In other words, private schools might group heterogeneously if they were larger. Let us ignore for now the question of why private schools are smaller—for perhaps they want to be small so they can avoid internal specialization—and just consider how public and private schools of similar size group children. We re-estimated the probit model, adding a control for eighth grade enrollment. What we found is that size matters, but that public and private schools still differ. Allowing for school size, an average student has a probability of being grouped homogeneously in a public school 10 percent higher than in a private school.

Why do private schools show a greater willingness to keep children of different backgrounds together? We think there are two reasons, both rooted in basic differences between political and market institutions. The first has to do with the very different structure of top-down control in the two institutions. Direct democratic control, as it is now structured, promotes the growth of bureaucracy around public schools. As we have argued, this bureaucracy generally tends to rob public schools of the autonomy that they need to exercise professional discretion and to organize themselves as effective educational teams. This bureaucracy also tends to do something very particular that affects how public schools deal with diversity. It prescribes how public schools deal with diversity. Public schools are required by law—federal, state, and local—to run various gifted and talented programs, enrichment programs, remedial programs, vocational programs, and numerous other programs. They are also required to utilize objective criteria—usually test scores—in assigning children to programs. A system of externally imposed rules determines how children will be organized and served.

There is more to this system, however, than the bureaucracy that implements it. The bureaucracy is not the source of the rules that limit how schools respond to diversity. The source is democratic authority, exercised by boards of education, state legislatures, and the U.S. Congress. As we observed in chapter 2 of *Politics, Markets, and America's Schools*, this authority is exercised in a distinctive way. Groups that vie for control of public authority insist on nailing down their political victories in detailed legislation that makes it difficult for subsequent victors to influence how legislation is implemented.

Groups want to limit discretion in schools not only because they distrust the professionals that work there, they also want to guard against the uncertainty of what future political decisions may bring.

What this distinctive political process means for equality in public schools is that the public schools are likely to be required to provide different services to different students—even if everyone agrees this practice mainly accentuates differences. For example, there is broad agreement among educators that disadvantaged children are hurt more than helped by programs that pull them out of regular classrooms for remedial work. Yet, the politics of "compensatory education" leads to demands for special treatment that can be easily monitored and documented—hence, veritable mandates for "pull-out" programs (Doyle and Cooper 1988). If schools were free to help disadvantaged children however they saw fit, what would guarantee that those children would actually get something extra? The politics of compensatory education is a thirty year saga of ever-tightening constraints. Although it is the classic case, it is not unrepresentative of the limitations that public schools face as they try to manage diversity. Public schools are basically required to treat different children differently.

Private schools are generally not subject to such requirements. They are managed by administrative structures that do not grow out of public authority. There is no politics of comparable consequence and there is no political uncertainty. The administrative structure exists to facilitate the voluntary relationships between individual schools and families—which is to say it scarcely exists at all. On most matters, including the management of student diversity, private schools are far freer than public schools to organize as they see fit. Private schools may treat different students differently or they may try to treat all students the same. If they want to treat all students the same, private schools may design grouping practices to do so—or they may simply limit their enrollment to prevent grouping from being feasible or necessary.

How private schools manage diversity will depend more on demands from families than on the requirements of bureaucracy. Which brings us to a second important difference between educational markets and political institutions, as they are currently structured. In an educational market, parents shop for the school that they believe is right for their child. Placing the child in a particular school is the parents' way of getting "something special" for the child. The odds are great that this school will not be large in size offering different things to different people. In today's public system, parents do not have the opportunity to shop or choose among schools to nearly the degree that parents do in the private market. Children are assigned to public schools, and at least within legal jurisdictions, there is not supposed to be anything special about any schools. The schools are supposed to be the same. If public school parents want "something special" for their child they must either work through the political process, which we just described, or they can apply pressure at the school site for special treatment. Public schools are likely to feel more direct pressure from parents than private schools do for the creation of ability groups and special programs, and the placement of particular children in them.

Overall, then, we believe public and private schools show different propensities to separate children of different backgrounds because these schools belong to different institutional systems. Direct democratic control encourages the development of bureaucratic classification systems; market control discourages this. Market control also defuses pressure at the school site for special treatment; political control increases it. Despite these differences, educators in both sectors tend to group children homogeneously. But there is a substantially greater willingness in private schools to keep different children together, to give all kids the same educational opportunity.

2.3 The operation of ability groups. Once schools decide to group kids by ability—and most schools do—there are still major steps schools can take to promote equality. They can ensure non-discrimination in group placement. They can extend the opportunity to participate in accelerated groups to the largest number of students possible. They can work to provide an equally high quality learning experience in groups at every level.

In our analysis we considered how public and private schools differ in all these regards. To begin, we found that private schools place more children—about nine percentage points more children—than public schools do in high math ability groups. Of course, private schools may have a higher percentage of very able students than public schools do. So we estimated a model of ability grouping in which the many influences on grouping can be compared. The model is a probit of the placement of a child into one of two categories, the high math group or a lower math group. What the model ultimately revealed is that the chances of being placed in a high group, all else being equal, are noticeably higher in private schools than in public. An average child has a .480 chance of being placed in a high group in private school but only a .378 chance in public school.

The model also provided some interesting information about how group placement decisions are apparently made. In all schools, public and private, ability grouping depends mostly on individual test scores and prior grades. In both public and private schools, there is evidence of affirmative action on behalf of black students. All things being equal, a black student is somewhat more likely than a white student to be placed in a high math group. Why this occurs is unclear. It may be that schools are more willing to give black children the benefit of the doubt in close cases because their scores are generally low and they are therefore underrepresented in high groups. Whatever the case, if we accept test scores and grades as valid placement criteria, there is no evidence of racial discrimination against black students in ability grouping.

Black and disadvantaged students enjoy another edge in high grouping as well. All things being equal, it is harder to get into a high group in a school where there is lots of competition for spaces, in a school that is high on average in test scores or socioeconomic status. Minority and disadvantaged children tend to attend schools with less competition for high groups and thus, if qualified, are more likely than kids in more competitive schools to get a high placement. This, and the lack of blatant discrimination, does not mean that disadvantaged children are grouped ambitiously to any great degree; they still dominate the low groups. Our observation is simply that matters could be significantly worse.

In eighth grade—or actually just prior to it—schools make an additional grouping decision, a decision that can prove far more important than the assignment of students to ability groups. At this juncture, schools decide which students will take algebra during eighth grade and which students will wait until ninth grade or longer. The importance of this decision is that eighth grade algebra tends to be a gatekeeper for the academic or college preparatory track in high school. Students who take algebra in eighth grade usually go on to take an accelerated sequence of mathematics classes through the twelfth grade and to follow a curriculum aimed at attending a competitive four year college. In comparison, students who do not take algebra in eighth grade very often take less mathematics and less advanced mathematics down the road and follow a general or vocational curriculum. Of course, the mathematics courses and high school curriculum that students take may be largely a reflection of student preparation or ability. But schools do make course assignments and schools do have the option of ambitiously assigning students to challenging programs—or of letting students just slide by.

Public and private schools differ significantly in their willingness to place eighth graders in algebra. We found that 60 percent of private school students are placed in (full- or part-time) algebra while only 42 percent of public school students are. We also found that this difference is a result of the schools and not of the students in them. We estimated a model of algebra enrollment that asked:

Is the student taking algebra in eighth grade or not? The estimates indicate that an average child has a .568 chance of being placed in algebra by a private school but only a .401 probability in a public school—provided that algebra is offered in these schools as a separate course.[7] In all schools, placement is most powerfully influenced by math scores and socioeconomic status. As with ability groups, it is tougher, all things being equal, to get into algebra in an academically competitive school. And again, there is no evidence of racial discrimination. If anything, there is affirmative action (in both sectors) on behalf of blacks, Asians, and to a very slight extent, Hispanics. All of these influences notwithstanding, there is strong evidence that private schools provide a sizable boost to algebra-taking—and to enrollments in high math groups more generally.

Why might this be? One possibility is that in ways we simply have not measured, private school students are better prepared for algebra and accelerated math than public school students are. We cannot rule this explanation out completely. However, we controlled for the most direct evidence that schools have of math preparedness—prior math grades and math scores on standardized tests. We also controlled for a host of student background characteristics that might influence course assignments. And, we allowed for competition within schools. In light of this, it seems unlikely that the ten to twenty point placement probability differences for algebra and high math groups are all due to student differences.

We think the differences more likely derive from the organization of public and private schools and the institutional contexts in which these schools operate. Public schools are organized to be all things to all people, to treat different kids differently, and to meet the needs of many and varied constituents. This has come to mean schools that are internally differentiated with lots of programs, levels, and tracks. In such schools, it makes sense to offer different students different mathematics options in eighth grade—none better and none worse, all simply appropriate for different kinds of kids. Private schools tend to be more specialized or focused. They have a vision of what their graduates should achieve and they try to do the same for all of their students. Private schools therefore tend to offer few electives and to keep all students on the same path, traditionally an academic one.

---

[7]Some schools, particularly smaller Catholic schools, offer only one eighth grade math course. Although not entitled algebra, such a singular offering will often include the advanced math necessary to prepare students for college-track math in high school.

Public schools have differentiated organizations because they are subject to multiple layers of political control that impose bureaucratic complexity. Private schools tend to have simpler organizations because they lack political control and must instead meet the demands of clients. In education, the market test is easiest to meet with a coherent teamlike organization, not a loosely connected comprehensive one. Perhaps a private school could meet such a test by focusing on goals other than academic excellence—religion, for example—and placing nobody in algebra in eighth grade. But parents who are choosing schools generally seem to care about academic results. And a pretty good recipe for academic results is a rigorous academic curriculum. Academic opportunity therefore is more widely—and equally—extended in private schools than in public.

Now, it might still be that the differentiated approach to student organization is a sound and equitable one. It may be better for all students not to push slower learners into tough classes or to burden bright students with slower classmates. It may be better for all students if students are grouped by ability and are offered first rate programs appropriate to their different levels of preparation. Since both public and private schools engage in a good deal of ability grouping, it is worth looking closely at the quality of the learning experience in different groups.

In our analysis we looked at a number of indicators of educational quality contained in the student questionnaire. What these indicators showed is that, at least in the eyes of students, the educational environment is better in private schools than in public. On every indicator, a higher percentage of private students than of public students gave highly favorable responses. And on several questions bearing directly on the learning experience—for example, "the teaching is good" and "teachers are interested in students"—the differences seem substantial.

Using these indicators, we then looked at differences within schools. We estimated regression models of each measure of the learning environment in public and in private schools. The models predicted an individual student's response to each measure as a function of the average response of other students in the student's school, the student's own socioeconomic status, and the student's ability group in mathematics. The models enable us to estimate whether children in higher groups experience different learning conditions from children in lower groups, controlling for the average learning condition in each school and a proxy for the orientation of each child to learning—socioeconomic status.

Estimating separate models for public and private schools enabled us to compare equality across sectors.

The results are not perfectly consistent. Generally, the educational conditions in high groups are more positive than they are in lower groups, in both public and private schools. However, the differences between groups are smaller than criticisms of grouping would lead one to expect. And the disparities are not generally greater within public schools than within private schools. On some indicators of educational conditions—for example, "teachers are interested in students" and teachers "put down" students—the higher and lower groups differ more in public schools than in private schools. On other indicators—for example, "teachers praise my efforts"—private ability groups are farther apart than public ability groups are. In both public and private schools, it seems, the best students have a somewhat better experience than average or worse students—when those schools use ability grouping.

Yet two differences between public and private schools do seem to exist. First, the educational conditions within all math ability groups are generally better in private schools than in public schools. Disparities exist within schools in both sectors, but conditions vary around higher means in private schools than in public schools. Second, in schools that serve mostly lower socioeconomic status students—a subject we examine closely in the final part of this chapter—the disparities in group conditions are significantly greater within public schools than within private schools. This finding echoes the results of earlier studies of Catholic schools serving poor families. For example, sociologists, Coleman and Hoffer (1987) and Bryk, Lee, and Holland (1992), argue that the undifferentiated Catholic education program and philosophy produce a "common school" effect for children of differing backgrounds.

Why might public and private schools display their various internal differences? Researchers have put forward a number of explanations. We think that the institutions of public and private education provide important clues as well. Public schools, we proposed earlier, are bound by administrative constraints to operate different programs and tracks. They are not free to push all students into ambitious groups or to ignore objective indicators that would suggest a different or lower placement. Private schools are free to do whatever is likely to satisfy parents and to use their best professional judgment in placing students. Private schools, as we have seen, still judge that many students are not up to the challenge of accelerated programs. But private schools also believe that the most ambitious placement feasible is the one that is likely to raise a student to his full potential. Of course, getting kids to realize their potential is an attractive strategy for satisfying parents. Public schools want to satisfy parents, too. But they must also satisfy higher authorities that mandate how different students must be served. The result, we think, is a higher rate of ambitious placements in private schools.

As for differences in educational experiences within schools, we think institutions also hold part of the answer. Private schools have a powerful incentive to provide the children of all of their families the same educational quality: all parents are paying the same tuition and expecting the same quality. If it is within their power to provide equal quality, private schools will strive to do so. Public schools undoubtedly would like to do this also; parents voting and paying taxes are equally entitled to quality, too. The problem, we think, is that public schools are not as free as private schools to provide equal quality. In particular, public schools are not free to assign teachers to any class or group they please; collective bargaining agreements often give teachers the right to decline assignments—to teach difficult kids, for example—on the basis of seniority or to choose assignments, such as working with the gifted and talented. In general, public schools are not as free as private schools to shape their organizations or to determine the content of their educational programs. Another consequence of these limitations is that public schools cannot as easily as private schools guarantee equality to students, once students are separated.

2.4 High school tracking. Ability groups and class assignments in middle school are precursors of broader and more significant divisions in high school. After eighth grade, students are often organized into general programs of study or tracks that determine the amount and level of academic coursework that students take until graduation. These tracks—most often labeled academic, general, and vocational—prepare children for very different post-graduation experiences. Academic track students are readied for four year colleges or universities; students in other tracks are schooled for work or less academic forms of higher education, such as community colleges.

Tracking has been the target of enormous criticism because it is perceived to be discriminatory and detrimental to students in non-academic tracks.[8] Tracking has also been the subject of extensive research, especially by educational sociologists, who see a potentially strong link between tracking in schools and economic stratification in society.[9] That research has plainly shown that racial

[8] See Oakes and Persell.
[9] Among many possible sources, see especially Garmoran and Mare (1989); Alexander et al. (1978); Heyns (1974); and Alexander and Cook (1982).

minorities and poor children are overrepresented in non-academic tracks; however, it has not shown that that overrepresentation is the result of discrimination. Research has also documented wide gaps in achievement between students in different tracks, but it has not demonstrated that those gaps are caused or exacerbated by differences in educational quality between tracks. More troubling for tracking is the fact that little evidence supports its supposed benefits: average achievement seems to be no higher in tracked schools than in untracked ones. Evidence on all of these points, however, is quite debatable. The argument over the merits of tracking therefore rages on.

Our interest in the tracking debate derives from the possibility that schools in different institutional systems may have inherent tendencies to track differently. This is a vitally important consideration if we are concerned with improving schools — raising levels of educational achievement and reducing levels of inequality. If tracking, as it is practiced in public schools today, turns out to be inefficient, inequitable or both, it is crucial to know why it is so practiced and how it can be changed. If high school tracking practices, like middle school grouping practices, have deep institutional roots, it may prove very difficult to change tracking without changing institutions, too.

It is well known that private school students are more likely to enroll in an academic track than public school students are. Among tenth graders in the NELS:88 First Follow-up Survey, well over half of all private school students are taking a college prep program while only a third of public school students are.[10] In our analysis we estimated a model that attempts to determine why. The model attempts to predict whether a student is in an academic track or not.

What the model shows, first, is that track placements work very similarly to ability group decisions and class assignments in middle school. The strongest influence on track placement, by far, is prior academic achievement — measured in this analysis by eighth grade tests in math, reading, science, and history. A student's socioeconomic status does have some impact, with higher status children favored. But there is no evidence of racial discrimination against minorities. In fact, there is strong evidence (in both sectors) of affirmative action on behalf of black youngsters. All else being equal, a black child is more likely than a white child to be placed in an academic program. As with middle schools, there is also evidence that competitive high schools, those high in

[10]Our estimates are from student self-reports. Information from principal surveys suggests that private school students may sometimes report their track as general when in fact it is academic. Our student data may therefore underestimate private student enrollment in academic programs.

average test scores and socioeconomic status, make it tougher for kids to be placed in the top programs. This, too, may provide a boost for disadvantaged kids who are usually not in competitive schools.

Once all of this is taken into consideration, however, a strong private school effect still seems to remain. A child who is average on every variable specified in this model would have only a .302 probability of being placed in an academic track in a public school but a .425 probability of being so placed in a private school. It is true that private school students may be more academically inclined than public school students are. But that greater inclination would have to manifest itself to private schools in subtle yet powerful ways, for the model allows for all of the indicators that schools are said to consider in placing students in tracks. It is therefore unlikely that the public-private difference in tracking probabilities is not due, in some large part, to differences between public and private schools. As we explained before, there are good reasons to expect private schools to be more ambitious in their grouping practices.

Of course, this difference does not mean that the private form of organization is superior on grounds of efficiency or equality. Private schools do extend the college prep opportunity to more students. But in so doing, they could compromise the quality of their advanced courses. Public schools might help children just as well or better than private schools do by offering quality instruction, tailored to different levels of preparation, to students in different tracks. In the analysis we tried to explore these possibilities.

First, we compared educational conditions in academic and non-academic track classes. The models that we employed are essentially the same as those that we used to compare conditions in eighth grade ability groups. The results, however, are somewhat different. Again, there is a tendency for the educational experience to be better for students in academic classes than for students in non-academic classes, in both sectors. And again, differences in experiences are not as large as criticisms of tracking would lead one to believe they should be. However, the disparaties in educational experiences are generally greater within public schools than within private schools.

2.5 Achievement consequences. The evidence we have seen so far indicates that private schools may do a better job than public schools of providing equal educational outcomes. Private schools strive to do this by offering relatively high proportions of their students the best academic opportunities without compromising the quality of those opportunities for anyone. We have also seen some evidence that for students who do not make it into top groups or programs, the experience may be somewhat better for private students than for public. Now, we want to see if these organizational differences have consequences for student achievement.

To do so, we estimated an elaborate regression model of tenth grade combined math and reading scores.[11] The determinants of achievement include prior (eighth grade) math and reading achievement, and prior history and science achievement, which we included as a proxy for academic ability more generally. The model also includes a generous set of controls for individual back ground—socioeconomic status, race, sex, and the number of parents in the home. In addition, the model allows for regional variations and for differences between urban, suburban, and rural settings. Finally, the model controls for differences in eighth grade schooling—for students who switch between public and private schools at the start of high school.

All of the coefficients in the model behaved as expected. Achievement in tenth grade is best predicted by achievement in eighth grade. The coefficients of greatest interest to us are those distinguishing private schools from public and academic track students from non-academic. These coefficients reveal three important things. First, private schools provide an independent boost to student achievement relative to public schools, after all else is considered. Second, academic track coursework increases achievement beyond levels that would be expected from identical students doing non-academic coursework. And third, students in the academic track end up closer to their non-academic track schoolmates in the private sector than in the public sector.

Generally, we also find that academic track students do equally well, all else being the same, in public and private schools. In other words, by operating a more inclusive academic track, private schools do not compromise the education of their brightest students. Students in the more exclusive academic track in public schools perform no better. Since private schools are providing the highest academic opportunity to more students than public schools are, private schools are also boosting the achievement of more of their better students than public schools are.

2.6 Summary. All things considered, the private sector seems to do a better job of promoting equality within schools than the public sector does. Both sectors seem to be non-discriminating in their internal organizing decisions. But

---

[11] We do not model the history and science tests because scores in those subjects can be strongly and legitimately influenced by school-to-school variations in curriculum sequences.

private schools maintain more equality when students are separated, and they succeed more in keeping diverse students together and in extending opportunity widely. Private schools also do a better job of maintaining a decent threshold of quality for students in the lower parts of the ability distribution. The end result is that students in private schools are more likely to exhibit equal educational outcomes than students in public schools are.

3. Equality Between Schools

In *Politics, Markets and America's Schools* we argued that the quality of a school depends foremost on the quality of its organization—its focus, expectations, leadership, professionalism, and teamwork. Organization was the one overarching characteristic of schools that most influenced student achievement once student background characteristics were taken into account. School organization, we also argued, is strongly influenced itself—most strongly by what we called autonomy. The best predictor of the quality of school organization is the freedom of a school from bureaucratic authority. The freer schools are to staff their own organizations and to define their own educational programs, the more likely they are to be organized effectively. The ultimate problem for public schools, we argued, is that they are part of institutional systems that routinely function to deny schools autonomy and in turn to undermine their organizations and performance. Private schools enjoy an enormous advantage in this regard because the market system of which they are a part promotes autonomy and rewards effective organization and performance.

This does not mean, however, that private schools should consistently outperform public schools, for there are other factors involved. Public schools, we observed, tend to be granted ample autonomy if they are part of suburban school systems, which are usually small, homogeneous and relatively free of political conflict and uncertainty. Public schools can also be granted substantial discretion if the students they are educating are not serious academic or behavior problems. By the same token, private schools can find themselves constrained by authorities if their students are unusually difficult. On average, then, we expect private schools to have greater autonomy than public schools and a greater chance for success. But we also expect the performance of public and private schools to vary a good deal and to overlap.

This hypothetical variation has important implications for the distribution of schools that might exist in a system of education based on school choice. As critics have observed, a choice system might concentrate difficult students in a limited number of schools and exacerbate inequality across the educational system. As they point out, our analysis shows that autonomy, organization, and eventually, performance are influenced by the caliber of the student body. A choice system might then breed differences between schools and make inequality worse.

We do not believe this would happen. In part, equality is a matter of system design. A system of school choice can be designed to protect or even promote equality between schools. As we have said and recommended, parents can be prohibited from adding to tuition payments made by the government. Schools can be required to accept certain numbers of educationally disadvantaged children. Parents can be assisted by the government in making informed school choices. Equality, however, is more than a matter of design. We also think it is a systemic characteristic, better protected by markets than by political institutions as we now know them.

In our view, the quality of a school is likely to depend foremost on its autonomy to solve its own problems and on the severity of the problems it must solve. In a market system, autonomy will generally be high. In a system of schools subject to direct democratic control, autonomy will vary with the structure of democratic institutions. Autonomy will generally be high in small, politically homogeneous systems and low in large, politically heterogeneous systems. All else being equal, autonomy will always be higher in market systems than in systems subject to direct political control. Overall, autonomy will tend to vary much more in political systems than in market systems because political institutions vary much more in basic structure than markets do. This is especially true in the United States where 15,000 school districts and 50 state governments create a literal multitude of institutional settings for schools.

If autonomy varies much more in political systems than in systems based on markets, then so, too, should school quality. Markets should exert a homogenizing influence on schools, providing relatively equal opportunities to schools to organize effectively and weeding out schools that do not organize effectively. Political institutions should present schools a wider variety of organizing situations—from highly constrained to relatively free—and should basically tolerate the operation of schools consistent with these constraints, regardless of their performance. Private schools should therefore vary less in quality than public schools do.

Except under one condition. If school choice worked to sort children into an array of schools that vary dramatically in student composition, then the homogenizing influence that markets exert on school organizations might be offset by the diversifying influence markets can exert on school enrollments. In a market, every school would still enjoy more autonomy than it would have in today's political system, all else being equal. But the schools in a market system might serve a more disparate set of student bodies than the schools in the political system serve and consequently develop school organizations that vary more, not less, than politically controlled schools vary. For example, if a market were to sort kids into schools that range from selective academies for child prodigies to holding pens for juvenile delinquents—a specter often painted by market critics—then the benefits of autonomy might indeed be offset. A politically controlled system, with variable bureaucratic constraints but less variable student bodies, might then provide more equal educational results, from one school to the next, than a market system would provide.

There is no way to know for certain how a public system of school choice would sort children into schools. As we said, sorting is substantially a matter of design. And public authorities can take measures to ensure that student bodies do not vary widely in average ability or behavior. The most important of such measures is guaranteeing that every child has available to him or her the same price of admission. Today, the composition of schools in both the public and the private sectors is strongly influenced by the ability of families to pay—tuition in private schools and housing costs in public schools. Many public schools therefore serve student bodies in which every child lives in poverty while other public schools serve children who are uniformly rich. The same goes for private schools. Although the families in private schools must all come up with some tuition money (unless they are offered complete scholarships), certain private schools charge $10,000 and attract children of economic privilege while others charge $750 and serve children who are decidedly poor.

A look at private schools today therefore cannot tell us everything we might need to know about the composition and organization of schools that a public system of choice might produce. On the one hand, today's private schools serve only a fraction of the student population and provide only a limited view of how choice might work. On the other hand, today's private schools may provide a good view of how choice might operate at its "worst"—where parents are charged widely varying tuitions, where ability-to-pay influences enrollments, and where the admissions process is completely unregulated. In other words, today's private schools may help tell us how schools will differ in quality when their student bodies are sharply stratified along class lines but when all schools nevertheless enjoy the organizational benefits of markets and autonomy.

3.1 Socioeconomic status and school performance. We begin our analysis with an overview of the schools in today's public and private school systems. First, we considered the full distribution of schools in each sector. Some of what we found is completely unsurprising. The average private school has students that are higher in socioeconomic status than the average public school has. This is a sizable difference—.865 standard deviations—and surely reflects the fact that parents who make tuition payments, however small, have more income than parents who do not. We also found that private schools post average math and reading scores that exceed public school scores by .753 standard deviations. Given the public-private difference in average school SES, this test score difference is likewise unsurprising.

What is surprising, however, is what we found when we shifted our attention from the means of the distributions to the variances. We found, first, that the socioeconomic status of private schools varies considerably more than the socioeconomic status of public schools. The variance of the average SES of student bodies in the private sector is two-thirds greater than the comparable variance in the public sector. Even though private school families represent a narrower and more affluent part of the total distribution of socioeconomic status, the schools that they attend vary more than the schools attended by public school families in average socioeconomic status. As we suggested, the fact that private schools operate at widely varying costs and charge widely varying tuitions produces a distribution of schools that varies much more than public schools vary in the class composition of each school. Private schools may then provide a good test of how school quality might vary when schools are socioeconomically stratified but free to operate as they judge best.

What then is the surprise? Despite the greater variation in socioeconomic status across private schools, there is less variation in test scores across private schools than across public schools. From school to school, the private sector is more diverse than the public sector in student background but less diverse in test scores. This is rather remarkable because test scores are well predicted (and influenced) by family socioeconomic status. All things being equal, private schools ought to have a wider distribution of average test scores than public schools do because private schools have a wider distribution of average class backgrounds. It appears, however, that all things are not equal. Test scores and class background do not seem to have the same relationship to each other in the two sectors.

Why might this be? One explanation—the one we proposed—is that private schools are more equal in quality than public schools are. The differences between the best and the worst private schools are not as great as the differences between the best and the worst public schools. Thus, the marketplace can organize children into schools that differ on average more than public schools differ in socioeconomic status. But because private schools are more similar in organization and effectiveness than public schools are, children in socioeconomically disparate private schools end up reaching more similar levels of academic achievement than children in less disparate public schools. If this interpretation of these data is correct, the equalizing effect of a market system may indeed be great. Private schools are two-thirds more diverse than public schools in average class background but slightly less diverse in average student performance.

There are, however, other possible explanations for these distributions. One is that the socioeconomic variance of private schools is deceptively large, inflated mostly by extraordinarily affluent independent schools. The test score variance of private schools only looks narrow by comparison because these affluent schools cannot post the extraordinary test scores that would be required to match their socioeconomic status. Another possible explanation is that the socioeconomic variance of private schools is deceptive in a different way. Private schools may indeed serve groups of children that vary from unusually poor to unusually rich, but the families at the lower end of the distribution may be unrepresentative of the poor. The poor families in private schools may be unusually interested in or supportive of education, and more to the point, the children of these families may bring relatively strong achievement levels to private school with them. In other words, economically poor students in private schools may be something of a disadvantaged elite that private schools are fortunate to enroll but that private schools do not especially help to learn.

To evaluate these explanations, we divided schools into two categories—schools with student bodies above the median SES of all schools, which we label "rich," and schools with student bodies below the median of all schools, which we label "poor." This division enables us to look separately at schools that serve mostly advantaged children and schools that serve mostly disadvantaged children.

Looking first at "rich" schools, we found that private ones in this category are more affluent on average than public ones and that the private distribution of schools is wider than the public distribution. When we look at test scores, moreover, we found precisely the same thing. The average test score of private schools is higher than the average test score of public schools, and the distribution of average test scores is wider in the private sector than in the public sector. In "rich" schools it appears that the socioeconomic make-up of the student body and the achievement of the schools are in much the same relationship in the public and the private sectors. It does not appear that extraordinary affluence in certain private schools is the source of the equalizing relationship found in the sample of all schools.

What about "poor" schools? Several things are of interest. First, the private schools in this category are indeed poor. Their children average nearly one standard deviation below the median socioeconomic status of all schools, and their children are lower in socioeconomic status than the children of "poor" public schools. The "poor" private schools are, however, more socioeconomically diverse than the "poor" public schools, their respective variances differing nearly two-to-one. If average test scores were predicted by socioeconomic status, as they are in "rich" schools, the variances of test scores in "poor" private and public schools would differ similarly. They do not. The variance of "poor" private school test scores is less than the variance of "poor" public school scores—despite the greater socioeconomic diversity of the private sector—and private scores are one third of a standard deviation higher.

Unless students in "poor" private schools are academically rich in some still undisclosed way, it appears that the public and private systems differ in the distribution of quality schools, with the key difference manifest in schools serving relatively disadvantaged children. In the private sector, "poor" schools are more disadvantaged and more diverse than "poor" schools in the public sector, yet test scores in "poor" private schools are higher and less diverse than scores in their public counterparts. Private schools serving poorer children seem to be doing a better and more equal job of promoting academic achievement than public schools serving comparable children. If this is so, the greater equalizing effect that private schools as a whole seem to have would be primarily attributable to the threshold of quality that private schools appear to meet for the education of even the most disadvantaged.

3.2 A closer look at students in "poor" schools. So far we have considered only the average socioeconomic status of families as we have tried to understand potential causes of performance in "poor" schools. But what about other student characteristics? Do public and private school children differ in other ways that might explain their different test scores? We began by considering one leading possibility, family composition. We found that students in "poor" public and private schools are not very different in this regard. Many of these kids, more than in the general population, come from homes where the mother and father are not both present. Private school children have a slight edge in living with their mother and father together, but private school children are also more likely to live with their mother alone. If living without both parents in the home is a handicap—and research suggests that it is—children in "poor" public and private schools are equally disadvantaged (United States Congressional Research Service 1987). There are no statistically significant differences.

Much the same is true of family size. Research suggests that children from larger families fare slightly worse in school than children from smaller families, all else being equal (United States Congressional Research Service 1987). The reason is not entirely clear, but undoubtedly has something to do with sibling rivalry for parent attention. At any rate, children in "poor" public and private schools come from families that are not significantly different in total size. The story is similar for race. There is not a statistically significant difference in the percentage of white students in "poor" public and private schools. There is a difference, however, in the percentage of black students—though not in the expected direction. "Poor" private schools, not public schools, enroll a higher percentage of black students—26.5 percent in the former, only 18.0 percent in the latter.

Finally, we considered parent education, a component of socioeconomic status, but probably the best predictor of student achievement among individual measures of family background. Here we found some difference, in the expected direction, between public and private school families. Most noticeably, "poor" private schools enroll only half as many students with parents lacking a high school degree as "poor" public schools do. This difference is then mirrored in small private school advantages at some but not all higher levels of education. Overall, however, the differences in parent education are not large enough to be confidently labeled statistically significant. The differences are close enough to accepted significance levels not to be ignored, but they may also be meaningless.

In total, the student bodies of "poor" public and private schools look pretty similar. There are no significant differences between them on the measures of family background that are most strongly associated with student achievement. To be sure, the student bodies still differ in one potentially crucial respect: the families of the private school kids decided to sacrifice and pay for private school while the families of the public school kids decided not to make the same sacrifice. In our analysis we cannot measure or control directly for this difference. But before we concede too much importance to this analytical hurdle, it is important to bear in mind that we are interested not primarily in whether or why private schools are better on average than public schools. We are concerned with whether and why private schools produce less variable results.

If we assume that every private school child gets an unmeasurable boost from unusually supportive parents, we have reason to expect higher achievement from every child in private school than in public school, all else being equal. But we have no reason to expect the distribution of achievement among those equally advantaged private school children to narrow relative to the distribution of achievement among children in public schools. We would only expect unmeasured parental influences to reduce achievement variation among private schools relative to public schools if we expected parental influences to be stronger in private schools than in public schools and less variable too. Researchers tend to agree that unmeasured parental influences are generally stronger in private schools than in public. But whether such influences are also less variable in private schools is unclear. There is good reason, then, to look beyond families, and to the schools themselves, to understand differences in the distribution of achievement across public and private schools.

3.3   The organization of public and private schools. Schools perform differently, we believe, because they are not all equally well organized for the task. This is true of differences between successful and unsuccessful public schools, private schools, or both. The immediate cause of school performance is not the institutional system; the immediate cause is school organization. Institutions are important primarily because of their influence on school organization. Market institutions, we think, produce school organizations that are more effective and more equal than those that current political institutions produce. We have now seen indirect evidence that this may be true. Private schools have higher and less variable average test scores than public schools do, especially among the less advantaged schools, and these differences are not well explained by the kinds of students in the schools.

Might these differences be explained by organization? We do not have space for a complete exploration of this possibility, but the evidence suggests that organization is important. We saw this first when we considered several basic measures of school organization, and the scores of "rich" and "poor" public and private schools on them. Several important relationships emerged from these indicators. The first is that organizational conditions (in the view of school principals) are much better in "poor" private schools than in "poor" public schools. For example, in most "poor" private schools, principals strongly agree that "teachers encourage students to do their best, and that "teachers do not have negative attitudes toward students." The same is true in only half of the "poor" public schools. The differences are equally stark on all indicators. Perhaps these differences explain why "poor" private schools, despite being lower in socioeconomic status than "poor" public schools, post noticeably higher test scores.

Another interesting relationship concerns variation within sectors. On average, the differences in key organizational conditions between "rich" and "poor" schools are of similar magnitude in the public and private sectors. In public and private schools alike, principals in "rich" schools are about 5 percent more likely than principals in "poor" schools to agree strongly that educational conditions in their schools are positive. On some indicators—for example, "teachers do not have negative attitudes toward their students"—the differences between "rich" and "poor" schools exceed 10 percent while on other indicators "rich" and "poor" are very similar. And other indicators show the gaps between "rich" and "poor" schools to sometimes be greater for public schools and sometimes greater for private. Overall, the sectors display similar amounts of variation from schools serving privileged students to schools serving the disadvantaged. What's interesting about this finding is that private schools serve a wider range of socioeconomic groupings than public schools do, and should therefore display more disparate school conditions—if student characteristics overwhelmingly determine school climate. The fact that the private and public sectors are equally homogeneous in school organization suggests that the market forces shaping private schools may have a more equalizing influence on school quality than the political and bureacratic forces molding public schools.

This evidence, moreover, is not the strongest indication that markets may have benefits for educational equity. For what is most remarkable about the organizational attributes of the schools we examined is not that "poor" private schools look better than "poor" public schools or that "poor" private schools are more similar to their "rich" counterparts than expected. What is most strking about "poor" schools in the private sector is that, on these indicators of school organization and climate, they look better than "rich" school in the public sector. On average, principals in "poor" private schools are over 20 percent more likely than principals in "rich" public schools to agree strongly that key conditions in their schools are positive. For example, while 61 percent of principals in "rich" public schools strongly agree that "teachers encourage students to do their best," 90 percent of principals in "poor" private schools do the same. The major point about private sector organization, it seems, is not that market pressures encourage private schools to be more alike in quality than public sch ools—though this seems to happen—it is that market pressures encourage all schools, including especially those serving the disadvantaged, to develop important attributes of effective school organization—teamwork, high expectations, and attention to individual needs.

These conclusions are reinforced by additional indicators of organizational effectiveness that are also examined—extra hours that teachers spend working with students and teacher absenteeism. Here we found the same public and private differences as before. The greatest public-private differences occur in "poor" schools. There we found 15.7 percent of public school teachers giving less than five hours a week in extra time to students but only 1.6 percent of private school teachers being so stingy. The modal number of extra hours spent by private school teachers is 10.5 to 14 per week; the mode for public school teachers is 5.5 to 10. Among teachers in "poor" private schools, only 6.3 percent are absent more than two days in a semester; among teachers in "poor" public schools, the figure is 37.3 percent. Teachers in "poor" private schools exhibit greater devotion to their work than teachers in "poor" public schools do.

In fact, teachers in "poor" private schools show greater commitment than teachers in "rich" public schools. And this is the most important finding for evaluating equity under political and market conditions. Even when private schools serve very disadvantaged students, they manage to develop the atttributes of effective organization.

4. Conclusion

The analysis summarized in this paper is the beginning, and not the ending, of an investigation that we hope will help clarify fundamental sources of inequality in American education. Our suspicion is that the institutions responsible for running American education bear major responsibility for inequality—not because of ill-intent or poor design, but as a result of their normal functioning. Driven by political conflict, these institutions have developed a bureaucratic control structure that seems to have institutionalized inequality. Within schools, the structure reinforces a system of student classification and educational specialization that exacerbates differences in achievement among students— differences that often run along class and racial lines. Between schools, the structure imposes the most burdensome constraints on the schools that can least tolerate them—schools serving the disadvantaged—and pushes those schools even further behind schools serving the advantaged. Public education consequently produces results that are not only lackluster, they are unnecessarily unequal.

We say unnecessarily because, as we saw in our look at private education, it is plainly possible to do better. Public education is not overtly discriminatory in its dealings with disadvantaged students; indeed, there is some evidence of affirmative action on their behalf. But public education could do much more. It could place children of different abilities together in the same groups and classes more often than it does now, exposing slower students to the curriculum and expectations provided to swifter students. It could provide accelerated programs to a higher percentage of students. It could ensure that children organized into different groups, classes, and tracks are provided programs and teachers equally high in quality. And, it could work to provide schools now stymied by urban bureaucracies the kind of autonomy that promotes effective organization in urban private schools. If public education took these steps, it would surely raise the achievement of its most disadvantaged students and, without jeopardizing the achievement of its best students, raise the average achievement of the system as a whole.

The problem is, these steps cannot easily be taken. If we are correct, the qualities of organization that breed inequality within and between public schools are rooted in the institutions that govern public schools. Unless these institutions are changed, the organization of public schools is unlikely to change—at least in any substantial way. School reformers, after all, have been criticizing tracking and bureaucracy for years; yet, efforts to solve these organizational problems have been largely to no avail. We believe institutional reform is necessary. And we believe the market provides the most promising model for carrying it out.

In *Politics, Markets, and America's Schools*, we made the case for institutional reform, based on markets, primarily on grounds of educational efficiency and effectiveness. Now, we would consider taking the case one step further. Markets appear better suited than institutions of direct democratic control to promoting educational equality. Markets seem to encourage the more equitable treatment of students within schools and the more equal distribution of quality across different schools. With public regulation aimed at further promoting their fair operation, markets would appear to provide a more promising foundation on which to rebuild public education than the institutions that now govern them. In any case, if the inequality and ineffectiveness that now plague American education are to be substantially reduced, research and reform must work harder to get to their roots.

References

Alexander, K.L., and M.A. Cook (1982). "Curricula and coursework: a surprise ending to a familiar story," *American Sociological Review* 47, 626-640.
Alexander, K., M. Cook, and E. McDill (1978). "Curriculum tracking and educational stratification: some further evidence," *American Sociological Review* 47, 47-66.

Ball, S.J. (1981). *Beachside Comprehensive: A Case Study of Secondary Schooling* (Cambridge University Press, Cambridge).

Bryk, A., V. Lee, and P. Holland (1993). *Catholic Schools and the Common Good* (Harvard University Press, Cambridge).

Camarena, M. (1990). "Following the right track: a comparison of tracking practices in public and Catholic schools," in R. Page and L. Valli, (eds.), *Curriculum Differentiation* (SUNY Press, Albany, NY), chapter 8.

Chubb, J.E., and T.E. Moe (1990). *Politics, Markets, and America's Schools* (Brookings, Washington, DC).

Coleman, J.S., and T. Hoffer (1987). *Public and Private High Schools: The Impact of Community* (Basic Books, New York).

Doyle, D.P., and B.S. Cooper (eds.) (1988). *Federal Aid to the Disadvantaged* (The Falmer Press, London).

Educational Testing Service (1991). *Psychometric Report: NELS:88* (ETS, Princeton, NJ).

Gamoran, A., and R. DeMare (1989). "Secondary school tracking and educational inequality: compensation, reinforcement, or neutrality," *American Journal of Sociology* 94(5), 1146-83.

Gutmann, A. (1987). *Democratic Education* (Princeton University Press, Princeton, NJ).

Heyns, B. (1974). "Social selection and stratification within schools," *American Journal of Sociology* 79(6), 1434-1451.

Lee, V., and A. Bryk, (1988).   "Tracking and achievement in public and Catholic schools, " *Sociology of Education* (April), 80-94.

Oakes, J. (1985). *Keeping Track: How Schools Structure Inequality* (Yale University Press, New Haven, CT).

Persell, C.H. (1977). *Education and Inequality* (Free Press, New York).

Slavin, R.E. (1990). *Cooperative Learning: Theory, Research, and Practice* (Allyn and Bacon, Boston).

United States Congressional Research Service (1987). *Student Achievement: An Explanation of Trends* (Government Printing Office, Washington, DC).

Chapter 17   Postal Service in the Nineties

Jess S. Boronico, Michael A. Crew, Paul R. Kleindorfer

1. Introduction to the Nature of Postal Services

Postal service is big business. Consider the United States. The United States Postal Service handles over 40% of the world's mail, with a work force of over 700,000 and with revenues of nearly $50 billion. Over the years, the Postal Service has moved from a department of government to a public enterprise organization, and is introducing high-tech equipment with further changes in progress. At the same time traditional postal service is facing competition not only from other types of delivery services but also from electronic communications. Competition has been made stronger by advances in microelectronics, telecommunications, and computers. Postal service will need to respond to the competition by adopting new technologies, being more flexible in its pricing and product mix, addressing issues of quality in part by using quality to differentiate its products, and by pricing efficiently. This paper will begin to address such issues drawing upon the recent literature on competition and sustainability of natural monopoly.

Modern postal service was originally recognized by Rowland Hill (1837) as presenting complicated organizational problems. It is a chain of activities consisting of collection, mail processing (e.g. canceling, and sorting), transportation, and final delivery. Traditionally, these activities have been highly labor intensive with horses giving way to vans and the railroad being supplanted by the airlines for long distance mail carriage. Such advances as occurred took place primarily in suppliers to postal service. Processing mail,

P. T. Harker (ed.), The Service Productivity and Quality Challenge, 471–492.
© 1995 Kluwer Academic Publishers. Printed in the Netherlands.

especially sorting, was a highly labor intensive activity, with around 80% of the U.S. Postal Service's expenditures being accounted for by labor. However, with technological advances postal service has started to adopt high tech methods of mail processing. These include methods of coding, such as barcoding, together with optical character recognition and remote video encoding devices, which have the potential for speeding up sorting and other mail processing operations. We illustrate some of the potential and effects of technological change by reference to the United States Postal Service's plans for automation for 1995, the so-called ABC (Automated Barcoding) environment. Our Figure 1 is a simplified illustration of how technological innovations are being incorporated into postal service, at least for large facilities.[1]

AUTOMATED SORTING OF ORIGINATING MAIL (OUTGOING SORT)

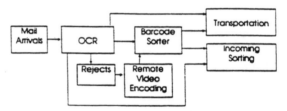

AUTOMATED SORTING OF DESTINATING MAIL (INCOMING SORT)

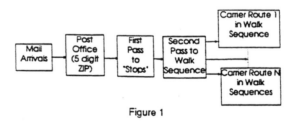

Figure 1

---

[1] In this simplified illustration, we confine our attention to sorting of originating mail and destinating mail, ignoring earlier steps in the processing of mail, e.g., facing and canceling.

Consider Figure 1. The arriving (canceled) mail is fed either into a multi-line optical character reader (OCR) or a barcode sorter depending upon whether it is pre-barcoded or not. Letters without barcodes are fed into an OCR. The OCR puts a barcode on every piece of mail. Three streams of mail emerge from the OCR. One stream goes to "incoming" sorting which consists of all the mail to be sorted for delivery by this (originating) center. Another stream goes directly to transportation to other centers and offices. Another stream goes to the barcode sorter, while a final stream is rejected, because the OCR is unable to read all of the mail passing through it.[2] Ideally, the vast majority of the mail fed into the OCR is read correctly and gets a barcode put on it. However, mail that is rejected is sent to a new technology, known as remote video encoding. This technology employs innovations in computer technology and telecommunications. It starts by placing an identifying mark on the letter by "lifting" an image of the address and storing in a computer. The computer then attempts to read the images that have been stored. Any images which the computer cannot read completely are then stored by the computer until they can be transmitted to a remote key-board operator who then completes the address. Successful completion of this operation results in a barcode being placed on the letter. The breakthrough with this technology is its use of computers and telecommunications. These make it possible to process OCR rejects much more cheaply than using conventional methods. The potential cost savings stem from a number of sources. Labor costs are likely to be lower, because operators do not require the training and "scheme" knowledge of existing operators of say letter sorting machines or manual sorting. In addition, the video center can be located where labor is cheaper and it can be contracted out thus avoiding the employment of potentially high priced postal union labor and potentially gaining the benefits from competitive contracting. It is even possible that such work might be performed at home on personal computers.

Returning to Figure 1, letters with barcodes are then sorted by the barcode sorter and either routed to the appropriate transportation mode or placed with the mail processing center's destinating mail for sorting by the barcode sorters to the individual carrier routes. Ultimately this will result in mail being sorted in walk sequence for each carrier. How this might operate is shown in the lower part of

---

[2] The OCR operates at a very high speed, (around 10 letters per second) reducing its ability to read addresses that are not clearly typed.

Figure 1. All mail arrivals are assumed to be barcoded. Some of this mail consists of destinating mail from other offices while some of it originated in this office. The mail is first sorted to post office or 5 digit Zip code. Further sorting of the mail requires a sorting scheme. The scheme has to operate within the constraints of the hardware. For example, it would take too many bins to sort the mail to carriers and then sort to walk sequence for each carrier. Instead a scheme like the one in Figure 1 is required. Here the mail is first sorted according to "stops" where a stop is just that, each stop on a carrier's route whether it be an apartment house, office or residence. Thus, a first pass is made at the end of which bin i will contain the mail for stop i for each carrier. A second pass is required that will then sort each bin to carrier route in walk sequence. Notice that the first pass can be performed a number of times but the second pass can only be performed once just before the carrier is about to set out on his route.

While these kind of changes in technology will result in a net reduction in costs for postal services, they will create additional problems. Not least is the creation of a new and apparently very inflexible peak at the second pass of the sortation to carrier route in walk sequence. One effect of this may be to drastically reduce the benefits from destinating sorting at off peak times since only first pass sorting can be done at this stage. In addition, the gains from having customers to prebarcode is likely to increase relative to the gains from having them presort mail. This raises questions of appropriate discounts for such customer co-production activity. Finally, issues of capital recovery associated with the much more capital intensive environment of postal services will present major new challenges in the nineties.

In addition to coming to terms with the implications of technological innovations, postal administrations have to face increased competition. For example, mail may be "presorted" by private firms, which are, in effect, competitors of the postal administration in providing this element of overall postal service. The presorting may take on various forms. It may be sorted completely so that the carrier does not even have to sort it himself for his walk. In this case, the presort supplier would likely drop the mail off at the destinating office. However, as the postal authority itself begins to develop more and more sophisticated forms of sorting, such as that described in Figure 1, the value of presorting may be reduced. Indeed, it may be more valuable to have mail pre-barcoded in such a system, but leave all sorting to the destinating post office in the postal administration. Thus, new technologies might not only eliminate the need for the carrier to sort the mail for his walk, but also reduce the value of the output provided by competitors such as presort companies. Normally a significant part of a carrier's day is spent in the office sorting his mail in readiness for his walk with the potential for significant labor savings. Similarly, traditional presort discounts may have to be reduced and barcode discounts possibly increased. Such changes will have a significant effect on the way postal services and their competitors do business. Not only will they result in the obvious substitution of capital for labor but they will necessitate changes in pricing policy in determining appropriate discounts for customer co-production activities, such as presorting and pre-barcoding, which compete with similar services provided by the postal administration.

Competition in postal services extends well beyond co-production activities, of course. Competition from courier services and facsimile transmission services (FAX) have already had a substantial impact on postal services. Private delivery services such as Federal Express, United Parcel Service, TNT, Airborne and DHL, are clearly strong global competitors. Similarly, facsimile transmission competes with both first class letter mail as well as courier services. Fax machines have lower marginal costs than traditional mail services and enjoy the added advantage of being able to interface with computer terminals directly, and are growing in appeal. Commercial FAX business alone accounts for over $5 billion annual turnover.

European nations face significant competition in the area of international mail, where inefficient rates, built in cross-subsidies and problems with service quality have opened the door for entry by competitive express carriers. This has also led to such services as remailing, in which, for example, mail destined for country A and mailed in country B is routed through country C in order to take advantage of inefficiently low rates (in the form of "terminal dues payments") between countries C and B.[3]

Another area of growing competition is electronic mail (E-Mail). Significant cost savings can result from E-Mail services. For example, one-page transmissions can be 10-540% cheaper than the equivalent transmission utilizing FAX. Longer reports offer even greater economies. The current problem of interaction between local area networks and public carriers, and increased costs

---

[3] For details on international competition, see Crew and Kleindorfer (1992a, 1992b).

for transmissions along complex routings, have prohibited E-Mail from currently making greater impact on postal services. However, this may be expected to change given the underlying economies of E-Mail for computer intensive customers.[4]

Without a doubt, postal services are facing significant competition and technological change. The issue of how postal services should react to the influx of competition is an open, but vital question. Increasingly, postal regulators have answered this question with a pro-competition policy, including encouraging the commercialization of the postal administration in the areas of technological innovation, service quality and new services to allow the postal administration to compete effectively. Two basic questions which arise in implementing this policy concern the definition of "efficient entry" and the management of service quality and innovation. The economic foundations of these will be the subject of our next two sections.

2. Natural Monopoly, Efficient Entry and Sustainability

Postal service has traditionally been and, with few exceptions, still is provided by public enterprise vested with a statutory monopoly. Even in Britain where extensive privatization has taken place under the Thatcher governments, the British Post Office remains one of the few public enterprises with a guaranteed but weakening statutory monopoly. In Germany the Bundespost continues as a public enterprise with a statutory monopoly in both post and telecommunications. While there are no obvious signs that the public enterprise monopoly is going to be replaced soon, the Bundespost has demonstrated an awareness of competition and has already taken steps to divide its operations into business units, which provides the potential for mitigating cross subsidies and, where efficient, promoting competition and/or privatization. Similar signs of

---

[4] Adie (1989) has argued that about half of today's first-class mail could be transmitted via some form of electronic transmission (see Adie 1989), so that E-mail and FAX competition will only grow. In addition, there is potential competition by banks in electronic funds transfer. Indeed, in Europe a much larger proportion of bills are paid through banks directly rather than the popular method in the U.S. of mailing checks.

"commercialization" of postal services are visible elsewhere (Dobbenberg, 1992). However, postal service plays such a key role in the economy that it is critical to ensure that such commercialization activities do not undermine the viability of an efficient postal service nationally and internationally. This is especially important if the requirement of universal service within a country is imposed with a uniform tariff. If there are economies of scale or scope in the delivery of postal service, then universal service at uniform rates may, under certain circumstances, promote entry by competitors with resulting erosion of these scale and scope economies. This is one of the central issues confronting postal administrations worldwide and it will be a focus of our analysis in this section. We begin with a discussion of the related notions of "natural monopoly" and "sustainability", drawing upon the earlier work of Elizabeth Bailey, William Baumol, John Panzar, and Robert Willig.[5] Their analysis was motivated by the entry that was starting to take place in telecommunications in the seventies. Many of the same issues of efficiency and network access carry over into postal service today.

Is postal service a natural monopoly and, if so, should postal administrations enjoy protected franchises? While this issue has not been definitively settled, empirical and conceptual analysis of this issue have led several to argue (see, e.g., Owen and Willig (1983) and Panzar (1991)) that the local delivery network in postal service has the clearest claim to being a natural monopoly, just as the local exchange network does in telecommunications. Other aspects of postal service do not appear to exhibit the required dominant economies of scale or scope required for a clear claim to monopoly status. If this continues to be so under the technological environment of the future, then competition in other functional areas (collection, sorting, etc.) of postal service could add significantly to postal efficiency. It would remain only to protect the viability of the overall postal network (to assure continuing universal service) and to assure open and equal access for all competitors to the local delivery network, which would continue to enjoy protected franchise status, at least for addressed letter mail distributed by mail carriers. In this context, equal access means that all competitors, including the postal administration, would pay the same per unit price for use of the local delivery network, with prices possibly differentiated by service class.

---

[5] For a comprehensive treatment of sustainability see Baumol, Panzar, and Willig (1988).

Multi-product issues and economies of scope are especially important in understanding the long-run sustainability of monopoly if entry is allowed into the monopoly sector. In a single-product world, if a natural monopoly is truly "natural," it is the dominant form of organization and its scale economies are such that competitors cannot undercut it. Its price would be sustainable against entry.[6] We illustrate this in Figure 2. As long as the competitor's average costs AC_c exceed the monopoly price given by P_m, the single-product monopoly is sustainable against entry by competitors. Attempts by regulators to lower the price below P_m will make the industry even less attractive to potential entrants. Thus, in the traditional single-product case, sustainability of natural monopoly is not an issue.

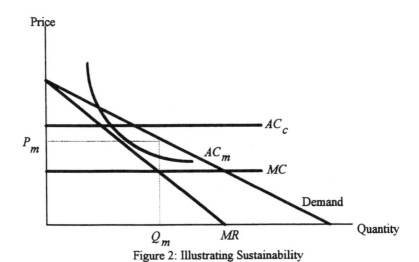

Figure 2: Illustrating Sustainability

---

[6] Panzar and Willig (1981) provide a more rigorous definition of this and also show that economies of scope exist if and only if the cost function in respect of the input shared by each output is subadditive.

Contrast this with the multiproduct monopoly where subadditivity and/or economies of scope exist. Here prices may be set, we assume by the regulators, such that entry to some markets becomes attractive. In this case the monopoly would not be sustainable against entry. Sometimes the reason for entry is obvious, namely that some prices are set too high in order to subsidize other prices. Cross-subsidization, however, is not the only reason why prices are not sustainable. Indeed, as Faulhaber (1975) has demonstrated, it is possible for a cost structure to be subadditive and yet, in the absence of regulation, it is not possible to have a set of prices that are sustainable. A natural monopoly is called *sustainable* if there is some break-even price vector which will not attract entry from a competitor using the same production technology as the monopolist. Sustainability is a central concept in understanding when entry restrictions are required in order to garner scale and scope economies associated with a natural monopoly. As discussed above, this is especially important for multiproduct firms like postal administrations which use common inputs. It can very well be the case that every allocation of common costs leads to some subset of product paying more than the cost of producing the given subset independently. In such a case, there would clearly be incentives for competitive entry, and the monopoly in question would not be sustainable. As noted by Baumol, Bailey and Willig (1977), this does not mean that the monopoly could not ward off entry by adjusting its price-output configuration. Unsustainability of a given price vector simply means that the price in question will attract entry. If there is no sustainable price vector, there is arguably a case for entry restrictions.

Interest in sustainability issues has gained momentum with recent deregulation moves, both in telecommunications and postal service, which have been directed at encouraging dynamic efficiency and productivity by allowing competitive entry into some of the markets of the multi-product monopolist. Let us first consider an example, based on Panzar (1980).

Consider the following cost function for a 2-product firm, e.g. a postal administration offering two classes of mail service:

$$C(X_1, X_2) = F + C_1 X_1 + C_2 X_2, \qquad (1)$$

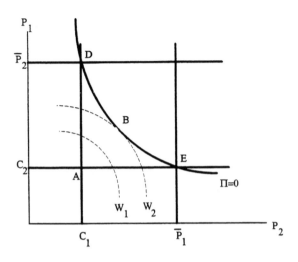

$$- - - - - - - - - - - - - - - - - - = \text{Iso-quants of welfare function}$$

Figure 3: Illustrating Sustainability (Based on Panzar (1980))

This cost function exhibits both economies of scale and scope. Suppose demand
for the two products is independent, i.e., $X_i(P)=X_i(P_i)$, i=1,2. We represent in
Figure 3 the locus of zero-profit points such that

$$\Pi (P) = \sum_{i=1}^{2} [P_i - C_i] X_i (P_i) - F = 0 \qquad (2)$$

Similarly, let P_i represent the lowest price at which a stand-alone firm (using the
same technology (1)) could break-even, i.e.,

$$\overline{P}_i = \text{Min}\{P_i \geq 0 \mid [P_i - C_i]X_i(P_i) = F\}, \quad i = 1, 2 \qquad (3)$$

From Figure 3, it is clear that the only break-even price vectors which could be sustainable lie on the locus DE. In fact every price P^m on DE is sustainable since (we assume) an entrant must set prices to attract any demand. However, any such price vector would clearly allow the entrant only to make losses. Moreover, any price vector to the right of (resp., above) could easily be challenged by a stand-alone firm marketing only product 1 (resp., only product 2). Thus, the locus DE is the set of all sustainable prices for this example. For reasons discussed below, we are particularly interested in whether the Ramsey optimal prices are sustainable (point B in Figure 3). From (2), it is clear that $P_i^* > C_i$, i=1,2 , so that the Ramsey solution clearly lies on the locus of DE. Thus, in this case, the Ramsey solution is sustainable.

As it turns out, a somewhat stronger property holds, even under more general cost conditions. Baumol, Bailey and Willig (1977), hereafter BBW, point out that for a monopolist to ascertain that price-output vectors other than the Ramsey solution are sustainable may require "global information about demand and cost functions for its products" (BBW, 351). Thus, when the Ramsey solution is sustainable, it may be the only safe bet for the monopolist to thwart competitive entry, if such is allowed. In this sense, one may think of entry threat to a monopoly as a "weak invisible hand" (BBW) inducing efficient (Ramsey) pricing. BBW establish general conditions under which the Ramsey solution is sustainable.[7]

For the postal context, perhaps the most important lesson to be taken from this discussion is that to the extent that the local delivery network for letter mail remains a natural monopoly it may be necessary to protect this monopoly from inefficient, cream-skimming entry and, for reasons of universal service, to assure the continuing viability of the overall postal administration as an end-to-end service provider.[8] It will also clearly be important to promote competition in those areas of the postal value chain other than the local delivery network, where this will not significantly affect the viability of the postal administration as an

---

[7] These are that: the services be weak gross substitutes, that the cost function exhibit decreasing average cost along every ray, and that the cost function be transray convex (which implies economies of scope).

[8] See Dobbs and Richards (1992) for further discussion.

end-to-end provider of postal services. How this might happen is the next focus of our attention.

As explained in the previous section, postal service may be viewed as a chain of interconnected services: collection, facing, sorting, transportation, etc. Each of these vertically aligned services are required in order to complete one full unit of postal service. A fundamental question in this context concerns whether various entrants will be allowed to compete in providing subsets of the total set of services required for full postal service. For example, will entrants (either separate service bureaus or postal customers themselves) be allowed to collect, sort and deliver mail to the final delivery zones, leaving final local delivery to the postal administration? If so, what discounts off full mail service should be granted for the subservices supplied by these entrants? This issue is at the heart of the question of sustainability and competition in postal services raised above.

If discounts are set too high, then inefficient entry will occur by service providers of these discounted services who are responding to the large discounts in setting up operations. This loss of business to the postal administration may not just erode revenues but it may represent real losses in economic efficiency to the extent that the postal administration could do the same service more cheaply than some of the entrants. The resulting losses in revenue and volume, together with the remaining universal service obligation, could severely damage the viability of the postal administration.

On the other hand, if discounts are set too low, then otherwise efficient competitors will not enter the market place and the postal administration will be providing services which could be provided more cheaply by these competitors. This could discourage such activities as pre-barcoding by business customers who could barcode and presort their outgoing letters rather easily for large mailings if they had a reasonable incentive to do so. The lost economies from failing to accomplish these activities could clearly be significant, especially since the vast majority of mail in most countries is sent by business customers.

Recent research suggests a solution to this problem. We review here a simple version of the model suggested by Panzar (1992). In this model, we assume two services, which are substitutes for one another. The first is "full service" and the second is "basic service." We think of full service as entailing all service steps required for the basic service (e.g., local delivery) plus some additional, separable services (e.g., collection, barcoding, presorting). In a simple two-stage model of postal service, we can express this relationship as

FULL SERVICE = BASIC SERVICE + SEPARABLE SERVICE

We imagine in this model that the basic service is imbued with natural monopoly characteristics, while the separable services do not enjoy clear advantages from monopoly provision. If the marginal cost of the separable service for the postal administration is c/unit, then Panzar argues that the postal administration should offer a discount off full service of c/unit if only the basic service is used. Thus, assuming a break-even constraint, the price for "full service" would just be the average cost of providing full service, and the discount for entrants who only use the basic service would be equal to the marginal cost c which the postal administration avoids if it provides one unit less of the separable service. As long as the postal administration is not challenged by entry into the basic service market, no sustainability issues arise. Interpreting basic service here as local delivery service, we see that the implication of this logic is that monopoly services (e.g., access to the local delivery network) should be priced at average cost (thus assuring full cost recovery), while separable services (prebarcoding, presorting, etc.) should be priced at the average-cost tariff minus a discount equal to the marginal cost of providing these separable services. This provides precisely the correct entry signal to potential competitors. Those which can perform the separable services less expensively than the postal administration will enter and those which cannot do so will purchase these separable services from the postal administration. Because this scheme prices components of the postal value chain to encourage entry only when it is efficient, we follow Baumol (1991) in referring to this scheme as "efficient component pricing".

An important aspect of efficient component pricing is that all participants in the postal services market, including the postal administration, face the same "price" for using the basic service. In this sense, efficient component pricing may also be thought of as "equal access pricing" for use of the local delivery network. As Panzar (1992) points out, under equal access pricing, while access charges for the basic service should be nondiscriminatory with respect to competitive service providers, they may vary across classes and categories of mail. In particular, in a multiproduct version of the above efficient component/equal access proposal, prices for access charges to the basic service could and should be set by the traditional Ramsey rule, described more fully below, to recover total costs. According to this rule, those classes of mail with lower price elasticity of derived demand (i.e., the demand faced by the postal administration) for basic service should be charged higher prices for use of the local delivery network (the basic service in the model above) even though the local delivery service provided to these different classes of mail might be indistinguishable.

An example, suggested by Dobbs and Richards (1992a) may be useful in illustrating the approach proposed by Baumol [1991], to which we will henceforth refer as "Top-down Efficient Component Pricing" (TECP). Under TECP, the discount of each link in the postal value chain for each class of mail is set equal to the LRMC (or avoided long-run marginal cost) of processing a unit of mail according to the service standards of the indicated class in that link of the postal value chain. We call this "Top-down" because the reference point against which discounts are set is the price of the highest cost class (First Class mail) required to make the entire price structure break even.

In this highly simplified example the price charged by a postal authority for drop-shipment of mail at the local delivery network would be derived as follows:

First Class mail	P
First Class presort	$P_p = P - m$
Drop-ship	$D = P - m - t$

We use the following notation in the above:
   m = avoided cost of presorting
   t = avoided cost from drop-shipment (e.g savings in transportation)

In the above TECP scheme, the process begins with specifying P, the price of First Class mail. P is chosen so that the authority breaks even when other prices are determined from the above TECP scheme and the cost structure of the postal authority. This particular implementation of TECP enjoys several desirable properties. First, it is relatively transparent for regulatory purposes. Second, it has desirable entry signalling properties, in that only entrants with lower costs than the postal authority will have an incentive to enter various activity segments. Finally, this implementation is conservative relative to the financial viability of the postal authority, in that it places the total responsibility for recovery of fixed costs on the local network where the postal authority has a monopoly.

TECP is not the only approach to break-even pricing consistent with the dictates of efficient component pricing, as laid out by Baumol [1991]. These dictates would include the following for the total pricing structure:

1.   The pricing structure should lead to overall break-even operations.

2.   The revenue from any activity in the postal value chain should not exceed the stand-alone cost for an efficient producer performing that activity only.

3.   The revenue from any activity in the postal value chain should be no lower than the incremental cost for the postal system to perform that activity.

It can be shown under reasonable conditions that TECP satisfies these three conditions but there may be other price structures that also satisfy these, including some form of Ramsey pricing, or "partial" Ramsey pricing, where some prices might be based upon the inverse elasticity rule and others based on avoided cost discounts equal to LRMC. While developing Ramsey and partial Ramsey solutions is beyond the scope of this paper we would expect that Ramsey type solutions would offer greater efficiency gains than the more constrained TECP approach, but would be less transparent and more difficult to compute and estimate. This discussion suggests several open questions concerning optimal tariff structure when competitive entry is possible including the differences in welfare between Ramsey and TECP, the structure and sustainability of Ramsey prices, and the implications for revenue stability and dynamic efficiency.   While some progress has been made in addressing these questions in both a general setting as well as in the postal context (see Crew and Kleindorfer [1992a]), these remain open research questions. At present, a reasonable approach would appear to be the TECP approach which approach which motivates efficient entry[9], yet provides a conservative approach to cost coverage for the postal system and equal access to the local delivery network.

Summarizing, this section has discussed the important notions of natural monopoly and sustainability. These issues are especially important when the postal administration is expected to provide universal end-to-end service in an

---

[9] Given the results of Crew and Kleindorfer [1992a, Chap 6], the level of entry implied by TECP may be lower than welfare optimal, with the result that excessive entry is likely to be avoided by this approach.

economy at uniform and reasonable prices. Determining conditions under which entry is efficient, and does not undermine the viability of such universal service, is complicated and ultimately rests upon judgement. However, we have argued that efficient component pricing, with equal access pricing of those aspects of postal service which are imbued with natural monopoly characteristics, provides a reasonable starting point for pricing to assure both efficient entry and sustainability of those aspects of the postal service for which monopoly provision is desirable.

3. Concluding Remarks

Our review in section 2 of the nature of the postal service demonstrates that postal service has much in common with other natural monopolies, particularly telecommunications. Like telecommunications the local delivery network is the source of the natural monopoly. In telecommunications, the local loop is a natural monopoly in both call origination and termination,[10] but in postal services the natural monopoly of the local network is confined to delivery with collection offering few scale economies. Like telecommunications most of the total "traffic" is local, either within the local delivery network, or between nearby delivery networks. Long distance traffic, as in telecommunications, can be performed by separate companies. However, unlike telecommunications, subscribers are not wired to the network, nor are competitors physically tied to the local delivery network. This makes postal service potentially subject to more competition than telecommunications. The only argument for using the local delivery network is that it is efficient to do so. Unlike local telephone service postal service has no monopoly of delivery to an address.[11] Postal

---

[10] Traditionally this was certainly correct. However, increasing competition, in the form of bypass, has begun to occur. Further down the road competition from another carrier such as a CATV operator may also become important.
[11] In the U.S. the Private Express Statutes do give the Postal Service a monopoly in using the mail box at an address. (Others may use the box provided they affixed postage on the item placed in the box reserved for U.S. mail.) In the U.K. Royal Mail has a monopoly on letters with postage less than one pound Sterling.

administrations do face a universal service obligation and this makes cream-skimming by competitors a pervasive concern among postal regulators.

Sustainability of postal service is accordingly a significant issue as we argued in Section 3. The extent of scale and scope economies in postal economics is an important issue for determining not just the extent of protection and regulation required for postal service, but the nature of the services to be offered by postal authorities. It is with this background that our analysis proceeded using the traditional welfare economic framework to evaluate policy, namely the framework of net benefit maximization and its associated Ramsey conditions to take into account a financial viability constraint.

Another important issue for postal service is the cost-benefit tradeoff of service reliability which is addressed in Boronico (1992) and Crew and Kleindorfer (1992a). The results derived are not only consistent with traditional microeconomic theory but also intuitive. Reliability or service quality should be set to equate the marginal costs of increasing reliability with the consumers' marginal willingness to pay for this increased reliability. Of course, understanding these benchmarks in theory is quite different from implementing them in practice, which is further complicated by the existence of regulation.

The issue of regulation of postal service is currently very important in face of the changes that are taking place in postal and delivery services and the ensuing regulatory debate.[12] Given the increasing competition in postal services, we might expect that postal services (de-)regulation will be very similar to the traditional public utilities, especially telecommunications. Perhaps the current overriding concern about regulation amongst economists is the deleterious effects it has on internal efficiency. Traditional forms of regulation are of a cost-plus nature and result in an attenuation of incentives for cost minimization. Recent theoretical advances (see Crew and Kleindorfer, 1992a) have examined the information asymmetries that exist between regulators and regulated firms and shows how inefficiencies can be reduced, though not eliminated. The message is that regulatory systems vary in their level of inefficiency. Because of information asymmetries efficiency cannot be achieved

---

[12] In Europe the debate is proceeding albeit slowly but very intensely with the Green Paper, "On the Development of the Single Market for Postal Services," Commission of the European Communities, Brussels.

with regulatory systems. The best that can be done is to choose one that offers minimal inefficiencies subject to equity constraints on process and outcome.

In some respects, however, the situation in the postal sector is more promising, as there do not seem to be the major cross subsidies between long distance and local that exist in telecommunications. In addition, the "baggage" of rate-of-return regulation does not exist. Similarly, the problem of transactions-specific or sunk investment is significantly less but growing as noted in our previous work (Crew and Kleindorfer 1992b). Finally, postal and delivery markets are characterized by strong actual and latent competition, weakening the case for subsidies to entrants which characterized the regulated telecommunications markets some years ago.

Some further research and policy implications stem principally from the above discussion. Pricing, capacity and technology planning and the associated problems of service offerings, reliability and service quality provide one important area of future research. Regulation presents the other opportunity for research. Both have important implications for policy. The key will be to assist postal administrations in their efforts to commercialize their operations, in both quality of service and innovation of new services, and to assist regulators and postal policy makers to ensure continuing incentives for regulation and efficiency through appropriate pricing and entry policies. Understanding these key issues in the context of rapid technological change and competition will present the major challenges for research and policy for postal service in the nineties.

Linking recent advances in the economic theory of postal services to related managerial issues will be key in the above two areas of expanding commercialization of the postal sector and regulatory processes. In particular, the theory outlined here needs to be coupled with available methodologies in marketing, operations, performance measurement, monitoring, accounting, technology and systems planning. New approaches by postal management to the kind of postal service provided would include making the local delivery loop more efficient, and devising means of generating additional traffic for the local delivery network. The projected ABC environment of the USPS and other postal administrations will provide highly automated sorting at the level of final delivery, providing carriers with their mail fully sorted ready for delivery. Such a system might pave the way for new products, such as barcoded mail dropshipped to the destinating sorting office. One thing is clear: postal management will need to be innovative in devising new products, showing less concern for maintaining all the vertical links in the chain and more concern for the efficiency of the local delivery network. A fundamental focus of postal management in the 90's must be to provide reliable, customer-oriented services in all accessible links of the postal value chain.

This commercialization of mail service may also raise the question of privatization. Although we have not addressed the subject of privatization in this paper, we do consider it another important issue facing postal administrations and regulators. With the great inroads made by privatization into utilities, it would not be surprising if privatization of postal administrations were to be an issue in the future. In this event, the design of formal regulatory institutions to bolster or replace current commission and ministerial oversight will take on more urgency.

Finally we should not forget that, except for the U.S., postal regulatory institutions are not well developed. This might be viewed as a disadvantage, but it also implies that there exists an opportunity in postal service for innovations in the design of regulatory institutions relatively unencumbered by the rent-seeking apparatus that is a feature of developed regulatory structures. In these circumstances design of regulatory institutions has the potential to provide significant potential benefits to postal services and their customers. It is important that economists and policy-makers respond to the challenge.

References

Adie, D.K. (1989). *Monopoly Mail* (Transactions Publishers, New Brunswick, N.J).

Baumol, W.J. (1991). "Modified regulation of telecommunications and the public interest standard," London (mimeo).

Baumol, W.J., E.E. Bailey, and R.D. Willig (1977). "Weak invisible hand theorems on the sustainability of natural monopoly," *American Economic Review* 67, 350-65.

Baumol, W.J., and D. Bradford (1970). "Optimal departures from marginal cost pricing", *American Economic Review* 60, 265-83.

Baumol, W.J., J.C. Panzar, and R.D. Willig (1988). *Contestable Markets and the Theory of Industry Structure,* revised edition, (Harcourt, Brace Jovanovich, New York).

Boiteux, M. (1971), "On the management of public monopolies subject to budgetary constraints", *Journal of Economic Theory* 3, 219-40.

Boiteux, M. (1960). "Peak load pricing", *Journal of Business* 33, 157-79.

Boronico, J.S. (1992). *An Economic Analysis of some Reliability-Constrained Service Systems*, unpublished Ph.D. dissertation, Department of Decision Sciences, University of Pennsylvania (Philadelphia, PA).

Coase, R.H. (1947). "The economics of uniform pricing systems", *Manchester School Economics& Social Studies* 15, 139-56.

Coase, R.H.(1961). "The British Post Office and the messenger companies", *Journal of Law and Econ.* 4, 12-65.

Crew, M.A., and P.R. Kleindorfer (1979). *Public Utility Economics*, (St. Martins Press, New York).

Crew, M.A., and P.R. Kleindorfer (1986). *The Economics of Public Utility Regulation* (MIT Press, MA).

Crew, M.A., P.R. Kleindorfer and M. Smith (1990). "Peak load pricing in postal services", *Economic Journal* 100(402), 793-807.

Crew, M.A., and P.R. Kleindorfer (1991a). "Peak load pricing of postal service and competition", in M.A. Crew and P.R. Kleindorfer (eds.) *Competition and Innovation in Postal Services* (Kluwer Academic Publishers, Boston, MA), 37-57.

Crew, M.A., and P.R. Kleindorfer (1991b). *Competition and Innovation in Postal Services* (Kluwer Academic Publishers, Boston, MA).

Crew, M.A., and P.R. Kleindorfer (1992a). *The Economics of Postal Service* (Kluwer Academic Publishers, Boston, MA).

Crew, M.A., and P.R. Kleindorfer (1992b). *Regulation and the Evolving Nature of Postal and Delivery Services* (Kluwer Academic Publishers, Boston, MA).

Dobbs, I.M., and P. Richards (1992). "Policy implications of postal network access," in M. A. Crew and P.R. Kleindorfer (eds), *The Economics of Postal Service*, 261-72.

Dobbs, I.M., and P. Richards (1992). "Entry and component pricing in regulated markets," Newcastle-upon-Tyne Discussion Paper.

Estrin, S., and D. de Meza (1988). "Should the Postal Office's statutory monopoly be lifted?", *London School of Economics* (mimeo).

Estrin, S., and D. de Meza, D. (1990). "The postal monopoly: a case study," *Economic Review*, 2-7.

Estrin, S., and D. de Meza (1991). "Delivering letters: should it be decriminalized?", in M.A. Crew and P.R. Kleindorfer (eds.), *Competition and Innovation in Postal Services* (Kluwer Academic Press, Boston, MA), 93-108.

Esogbue, A.M.O. (1969). "Dynamic programming and optimal control of variable multichannel stochastic service systems with applications," *Mathematical Biosciences* 5, 133-42.

Faulhaber, G.R. (1975). "Cross-subsidization: pricing in public enterprise," *American Economic Review* 65 (5), 1083-1091.

Gregory, D., "The friction of distance? Information circulations and the mails in early nineteenth-century England," *Journal of Historical Geography* 13, 150-154.

Hill, R. (1837). *Post Office Reform*.

Merewitz, L. (1971). "Costs and returns to scale in U.S. Post Offices", *Journal of the American Statistical Association* (September), 504-509.

Owen, B.M., and R.D. Willig. "Economics and Postal Pricing," in J. Fleischman (ed.), *The Future of the Postal Service* (Aspen Institute).

Panzar, J.C. (1980). "Sustainability, efficiency, and vertical integration," in B.M. Mitchell P.R. Kleindorfer (eds.), *Regulated Industries and Public Enterprise* (Lexington Books, Lexington), 171-86.

Panzar, J.C. and R. D. Willig (1977). "Free entry and the sustainability of natural monopoly," *Bell Journal of Economics* 8, 1-22.

Priest, G.L. (1975). "The history of the postal monopoly in the United States," *Journal of Law & Econ* 18, 33-80.

Scott, F.A. (1986). "Assessing USA postal ratemaking: an application of Ramsey pricing,", *Journal of Industrial Economics*, 279-90.

Senior, I. (1983). "Liberating the letter," (Institute of Economic Affairs).

Sherman, R., and A. George (1979). "Second-best pricing for the US Postal Service," *Southern Economics Journal* 45, 685-95.

Sherman, R. (1991). "Competition in postal service," in M.A. Crew and P.R. Kleindorfer (eds.), *Competition and Innovation in Postal Services* (Kluwer Academic Publishers, Boston, MA), 191-214.

Wattles, G.M. (1973). "The rates and costs of the United States Postal Service," *Journal of Law & Economics,* 89-117.

Contributors

Uday M. Apte is Associate Professor of Management Information Sciences at the Cox School of Business, Southern Methodist University, where he teaches courses in Operations Management. He received his Ph.D. in Decision Sciences from the Wharton School, University of Pennsylvania, where he taught for over eight years. His research and publications are in Service Operations Management and Management Information Systems, and several of his papers have received best paper awards. He has ten years of management experience in operations and information systems. He holds a B. Tech. (Chemical) from the Indian Institute of Technology, and an MBA from the Asian Institute of Management.

Pamela K. Armstrong is an Assistant Professor of Operations Management at Georgetown University School of Business. She received her B.Sc. in systems Engineering from the University of Arizona in 1984, her M.S.E. in Operations Research from the University of California at Berkeley in 1985, and her Ph.D. in Decision Sciences in 1993. Prior to attending the University of Pennsylvania, Dr. Armstrong was a systems engineer at AT&T Bell Laboratories and IBM.

Gabriel R. Bitran is presently the Head of the Management Science area of the M.I.T. Sloan School of Management. Professor Bitran is Editor-in-Chief of Management Science. He is a member of the editorial boards of the International Journal of Production Planning and Control, the Annals of Management Science series, and the Management Science Research series. He is also an associate editor of the Brazilian Journal of Operations Research and the Revista Latino-Ibero-Americana de Investigacion Operative. He has an M.S.c. and a Ph.D. in Operations Research from M.I.T. and a B.S. and an M.S.c. in Industrial Engineering from the "Escola Politecnica" of the University of Sao Paulo, Brazil. Professor Bitran's research interests lie in the field of operations management in manufacturing and the service industry. He has consulted with companies in the computer, semiconductor, electronics, telecommunications, steel, and automotive industries.

Severin Borenstein is an Associate Professor of Economics and Co-Director of the University of California Program on Workable Energy Regulation. He received his Ph.D. in Economics from M.I.T. in 1983. Dr. Borenstein has written extensively on the U.S. airline industry and on oil and gasoline markets. He has advised airlines, computer maintenance companies, oil companies, insurance companies, and state and federal agencies on antitrust and regulation issues. He has been a visiting professor of business economics at U.C. Berkeley's Haas School of Business and a visiting professor of strategic management at Stanford University's Graduate School of Business.

Jess S. Boronico is a professor of Management and Operations Research at Monmouth College. He received his Ph.D. from the Wharton School of the University of Pennsylvania in 1993 after completing the M.S. and B.S. in Mathematics at Fairleigh Dickinson University. Dr. Boronico's research interests lie in the determination of optimal reliability-constrained capacity policies for industries both in the manufacturing and service sectors. In addition to consulting for the USPS, he has worked with both the New Jersey and Pennsylvania Highway Authorities with regard to capacity and pricing decisions as they pertain to the design and control of the queuing processes at toll booths.

Richard A. Cavaliere is Assistant Professor, Department of Mathematics/CSC, Saint Joseph's University, Philadelphia, where he teaches courses in mathematics. He received his Ph.D. in Analytic Number Theory from Temple University, Philadelphia, in 1984. His research interests and publications are in the areas of Modular Forms and Integrals, Rational Periodic Functions, and Mathematical Modeling as Applied to Management Science and Computer Algebra Systems. Dr. Cavaliere was awarded the Sun Faculty Fellowship in 1989-90.

John E. Chubb is Director of Curriculum and Founding Partner of The Edison Project, as well as a Non-Resident Senior Fellow at the Brookings Institution. **Terry M. Moe** is Professor of Political Science at Stanford University and a Senior Fellow at the Hoover Institution. Drs. Chubb and Moe are the authors of *A Lesson in School Reform from Great Britain* (1992), and

Politics, Markets, and America's Schools (1990), both published by the Brookings Institution.

Robert W. Crandall is a Senior Fellow in the Economic Studies Program at the Brookings Institution. He hods an M.S. and a Ph.D. in Economics from Northwestern University. He has specialized in industrial organization, antitrust policy and regulation. His current research focuses on the regulation of the telephone and cable television industries. He is the author of After the Breakup: The U.S. Telecommunications Industry in a More Competitive Era, Up from the Ashes: The U.S. Minimill Steel Industry, Regulating the Automobile, The U.S. Steel Industry in Recurrent Crisis, Controlling Industrial Pollution, The Scientific Basis of Health and Safety Regulation, and Manufacturing on the Move. He was a Johnson Research Fellow at the Brookings Institution and has taught at Northwestern University, MIT, the University of Maryland, and George Washington University. Mr. Crandall has served as Assistant, Acting, and Deputy Director for the Council on Wage and Price Stability, and as a Member of the Reagan Campaign Task Force on Regulatory Policy.

Michael A. Crew is Professor of Economics and Director of the Center for Research in Regulated Industries, Rutgers University. He received his B.Com. in 1963 from the University of Birmingham and his Ph.D. from the University of Bradford in 1972. He has taught Economics at the Graduate School of Management, Rutgers University since 1977. Prior to joining Rutgers, he taught at several universities and colleges including Wesleyan University, Harvard University, Carnegie-Mellon University, and the University of Strathclyde. His principal research interests are regulatory economics, peak-load pricing, and the theory of monopoly. His current research includes the economics of postal service, economic depreciation, diversification and deregulation issues for utilities, and environmental problems of utilities. His publications include five books, ten edited books, and numerous articles in such journals as *American Economic Review*, *Economic Journal*, *Bell Journal of Economics*, *Journal of Political Economy*, *Journal of Regulatory Economics* and *Public Choice*. He has served on several editorial boards, as well as being the founding editor of two journals, *Applied Economics* and the *Journal of Regulatory Economics*. He has consulted on pricing, economic costing, and regulatory economics for a number of major corporations, including AT&T,

BellSouth, Jersey Central Power and Light, New York Telephone, and the United States Postal Service. Dr. Crew served on the Board of Directors of Energy Initiatives, Inc. from 1984-1988.

Edward R. Dean is the Associate Commissioner, Office of Productivity and Technology, U.S. Department of Labor. He received a B.A. from Yale University and a Ph.D. in Economics from Columbia University in 1963. He taught in the Economics Departments of Columbia University and Queens College, City University of New York prior to joining the federal government in 1973. He came to the Bureau of Labor Statistics in 1983.

Ranjit S. Dighe is a Teaching Fellow in the Department of Economics at Yale University. He received his B.A. in Economics at Oberlin College in 1987 and his M.A. in Economics at Yale University in 1991. He was a research assistant at the Urban Institute in Washington, DC from 1987 to 1989.

Joseph F. Francois is an Economist with the GATT Secretariat in Geneva. Dr. Francois received his B.A. in Economics and History and his M.A. in Economics from the University of Virginia, and received his Ph.D. in Economics from the University of Maryland. Prior to joining the GATT, Dr. Francois served as Chief of Research and Acting Director of Economics at the U.S. International Trade Commission (ITC) and as Senior Economist for the international law and trade consulting firm of Mudge Rose Guthrie Alexander & Ferdon.

Harold O. Fried is Associate Professor of Economics at Union College. He received his Ph.D. in Economics from the University of North Carolina at Chapel Hill in 1980. His research focuses on the evaluation of performance and measurement of efficiency.

Jonathan Galst is an attorney at Covington & Burling in Washington, D.C. He has published an article on regulatory preemption in the telecommunications sector, entitled " 'Phony Intent'?: An Examination of Regulatory-Preemption Jurisprudence," 67 N.Y.U. L. Rev. 108 (April 1982). Jonathan graduated, *magna cum laude*, from New York University School of Law (1992), where he was the Managing Editor of the Law Review. He graduated, *magna cum laude*, from the Wharton School and the College of Arts and Sciences of the University of Pennsylvania (1988).

Stephen M. Gilbert is an Assistant Professor of Operations Management at the Weatherhead School of Management, Case Western Reserve University. He received his Ph.D. in Operations Management from M.I.T. in 1992. Prior to that, he received an M.S.I.E. from Stanford University in 1985, and a B.S.I.O.E. from the University of Michigan in 1984. Professor Gilbert's research interests are in the modeling and analysis of processes for creating and delivering products and services.

Patrick T. Harker was director of the Fishman-Davidson Center for the Study of the Service Sector from 1989 to 1994, and professor of Decision Sciences at the Wharton School of the University of Pennsylvania. He is currently UPS Professor of Transportation and Chairman of the Systems Engineering Department at the School of Engineering and Applied Science of the University of Pennsylvania. Dr. Harker was a 1991-1992 White House Fellow and Special Assistant to the Director of the U.S. Federal Bureau of Investigation. From 1986 to 1991, he was a National Science Foundation Presidential Young Investigator.

G. G. Hegde is Associate Professor of Business Administration at the Katz Graduate School of Business, University of Pittsburgh. He received his Ph.D. in Production and Operations Management at the University of Rochester. His research interests are interdisciplinary, and include manufacturing and service strategy, performance measurement for continuous improvement, engineering and manufacturing cost interface, and quality and productivity,. In addition to his teaching emphasis on courses in Operations Management, he teaches a wide variety of courses including Probability and Statistics, Econometrics and Cost Management for Manufacturing Competitiveness. Dr. Hegde taught at Duke University in Fall 1992.

Bernard M. Hoekman is a trade economist in the Finance and Private Sector Development Division of the World Bank, and a research fellow of the center for Economic Policy Research in London. Before joining the World Bank, he was an economist in the Economic Research and Analysis Unit of the General

Agreement on Tariffs and Trade. Dr. Hoekman graduated from the Erasmus University of Rotterdam, the Netherlands in 1983 and received his Ph.D. in Economics from the University of Michigan in 1988.

Paul R. Kleindorfer is the Universal Furniture Professor of Decision Sciences and Economics. He is a 1961 graduate of the United States Naval Academy and a 1970 graduate of Carnegie-Melon University. He has enjoyed appointments at Carnegie, M.I.T. and several international institutes. Dr. Kleindorfer's research interests include quality, technology choice and logistics, and the results of this research have appeared in numerous journals and books in the management and economics literatures. Dr. Kleindorfer has recently investigated the effects of increasing international competition on pricing policies, technology strategy and quality deployment in both telecommunications and postal service.

Kent Kunze is a senior economist and project director with the Division of Industry Productivity and Technology Studies, Office of Productivity and Technology, U.S. Bureau of Labor Statistics. He directs the development of new industry productivity measures. Dr. Kunze received his B.S. in Economics in 1971 and his Ph.D. in 1979 from the University of Utah. He was a member of the faculty of the University of Utah prior to coming to the Bureau of Labor Statistics in 1976.

David E. Lebow is an economist at the Federal Reserve Board. He received a Ph.D. in Economics from Princeton University in 1989 and a bachelor's degree in economics from the Massachusetts Institute of Technology in 1983. Prior to joining the Federal Reserve Board, he was a research fellow at the Brookings Institution and worked at the World Bank.

Thin Yin Leong is a lecturer at the Department of Decision Sciences, Faculty of Business Administration, National University of Singapore where he teaches Business Logistics and Operations Management. Dr. Leong received his B.Eng. in Mechanical and Production Engineering from NUS in 1981, and his Ph.D. in Management from M.I.T. in 1990. His research interests are in analysis and modeling of manufacturing and service operations, production planning, inventory control, capacity planning, transportation planning and system design.

Jiatao (J.T.) Li is Assistant Professor of Strategy and International Management at the University of Hawaii. His current research focuses on international business strategy, multinational networks, international expansion and performance, and global competition in service industries. Recent publications include "Ownership Structure and Board Composition: A Multi-country Test of Agency Theory Predictions" (*Managerial and Decision Economics*, 1993), and with S. Guisinger, "The Globalization of Service Multinationals in the 'Triad' Regions: Japan, Western Europe, and North America" (*Journal of International Business Studies*, 1992). Dr. Li received his Ph.D. in Strategy and International Management from the University of Texas at Dallas in 1992.

C.A. Knox Lovell is the C. Herman and Mary Virginia Terry Distinguished Professor of Economics at the University of Georgia. Dr. Lovell received his A.B. from the College of William and Mary, and his Ph.D. from Duke University. He has held visiting positions at the University of British Columbia, the University of Pennsylvania and the University of Adelaide, and he has been a frequent visitor at CORE, Université Catholique de Louvain. He is Editor-in-Chief of *The Journal of Productivity Analysis* and Associate Editor of *Management Science*.

Jeffrey K. MacKie-Mason is an Associate Professor of Economics and Public Policy, and an Associate Research Scientist in Public Policy at the University of Michigan. He also is a Faculty Research Fellow at the National Bureau of Economic Research. He received his Ph.D. in Economic from M.I.T. in 1986, and his M.P.P. in Public Policy from the University of Michigan in 1982. He has written on antitrust economics, corporate behavior, computer network and telecommunications pricing. He has advised computer maintenance companies, telecommunications switching companies, manufacturers and hospitals on antitrust issues. He has been a National Fellow at the Hoover Institution, Stanford University, a Visiting Research Scholar at the Department of Economics, University of Oslo, Norway, and a Visiting Research Scholar at the University-Wide Energy Research Group, University of California at Berkeley.

Richard O. Mason is Carr P. Collins Distinguished Professor of MIS, Cox School of Business, Southern Methodist University. He received his Ph.D. from the University of California, Berkeley. Formerly, he was Professor at the University of Arizona, Professor and Associate Dean at USC, and Professor and Assistant Dean at UCLA. He serves as an officer of TIMS and ICIS, and is a member of the Russian Academy of Natural Sciences. His research focuses on information systems-strategy, history, and social and ethical implications. He has published numerous books and articles. He was awarded a Fulbright Scholarship to the University of Umea, Sweden in Spring 1993.

Edward K. Morlok is the UPS Foundation Professor of Transportation and Professor of Systems Engineering in the Department of Systems, University of Pennsylvania. Dr. Morlok received his B.E. in Mechanical Engineering from Yale University in 1962, a Certificate in Transportation from the same institution in 1963, and the Ph.D. in Civil Engineering/Transportation Systems from Northwestern University in 1967. He worked for the U.S. Department of Commerce (Transportation Systems Division) and was on the faculty of Northwestern University prior to coming to Penn. He received the von Humboldt Foundation's U.S. Senior Scientist Award in 1980-81.

Janet S. Netz teaches economics at Purdue University. She received her M.A. and Ph.D. in Economics from the University of Michigan, and her A.B. in Economics from the University of California at Berkeley. Dr. Netz has worked as a consultant on antitrust cases in the service industry.

Linda K. Nozick is an Assistant Professor of Civil and Environmental Engineering at Cornell University. She received a B.S.E. in Systems Analysis and Engineering from the George Washington University in 1989, an M.S.E. in Systems from the University of Pennsylvania in 1990, and a Ph.D. in Systems also from the University of Pennsylvania in 1992.

Johannes M Pennings is a Professor of Management at the Wharton School of the University of Pennsylvania. He received his B.A. and M.A. at Utricht University in the Netherlands and his Ph.D. from the University of Michigan. Before coming to Wharton, he taught at Carnegie Mellon University, Columbia University, and INSEAD. His research interests include organization design, executive compensation, and innovation. He is the author of *Organizational Strategy and Change* (Jossey Bass 1985), *New Technology as Organizational Change* (Ballinger 1987), and numerous articles.

Kenneth A. Reinert is an Assistant Professor of Economics at Kalamazoo College. Dr. Reinert received his B.A. and M.A. in Geography from Boston University in 1980 and 1982, respectively. He received his M.A. and Ph.D. in Economics from the University of Maryland in 1985 and 1988, respectively. He served as International Economist and Senior International Economist at the U.S. International Trade Commission from 1988 to 1993 and as Visiting Assistant Professor of Economics at Wellesley College from 1992 to 1993.

John P. Sammon is Vice President of Conrail's Intermodal Service Group. Prior to being promoted to that position in July 1994, he was Assistant Vice President of Intermodal, the position he held while the paper in this volume was prepared. He joined Conrail in 1979 and has held a variety of marketing and sales positions in intermodal, forest product, petrochemical and automotive business groups.

Daniel E. Sichel is a research associate at the Brookings Institution. He received a Ph.D. in Economics from Princeton University in 1988, and a bachelor's degree in Economics and a master's degree in Public Policy from the University of Michigan in 1983. He was an economist at the Federal Reserve Board for five years prior to joining Brookings in 1993.

Lazar N. Spasovic is Assistant Professor of Management and Transportation in the School of Industrial Management, and the Center for Transportation Studies and Research, New Jersey Institute of Technology. Dr. Spasovic received his Diploma in Transportation Engineering in 1985 from the Belgrade University, Yugoslavia, M.S. in Civil Engineering in 1986 from the University of Maryland at College Park, and a Ph.D. in Systems Engineering from the University of Pennsylvania in 1990. For his dissertation research on planning tractor-trailer operation (drayage) in rail-truck intermodal transport, Dr. Spasovic received the U.S. Department of Transportation University Transportation Center Student of the Year Award.

Philippe Vanden Eeckaut is a doctoral student in economics at Université Catholique de Louvain, where he is a teaching assistant at College Jacques Leclerq and a research assistant at CORE. He has been a Visiting Scholar at the University of North Carolina at Chapel Hill. His research interests include efficiency and productivity measurement, especially in not-for-profit institutions.

Mark I. Wilson is an Assistant Professor teaching in the Political Economy field of James Madison College, and a Research Associate with the Institute for Public Policy and Social Research at Michigan State University. Dr. Wilson received his Ph.D. in Regional Science from the University of Pennsylvania. In addition to research on the globalization of services production, Dr. Wilson also addresses the economic and spatial behavior of nonprofit services.

Index

503

International Studies in the Service Economy

1. O. Giarini and W.R. Stahel: *The Limits to Certainty.* Facing Risks in the New Service Economy. 1990   ISBN 0-7923-0468-3

2. E. Weisman: *Trade in Services and Imperfect Competition.* Application to International Aviation. 1990   ISBN 0-7923-0900-6

3. J.C. Delaunay and J. Gadrey: *Services in Economic Thought.* Three Centuries of Debate. 1992   ISBN 0-7923-9230-2

4. O. Giarini and W.R. Stahel: *The Limits to Certainty.* 2nd Revised Edition. 1993   ISBN 0-7923-2167-7

5. P.T. Harker (ed.): *The Service Productivity and Quality Challenge.* 1995   ISBN 0-7923-3447-7

KLUWER ACADEMIC PUBLISHERS – DORDRECHT / BOSTON / LONDON